Christian responses to Islam

D1566346

MANCHESTER
1824

Manchester University Press

Christian responses to Islam

Muslim–Christian relations
in the modern world

EDITED BY
ANTHONY O'MAHONY AND
EMMA LOOSLEY

Manchester University Press

Manchester and New York

distributed exclusively in the USA by Palgrave Macmillan

Copyright © Manchester University Press 2008

While copyright in the volume as a whole is vested in Manchester University Press, copyright in individual chapters belongs to their respective authors, and no chapter may be reproduced wholly or in part without the express permission in writing of both author and publisher.

Published by Manchester University Press
Oxford Road, Manchester M13 9NR, UK
and Room 400, 175 Fifth Avenue, New York, NY 10010, USA
www.manchesteruniversitypress.co.uk

Distributed in the United States exclusively by
Palgrave Macmillan, 175 Fifth Avenue,
New York, NY 10010, USA

Distributed in Canada exclusively by
UBC Press, University of British Columbia, 2029 West Mall,
Vancouver, BC, Canada V6T 1Z2

British Library Cataloguing-in-Publication Data is available

Library of Congress Cataloging-in-Publication Data is available

ISBN 978 0 7190 8668 7 paperback

First published by Manchester University Press in hardback 2008

This paperback edition first published 2012

The publisher has no responsibility for the persistence or accuracy of URLs for any external or third-party internet websites referred to in this book, and does not guarantee that any content on such websites is, or will remain, accurate or appropriate.

Printed by Lightning Source

Contents

Notes on contributors

Chris Clohessy, of the Pontifical Institute for Arabic and Islamic Studies (PISAI) Rome, was born in South Africa. Having graduated in 2001, he is now a member of staff of PISAI, teaching Shi'a Islam and reaching a doctorate about Fatima, daughter of Muhammad, in the light of Christian theology. He is editor of the College's English language journal, *Encounter: Documents in Muslim–Christian Understanding*; and has published a number of papers including 'Islam in South Africa', *Encounter* (Rome), 242 (1998), 'Glimpses along the Sufi Path', *Encounter* (Rome), 265 (2000), 'Karbala', *Encounter* (Rome), 285 (2000); 'The Gospel of Barnabus', *Encounter* (Rome), 295 (2002); and 'Maiden of Paradise: Notes on Fatima, daughter of Muhammad', *Encounter* (Rome), 314 (2005).

Basil Cousins did postgraduate study and research on the encounter between Russia, the Orthodox Church and Islam at the Centre for Christianity and Interreligious Dialogue at Heythrop College, University of London. He has recently published 'The Russian Orthodox Church, Tatar Christians and Islam', *Eastern Christianity: Studies in Modern History, Religion and Politics* (London, Melisende, 2004); 'Russian Orthodoxy: contemporary challenges in society, interreligious encounters and mission' in *World Christianity: Politics, Theology and Dialogues* (London, Melisende, 2004); 'The Russian Orthodox Church and Islam', *One in Christ: A Catholic Ecumenical Review*, 41 (2006). He is researching and writing a book on the modern history and contemporary politics of the confrontation between Christianity and Islam in Russia.

John Flannery has undertaken postgraduate studies in Christian theology and other religious traditions and has recently carried out a research project on the Jesuit encounter with Islam and Buddhism in Asia at the Centre for Christianity and Interreligious Dialogue, Heythrop College, University of London. At present he is working on the history of Christian–Muslim relations in various historical and global contexts. His publications include, 'Through a glass darkly: the Jesuit encounter with Buddhism in Tibet', in A. O'Mahony (ed.), *Catholics in Interreligious Dialogue: Monasticism, Theology and Spirituality* (Leominister, Gracewing, 2005); 'The martyrdom of Queen Ketevan in 17th century Iran: an episode in relations between the Georgian Church and Rome', *Sobornost: Eastern*

Churches Quarterly, 27 (2005); 'Christ in Islam', *One in Christ: A Catholic Ecumenical Review*, 41 (2006); and 'The Syrian Catholic Church', *Christianity in the Modern Middle East* (London, Melisende, 2008).

Stanisław Grodź did postgraduate study and research into historic and contemporary encounters between Christianity and Islam at the Centre for Islam and Christian–Muslim Relations, Selly Oak College, University of Birmingham, and on contemporary African Christian theology. He is currently a lecturer in Theology and Christian–Muslim relations at the Catholic University of Lublin, Poland. Previously he lived in Ghana and West Africa for a decade. Recently publications include: 'Towards universal reconciliation: the early development of Amadou Hampâté Bâ's ecumenical ideas', *Islam and Christian–Muslim Relations*, 13 (2002); 'Faith in Jesus Christ as expressed in African concepts?', *World Christianity: Politics, Theology and Dialogues* (London, Melisende, 2004); '"Vie with each other in good works": what can a Roman Catholic missionary order learn from entering into closer contact with Muslims?', *Islam and Christian–Muslim Relations*, 18 (2007).

Michael Ipgrave is Archdeacon of Southwark Cathedral. He has been Interfaith Relations Adviser to the Archbishops' Council of the Church of England 1999–2004, including the establishment of a national Christian–Muslim Forum in England for the Archbishop of Canterbury. Publications include *Christ in Ten Thousand Places* (London, Darton, Longman and Todd, 1994) and *Trinity and Inter Faith Dialogue* (Oxford, Peter Lang, 2003), as well as various articles, notably in *The Road Ahead: A Christian–Muslim Dialogue* (London, Church House Publishing, 2002), and *Scriptures in Dialogue* (London, Church House Publishing, 2004).

Anthony H. Johns is Emeritus Professor and Visiting Fellow at the Division of Pacific and Asian History, at the Research School of Pacific and Asian Studies, Australian National University. He has published widely in a range of academic journals including, 'Muslim communities in Australia: an opportunity for interfaith conciliation', *Encounter* (Rome), 234–5 (1997); 'The need to rediscover compassion in Australasia', *Islamochristiana*, 26 (2000); 'Perspectives of Islamic spirituality in Southeast Asia: reflections and encounters', *Islam and Christian–Muslim Relations*, 12 (2001); 'Three stories of a prophet: Al-Tabari's treatment of Job in *Surah al-Anbiya*' 83–4', *Journal of Qur'anic Studies*, 3–4 (2001–2); 'Jonah in the Qur'an: an essay on thematic counterpoint', *Journal of Qur'anic Studies*, 5 (2003). He also recently co-edited a volume on *Islam in the Modern World* (London, Routlege, 2005). He was honoured by the publication: *Islam: Essays on Scripture, Thought and Society. A Festschrift in Honour of Anthony H. Johns*, edited by Peter G. Riddell and Tony Street (Leiden, E. J. Brill, 1997).

Philip Lewis is Interfaith Advisor to the Anglican Bishop of Bradford and a lecturer in Peace Studies, University of Bradford. He is author of *Islamic Britain: Religion, Politics & Identity among British Muslims* (London, I. B. Tauris, 1994, reprinted 2004); 'Between Lord Ahmed and Ali G: which future for British

Muslims?', in W. A. R. Shadid and P. S. van Koningsveld (eds), *Religious Freedom and the Neutrality of the State: The Position of Islam in the European Union* (Leuven, Peeters, 2002); 'Christians and Muslims in the west: from isolation to shared citizenship?', *International Journal for the Study of the Christian Church*, 3 (2003). He has also published articles in *The Tablet* and *The Church Times*.

Emma Loosley is Lecturer in Oriental Christian and Islamic Art at the University of Manchester, and has an expertise in Eastern Christianity in the Middle East. Between 2001 and 2003 she lived in the monastery of Dayr Mar Musa in the mountains of Syria, which has become a major centre for Christian–Muslim relations in the Middle East. Her research interests include the evolution of Christian art, the architecture of monasticism, pilgrimage, cross-currents at the fringes of the Roman and Persian empires and the transition from Christian to Islamic art. Publications include *The Architecture and Liturgy of the Bema in Fourth to Sixth-Century Syrian Churches* (USEK, Kaslik, Lebanon, 2003); with P. Dall'Oglio, 'La communauté d'Al-Khalil: une vie monastique au service du dialogue islamo-chrétien', *Proche-Orient Chretien*, 54 (2004); 'A spiritual odyssey: the Maronite self-image in the twenty-first century', *Royal Bulletin of Inter-Faith Studies*, 7–2 (2005); 'Brothers and brotherhoods: reflections on Christian and Islamic views of monasticism', *International Journal for the Study of the Christian Church*, 7: 3 (2007).

Fiona McCallum, Department of International Relations, St Andrew's University, Scotland. She has a specialist interest in Christianity in the Modern Middle East; recent publications include: 'Desert roots and global branches: the journey of the Coptic Orthodox Church', *Bulletin of the Royal Interfaith Studies*, 7: 2 (2005); 'The Maronite patriarch in the contemporary ear: tradition and challenges', *Christianity in the Modern Middle East* (London, Melisende, 2008); 'The role of the Maronite patriarch in Lebanese history: the patriarch of Lebanon?', *Chronos*, 15 (2007).

Barbara Mitchell did postgraduate research at the Centre for Christianity and Interreligious Dialogue Heythrop College, University of London. At present she is researching the contemporary encounter between Christianity, Islam and Muslim–Christian relations in Britain. Her publications include, 'The Church of England and Islam', *One in Christ: A Catholic Ecumenical Review*, 41 (2006).

Anthony O'Mahony is director of the Centre for Christianity and Interreligious Dialogue at Heythrop College, University of London. He has a particular research interest in Eastern Christianity, Christian theology and politics, and Christian–Muslim relations. His publications include: *Palestinian Christians: Religion, Politics and Society in the Holy Land* (London, Melisende, 1999); *The Christians Communities in Jerusalem and the Holy Land: Studies in History, Religion and Politics* (Cardiff, University of Wales Press, 2003); with Michael Kirwan (SJ), *World Christianity: Politics, Theology and Dialogues* (London, Melisende, 2004); *Eastern Christianity: Studies in Modern History, Religion and Politics* (London,

Melisende, 2004); *Christianity in the Middle East: Studies in Modern History, Theology and Politics* (London, Melisende, 2008).

Peter G. Riddell is Professor and Director of the Centre for Islamic Studies at the London School of Theology. He wrote his PhD thesis on Islam in Southeast Asia at the Australian National University, and held a post-doctoral fellowship at the Hebrew University of Jerusalem (Israel). He has previously taught at the Australian National University, the Institut Pertanian Bogor (Indonesia), and the School of Oriental and African Studies, University of London. His books include: *Transferring a Tradition* (Berkeley, University of California, 1990); *Islam: Essays on Scripture, Thought and Society*, edited with Tony Street (Leiden, E. J. Brill, 1997); *Islam and the Malay-Indonesian World* (Hawaii, University of Hawaii Press and London, Christopher Hurst, 2001) and *Islam in Context* (Grand Rapids, Baker, 2003). Recent articles include: 'The diverse voices of political Islam in post-Suharto Indonesia', *Islam and Christian–Muslim Relations*, 13 (2002); 'Muslims and Christians in Malaysia, Singapore and Brunei', in *Christians and Muslims in the Commonwealth* (London, WIFT, 2001); and 'Arab migrants and Islamisation in the Malay world during the colonial period', *Indonesia and the Malay World*, 29 (2001). In 2003 he gave the London Lectures in Contemporary Christianity, which have been published as, *Christians and Muslims: Pressures and Potential in a Post-9/11 World* (London, Inter-Varsity Press, 2004).

Andrew Unsworth is a catholic priest of the Diocese of Liverpool, he has undertaken postgraduate work at the Centre for Christianity and Interreligious Dialogue at Heythrop College, University of London, on the Holy See, Islam and Muslim–Christian relations in the modern world. His most recent publications are: 'John Paul II, Islam and Christian–Muslim relations', *Catholic and Shi'a in Dialogue: Faith and Reason in Theory and Practice* (London, Melisende, 2006); with Barbara Wood, 'Pope Benedict XVI, interreligious dialogue and Islam', *One in Christ: A Catholic Ecumenical Review*, 41 (2006); 'Louis Massignon, the Holy See and the ecclesial transition from 'Immortale Dei' to 'Nostra Aetate', *Aram: Society for Syro-Mesopotamian Studies*, 20 (2007–8).

Rocco Viviano recently completed postgraduate study on the theology of interreligious dialogue and research into contemporary Christian–Muslims relations in the Philippines at the Centre for Christianity and Interreligious Dialogue at Heythrop College, University of London. He now lives and teaches in Manila in the Philippines. Recent publications include: 'Responses of the Catholic church to Islam in the Philippines from the Second Vatican Council to the present-day', *World Christianity: Politics, Theology and Dialogues* (London, Melisende, 2004).

1

Christianity and Islam: between history and theological encounter

Anthony O'Mahony

The Christian–Muslim engagement may be experienced at many levels: theological, political, cultural and global. Today looking at the world as a whole, Christians and Muslims together make up half the global population. Statistics are almost inevitably estimates; however Christians make up 33% (approximately 2 billion) and Muslims 18% (1.3 billion).[1] However, some say that today we are witnessing a 'clash of theologies' that has deep echoes in religious tradition and history and in contemporary politics with global implications.[2]

Christian–Muslim relations increasingly must be set within a context of global religious resurgence.[3] This religious-political context is opening up dynamic encounters, which go far beyond the classic historic relationship between Europe and Islam across the Mediterranean or in the Balkans. It also goes substantially beyond the European discussion on the relationship between church and state, and religion and politics, in the public arena.[4]

Today Christian–Muslim relations take place in a multiplicity of contexts, for example in Asia, where both Christians and Muslims form majorities and minorities, or share a minority situation such as in 'secular' but 'Hindu' India.[5] Or Africa, where in some states the Christian–Muslim divide is of determining political influence, such as in Nigeria and Sudan or Ethiopia and Eritrea.[6] The nature of Christian–Muslim relations in various states is also determining the scope of these states' international relations and alliances. We increasingly see external Islamic finance being given to local and regional Muslim groups to aid development politically and materially, particularly in Africa and Asia, so that Islam has a more powerful and higher profile in relation to political culture than previously held. This can be in the funding of Muslim political movements, the building of mosques and the funding of *da'wa*/Mission. In western European states and increasingly in North America, religious and cultural *da'wa*/Mission are particularly strong themes.

Other religious contexts are informing Christian–Muslim relations: conflict and encounter between China and Islam, at home and abroad; the Thai Buddhist state and the Muslim minority in the south of the country; Hindu–Muslim relations in South Asia; and Jewish-Muslim encounters.[7] The significance of the scale and importance of the Christian–Muslim engagement is not lost on other faiths, so we are finding increasingly other traditions, particularly Judaism but also Hinduism and Buddhism, are taking an active interest in the developments in the dialogue between Christianity and Islam.

We also witness a reconfiguration of Christian–Muslim relations in Russia, and some of the former Soviet Central Asian states are witnessing a growth in Islam. This is another layer of the complexity of Christian–Muslim relations.[8] In western Christian circles there is little understanding of the political and religious encounter between Islam and the Eastern Orthodox churches, which form majorities in Russia and some Balkan states, or minorities in the Middle East, such as the Patriarchates of Antioch, Constantinople, Alexandria or Jerusalem. We in the west, also generally have poor knowledge and understanding of the Oriental churches – Armenian, Coptic, Ethiopian, Syrian – and their contribution to understanding the Islamic tradition that they have historically experienced over many centuries. To sustain a more robust theological and political reflection on the Christian–Muslim encounter it is necessary to expand our 'canon' of understanding from this historical experience.[9]

We also notice a growth in transitional ideology, and the influential thought of Sayyid Qutb, traces of which can be found across the Muslim world, for example in Qutb's wish to delegitimatise states governed by non-Islamist Muslims; and the focus on the eternal combat between Christians and Muslims as found in a Qur'anic exegesis on their early relationship[10] and on the identity of the Christian tradition in relation to the corrective of Islam. The state of Israel is seen as a modern reflection of the Jewish rejection of Islam, and of the early Muslim overthrowing or destruction of the Jewish community in Medina, which led to the establishment of the first Islamic state.[11] The 'Constitution of Medina' is also put forward as the correct relationship of Muslims to Jewish and Christian believers, by both radical Islamists and 'moderate' Muslims.[12]

Further Christianity experiences Islam as a religious and theological challenge. Since the earliest period in its history, the Islamic tradition has been conscious of the religious diversity of the human race and considered it an issue of importance. Muslim tradition maintains that diversity of religions has been the hallmark of human society for a very long time, but it had not been its primordial condition.

Yohannan Friedmann has reminded us that according to the Islamic tradition Islam is not only the historical religion and institutional framework that was brought into existence by the Muslim prophet Muhammad in the seventh century, but also the primordial religion of humankind, revealed to Adam at the time of his creation. This is intimately related to the conception that Adam was a prophet, and to the notion that Ibrahim/Abraham was a Muslim in a metahistorical sense. At a certain stage in their development, however, Judaism and Christianity deviated from their pristine condition and became corrupt. A prophetic mission would have been required to ameliorate this situation. However, no prophets were sent to accomplish this task between the missions of Jesus and Muhammad and, consequently, true religion ceased to exist. Only with the emergence of Islam in the seventh century was the situation transformed.[13]

It is thus that Christianity locates the challenge of Islam, not just as a historical encounter, which is of importance; or as a political force in the modern world; but also as a theological challenge. There is an intimacy to the Christian–Muslim encounter, which offers a familiarity, but allows for little theological commonality due to difference. Thus throughout the centuries since the rise of Islam, Muslim–Christian relations have revolved around this double axis of familiar, biblical appeal and strenuous, religious critique. It is this story that these chapters attempt to tell in a contemporary sense set against the global encounter between Christianity and Islam in the modern world.

Notes

1 Goddard, H., 'Christian–Muslim relations: yesterday, today and tomorrow', *International Journal for the Study of the Christian Church*, 3: 2 (2003), 1–14.
2 Emilio Platti of the Dominican Institute for Oriental Studies in Cairo: 'Risques respectifs du souci de fidelité dans l'Islam et dans le christianisme', *Christianisme, Judaisme et Islam: Fidelité et ouverture* (sous la direction de Joseph Dore) (Paris, Editions du Cerf, 1999), pp. 223–42 and 'Islam et Occident: "Choc de théologies"?', *Mélanges Institut Dominicain d'études orientales du Carire*, 24 (2000), 347–79.
3 Thomas, S. M., 'Taking religious and cultural pluralism seriously: the global resurgence of religion and the transformation of international society', *Millennium: Journal of International Relations*, 29: 3 (2000), 815–41; 'Religious resurgence, postmodernism and world politics', in Esposito, J. L., and Watson, M. (eds), *Religion and Global Order* (Cardiff, University of Wales Press, 2000), pp. 38–65.
4 Lewis, P., 'Christians and Muslims in the west: from isolation to shared citizenship?', *International Journal for the Study of the Christian Church*, 3: 2 (2003), 77–100; 'Christian–Muslim relations in Britain: between local and Global', in O'Mahony, A. and Siddiqui, A. (eds), *Christians and Muslims in the Commonwealth* (London, Al-Tajir and World of Islam Festival Trust, 2001), pp. 182–97.
5 Michel, T., 'Implications of the Islamic revival for Christian–Muslim dialogue in Asia', *International Journal for the Study of the Christian Church*, 3: 2 (2003), 58–76; Riddell, P., 'Malaysian Christians and Islamization', in O'Mahony, A. and Kirwan, M. (eds), *World Christianity: Politics, Theology, Dialogues* (London, Melisende, 2004), pp. 226–56, 372–415.
6 Hock, K., 'Christian–Muslim relations in the African context', *International Journal for the Study of the Christian Church*, 3: 2 (2003), 36–57.
7 Kramer, G., 'Anti-Semitism in the Muslim world: a critical review', *Die Welt des Islams*, 46: 3 (2006), 243–76.
8 Cousins, B., 'The Russian Orthodox Church, Tatar Christians & Islam,' in *Eastern Christianity: Studies in Modern History, Religion and Politics* (London, Melisende, 2004), pp. 338–71; 'Russian Orthodoxy: contemporary challenges in society, interreligious encounters & mission', in O'Mahony, A. and Kirwan, M. (eds), *World Christianity: Politics, Theology and Dialogues* (London, Melisende, 2004), pp. 308–46.
9 For those interested in the modern history of Christianity in the Middle East see the volumes edited by O'Mahony, A.: *Eastern Christianity: Studies in Modern History, Religion and Politics* (London, Melisende, 2004); *The Christian Communities of Jerusalem and the Holy Land: Studies in History, Religion and Politics* (Cardiff, University of Wales Press, 2003); *Palestinian Christians: Religion, Politics and Society in the Holy Land* (London, Melisende, 1999); *Christianity in the*

Middle East: Studies in Modern History, Theology & Politics (London, Melisende, 2007); *Christianity and Jerusalem: Modern Theology and Politics in the Holy Land* (Leominster, Gracewing, 2007).

10 Carré, O., 'Juifs et chrétiens dans la société islamique idéale d'aprés Sayyid Qutb (m. 1966)', *Revue des sciences philosophiques et theologique*, 68 (1994), 50–79.

11 Nettler, R. L., 'A post-colonial encounter of traditions: Muhammad Sa'id Al-Ashmawi on Islam and Judaism', in Nettler, R. L. (ed.), *Medieval and Modern Perspectives on Muslim-Jewish Relations* (Luxembourg, Harwood Academic, 1995), pp. 174–85.

12 Rubin, U., 'The "Constitution of Medina": some notes', *Studia Islamica*, 62 (1995), 5–24.

13 See the important works by Friedmann, Y., *Tolerance and Coercion in Islam: Interfaith Relations in the Muslim Tradition* (Cambridge, Cambridge University Press, 2003); 'Classification of unbelievers in Sunni Muslim law and tradition', *Jerusalem Studies in Arabic and Islam*, 22 (1998), 163–95; 'Islam is superior . . .', *The Jerusalem Quarterly*, 11 (1979), 36–42.

2

Ecumenical Christian responses to Islam in Britain

Michael Ipgrave

In what ways do Christians from across the ecumenical range of churches respond to the presence of Islam and Muslims in Britain? To ask that question is to inquire into the perception, or perceptions, of Islam held among Christians; the extent to which such perceptions correlate with the objective reality of the Islamic presence in Britain is a different question, which I shall not explore in this chapter.

Responses to Islam among Christians will operate on many different levels – instinctive, theological, sociological, pastoral, and so on. To chart a way through this complexity, I shall take as a starting point the typology proposed by David Lochhead for the different ways in which communities of belief relate to one another.[1] He emphasises that different relationships are not simply created by different theologies, but also provide contexts within which different theologies develop:

> Instead of approaching the problem as one of the history of ideas, I propose that we look at the problem as one in the sociology of knowledge. What kind of theology would we expect from a community that is related in a specific way to another community of a different religious tradition?[2]

> It is very dubious to assume that the bad record of Christians in relating to other religious traditions is the fault of certain Christian ideas. It is equally as likely that the bad ideas are projections of bad relationships.[3]

Lochhead identifies sociologically four 'ideological types' of relationship between different communities: respectively, isolation, hostility, competition, partnership. He further proposes that a fifth relationship is needed, distinct from these, to express an authentically Christian response: that of dialogue. Developing his proposal a little, we may suggest that in the first four relationships theology is more or less conditioned by context, whereas the fifth represents an opportunity to reverse the dynamic, so as to create a relationship motivated and governed by theological principles. This is perhaps a distinction easier to maintain in theory than practice,[4] but it does point to two key questions to address in forming any perspective on the range of Christian responses to Islam in Britain: first, what theologies emerge from the perceptions of Muslim communities which

Christians currently hold, and the relationship with them in which they are now engaged; second, what theological motifs are important for Christians in moulding a truly dialogical attitude to, and relationship with, Muslims?

In this brief survey I shall first look at examples of Lochhead's four relation-ships of, respectively, isolation, hostility, competition and partnership, and note the theologies on which they rely. I shall then question the parameters of a theo-logy appropriate for his fifth relationship, the dialogical. It is of course difficult to separate out these different strands clearly, and it would be misleading to draw too sharp boundaries between them. The delineation of ideologies is to serve just as a heuristic tool to provide some orientation in a complex area. In this connection, Lochhead himself gives the example of one and the same Christian work on Islam which may assert that:

> (1) Muslims are outside the light of the Gospel (isolation) (2) Islam is funda-mentally opposed to the purposes that God has revealed in Jesus Christ (hostil-ity) (3) the Gospel speaks more fully to the human condition than does the Qur'an (competition), and (4) Muslims are fellow monotheists (partnership). One of the types of attitudes will likely dominate the work, but all of the types may be present.[5]

Isolation

Lochhead's first relational ideology is that of isolation, where either community 'defines reality for itself'.[6] Indifference of this kind to Islam and Muslims is a common experience through much of British Christian life, for a variety of reasons. Churches located in places where daily contact with Muslims is not a possibility may feel that this is an issue of no concern to them – 'We don't have that problem here'. Even in areas with a significant Muslim population, the lack of interaction may serve effectively to insulate one community from another. Churches struggling to deal with their own internal challenges may simply not have the interest, motivation, energy or confidence to take seriously an engage-ment with the religiously other. Yet the 'isolation' model cannot be total in contemporary Britain, for this is a society where media images of Islam are increasingly pervasive – and prevailingly negative.[7] Any ideological isolation of British Christians as members of churches is therefore found in a context where their conceptual isolation as consumers of media is not a possibility, and this sets up a disjuncture which is unsatisfactory and unsustainable. It cannot be right for Christian people to form their attitudes towards people of another faith on the basis solely of secular opinion, without any attempt at the ecclesial forma-tion of a Christian mind on the question.

The theology which lies behind an isolationist ideology, insofar as it is articu-lated, is likely to be the remnants of a 'Christendom' model: the assumption that Britain is to be identified as a Christian country in a way that means that other faiths can be safely ignored. At most, the primary Christian engagement is seen to be with the absence of belief in a secularising society, rather than with differ-ent patterns of belief in a multifaith society. Much of the pressure to move beyond this attitude seems to be led by lay church members who are encounter-ing Muslims and Islam on a daily basis.

Hostility

In Lochhead's second ideological type, hostility, 'the impact of another construction of reality is experienced as a threat'.[8] This kind of attitude among British Christians draws on latent negative images of Islam, Muslims and Muhammad which are of surprising longevity and power in the western European tradition.[9] It is fed by the concern which many Christians feel over the situation of their co-religionists who are members of minority communities in Muslim-majority states, particularly in relation to issues such as freedom to convert or to evangelise. It also often expresses a particular anxiety closer to home, about the growth of Islam in Britain. Three examples may be mentioned briefly, all of which fall within Lochhead's ideological spectrum of hostility, though they range from a position close to 'isolation' to an attitude which moves almost into the terrain of 'competition'.

Examples of extreme hostility to Islam, influential among some conservative evangelical Christians, are to be found in the published and web-based writings of David Pawson.[10] Pawson expects Islam to supplant Christianity as the dominant religion in Britain, a consequence which he ascribes to the laxity and error of most contemporary Christianity. In common with much writing of this kind, he believes this insight to be given him through a specific prophetic message, which was given to him while listening to a lecture by Patrick Sookhdeo:

> In the middle of his talk, both unexpected and unrelated to its contents, I was suddenly overwhelmed with what could be described as a premonition that Islam will take over this country (England). I recall sitting there stunned and even shaking. We were not just listening to an interesting lecture about a religion and culture, which others believed and practiced. We were hearing about our future![11]

Sookhdeo's own organisation, the Barnabas Fund, is much more widely influential in the historic churches. It presents a more nuanced approach, drawing particularly on overseas experiences, hostile to Islam but drawing an important distinction between attitudes to the religion and to the people who follow it:

> Islam is a religious system but Muslims are individual human beings, the overwhelming majority of whom want nothing more than to live in peace and security and enjoy life with their families . . . However, it is also important that we do not turn a blind eye to the real problems that exist in the teachings of Islam the religion.[12]

These 'real problems' include: the acceptance of violence as an 'acceptable stratagem' for Islamic expansion; an exteriorising and legalistic approach to ethics; an emphasis on community at the expense of individuals; a lack of distinction between religion and state. Islam is presented as a unified and monolithic system, and in the British context is seen to have clear strategic aims:

> Muslims have been able to capitalise on the post-September 11th situation and have launched a major endeavour in the United Kingdom. This aims firstly to change the British perception of Islam from negative to glowingly positive, secondly to ensure that Islam becomes firmly ensconced in all the structures of our society, and thirdly to convert individuals to the Islamic faith.[13]

An interesting recent development has been the convergence of this approach with secular views in the effort to exclude Islam from public recognition or Muslims from legal protection on the basis of their religious identity. This is seen, for example, in the controversy over the British government's repeated attempts to introduce legislation against incitement to religious hatred – a debate in which the Barnabas Fund has been strenuous in campaigning against any restrictions on freedom to criticise another religion. There are points at which this argument comes close to the position that it is better to have a wholly secular society than one in which Islam has influence. Thus Sookhdeo offers a significantly 'privatised' view of religion:

> In Islam there is no distinction between religion and the state . . . Christianity does not offer a blueprint for the way society should be governed. The teachings of Christianity have, at least since the reformation, primarily been seen as something to be practised by individuals as a matter of personal belief.

A third example of the ideology of hostility can be found in the vast, detailed and much-used website 'Answering Islam', which states of itself:

> We have no goal to be 'politically correct' and know that many Muslims do not like our conclusions. We believe the Bible to be the word of God and Islam to be 'another message' that is not compatible with God's Word as revealed in the Bible.[14]

However, the website, while seeking consistently to refute Islamic claims, emphasises also the importance of accurate information, fair representation and cogent argument, and in this way moves the debate into the area of apologetics, which is close to Lochhead's third ideological type, 'competition'.

Theologically, there is in general within the trajectory of 'hostility' a rejection of any identification of Allah with the biblical God.[15] This can reach to the extent of seeing Allah as a false spirit intentionally deceiving people into the acceptance of Islam, with the consequence that Muhammad must be seen as a false prophet.[16] Such an attitude can then apply directly to Islam the strictures and warnings recorded in Old and New Testaments as directed against false and dangerous cults. The relationship between theology and practice here becomes mutually reinforcing: on the one hand, the negative theological assessment of Islam emerges from a relationship of hostility, but on the other hand that assessment itself in turn can prohibit the development of more cordial relationships through inhibiting any sense of mutual trust.

Competition

The third relationship identified by Lochhead, that of competition, describes the viewpoint of a community for whom another community 'is not totally outside the truth, but the full truth is to be found only in the beliefs and practices of our own community'.[17] For Christians who take this type of attitude, the entry of Islam into Britain, and of Muslims into public space, is cautiously welcomed insofar as it can be seen to have contributed to a raising of the profile of religion in the public space, and so to a strengthening of the case for Christian involvement also. At same time, there is an emphasis on the need to advance distinctively Christian interests in society. Most importantly, the profile in Britain of Islam and Muslim communities is seen as both a challenge and a stimulus to Christianity and Christians.

This is probably the position of the majority of engaged Christian churches at the present, in instinctive terms at least. In the Church of England, for example, this results in a double emphasis in Christian–Muslim relations. On one hand, as an established church charged with some sense of spiritual responsibility for the whole of society, Anglican leaders have devoted considerable energy to the effort to ensure that Muslim communities (together with other religious minorities) should have fair access, necessary protection and appropriate recognition in public life. This is a concern which is being worked out in a variety of areas such as: bishops in the House of Lords taking seriously the requests of Muslim communities for legislative protection from religious discrimination and incitement to religious hatred; chaplains ensuring that appropriate arrangements for the spiritual care of Muslim patients and prisoners are in place in hospitals and prisons; church aided schools making provision for the religious and cultural needs of Muslim pupils; Christian leaders and opinion formers seeking to influence, and where necessary to correct, media representations of Islam and of Muslims. In these and similar situations there is evident a desire to ensure that Muslims are not disadvantaged from participation in society because of their religious commitment.

On the other hand, and particularly at the local level of parish churches, there is a balancing insistence on maintaining the distinctive imperatives of Christian mission and ministry. This is particularly clearly demonstrated in the significant Church of England research and consultation exercise called 'Presence and Engagement'.[18] This project sought to identify the challenges and opportunities facing parish churches in neighbourhoods with a significant population of people of other faiths. These were identified by using the 2001 census figures on self-declared religious affiliation, which showed that 900 of the 10,000 or so parishes of the Church of England serve communities where at least 10% of the population identify themselves as belonging to a faith other than Christianity.[19] In the great majority of cases, the most significant of these other faith communities are Muslim.[20] Islam is therefore ineluctably part of the daily context within which many Anglican churches in this country exercise their ministry and mission – and the same would doubtless be true of other churches also. The qualitative results of 'Presence and Engagement' are still being processed but they already seem to show, alongside the development of links with established Muslim leadership and institutions by clergy and churches, a growing pastoral and missionary outreach by parishes to individual Muslims.

This duality characterises a 'competition' approach, where there is a recognition that – to put it in non-theological terms – other religions are playing on the same ground, and broadly according to the same rules, as Christians. The three priorities for parishes which are identified in the *Presence and Engagement* report fit within this paradigm as key challenges which churches will need to address in order to be able to compete effectively at local level:

The *identity* of Christians as a presence among people of other faiths: For Christian communities corporate identity is . . . related in the presence of other religions to questions about the unique identity of the Gospel and the specific claims of Jesus Christ. Where churches have become a religious minority, a proper sense of Christian identity becomes particularly important . . . to engage with people and communities of other faiths than our own is to enrich our identity, not to diminish it.

The building up of *confidence* for engagement with local communities: Anxiety and loss of confidence can sap the ability of a congregation to remain people of outgoing hope and hospitality and turn them inwards . . . the loss of status and position . . . can be the means for local churches to lead people back to a confidence in God rather than in inherited structures and ways of doing things.

The *sustainability* of an engaged Christian presence: The ability of a local church to remain sustainable in financial and material senses often appears to be in doubt . . . What are the ways in which churches can be adventurous and enterprising? . . . Even more important are the issues of spiritual and theological sustainability. What are the sources which sustain churches spiritually in such situations?[21]

A theology appropriate for competition will presuppose at least some overlap in the understanding and identity of God as experienced by Christians and Muslims, while also being very aware of the significance of the differences and even contradictions between the two theologies.[22] There are often very cordial relationships at a personal level with Muslims, particularly striking between evangelical Christians with a strong evangelistic motivation and those Muslims who have some explicit commitment to the task of *da'wa*, 'invitation' into the path of Islam. The impulse to commend Christian truth forms one major motivation for Christians actually to engage with Muslims, and can naturally find expression in a competitive attitude.

Partnership

Lochhead explains that his fourth relational type, partnership, refers to a situation where one community's perception of another is that 'similarities [between the communities] are primary and essential while differences are secondary and accidental';[23] such a perception then opens up the possibility of working together in partnership on the basis of shared values and common goals. It is possible to discern two overlapping dimensions of a partnership approach which appeal to Christians in Britain today: first, a concern for cohesion within divided communities where Muslims find themselves in an isolated or marginalised situation; second, a desire to contribute together to the common good of society, where Islamic values can be seen as congruent with what Christians have to offer.

Recognition of the importance of community cohesion stems from an awareness of the dangers of serious division and alienation among disenchanted British Muslims, particularly where this is married to educational and economic disadvantage, and in places where communities are effectively separated from one another by territorial, educational or other socio-economic pressures. Awareness of this was one factor contributing to the notably strong stand taken by most British churches against the Iraq war.[24] More widely, the churches' continued involvement in areas from which so many other organisations have withdrawn, and clergy's continued presence in neighbourhoods in which other professionals are daytime visitors, can provide them with the credibility necessary for them to be able to act as the enablers and guardians of safe spaces for meeting and sharing across religious divides. This is a model of partnership as a response to a perceived problem, but it can in turn grow into a more positive and proactive approach through the building up of trust to work together.

An innovative example of the commitment of Christians and Muslims to work together in partnership for the common good is seen in the Archbishop of Canterbury's *Initiative in Christian–Muslim Relations*. A small group of Christians and Muslims were commissioned by the archbishop to spend time listening intensively to the concerns and insights of Muslims in five English cities, and of Christians living alongside Muslims, with the aim of seeing what structures of meeting and dialogue might strengthen and develop Christian–Muslim relations in this country. One outcome is the establishment of a national Christian–Muslim Forum, launched by the archbishop in January 2006. The rationale for this kind of cooperation is expressed in the following way in the report of the initiative:

> Our present time constitutes a critical context for Christian–Muslim relations. It is fraught with the dangers of distrust, division and destruction. At the same time, it offers to Christians and Muslims, each building on their faith in God, the possibility of new and creative partnerships nurtured by a growing trust in one another and directed towards the common good. We can no longer ignore one another's presence, and this challenge meets us not only in our social interaction but also as people of faith. The question facing us is not simply: 'How can we live and work together as different communities in our society and world?', but: 'How do we understand and relate to one another within the purposes of God?'[25]

There is an attempt here to construct a shared theological foundation which will prove sufficient to carry the weight of a practical partnership which will enable Christians and Muslims to contribute together to society from their values and wisdom born of prophetic faith. This does not require an absolute identification or reconciliation of differing views of God's nature and purposes, but it does require a significant convergence of values, and so points to a recognition of one another as communities entrusted with the burden and joy of the divine word for the world. There seems in fact to be an understandable tendency within an approach of this kind to bracket out more specifically theological questions (such as those relating to prophetic status, incarnation, Trinity, or the sufficiency of scripture). At the best, there is the hope that the experience of practical working together can create the atmosphere of trust, respect and understanding in which such contentious differences can be creatively addressed.[26] If the reality of disputed questions is not held alongside the recognition of agreed common ground, though, there is a danger of shutting out from the relationship precisely those distinctive affirmations of our respective faiths which mark out our identity and commitment as faithful Christians or Muslims.

Theological motifs for a dialogical relationship

The possibilities and limitations of even a 'partnership' approach, and the need constantly to hold it up to a critique founded on the core affirmations of faith, bring me to the second question to be addressed in charting Christian responses to Islam – namely, 'what theological motifs are important for Christians in moulding a truly dialogical attitude to, and relationship with, Muslims?' Whereas the first four ideological types may be reflected in theological attitudes, I argue that here the relationship between the 'history of ideas' and the 'sociology of knowledge' should be reversed: a coherent theology is needed to generate and hold together a balanced involvement in dialogue. This involves a move from description to prescription, which in turn suggests a more personal statement of aspirations for parameters to govern future Christian dialogical responses to Islam and Muslims. In the remainder of this chapter, therefore, I list seven factors which seem to me to be essential for this.

Firstly, Christians need to be motivated by gospel imperatives to adopt an orientation of welcoming the Muslim other in a way that avoids the risk that '"the other" is totalised into "more of the same"'[27] – in other words, in a way which respects the boundaries of their distinctiveness as genuinely other. It is impossible to read the New Testament without recognising the centrality in Jesus' ministry of the giving and accepting of hospitality, the inclusive and open welcome to those who are different to share in fellowship. At the same time, this evangelic hospitality is without any pressure to assimilate, to conform the guest to the expectations or norms of the host.[28] Ethically, Derrida has coined the neologism 'hostipitality' to point to the way in which hosts can subtly deploy strategies of hospitality to express an underlying hostility to strangers through neutralising their otherness by an expectation of their assimilation.[29] This has a clear correspondence in terms of social policy to the view that integration is a duty laid solely on those who are different, with no challenge to the host community also to integrate its attitudes and practices to welcome the other. A Christian understanding of hospitality, though, will begin from the rather different premise of recognising that all humans are guests of the God who is a generous host to the whole world, yet comes among his people as a stranger seeking welcome. This gives indeed a clear mandate for the practice of hospitality, yet insists that that hospitality needs to have mutuality, vulnerability and readiness to change built into its definition as an expression of the true reconciliation which God seeks.

In the context of Christian–Muslim relations in Britain, such a theologically formed practice of hospitality must be sufficiently robust to be able to withstand both the weight of negative and defamatory imagery from the past that infects mutual perceptions and the forces of current geopolitical rhetoric and pressures that seek to pull communities apart. While recognising the global connections both Christians and Muslims have with co-religionists in other countries, it will have to be firmly rooted in the local contexts of the British towns and cities where members of the two faiths live in geographical proximity to one another, being courageous and sensitive enough to cross the territorial and cultural boundaries which separate them. It will be an instance, modulated for the specific situation of this encounter in Britain, of the 'ethical heterology' set by Michael Barnes as a *sine qua non* of interfaith relations.[30]

Secondly, alongside this ethical heterology, and providing a theological support for it in the motif of Christians and Muslims as co-guests of the divine, is to be set what could be called a 'spiritual homology' of God: a way of understanding from an authentically Christian (and, therefore, a Trinitarian) perspective the identity of the divine being who is at the centre of Islamic faith and worship. As seen in the discussion above of the ideology of relationship as 'hostility', the identity or otherwise of the Islamic Allah with the biblical God is a contentious issue for some Christians, and it is certainly not sufficient simply to assert the 'sameness' of the two in an undifferentiated way. Kenneth Cragg, for example, recognises the need for a more nuanced use of language when he writes:

> Those who say that *Allah* is not 'the God and Father of our Lord Jesus Christ' are right if they mean that God is not so described by Muslims. They are wrong if they mean that *Allah* is other than the God of the Christian faith.[31]

The second part of Cragg's analysis, though, underlines the critically important point that the God worshipped by Muslims is not to be seen as another divine being distinct from 'the Christian God'. Indeed, the logic of monotheism itself allows for no such entity, other than in the categories of the 'false divinities' repudiated by all the prophetic religions which claim descent from Abraham. The ecumenical parameters of this theological homology have already been clearly set by the unambiguous affirmation of the Second Vatican Council:

> [Muslims] worship God, who is one, living and subsistent, merciful and almighty, the Creator of heaven and earth, who has also spoken to men.[32]

Within these parameters, due space will indeed need to be given for recognition and discussion of the very significant differences in the way that Islamic, as compared to Christian, faith apprehends the one God, and in particular to the question of how far Trinitarian belief is reconcilable with an Islamic account of *tawḥīd*, divine unity.[33] Nevertheless, without an acknowledgement of the basic identity of the God who sustains both communities of faith, any serious dialogue seems doomed to failure.

Thirdly, Christians need to develop an apparatus for discerning the presence and activity of God within Islam as a structured way of belief and practice, as well as among individual Muslims. Two related motifs, one Christological and one Pneumatological, might provide resources for such discernment. The former is the theme of *semina Verbi* which is evident behind the text of *Nostra Aetate*, speaking of elements of other religions as a *praeparatio evangelica* sown by the Logos in human hearts to lead them towards the fullness of truth revealed in Jesus Christ.[34] There are conceptual difficulties involved in applying this analysis directly to Islam, in that it is not immediately apparent how a religion post-dating Christ can serve as a pointer towards, rather than away from, the Christian revelation. However, the *semina Verbi* theme can be complemented by the idea of other religions as 'sites of the Spirit's operation'.[35] The insistence that discernment of this can be made in structural terms is made by Pope John Paul II's later exegesis of a key conciliar text:

> The Spirit's presence and activity affect not only individuals but also society and history, peoples, cultures and religions. Indeed, the Spirit is at the origin of the noble ideals and undertakings which benefit humanity on its journey through history: 'The Spirit of God with marvellous foresight directs the course of the ages and renews the face of the earth.'[36]

From an Anglican perspective, a similar, though perhaps slightly more radical, Pneumatological approach is represented by John Taylor's description of a religion as 'a people's tradition of response to the reality that the Holy Spirit has set before their eyes'.[37] These Christological and Pneumatological ways of affirming the possibility of a divine operation within Islam, though, do not need to imply that it is a separately sufficient framework of revelation or salvation alongside Christianity. The process of discerning the presence of Word or Spirit in Islam would still be governed by the criteria supplied by the Christian faith which is expressed in Trinitarian belief.[38]

Fourthly, alongside the discernment of these resonances, truthful dialogue between Christians and Muslims requires a full and honest acknowledgement of the real differences presented by the mutually incompatible claims of a finality of revelation made available in the events of Jesus or Muhammad respectively. It is important to be accurate about the terms to be set against one another here. For Christians, the fullness of God's self-revelation is lived out in the life, death and resurrection of the human Jesus of Nazareth: the Word of God is expressed most adequately, we might say, in 'body language'. For Muslims, on the other hand, the divine message in its completeness is delivered in written form as a scripture revealed through the prophetic agency of Muhammad. As in one religion we speak of the Word's 'incarnation' or enfleshment, so in the other we may speak of 'inlibration' or embookment:[39] thus, the pairs of terms to be set alongside one another from the two revelatory events are neither Jesus and Muhammad, nor Bible and Qur'an, but rather Jesus and Qur'an.

Nevertheless, despite these differing accounts of the method by which the final revelation is understood to be transmitted and received, there is a deep and irreducible dividing line between Christian and Islamic faith as to the historical point at which that finality is realised: in the first-century life of Jesus, or in the seventh century life of Muhammad? Moreover, because its final revelation is the chronologically earlier of the two, it is more problematic for Christian theology to give a theologically satisfying account of Islam, a spiritually adequate response to the figure of Muhammad, than it is for Islamic theology to account for Christianity or Jesus.[40] Indeed, Muslims not infrequently remark on the imbalance between the detail of their own accounts of the other – where Christianity is usually seen as a divinely inspired, if partially corrupted, monotheism, and Jesus is honourably enrolled among the succession of prophetic messengers – on the one hand, and the silence of the Christian other in relation to key elements of their own faith on the other hand.[41] Yet this imbalance is a natural consequence of the relationship of contested finality which links the two faiths, and it can only be redressed (by giving a Christian reading of the Qur'an, or a Christian appreciation of Muhammad) from a position which fully recognises the significance and permanence of that unresolved relationship.

Fifthly, these points lead to recognition of the importance of a method of scriptural intertextuality as one of the key ways in which believers of the two faiths can effectively relate dialogically to one another. Bible and Qur'an are respectively our foundational texts; to insist on their primacy in dialogue is to ensure that inter faith engagement is rooted in the core concerns and impulses of both faiths: it prevents a concentration on issues which are easily capable of a superficial resolution, by holding in the centre of the conversation also those questions which are less tractable. As neither scripture can be relegated to the role of being the possession of its own community, but has about it a givenness which stands over and above the community, the dialogue can come to have an objectivity and independence which releases it from the danger of being locked into personalised disagreements:

> Put the scriptures at the centre of our dialogue, and the deadlock can be avoided. The disputes are now less about us and our opinions and more about something that has a claim on us and to which we give greater allegiance than we do our own convictions . . . In an important sense, *we are not so much agents of a dialogue as instruments of a dialogue whose main protagonists are our respective scriptures.*[42]

Moreover, this 'dialogue of scriptures' inextricably involves God. While, as noted above, the role of Bible and Qur'an is not equivalent in terms of Christian and Islamic revelation respectively, it remains true that in both faiths the scriptures can be seen as instruments through which God engages in a dialogue with his people and with his world. Because He is unlimitedly God and those who record and read the scriptures are limitedly human, the texts envelop an unexhausted richness of the divine Word which will always reach beyond the interpretations which either community of faith can assimilate. In a scriptural dialogue, as Christians read the Qur'an in the company and under the guidance of Muslims, or Muslims similarly read the Bible with Christians, some of this inexhaustibility of divine communication in the text may be released to the other reader both through and beyond the reading supplied by its own readers. Gavin D'Costa's more generally applicable comments about 'auto-interpretation' and 'hetero-interpretation' have a particular relevance to this dynamic of intertextual reading through which the distinctive dialogue of God with either community may become open in a different way to the other:

> Affirmation requires both a serious engagement with the other religion on its own terms, which is an on-going process, and also allows for what I will call legitimate hetero-interpretation, that is, a theological evaluation of the meaning of that religion, or various parts of it, that may not necessarily be in keeping with the sense of those within that tradition – what I call auto-interpretation. While auto- and hetero-interpretations may coincide, the latter is always reliant on auto-interpretation.[43]

Sixthly, there needs to be for Christians a theological framework to hold together and mutually balance the different aspects and modalities of dialogue with Muslims – which can be helpfully enumerated according to the fourfold schema of: (1) dialogue of life; (2) dialogue of collaboration in social involvement for justice and peace; (3) theological dialogue in search of the truth; (4) dialogue of the sharing of religious experience.[44] Of these four dimensions, the first represents the foundational and all-encompassing matrix of Christians and Muslims enriching one another's lives through practising their respective values, while the three latter strands focus particularly on the social, intellectual and spiritual aspects of dialogue in turn. If these three are not held together, and grounded in the former, an undue emphasis on one or the other may reduce dialogue respectively to shallow and platitudinous activism, to the aridity of sterile argumentation, or to a syncretistic swapping of spiritual techniques.[45]

There is perhaps in the British context of Christian–Muslim relations a most pressing need to hold together the second and third of these four forms of dialogue, i.e. the social and the intellectual, which Vatican II linked as *collaboratio* and *colloquium*:

> The Church urges her sons to enter with prudence and charity into discussion and collaboration (*colloquia et collaboratio*) with members of other religions.[46]

The challenge here is not only the general one of how *praxis* is to be effectively related to reflection; more specifically, in Britain it reflects the need to bring into contact the distinct worlds of academically rigorous dialogue between Christian and Muslim theologians and of neighbourhood-level cooperation between Christian and Muslim communities. If *colloquium* in the search for truth has a tendency to focus on difference while *collaboratio* must build on shared values, then in Lochhead's terms, the need is for a dialogue holding together 'competition' and 'partnership' models.

Finally, Christians need to be able to give a theologically informed account of public space, an arena both for the advancement of Christian values and also for the accommodation of an Islamic presence. This is a particularly complex issue within the British context, where there are long histories of the shaping of public life by Christian influence.[47] Christian individuals and communities who are enthused and renewed by the encounter with Islam to reclaim the public square as an arena for the sharing of Gospel truth and values have at the same time to ensure the provision of a space within which the sometimes different truths and values of Islam (and of other faiths) can publicly flourish and play their own part in nurturing civic society. Moreover, an adequately Christian view of the public world which can incorporate diversity of this kind still must aim to maintain an overall connected account of society which either does not surrender all to a starkly secularised ideology, or at least can find a convincing Christian basis for secularity. Beyond this again, there lies the positive challenge of finding a theological basis for Christians and Muslims to work together in promoting the common good of a society which seems to be increasingly unsure of how to handle issues of religious identity and interaction. In the English context at least, all this points to the principle of an established religion being extended and diversified in ways which make its public workings increasingly hospitable to Muslims as well as Christians:

> It is part of our role, I believe, to seek to provide space and access, opportunity and the right atmosphere for the many dealings and interactions between faith communities and the wider society, however and wherever we can.[48]

To develop a theological foundation adequate for understanding a society which is in this way simultaneously Christian, diverse and secular, though, is a responsibility not for one denomination alone, but for churches of all traditions working together. The same is true of the other six parameters I have proposed as imperatives for developing a dialogical relationship between Christians and Muslims: they represent a major ecumenical challenge for Christians to build their responses to Islam and to Muslims in Britain on a firm theological foundation.

Notes

1 Lochhead, D., *The Dialogical Imperative: A Christian Reflection on Interfaith Encounter* (London, SCM, 1988).
2 Ibid., p. 2.
3 Ibid., p. 3.
4 Lochhead himself admits that dialogue is evident among Christians only 'infrequently, ambiguously and fragmentarily' (p. 81). It seems to me that his account of this 'fifth relationship' is unrealistically optimistic as a description of an actually existing phenomenon – in particular, it does not take seriously the element of 'negotiation' in inter faith dialogue. See Ipgrave, M., *Trinity and Inter Faith Dialogue: Plenitude and Plurality* (Bern, Peter Lang, 2003), pp. 306ff. Nevertheless, it serves as a useful shorthand for the ideal of a theologically governed relationship.
5 Lochhead, *The Dialogical Imperative*, p. 28.
6 Ibid., p. 7.
7 The seminal report on this question remains that of the Commission on British Muslims and Islamophobia, *Islamophobia: A Challenge for Us All* (London, Runnymede Trust, 1997). The Commission's findings are corroborated by a number of detailed surveys, e.g. Poole, E., 'Framing Islam: an analysis of newspaper coverage of Islam in the British press', in Hafez, K. (ed.), *Islam and the West in the Mass Media: Fragmented Images in a Globalizing World* (Cresshill, NJ, Hampton, 2000), pp. 157–80.
8 Lochhead, *The Dialogical Imperative*, p. 12.
9 The evolution of these images is charted with detail and eloquence by Daniel, N., *Islam and the West: The Making of an Image* (Oxford, Oneworld, 1993).
10 Notably, Pawson, D., *The Challenge of Islam to Christians* (London, Hodder & Stoughton, 2003).
11 Ibid., p. 6. He goes on to say of this revelation: 'I hope I am wrong. I hope it is a false prophecy'.
12 Sookhdeo, P., *A Christian Perspective on Islam*, December 2001, on www.barnabasfund.org. Subsequent references are all to this article. See also the more recent article, 'Islamization of Europe' (August 2005) on the same website, and

the booklet from the Institute for the Study of Islam and Christianity, *Islam in Britain* (Pewsey, Isaac, 2005).

13 Sookhdeo, *A Christian Perspective on Islam.*

14 www.answering-islam.org.uk/Hoaxes/israeliweb.html.

15 It is interesting to note that this in one sense mirrors the extreme Wahhabist views of those Muslims who regard Christians as *mushrikūn*, 'those who associate another with God' (i.e., polytheistic pagans) because of their belief in the Trinity.

16 This is a theme developed in pamphlets and booklets with titles such as: *Who Is This Allah?, Who Is Allah in Islam?, Allah – Is he God?,* and *Allah or the God of the Bible – What Is the Truth?* See Ipgrave, M., 'God and Inter Faith Relations: Some attitudes among British Christians', in Mortensen, V. (ed.), *Theology and the Religions: A Dialogue* (Grand Rapids, Eerdmans, 2003).

17 Lochhead, *The Dialogical Imperative*, p. 18.

18 The findings of this exercise were presented to, and endorsed by, the General Synod in July 2005 in the report *Presence and Engagement: The Churches' Task in a Multi-Faith Society* (London, Archbishops' Council, GS [General Synod] 1577, 2005).

19 GS 1577, p. 27. In the Diocese of London, the figure is 296 parishes out of 413, i.e. 72% of the total. 556 parishes nationwide fell within a still higher measure of religious diversity – those where the population included at least 25% of other faith communities combined or at least 10% of any one faith community other than Christianity – GS 1577, p. 28.

20 In the twenty Church of England parishes with the highest proportions of people of other faiths, Muslims were the biggest community in all but one parish – GS 1577, p. 29.

21 GS 1577, pp. 16f.

22 One classic and widely influential exposition is Chapman, C., *Cross and Crescent* (Leicester, InterVarsity, 1994). On the contentious question of the identity of the Islamic Allah with the biblical God – generally denied in a 'hostility' paradigm – Chapman judiciously writes that there is 'enough in common between the Christian's idea of God and the Muslim's idea of God for us to be able to use the same word for "God"' (Ibid., p. 228).

23 Lochhead, *The Dialogical Imperative*, p. 23.

24 See Churches' Commission on Inter Faith Relations, *Responding Locally to the War in Iraq* (London, Churches Together in Britain and Ireland, 2003).

25 *Archbishop of Canterbury's Listening Initiative in Christian–Muslim Relations: Final Report of the Planning Group* (London, Archbishops' Council, 2004), p. 3.

26 Expressed, for example, in the report's recommendation that: 'Underpinning and accompanying all the practical work in Christian–Muslim relations with which the Forum is concerned there needs to be a continuing theological exploration together of those core elements in both our faiths which inform our involvement. Such an exploration would take account of both the resonances and the dissonances in our understanding of how divine guidance is given' – Ibid., p. 28.

27 Barnes SJ, M., *Theology and the Dialogue of Religions* (Cambridge, Cambridge University Press, 2002), pp. 184f.

28 A similar practice of hospitality-affirming-difference can be discerned in the passages of the Hebrew scripture which mandate right treatment of the *gēr*, the 'resident alien' in the midst of Israel, though in subsequent Jewish tradition these

are reinterpreted as referring to Gentile converts to Judaism, i.e. assimilative pressures are reintroduced. See Goshen-Gottstein, A., 'Judaism: the battle for survival, the struggle for compassion', pp. 34ff, in Goshen-Gottstein, A. (ed.), *Religions, Society and the Other: Hostility, Hospitality and the Hope of Human Flourishing* (Jerusalem, Elijah Interfaith Academy, 2003).

29 Derrida, J., 'Hostipitality', in Anidjar, G. (ed.), *Acts of Religion* (New York, Routledge, 2001).

30 Barnes, Theology, p. 62 eloquently summarises Michel de Certeau's understanding of heterology as: 'the deconstruction or uncovering of unavowed forms of enclosure'.

31 Cragg, K., *The Call of the Minaret* (New York, Orbis, 1985), p. 30.

32 *Nostra Aetate*, cap. 3 – in Abbott, W. (ed.), *The Documents of Vatican II* (London, Chapman, 1966). Even more remarkable, particularly given the period in which it was made, is the statement of Pope Gregory VII in a letter written to Anzir, the Muslim King of Mauritania in 1076: 'We and you must show in a special way to the other nations an example of this charity, for we believe and confess one God, although in different ways, and praise and worship Him daily as the creator of all ages and the ruler of this world' – cited in Neuner SJ, J. and Dupuis SJ, J. (eds), *The Christian Faith: Doctrinal Documents of the Catholic Church* (London, Harper Collins, 1992), p. 302.

33 A striking and high-profile recent exploration of these issues is to be found in a lecture delivered by the Archbishop of Canterbury at the al-Azhar university on 11 September 2004 – text on www.archbishopofcanterbury.org. See also Ipgrave, M., 'Trinitarian theology at al-Azhar: reflections on a lecture by Archbishop Rowan Williams', *Mission*, 11: 2 (2004), 313–28.

34 *Nostra Aetate* cap. 2, which refers in explicit terms to the similar motif of the *radius veritatis* enlightening all people (see Jn 1.9). The connection with *semina Verbi* is made by Pope John Paul II himself, in McPhee, J. and McPhee, M. (trans.), *Crossing the Threshold of Hope* (London, Jonathan Cape, 1994), p. 81.

35 See D'Costa, G., *The Meeting of Religions and the Trinity* (Maryknoll, Orbis, 200), pp. 109ff.

36 From the 1991 encyclical *Redemptoris Missio: On the Permanent Validity of the Church's Missionary Mandate*, cap. 28. The quotation at the end is from *Gaudium et Spes*, cap. 26. As D'Costa observes (*The Meeting of Religions*, p. 113), in the original citation Vatican II does not 'refer to cultures and religions, and the Pope clearly wants to push beyond any individualist reading of *Gaudium et Spes*'s far-reaching affirmations'.

37 Taylor, J. V., *The Go-between God: The Holy Spirit and Christian Mission* (London, SCM, 1972), p. 182. Taylor immediately went on to clarify his meaning as follows: 'I am deliberately not saying that any religion is the truth which the Spirit disclosed, nor even that it contains that truth. All we can say without presumption is that this is how men have responded and taught others to respond to what the Spirit made them aware of'.

38 In just the same way, a Muslim appraisal of Christianity might find within it elements of authentic monotheism, and still insist that these are to be judged according to the norms of *tawḥīd*.

39 The language of 'inlibration' appears to have been first coined by H. Wolfson in *The Philosophy of the Kalam* (Cambridge, Mass., Harvard University Press, 1976), p. 246. See also the earlier comment by R. C. Zaehner: 'For the Word made flesh

Muslim theology substitutes the Word made book': *At Sundry Times: An Essay in the Comparison of Religions* (London, Faber & Faber, 1958), p. 198 – though the use of the verb 'substitute' is perhaps unfortunate here.

40 In this sense, the relationship between Christianity and Islam broadly parallels the relationship between Judaism and Christianity, in that in both cases the later religion comes into the world with an already felt need to define itself in terms of, and over against, the earlier religion, whereas the earlier has neither immediately available resources nor instantly pressing need to do so in relation to the later.

41 The most dramatic sign of this deficit in Christian theology is perhaps the entire absence of any reference to the prophetic figure of Muhammad (or to the Qur'an which he delivered) among the otherwise warmly sympathetic comments on Islam in *Nostra Aetate*, cap. 3.

42 Volf, M., 'Hospitable readings: comments on *Scriptures in Dialogue*', in Ipgrave, M. (ed.), *Bearing the Word: Prophecy in Biblical and Qur'ānic Perspectives* (London, Church House Publishing, 2005), p. 25. The italics are Volf's own.

43 D'Costa, *The Meeting of Religions*, p. 100. D'Costa's 'auto-interpretation' would in my example correspond to Muslims' reading of a Qur'ānic passage, and 'hetero-interpretation' to Christians' reading of the same text in dialogue with that Muslim reading (or the converse stances for the Bible).

44 This fourfold classification, which has been quite widely adopted ecumenically, was first proposed in a document from the Vatican's then 'Secretariat for Non-Christians' (now the 'Pontifical Council for Interreligious Dialogue') with the rather cumbrous title: *The Attitude of the Church Towards Followers of Other Religions: Reflections and Orientations on Dialogue and Mission* (Vatican, Secretariat for Non-Christians, 1984).

45 I have argued elsewhere (*Trinity and Inter Faith Dialogue*, pp. 325ff) that Trinitarian belief gives a Christian theological framework to hold these different dimensions together.

46 *Nostra Aetate*, cap. 2.

47 'Histories' in the plural, because the national stories of the four nations which comprise the United Kingdom of Great Britain and Northern Ireland have been quite distinct in terms of their religious shaping, e.g. in the part (if any) played by a 'national' or 'established' church.

48 Archbishop George Carey, 'Holding together: church and nation in the twenty-first century', lecture delivered at Lambeth Palace on 23 April 2002 – text on www.archbishopofcanterbury.org.

3

The response of the Church of England to Islam and Muslim–Christian relations in contemporary Britain

Barbara Mitchell

Islam is the second largest religion in the world, with approximately 1000 million adherents.[1] The emphasis that Islam places on missionary activity means the number of Muslims living within western societies is increasing steadily, not just through birth and immigration but also as a result of conversion. It is therefore a faith which Christians in Britain must necessarily come into contact with as they pursue their daily lives.

The *umma*, the trans-national and cross-cultural unity that is shared by all Muslims, regardless of their nationality or ethnic background, is central to the teachings of their faith. However, it is wrong to regard Islam as a monolithic religion and Muslims living in Britain today are a mosaic of social, cultural, ethnic, economic and theological elements. A university-educated Muslim of Middle-Eastern origin living in London will often find as great a gulf between himself and a Muslim from Pakistan living in Bradford, as he would with a member of the Christian faith. Both these factors need to be taken into account when considering Christian–Muslim dialogue.

In this chapter I will briefly examine the role of the Church of England in modern society and outline the history and diversity of the Muslim community in Britain today, before examining the approaches that leading practitioners of interfaith dialogue within the Church of England have developed in seeking to expand Christian–Muslim dialogue.

The pastoral responsibility of the Church of England

The Church of England, the established church, consists of a network of parishes covering the entire country. When it came into being in the mid-sixteenth century, Britain was a wholly Christian country. The parish priest was regarded as having a pastoral duty towards all those who lived within the boundaries of his parish. This situation continues today, despite the enormous changes that have taken place within the social fabric of Britain. The Church of England continues to offer pastoral care to all, both baptised and unbaptised, and this must necessarily include those of other faiths.[2] In a debate at the General Synod in February 1988 about the church's legal obligation to marry adherents of non-Christian faiths in a church service it was stated:

Marriage is God's gift available to all people and mindful of the church's responsibility to minister to everyone in this country . . . there should be no change in the Church's responsibility to solemnise the marriage of all parishioners who request that ministry.[3]

Likewise, Anglican churches were encouraged to be sympathetic when other faith groups wished to use their buildings and facilities, provided certain criteria were met. This was to be seen as an appropriate means of building positive relationships between different worshipping communities.

Education is also an area where the Church of England encounters members of other faiths. 25% of all state primary schools and 6% of all state secondary schools are aided or assisted by the Church of England.[4] Many of these schools are in inner-city areas where immigrant groups predominantly live. Consequently, the education of many children from other faith backgrounds is undertaken under the auspices of the Anglican church. In some church primary schools over 90% of the pupils are from non-Christian backgrounds, but this situation is viewed positively by those responsible for developing the curriculum:

If children of other faiths are admitted to the school then those children will be co-pilgrims rather than co-custodians. The very presence of children of other faiths is a challenge for the universal relevance of the Christian faith as it is lived and expressed by those who claim it as their own.[5]

One example of this tolerant approach may be seen at Cheetham Church of England Community School in Manchester: 98% of the pupils in the school are Muslim and, as a response to this situation, the governors appointed a British convert to Islam as headmaster and employed a number of Muslim teachers. As far as possible school life has been adapted to the pupils' needs; prayers are said in the school hall at midday and in the afternoon, and when Ramadan falls during the winter months the fast is opened by pupils before they leave school for the day.[6]

The relationship between the Church of England and those of other faiths living in Britain is becoming increasingly important, as is the development of interfaith relations on an international level throughout the Anglican Communion. Much of this work is done ecumenically and focuses on cooperation, where possible, in service to the wider society. Rather than causing division, the unique situation of the Church of England within modern Britain is often valued by members of other faiths. It is felt that its position ensures that religion still retains a voice within a society that is becoming increasingly secularised.

The history of the Muslim community in Britain

The documented history of the Muslim community in England began during the reign of Elizabeth I. At this time Muslims were temporary visitors and it was only towards the end of the seventeenth century that a small number of Muslims became permanent residents. The expansion of trade in the late sixteenth century meant that it became necessary to cooperate with Muslims from North Africa and the Ottoman empire. Seamen from these areas were permitted to use harbours in England and Wales and there is evidence that a few Muslim traders chose to convert to Anglicanism during this period in order to remain in England.[7]

The most visible representatives of Islam in this early period were ambassadors at the royal court, whose position allowed them to practise their religion openly. However, their insularity did not endear them to the populace and the number of ambassadors from Muslim domains was reduced when James I, who was 'notoriously hostile to Islam', ascended to the throne.[8]

Another group of Muslims in Britain was those who were brought in as prisoners of war. Some of these returned home but others chose to remain. An anonymous writer, depicting London life in the early 1640s, described a sect of 'Mohametans . . . here in London' and in 1627 John Harrison reported there were nearly forty 'Turkes' living in London, employed in various trades.[9]

The Muslims who lived in seventeenth-century Britain do not seem to have remained as permanent residents and there is no evidence of the development of communal facilities to serve their religious needs. However, their presence in the country attracted the attention of John Locke (1632–1704). Writing at a time when relations between dissenting religious groups and the newly restored Stuart monarchy were of paramount importance he argued that if the state could tolerate those of other faiths, such as Jews and Muslims, it must also be capable of tolerating Christian Dissenters. Locke regarded Muslims favourably, as they were valuable economically and he saw no difficulty in allowing law-abiding Muslims to settle in Britain. For Locke, arguing from a political rather than a theological stance, a person's faith was irrelevant to their claim on citizenship; a view that continues to find resonance in contemporary Britain.[10]

A steadier flow of Muslim immigrants began in the mid-nineteenth century, starting with *lascars* who worked as cheap labour in port cities. Trade with the Middle East and South Asia increased following the opening of the Suez Canal in 1869 and Muslims began to settle in cities such as Cardiff, Liverpool and London. In some areas, Sufi Sheiks arrived to meet their religious needs and centres opened which became focal points for the Muslim community. Some *lascars* married local women and remained permanently in their adopted country, becoming the nucleus of an indigenous Muslim community.[11] In the first half of the twentieth century this community numbered about 15,000, living mainly in major port cities.

In the nineteenth and early twentieth centuries there was constant traffic between the colonies and Britain. This led to an increase in the Muslim population in Britain, ranging from the wealthy professional and merchant classes, often students, to the servants brought to Britain before being dismissed by their employers and left without means of support.[12]

Islam also exercised an influence on Britons who had travelled in Muslim countries and there was a number of high profile converts to Islam during the Victorian era. William Henry Quilliam, a solicitor who embraced Islam after a visit to Morocco in 1887, founded the mosque and Islamic Institute in Liverpool. Others included Lord Headley and M. M. Pickthall who were associated with the Woking Mosque and Mission, built in Surrey in 1889, which is still active today.[13]

The nature of the Muslim community in Britain changed radically after the Second World War. Following the Independence and Partition of India in 1947 there was a widespread relocation of displaced people. The demand for labour in Britain, which was seeking to rebuild its industrial base after the Second World War, resulted in many single males from Pakistan and India coming to Britain in the late 1950s and early 1960s for socio-economic reasons. The intention of these men was not to settle permanently in Britain but to earn money to support their relatives at home before returning themselves. However, the Commonwealth Immigration Acts of 1962 and 1964 limited the free movement of those seeking to travel between the countries of the Commonwealth and Britain. Consequently, many chose to settle in Britain permanently, bringing their wives and families to join them before such a move could be banned. Between 1955 and 1960 17,000 Pakistanis entered Britain and this increased to 50,000 in the eighteen months before the 1962 Act came into force.[14] This rise in population radically changed the face of the Muslim community in Britain. There was now a need to develop a religious infrastructure suited to the needs of the whole family: mosques, provision for religious education and shops to provide for dietary requirements. The Muslim community was enlarged again when Asians from East Africa were forced to leave their homes and settle in Britain in the mid-1970s. Consequently, some two-thirds of the Muslims in Britain today have their ethnic roots in the Indian sub-continent.

During the 1970s and 1980s, an increasing number of students and business people from the Far East, Middle East and Africa arrived. This group comprised a far more transient population than those from former British colonies, but it has had the effect of broadening the ethnic make-up of the Muslim community, as has the increasing number of converts from within the indigenous population.

Today the Muslim community in Britain centres on urban areas, with different ethnic groups concentrated in particular regions. In London Bangladeshis are found in the East End, Turks in the north, and Arabs and Iranians in Kensington. Pakistanis are the dominant group in Bradford and Birmingham, while the majority of Yemenis live in Sheffield and Malaysians favour Manchester.[15] Following the 1991 census it was estimated that there were between 1 and 1.5 million Muslims living in Britain. As there was no question about religious affiliation on the census form, this figure was based on the ethnic identity of the respondents and information given by the religious communities themselves.[16] In the 2001 census, when a question about religious affiliation was included, the number of people describing themselves as Muslim was 1,591,126. It is predicted that this figure will have trebled by 2020.

The contemporary position of Islam and Christian–Muslim relations in Britain

Islam emerged into a world in which both Judaism and Christianity were well established and from its earliest days Islam was faced with the question of how to relate to these pre-existing faiths. For some Muslims the entire 'infidel' world was to be regarded as one homogenous entity, which was united by their *shirk*.

On the other hand, some scholars, such as Ibn Abi Layla (d. 785CE) regarded Judaism and Christianity differently from religions such as Zoroastrianism, because Jews and Christians shared a belief in the unity of God and the prophethood of Moses.[17] These differing views are still reflected in contemporary attitudes of Muslims towards Christianity. However, whether or not Christians and Jews are regarded as being on a par with other 'non-believers' or in a special category, the difficulty for Christians seeking to dialogue with Muslims is that their faith is regarded as having been abrogated by the message brought to the world by Muhammad.

The earliest barriers to constructive dialogue between Muslims and Christians were theological; were Christians, with their doctrine of the Trinity, to be regarded as monotheistic believers? How was Jesus, so differently described by the New Testament and the Qur'an, to be understood? What about the nature of God's revelation to humankind? Could Christians regard Muhammad as a prophet and, if so, in what sense? Additionally, both Islam and Christianity saw themselves as universal, missionary faiths. The vocation of both Muslims and Christians was to spread their message among those whom they regarded as unbelievers. Was it possible with two faiths coming from this standpoint for a productive dialogue to develop between them? These questions remain pertinent in today's world. Scholars such as Sidney Griffith are returning to the period in which Islam emerged in order to discover ways in which contemporary Muslims and Christians may understand each other better.

Within the Qur'an both Jews and Christians were accorded special status as 'the People of the Book'. They were allowed to live in the domains of Islam on payment of *jizyah* and permitted to worship, although any form of missionary activity or church building was forbidden. The language of the doctrine of the Trinity proved a stumbling block for general Islamic acceptance of Christians as fellow monotheists. Kenneth Cragg, an Anglican bishop and leading Christian Islamacist, sees this as a misconception of Christian teaching by Muslims:

> The Christian faith in God as Father, Son and Holy Spirit is not a violation of faith in God's unity. It is a way of understanding that unity – a way, the Christian would go on to say, of safe-guarding that unity.[18]

Cragg developed this idea in a later book, *Jesus and the Muslim*, where he argues that the conviction of all three Semitic faiths is that God can only be known by humans in conjunction with the human situation. In Judaism, this is through the Covenant relationship between God and His people, in Islam through human prophethood and in Christianity 'finally and exclusively' in the person of Jesus.[19]

Despite Cragg's assertion, the person of Jesus remains problematic for Muslims. *Isa* is regarded as a prophet in the Qur'an, but in no sense divine. The Qur'an contains stories about his birth and miracles as well as divine pronouncements about him and conversations he had, both with God and other people. There are also many references to Jesus in Arabic literature from the eighth century onwards. *Isa* is regarded as a Muslim prophet who brought a revelation from God to humankind. His message has been distorted by its recipients, according to Muslim thought, and the Christianity that later emerged was a product of that distortion and not the faith that was intended by its founder. Nor can that message be considered except as forerunner to the revelation brought by Muhammad. Muslims point to the existence of four Gospels, the nature of the Epistles and the development of Christian theology to support their thesis that the teachings of Christianity are adjusted to 'cross-currents of time and opinion'.[20] Despite this, Muslims have continued to appreciate the person of Jesus, albeit in an Islamified form, which Christians may argue has its roots in the non-canonical apocryphal gospels. As Tarif Khalidi, a modern Muslim writer, expressed it:

> For early Muslims, there was no *prima facie* reason not to accept a Christian story, tradition, maxim or homily, provided it lay within the conceptual frame-work that Islam had already laid out for itself.[21]

In the way that the doctrine of the Trinity is an impediment to dialogue for many Muslims, the nature of the prophethood of Muhammad provides a major obstacle for Christians in their acceptance of Islam as a 'true' religion. Christianity has no problem accepting the revelation of God through the prophets of the Jewish Scriptures, many of whom are also acknowledged as prophets in the Qur'an. However, in Christian thought, those men were seen as preparing the way for the final and exclusive revelation of God in the person of Jesus. Muhammad post-dated the person of Jesus and so cannot be regarded as prophetic in the same sense by Christians. An additional difficulty for Christians is that conversion to Islam simply requires a declaration of belief in one God and in Muhammad as the messenger, or prophet, of God. Therefore, if Christians acknowledge an acceptance of the prophethood of Muhammad they place themselves in a position in which they may be regarded as renouncing Christianity. It may be tempting, in a spirit of reciprocity, for Christians to talk of Muhammad as a prophet in the same way Muslims show respect for Jesus. However, for Muslims this would undermine the very existence of their Christian faith, a situation that would not be conducive to profitable dialogue. Jacques Jomier, a French Dominican and Catholic scholar of Islam, recounts this cautionary tale:

> A Christian bishop, full of good intentions but not realising the effect of his words, proclaimed to the Islamic-Christian Congress in Tripoli that dialogue would be impossible as long as Christians did not accept a certain number of positions – and in particular that they should recognize the prophetic character of Muhammad . . . The next day the local papers announced in bold headlines that the bishop had been converted to Islam, which was hardly the intention.[22]

Two problems on the path to dialogue, but problems which dialogue itself seeks to redress, are Muslim perceptions of Christianity and Christian perceptions of Islam. Both religions have been moulded through events of history and by geographical distance from one another. It is only recently with the breakdown of colonialism and the advent of relatively cheap and rapid transport that large numbers of Muslims and Christians have come into regular contact with each other in this country. Consequently, old myths and stereotypes have lingered and fear of the other has kept communities separate. These need to be broken down if dialogue is to be initiated and be successful. Ataullah Siddiqui, a Research Fellow at the Leicester Islamic Foundation, writes:

> Muslims in a pluralist society . . . need to re-examine their perceptions about the people around them. The tendency to perceive all non-Muslims as inherently 'antagonistic' to Islam and to Muslims and 'perpetually' conspiring against them, needs re-thinking. There are very good souls and fine people beyond our own community.[23]

This statement reflects a very positive approach towards Christianity, which is not widely reflected within the Muslim community. The majority of Muslims living in Britain have their origins in countries, such as Pakistan, where Christianity is the faith of a small minority of the population. There is no need or desire to learn more about its beliefs or practices, as the traditional Islamic view is that Christianity is a failed religion. This belief, combined with a long held mistrust of Christianity that has its roots in historical events such as the Crusades and the missionary zeal associated with colonialism, means that overtures to dialogue tend to be instigated by Christians rather than Muslims. This may be illustrated by the very real fears that some Muslims had about the motivation behind the designation of the 1990s as the 'Decade of Evangelism' by Archbishop George Carey. For many Muslims the Anglican church may be seen as irrelevant to their lives, 'a disunited and waning force' which has been 'damaged by Carey's decade of de-evangelisation, spiritually arid, and increasingly compromised by concessions to liberal agendas', despite Dr Carey's efforts to develop a positive Muslim–Christian dialogue both in Britain and other provinces of the Anglican Communion. However, having said this, the same writer in the Muslim journal *Q News*, looked to the future and welcomed Rowan Williams as the new Archbishop of Canterbury, describing him as 'a man of intelligence and political courage, who is worth cultivating as an ally'.[24] In his first years in office Dr Williams has worked hard to build on the groundwork laid by George Carey in stressing the importance of all religious groups learning to sustain themselves in an increasingly complex environment while at the same time learning to work together for the good of society at large.[25]

Practical problems for Christian–Muslim dialogue in Britain

Islam is concerned with all aspects of a person's life; therefore there can be no separation between their religious beliefs and other aspects of life, as there appears to be, to Muslim eyes, in western Christianity. For Muslim communities who have arrived in Britain there is a desire to maintain their traditional lifestyle and this becomes increasingly important as subsequent generations are born and educated in Britain. One way in which continuity with life in the country of origin is maintained is by bringing imams from those countries to Britain to act as guides and mentors to the community. This is particularly true of Muslims whose roots are in Pakistan, many of whom came from rural areas with a high level of illiteracy. Many of those arriving in Britain spoke no English; in 1968, there were 600 imams in Britain, none spoke English nor had any knowledge of any faith but Islam. This situation has improved little over the past thirty-three years. Dr Zaki Badawi opened the Muslim College in 1990 with the express purpose of preparing imams to work specifically within British society,[26] but this venture initially had little impact on the majority of the Muslim population. Recent events have reopened this issue and changes are beginning to take place within the wider British Muslim society. However, with a leadership who had little knowledge or contact with British society or the English language it is not surprising that few moves to initiate dialogue came from the Muslim side.

The role of the imam, who is paid by the local mosque, is to lead congregational prayers, deliver a sermon on Friday and teach children at the *madrasa* held at the mosque. The traditional method of teaching is rote learning. This is understandable in a faith that places emphasis on the ability to recite the Qur'an by heart, but it has little resonance with a generation of children brought up within an educational system which encourages independence of thought and free discussion. Consequently some young people are rejecting the traditional Islam of their parents and replacing it either with secularism or with more radical forms of Islam, which allow no space for dialogue with Christianity.

Many Muslim groups tend to live in isolation from the wider society, especially those in poorer inner-city areas. The religious demands of Islam, prayer five times a day, the need for children to learn Qur'anic Arabic, the requirement to eat meat slaughtered according to Islamic law, means that Muslim communities tend to grow up within walking distance of a mosque. In the report by Lord Ousley following the riots in Bradford these areas were referred to as 'comfort zones', relatively self-sufficient cultural and religious worlds that can exist with minimal acknowledgment of the western world beyond them. In towns like Bradford, there are few opportunities for natural interaction between the Muslim and Christian communities. Schools in certain areas have a predominantly Muslim intake. The high unemployment rates mean that there are few chances of meeting non-Muslims in the workplace and the drinking culture associated with many sports in Britain means that Muslims have chosen to develop their own sports' leagues.[27] Consequently, there is little opportunity for dialogue to develop naturally between people going about their daily lives and both sides become more entrenched in their prejudices.

The problems of Bradford and Oldham, highlighted by the riots during the summer of 2001, may present a particular case, but the cultural background of Muslims from South Asia does not make it easy for them to develop social relationships with those outside their communities. The local intermarrying family groups (*biradari*) remain strong and limit social contact, especially for women, with those outside. Marriage partners and business contacts will be selected initially from the *biradari* and employment will be chosen that allows other members of the *biradari* to settle in close proximity to one another. The idea of honour and loyalty is very important and relationships outside the *biradari* run the risk of being misinterpreted as breaking the rules of traditional etiquette, with consequent alienation from the group.[28] Therefore, it is safer to confine relationships only to those who are members of the *biradari*: another barrier to dialogue with non-Muslims.

Language provides a further barrier between many Muslims and their neighbours. The demands of the *biradari* mean that many young Muslims are married to relatives from South Asia. Some of these spouses do not speak fluent English and women in particular are not encouraged to learn as traditionally they are not expected to take part in activities outside of their home or family circle.[29] The issue of language particularly affects South Asian Muslims as they need to be able to function in a number of tongues: within the home Urdu and Punjabi are commonly used, while Arabic is the language of prayer and the Qur'an. Therefore, mastery of English is an extra burden which some find hard to shoulder. This is less of a problem for those born and educated in Britain, who are often far more at home in English. However, this too can be a cause of tension, when they have a 'breakdown in communication' as a result of problems with their parents' mother tongue'.[30]

Conversely, many Christians remain ignorant of the religious activities of the Muslims who share their streets and towns. When describing Muslim life in Birmingham in the mid-1980s, Daniele Joly could comment: 'Most of this intense social and religious Muslim life' (e.g. Friday prayers, weddings and funerals) 'remains unknown and unnoticed by the wider British population. There are few material signs of it'.[31] Policy changes in many planning departments since the 1980s mean this is becoming less true. There are a greater number of material signs of the Muslim community: minarets are now visible on the sky-lines of many British towns and the public call to prayer is no longer totally forbidden. However, the private practice of Islam within the homes and families of British Muslims remains a closed book to many of their fellow citizens. As some sectors of the media continue to perpetuate myths and stereotypes about Islam, although the events of 11 September 2001 and 7 July 2005 have encouraged the development of a more balanced approach from serious journalists, it is not surprising that many Muslims prefer to practice their religion quietly, without interference from an outside world that many feel they have good reason to fear. On the other hand, if a more informed understanding of Islam is to be formed within the western mind, it is important that Muslims from all backgrounds continue to contribute confidently within British society, rather than leaving that role to politicised and vocal Islamist groups, whose contributions may only result in maintaining the stereotyped images.

Christian–Muslim dialogue within the contemporary Church of England

The response of the Church of England to the Muslim population within the country may be considered on two levels. On the one hand, there is the pragmatic approach of the ordinary parish clergy and lay people of their congregations. They wish to offer practical pastoral care to all people resident in their parishes, regardless of colour, race or creed, in fulfilment of Jesus' command to 'Love your neighbour as you love yourself'. On the other hand, there are specialists in the field of interfaith dialogue who wish to engage theologically with Muslim scholars and thereby enable their fellow Anglicans to grow into a deeper understanding of Islam and their relationship with its adherents.

Although the growing Muslim population in many towns and cities could not be ignored by members of the Church of England who lived in those environments, it was an issue regarded as being of little importance by many Anglicans. Following the terrorist attacks in the United States on 11 September 2001, the subsequent 'war against terrorism' and the London bombings in July 2005 the issue of Christian–Muslim understanding and dialogue became an issue which needed to be rapidly addressed by all Christians. Prayer vigils, often interfaith in nature, were held particularly at the start of the conflict in Iraq and there was a heightened interest from Anglicans to find out more about the faith of Islam, often as a means of discovering what they shared in common with their Muslim neighbours. The most high-profile event hosted by the Anglican church at this time was a seminar, 'Building Bridges', held on 17–18 January 2002 at Lambeth Palace at which forty eminent Christian and Muslim scholars from a wide variety of nationalities, denominations and cultures presented papers and discussed their various standpoints.[32] The hope was that the interest generated would act as a catalyst to promote further education and discussion among both Muslims and Christians, building on the many individual relationships and projects for mutual dialogue and cooperation that had already been established. This has created an important foundation for the urgent dialogue the events of 7 July 2005 have necessitated.

To illustrate the varied approaches of Christians within the Anglican church towards Christian–Muslim dialogue I have examined the work of three leading practitioners in this field, all of whom were present at the 'Building Bridges' seminar, who present contrasting approaches towards Christian–Muslim dialogue.

Bishop Kenneth Cragg

Bishop Kenneth Cragg was one of the pioneers in the field of Christian–Muslim relations in the second half of the twentieth century. Cragg is a prolific writer, having produced over thirty full-length books in addition to numerous articles, in which he draws on his wide experience of ministry in Jerusalem, Beirut, Cairo, Nigeria and England, as well as lecturing in universities on both sides of the Atlantic.

Kenneth Cragg comes from an evangelical Anglican background. He studied for the Anglican ministry at Tyndale Hall in Bristol before his ordination in 1936 and his first practical experience of Islam was while working with the British Syria Mission in Lebanon in 1939. Following further study in England he returned to the Middle East in 1956 as a residentiary canon of St George's Cathedral, Jerusalem. The title of his job was a misnomer, as much of Cragg's time was spent travelling throughout the region. Despite his evangelical upbringing Cragg always asked deep theological questions and was not satisfied with simplistic answers. This personal struggle with questions of criticism is reflected in his approach towards Islam, which is searching and not content with an easy reply.[33] Cragg's intention in writing his first book, *The Call of the Minaret* (1956), was to draw both Islam and Christianity 'out of the shadows of enmity and into the light of mutual understanding'.

From encouraging a deeper understanding of the nature and history of Islam, Cragg suggests that Christians should feel compelled to move on to some form of participation in the religion. From his own experience, he stresses that Muslims will tend to reject any unsolicited participation in their affairs, as they place high value on their own identity. This is particularly true of intervention by Christians because of the difficult history that lies between the two faiths. However, in a world in which people of different cultures and faiths now live in close proximity, some level of participation with the other is unavoidable. Christians, Cragg believes, are under an obligation stemming from the very essence of their faith, to offer hospitality to people of all backgrounds. One of the consistent themes of Cragg's writings is the need for communication and relationship between all human beings, who are estranged from each other and estranged from God.[34] Nevertheless, such an approach, however hospitably offered, requires sensitivity and knowledge on the part of the Christian.

Cragg identifies one of the problems affecting the beginning of any dialogue between Christians and Muslims as being the ignorance many Muslims have about Christianity. The view that Islam 'developed in an environment of imperfect Christianity' and that it claims that 'Islam represents what Christianity should have been and failed to be' means that Muslims have shown little inclination to make a detailed study of Christianity. As Cragg expresses it: 'This is the inward tragedy, from the Christian angle, of the rise of Islam, the genesis and dissemination of a new belief that claimed to displace what it had never effectively known'.[35]

Coming from evangelical, missionary roots, Cragg pays particular attention to the value of the Christian Scriptures, both in his writing and in his engagement with Muslims. The nature of their different scriptures is another area of contention that can arise within dialogue. The Qur'an is central to Muslim belief and their religious education focuses upon acquiring a sound knowledge of the text. It is important that Christians who wish to grow closer to Muslims develop an equally profound knowledge and understanding of their own Scriptures. Despite this assertion, Cragg is fully aware of the difficulties of presenting the Bible to Muslims as the revealed Word of God: the Biblical Scriptures 'do not square' with the Qur'an; neither the Old nor the New Testament foretells the coming of Muhammad; the existence of a multiplicity of translations is regarded as suspect; and, most importantly, the belief that Islam has abrogated Christianity. In this situation, Cragg suggests, 'the Christian must rely on the inherent worth of the Scripture and press for a new attention to their contents'.[36]

As a bishop, Kenneth Cragg is not looking at Islam just as an academic but also as a man of faith and as one who writes with passion about the Islamic world. It is this aspect of his work that has led to his theology being described as 'eclectic rather than systematic'.[37] For Cragg it is God who is at the centre of both faiths, a God who demands worship: 'Praise and theology are properly one. We conceptualise God in thought: we acknowledge Allah in our worship'.[38]

Cragg has been a significant scholar in Anglican–Muslim relations for the past fifty years. He followed in the steps of earlier Anglican missionaries in the Middle East, such as Temple Gairdner, who made serious studies of the Arabic language and Islam. In some ways, Cragg was a man before his time. However, in the wake of recent events, the value of Kenneth Cragg's scholarship and spirituality has come to the attention of a new, younger audience. Several of his earlier books have been reprinted in new editions and this has allowed him to relate ideas more precisely to the present world situation.

Dr Philip Lewis

Dr Philip Lewis is the interfaith adviser to the Anglican Diocese of Bradford. His knowledge of Islam was largely gained during his six years at the Christian Study Centre in Pakistan and during the period he has lived and worked in Leeds and Bradford. His personal experience in both the context of South Asia and in the inner-city areas of Britain enable him to speak with authority on Christian–Muslim relations within the Anglican church.

The main aim of Philip Lewis's writing would seem to be to educate non-Muslims in Britain about the lives and religious practices of their Muslim neighbours. It is often fear of the unknown that causes the misunderstandings that can so easily lead to tension and hostility between different groups. This has been particularly true in some northern industrial towns, such as Bradford and Oldham, which have suffered from racially motivated riots, particularly during the summer of 2001. In this respect, Philip Lewis's work is far more sociologically based than Kenneth Cragg's. He focuses on explaining the religious practices of South Asian Muslims within the context of their lives in contemporary Britain rather than discussing the theology and the grammatical nuances of Qur'anic Arabic.

Muslims had begun to settle in Bradford in the 1930s. During the Second World War others arrived to work in the armament factories. At this stage the numbers were small, there were only 350 immigrants from the Commonwealth living in the city in 1953. However, during that decade the numbers increased rapidly, particularly of Muslims from Pakistan who arrived to fill gaps in the labour market. They found work primarily in transport and the textile mills, which dominated the industrial landscape at that time. In the 1961 census 3,376 Pakistanis were recorded as living in Bradford, predominantly single males, most of whom did not intend to remain permanently in Britain. However, the numbers of Muslims living in Bradford increased rapidly with the advent of the Commonwealth Immigration Acts. By 1971 there were 12,250 Pakistanis living in the city. By 1981 this had risen to 32,100 and by 1991 to 48,933, or 1 in 9 of the population of the city. Demographic estimates suggest that with the youthful Muslim population this figure will treble by 2020, to 150,000.[39] This rapid growth of the Muslim population has led to the city being dubbed 'Britain's Islamabad'.

The rapid demographic change allied to the loss of the traditional industries of the area over the past twenty years has caused tensions between the immigrant and indigenous groups in the city. The original migrants in the 1950s and 1960s were attracted by work in the textile mills, which were the major employers in the region, but by the 1990s the majority of mills had closed, leading to high unemployment in the region, especially among unskilled workers. Unemployment has hit the Pakistani community in Bradford particularly badly. Most originated from the least developed rural areas of Pakistan, where educational facilities were poor. Many children are taken out of school for protracted family visits to Pakistan, which disrupts their education in Britain. English is rarely the language used in the home and greater stress is placed on learning Arabic, the language of a Muslim's spiritual life. Consequently, educational results among Muslim children in Bradford are poor, with only 29% of Pakistani pupils gaining five GCSEs at A–C grades in 1998, in comparison with 47% of white pupils and 54% of Indian pupils.[40]

Bradford has had a history of social unrest between the different ethnic and religious groups since the mid-1980s. At first, these focused on the school system, with a request in 1983 for *halal* meat to be provided at school and the 'Honeyford Affair' erupting in 1984.[41] The reaction to the publication of Salman Rushdie's novel, *The Satanic Verses*, in 1988 in Bradford led to another event which made national news. As a consequence, the very real issues that needed to be discussed at that time in Bradford, concerning the tension between preserving distinct cultural identity on the one hand and the encouragement of social integration on the other, were not fully aired.[42]

Philip Lewis uses his knowledge of a particular Muslim community to show that Islam in Britain is not the monolithic faith that people might imagine it to be, but rather a complex religion in which different traditions are represented. The experience of colonialism in South Asia was traumatic for many Muslims, as they had been conquered by a group of people that the Qur'an regarded as inferior to them (Sura 3.110). In his writings Lewis shows how Muslims developed different responses to cope with this situation, which have all transferred to the Bradford South Asian community: the reformist *Deobandis*; *Tablighi Jama'at* who place stress on the development of individual moral and spiritual renewal; *Barelwis*, a populist movement with links to Sufism whose interpretation of Islam leads to heated disputes with the *Deobandis*; *Jama'at Islam*, which aims to establish Islam as a complete political and religious ideology; and Islamic Modernism, a more overtly political group.[43] In order to establish a dialogue and rapport with Muslims within a community Lewis stresses that it is important to understand the stance and viewpoint of the particular group an individual comes from. In the same way Muslims need to appreciate that although all Christians share basic beliefs, different denominations place stress on different elements of those beliefs.

Despite his scholarly approach towards interpreting the situation in Bradford to aid Christians in their quest for mutual understanding with their Muslim neighbours, Philip Lewis's work has been criticised by elements of the Muslim community. His response to the Ousley Report, entitled 'Between Lord Ahmed and Ali G: which future for British Muslims?' was regarded as the work of an outsider looking into a community he could never truly understand while the title of the article was seen as perpetuating stereotypes.[44] In his defence, Lewis maintained that his aim was to initiate serious research into the factors that have lead to riots and that he was 'seeking to contribute to religious and cultural literacy for policy makers'.[45]

Lewis's work would seem to aim to give people the tools and knowledge to feel more confident about talking to their Muslim neighbours. He is, however, honest about the difficulties raised by this venture and suggests ways in which these may be overcome. Firstly, there are no easy routes to developing under-standing between Muslims and Christians. He talks about the need for develop-ing 'a place for honest perplexity in interreligious meeting', maintaining that perplexity has always been part of the Christian life, from the time of St Paul onwards. Secondly, he argues that the Wisdom Literature of the Bible, which was the product of Israelite religion meeting with and learning from other cul-tures in the Near East, might provide a model for Christians in their acceptance that truth may be found in other faiths. Thirdly, 'the law of the cross' shows that conflict is inescapable for Christians as they seek to establish justice and peace in the world. Although history has shown that such conflicts may divide Chris-tians, they may also find allies among those of other faiths, such as during the struggle against apartheid. Finally, Lewis argues that the Christian vocation is to go forward in confidence rather than certainty; in faith and hope, rather than knowledge. Christianity and Islam are both traditions with an eschatological hope and it is only at the end that the full nature of God will be revealed. God is a God of surprises and still has much to teach those who are willing to learn. It may be that some of God's truths are learned by our encounter with those of other faiths.[46]

Bishop Michael Nazir-Ali

Michael Nazir-Ali was born and educated in Pakistan. After theological educa-tion in England he served his title in the Diocese of Ely before returning to Pakistan, where he was consecrated Bishop of Raiwind in 1984. From 1989 until 1994 he served as general secretary to the Church Missionary Society before becoming the first Asian to be appointed as a diocesan bishop in England when he was installed as Bishop of Rochester in 1994. Like Kenneth Cragg, Michael Nazir-Ali's perspective is evangelical and, when assessing the importance of dialogue with other faiths, his primary source of guidance and authority is the Bible. For him dialogue is integral to the church's mission because all human beings have been created in the image of God and the coming of Jesus Christ as the Eternal Word of God has illuminated all human beings throughout the world. The Holy Spirit continues to be present in the world, working among 'men and women everywhere of all cultures, all kinds'.[47] The example offered by Jesus himself, Nazir-Ali maintains, points to the imperative of dialogue with others. Jesus' ministry was in Galilee, with its mixed ethnic population, rather than in the closed Jewish society of Jerusalem and it was to Galilee that he and his disciples returned after the resurrection.[48] As the church turned towards Europe its continual dialogue with the pre-existing cultures helped it to develop its theology. Dialogue with others continues to allow Christians to develop their own vocation and mission to the world:

> While Christians will want to present truth as they see it revealed in Jesus Christ there is always a sense in which dialogue with people produces a new kind of appreciation of some aspect of truth, even Christian truth. For me, my dialogue with Muslims has resulted in a fresh appreciation of the doctrine of the unity of God, which in some cases is seriously compromised by certain kinds of Christian Trinitarian theology.[49]

In a paper delivered at the 1998 Lambeth Conference Nazir-Ali stressed his view that 'God's saving design is revealed in Christ but extends to all' and therefore 'the Church should reject nothing which is true and holy in these religions'.[50] In countries where religions have lived closely together throughout history this understanding has gradually evolved, but the sudden social changes in Britain require a greater effort for those of different faiths to learn more of the other. In this, the Church of England has a special responsibility. As the established church it has the 'role of advocacy' for those of other faiths who 'may feel marginalised in national or social life'. This would include ensuring that they enjoy the 'same freedoms and facilities which Christians themselves enjoy'.[51] Such advocacy can only be undertaken if the other party is known and understood and therefore interfaith dialogue is essential for the Anglican church. For Nazir-Ali the dialogue between Muslims and Christians should be conducted to ensure that the different ways that both faiths see humans as stewards of God's creation should be harnessed for the good of society. Through such mutual understanding, they will hopefully develop a new appreciation of the tenets of the other.[52] In his views Nazir-Ali draws on the work of Kenneth Cragg when he says that Christians should approach the other in a spirit of 'hospitality', welcoming and meeting their needs, and 'embassy', sharing the Christian teaching of the Gospel with them. This would include working to find resolutions to problematical issues for many Christians, such as sharing church facilities with non-Christian faiths and multifaith worship.[53]

Conclusion

Christian–Muslim dialogue is an issue that has been on the agenda of the Church of England for many years. Initially this was almost exclusively within the context of overseas missions and the pioneering work of priests, such as Temple Gairdner and Kenneth Cragg, who ministered within Muslim societies, remains a foundation for an Anglican understanding of Islam today. Since the 1960s, the increasing Muslim population within Britain has encouraged the development of interfaith dialogue, particularly in inner-city parishes. As this work has grown the church has recognised the need for employing specialists in this field and many dioceses are beginning to address this issue following the lead and example of Philip Lewis and the Bradford Diocese. The tragic events of 11 September 2001 and 7 July 2005 have acted as a catalyst to these endeavours. Many Anglicans, who had previously had little or no contact with Muslims, now want to learn about Islam, rather than simply relying on the images portrayed by the media.

From the Muslim side, there is the problem of how a faithful British adherent of Islam, a religion which demands that a follower's whole life be submitted to the Will of God, can live in a primarily secular society where religion has been relegated to the position of 'leisure activity'. Is it possible to live an authentic Muslim life in *dar al-harb*? If one is free to practise one's religion in Britain is it therefore justifiable to shun the options of isolationism or assimilation and instead live in a position some Muslims have called *dar al-ahd* (abode of treaty)? Such questions may be resolved by dialogue with practising Christians who are faced with similar questions. The importance of this issue to the Church of

England may be best expressed in the words of Archbishop George Carey in 1996:

> In my view interfaith dialogue is not an option but a necessity . . . but the answer to the question 'How far can we travel together?' is not one we can answer when the journey has only just begun. It is something we shall only discover as we set out boldly on the way.[54]

Notes

1 Waines, D., *An Introduction to Islam* (Cambridge, Cambridge University Press, 1995), p. 1.
2 Lewis, P., 'Christian–Muslim relations in Britain', in O'Mahony, A. and Siddiqui, A. (eds), *Christians and Muslims in the Commonwealth* (London, Al Tajir-World of Islam Trust, 2001), pp. 187f.
3 Inter-Faith Consultative Group of the Board of Mission, *The Marriage of Adherents of Other Faiths in Anglican Churches* (London, Board of Mission of the Church of England, 1992), p. 4.
4 www.cofe.anglican.org/about/education/index.html (accessed July 2002).
5 Brown, A., *The Multi-faith Church School* (London, National Society, 1992), pp. 6, 11.
6 Ansari, H., *The Infidel Within* (London, C. Hurst & Co., 2004), p. 335.
7 Matar, N. I., 'Muslims in seventeenth-century England', *Journal of Islamic Studies*, 8: 1 (1997), 63–7.
8 Ibid., p. 73.
9 Ibid., p. 71f.
10 Mata, N., 'John Locke and the "turbanned nations"', *Journal of Islamic Studies*, 2: 1 (1991), 72–5.
11 Lebor, A., *A Heart Turned East* (London, Oxford Journals, 1998), p. 135.
12 Ansari, *The Infidel Within*, p. 33.
13 Lewis, P., *Islamic Britain* (London, C. Hurst & Co., 2002), pp. 11–12.
14 Shaw, A., *Kinship and Community* (Harwood, OPA, 2000), p. 30.
15 Lebor, *A Heart Turned East*, p. 133.
16 Commission for Racial Equality, *Ethnic Minorities in Britain* (London, Little Brown, 1999).
17 Friedmann, Y., 'Classification of unbelievers in Sunni Muslim law and tradition', *JSAI*, 22 (1998), 165f.
18 Cragg, K., *The Call of the Minaret* (2nd edn, Jerusalem, The Hebrew University, Oneworld, 2000), pp. 278f.
19 Cragg, K., *Jesus and the Muslim* (London, Oneworld, 1985), p. 11f.
20 Ibid., p. 9.
21 Khalidi, T., *The Muslim Jesus* (Harvard, Oneworld, 2001), p. 19.
22 Jomier, J., *How to Understand Islam* (Harvard, SCM, 1989), p. 141.
23 Siddiqui, A., 'Believing and belonging in a pluralist society', in Hart, D., *Multi-Faith Britain* (London, O Books, 2002), p. 30.
24 Richardson, M., 'Anglicans hail new patriarch', *Q-News* (July–Aug. 2002), p. 11.
25 Williams, R., 'Christian theology and other faiths', lecture delivered at Birmingham University, 11 June 2003.
26 Talk by Dr Zaki Badawi given at Hengrave Hall Conference Centre April 2002.

27 Lewis, P., 'Bradford – more than a race war', *The Tablet*, 21/07/01.
28 Shaw, *Kinship and Continuity*.
29 Ibid., p. 6off.
30 Lewis, *Islamic Britain*, pp. 66 and 179.
31 Joly, D., 'Making a place for Islam in British society', in Gerholm, T. and Lithman, Y. G. (eds), *The New Islamic Presence in Western Europe* (London, I. B. Tauris, 1988), p. 44.
32 Ipgrave, M. (ed.), *The Road Ahead* (London, Church House Publishing, 2002).
33 Ibid., pp. 4–5.
34 Ibid.
35 Cragg, *Call of the Minaret* pp. 219–21.
36 Ibid., pp. 254–7.
37 Lamb, *The Call to Retrieval* (London, Church House Publishing, 2002), p. 15.
38 Ibid., p. 15.
39 Lewis, P., *Islamic Britain* (new edn, London, I. B. Tauris, 2002), pp. 54ff.
40 *Minority Ethnic Issues in Social Exclusion and Neighbourhood Renewal* (London, Social Exclusion Unit, June 2000).
41 A controversy in 1984 in which a Bradford headmaster, Ray Honeyford, wrote an article in the right-wing *Salisbury Review* criticising the multicultural approach towards education by his local education authority.
42 Ibid., pp. 151ff.
43 Ibid., pp. 35–47.
44 Lewis, Philip, (2002) 'Between Lord Ahmed and Ali G: which future for British Muslims?', in Shahid, W. A. R. and van Koningsfeld, P. S.(eds), *Religious Freedom and the Neutrality of the State: The Position of Islam in the European Union* (Leuven, Peeter, 2002). Responses in *Q News*, 339–40 (Jan.–Feb., 2002), p. 9.
45 *Q News*, 341–432 (Mar.–Apr., 2002), p. 4.
46 Lewis, P., 'Against anxiety, beyond triumphalism', in Platten, S., James, G. and Chandler, A. (eds), *New Soundings* (London, Darton, Longman, Todd, 1997).
47 Nazir-Ali, M., *Mission and Dialogue* (London, SPCK, 1995) pp. 75f.
48 Ibid., pp. 79f.
49 Ibid., p. 81.
50 Nazir-Ali, M., *Citizens and Exiles* (London, SPCK, 1998), p. 120.
51 Ibid., pp. 126f.
52 Ipgrave, *The Road Ahead*, pp. 110f.
53 Nazir-Ali, *Citizens and Exiles*, pp. 123ff.
54 Quoted in *Islamophobia* (Runnymede Trust, London, SPCK, 1997).

4

The Orthodox church, Islam and Christian–Muslim relations in Russia

Basil Cousins

Without doubt, we are witnessing a religious resurgence globally. At the close of the nineteenth century, religious belief was described as an outgoing tide;[1] the twenty-first century has already witnessed one major religious tremor in 9/11. The tectonic plates of religion show no signs of settling down. The Russian Federation (RF) and Commonwealth of Independent States (CIS) undoubtedly form one of the key fracture zones, caught historically between the Islamic and the Christian plates. This chapter describes the crucial importance of Russia in the global engagement between the belief systems represented by a resurgent Islam, Russian Orthodoxy and the modern world. Orthodox Christian Russia considers that it has been the key bulwark against the steady encroachment of Islam into Europe for at least 500 years. It remains so today.

Since the 1905 Russian Revolution, the tensions between domestic Islam (Islam within the borders of the Russian Federation) and Russian Orthodoxy have been profoundly affected by the political developments of the twentieth century: the reduction in autocracy and faltering development of democracy between 1905 and 1917, the Communist Experiment from 1917 to 1991, and the modern era of uncertainty and rapid change following the transition from the Soviet period to Russian Independence. The events of 9/11 typified the meeting of these tectonic plates. Immediately it achieved global iconic status, to be followed by a series of substantial aftershocks – the Moscow theatre siege, the horrors of Beslan, the Madrid train bombing, and more recently the bombings in London and in Bali. In the background, smaller incidents are steadily occurring in Russia and elsewhere, which do not reach the international or even local press or community. Sadly we await other events which may achieve even greater horrific status. Against such a background, the fundamental challenge for the Russian Federation today is to build a relatively peaceful, cohesive and successful modern state able to compete and play its full role in the contemporary world. There are a number of key components to achieve such an aim – with economic success at the top of the list. However, this is dependant on a reasonable level of peaceful social cohesion.

This chapter focuses on the role of underlying belief systems in the creation and preservation of such cohesion across a highly diverse population. The term 'belief systems' is used in order to reflect the reality on the ground today in the

Russian Federation, whose population has been profoundly affected by the cata-strophic imposition of Communist social and anti-religious propaganda. The principal result is a highly secularised population. Belief systems include Atheism, Agnosticism, Buddhism, Christianity including Orthodoxy and other forms, Communism in its modern forms, Islam, Judaism, Shamanism, etc. Underlying these, there are over 180 ethnic groups speaking over 150 different languages.[2] Each ethnic group has its own historical tribal and national loyalties as well as underlying social and religious beliefs.

The prevention of disintegration of the Russian Federation still remains 'a high priority' and explains many of President Putin's current policies and actions. The terrorist atrocities so prevalent in parts of Russia today need to be seen in their full political/religious historical context. The Russian Federation may be regarded as a key historical hinge in the relationships between the competing forces of Islam and Christianity. Due to the very nature of both Russian Ortho-doxy and Islam, it is difficult to separate out religious motivations from political. One authority – Alexei Malashenko – points out that both 'actively interfere in secular, including political issues. But the Orthodox church, or . . . powerful elements within it "aspire to a monopoly of Russia's national state ideology"'.[3]

Given that Russia occupies such a potentially crucial position in the develop-ment of a 'new world order', questions arise as to whether it can, in practice, play a positive role – politically, economically and religiously – in a manner that benefits Russia itself and its neighbours in the global village. For at least the last five centuries, Russia has wanted to be seen as a world power. It came closest to achieving this ambition during the Communist period. Can it re-gear itself to play such an important role again effectively? What role will belief systems – particularly religious belief – play in achieving this? This is a unique opportunity for Russia to re-establish itself as a world leader by bringing into being a har-monious, productive society which will bring out the best in the amalgam (*sli-yanie*) of its different peoples with their heterogeneous customs and beliefs.

The Russian Orthodox church sees itself as crucial to the functioning of the Russian Federation. Although its basic theological concepts are broadly identical to those of western Catholic Christianity, it views its relationship to society at large in a very different manner. This gives rise to a number of issues concerning the theological identity of the Russian Orthodox church and its development as a multi-ethnic church – part of a universal expression of Christianity. There would appear to be a distinct possibility that it will remain a monoethnic church with strong nationalistic overtones. Such a development could well lead to con-flict with other religious and ethnic groups. Its missionary, social and educa-tional ambitions need careful examination in the light of such a scenario. Finally, one needs to ask if the real ambition of the Russian Orthodox church to be arbiter of genuine Russian culture in the contemporary situation is justified by the social realities on the ground in the Russian Federation – bearing in mind the growth of Islam across the Federation and the high level of secularisation of urban society – or is such an ambition a false pretension that will melt away under the unstoppable impact of historical forces.

Domestic Islam will play a crucial role in the achievement of a successful modern state by the Russian Federation. It is all too easy to be mesmerised by anti-western and anti-Russian attitudes and the terrorist acts perpetrated by the Islamists – the more extreme Muslim elements seeking world domination by whatever means. But there are powerful, more moderate elements across much of the Islamic world, including one particular movement – now called EuroIslam (formerly called Jadidhism) – which has developed since the mid-nineteenth century in Central Asia and Tatarstan.

Some important issues need to be addressed concerning the domestic Muslim community in the Federation. These include its urgent desire to achieve equal status both politically and religiously with Russian Orthodoxy in the Federation. In order to realise such an ambition, the Russian Muslim community needs to create a sufficient level of internal consensus to become an effective and cohesive social/political force. This presupposes that the Muslim community in Russia resists conversion to extreme Islamist philosophies, policies and actions. It needs to develop a version of Islamic belief and practice geared to the modern world in the Federation and CIS. Finally it is vital to understand its missionary, social and educational ambitions and how these are being played out in the context of the RF and the CIS.

The RF and CIS are physically immense – occupying one sixth of the world's landmass – the hinge between Asia and the west in general. The CIS was created by President Yeltsin out of the ruins of the Soviet Union. The sheer size is some-what misleading as it is heavily under-populated – some 140 million people in the Federation and 280 in the CIS as a whole. The population is affected by challenging geography across Siberia, the terrible effects of the Nazi invasions, as well as by Lenin's and Stalin's various purges in their attempt to force the creation of Homo Sovieticus. Some authorities reckon that without Commu-nism and the Nazi invasion the current population of the Federation would equal that of the United States – 290–300 million. Whatever the truth of that, there is no doubt that the RF and CIS have considerable economic strength with immense natural reserves – for example 50% of the proven global reserves of underground gas lie in Russia.

Historical perspective

Importantly, Russia bridges from west to east as well as north to south in Asia. As a result, it finds itself uncomfortably neither wholly identified with the west nor with the east. This discomfort has long driven the Russian sense of its special mission in the world as a whole – its classical axis of identity. The Tsarist Russian empire grew progressively by conquest. These conquests effectively began from the reign of Ivan IV – The Terrible – from the 1550s and continued right up the acquisition of Central Asia completed in 1900. This movement east and south was partly seen as a 'Sacred Mission', more pragmatically as a drive to 'Warm Water' – a geopolitical concept which obsessed the Russian ruling class more or less from the start. This geopolitical concept, sometimes expressed as 'The Great Game', has coloured Russian history throughout, dating back to the capture of Kazan and Astrakhan in the sixteenth century giving access to the Caspian Sea. It is no less important today in Russia's relationships with its southern neigh-bours – Iran and India, Iraq and Turkey as well as Afghanistan.

The period from Ivan IV to Catherine II was marked by the systematic suppression and attempts at the forced conversion of the conquered Muslim and Shamanist communities. The mission to convert the conquered Shamanist and Muslim tribes was all too frequently, if not generally, carried out as a semi-political/police operation, using a wide range of incentives, bribes, tax and service concessions as well as punishments. On occasions, mass baptisms were carried out by lay people with no priests involved. The conquest of vast swathes of territory east and south along the Volga in Siberia, and south towards the Caspian/Black Sea and Central Asia, triggered the mass migration of Russian peasants, some voluntary, some highly organised. The Russian Orthodox church generally followed in the wake of the ethnic Russian settlers and the military, establishing monasteries, parishes and bishoprics in the newly colonised centres. The net result of the somewhat dubious methods of conversion and poor religious education was the mass apostasies of so-called newly baptised native Christians to Islam throughout the nineteenth century as well as the steady advance of Islam among the pagan tribes.

The 'Whip and Cake' methods used by the Russian empire were, essentially, no different to the methods employed by Islam since the seventh century, but with markedly less long-term success or holding power. Catherine II was the first Tsar to seek to bring the Muslim communities under political control by creating the Ufa Spiritual Mohammedan Assembly in 1789 headed by a mufti – a senior Muslim cleric. The Tsarina had previously instructed the Holy Synod to issue a 'toleration of faiths' edict in 1773. These actions followed the very dangerous Pugachev Revolt in southern Russia involving many Muslims and Christian dissenters. Nevertheless, there were some genuinely spiritually effective Orthodox missionary initiatives. The somewhat surprising re-identification of 300,000–400,000 *Krestianin* (baptised Tatars) – in Tatarstan after 1991 evidences this.

The mass apostasies in the nineteenth century led to a significant rethink of missionary methods in the mid-nineteenth century by the Russian Orthodox church. One particular orientalist missionary – Nicolai Il'Minsky – stands out. He developed an imaginative method of primary education for baptised Tatar Children in their native language and established a teaching seminary for missionaries and teachers in Kazan supporting a widespread network of schools which followed the Il'Minsky method, financed by the St Guri Brotherhood.

The linguistic policies of Russia in its broadest historical sense are critical to the interrelationship between the principal religious beliefs and the education systems. They applied no less during the Tsarist period than they did during Soviet times. They are crucial to the functioning of the state as well as to the Russian Orthodox church and the drive for Russification of the entire population. They have a significant impact on the development of domestic Islam. Lenin sought and received key support from parts of the Russian Muslim community during the Civil War after 1917 but he quickly reneged on his undertakings. However, Stalin waited until the late 1920s to initiate a full-scale suppression of Islam in the Soviet Union. This was particularly tied in with his agricultural reforms and his drive for universal literacy. The persecution continued unabated until the Great Patriotic War (Second World War) when significant numbers of Muslims sided with the Germans fighting alongside the Bosnian Muslim SS

Regiment complete with military mullahs. Stalin shipped entire populations to Siberia, particularly from the Caucasus. In 1942 he subsequently allowed a limited religious revival, creating three new Muslim Spiritual Assemblies, each under a mufti. This Islamic Administration – the Muftiate – was continued after the war for foreign policy reasons. It has grown significantly since 1991 to include at least fifty Muftiates – broadly organised into two main groups – the Russian Council of Muftis (RCMT) under Mufti Ravil Gainutdin and the Central Spiritual Board of Muslims (CSBM) under Mufti Talgat Tadzhuddin. There is intense competition between these two groupings. Moscow plays one against the other but generally seems to prefer dealing with Talgat (CSBM).

In 1991, the Soviet Union had a population of 280 million, 50 million of whom were said to be Muslim. Today the population of the Russian Federation is 143 million of which some 20 million are Muslim. They are mainly focused in a belt of states to the east and south of Russia but there are significant city populations, e.g. in Moscow there are believed to be 1.5–2 million Muslims with half a million in St Petersburg. The number of illegal immigrants is unknown. There is considerable dispute about the number of Muslims in the Russian Federation – the real figure could well be very much higher, so much so that the question is beginning to be put; 'Could a Muslim become President of the Federation?'[4] The number of Russian Muslims has grown from 6% of the population in 1959 to 10–15% currently. Russian Orthodoxy is reported to account only for 15–20% out of the total Federation population of 142,893,540, of which 79.8% are ethnic Russians. Only a limited number of 'inorodtsi' (non-Russians) are Christian (say less than half a million).With the falling Russian ethnic population trends due to very low birth rates and poor life expectancy, the overall population will soon be evenly divided between Russian Orthodoxy and Islam.[5] The number of Mosques has grown from 300 in 1991 to over 8,000 currently while the number of religious schools has risen from none to 50–60, teaching 50,000 students.

Ethnic Russian self-perception

One of President Putin's key tasks is to create a successful national identity for the Russian Federation and a sense of peaceful, social cohesion across the Federation and the CIS. The impact of historically imposed secularisation remains deeply significant. With over 80% of the Federation's population currently made up of ethnic Russians, it is hard to visualise an overall identity, which will unite them in a common cause with the minorities who are largely Muslim. Some politicians even consider Russia to be monoethnic. Some older studies show that 60–80% of ethnic Russians claim to be Orthodox although when asked few have a firm grasp of the essential beliefs, mainly due to the anti-Christian and anti-religious policies of the Soviet state. Later studies put the much lower numbers. However, most sources put the level of practice by both Orthodox Christians and Muslims at about 3–4%.[6]

Alexander Solzhenitsyn[7] and others have expressed their fundamental belief in Russian uniqueness and the necessity of finding its own path of regeneration. He has stressed the central role of Russian Orthodoxy and promoted an ethnocentric national identity and consistently said that Russia must make its own way. We hear echoes of this in President Putin's responses to US statements about democracy. During the Early and Late Modern Period, particularly after the Fall of Constantinople in 1453, the Russian Orthodox church saw itself as the bulwark against the advance of Islam into Europe. The church grew ever more closely identified with the Tsar who became the effective head of the church. As a result, the church was identified with autocracy. It began to perceive itself as the only pure version of Christianity, giving rise to the concept of being the Third Rome. Strangely, this concept never translated itself into widespread missionary activity outside the Russian empire until the advent of Communism when a very serious attempt was made to convert the world to Russian Communism.

During the first millennium, Orthodoxy worked out the concept of *Symphonia* to describe a working relationship between church and state. This evolved into the almost complete symbiosis of the Russian church with the Tsarist state. There are many examples of the Tsar starting with Ivan IV giving detailed instructions to the church about, say, missionary work. Ethnic Russian political philosophy has been torn at least since the nineteenth century between the western-looking 'Europhiles' and the more eastward-looking 'Slavophiles', with another version known as 'Panslavism' focused on Slavic peoples everywhere. The orientation towards the European west was enthusiastically supported by Peter I (the Great) and Catherine II (the Great). Communism was the ultimate European import.

Slavophilism itself is complex, rooted in cultural, social, economic and political factors. It has a strong ethnic Russian origin, stressing religiosity and spirituality with an emphasis on national consciousness and a belief in the historic mission of Russia coupled with national identity. Panslavism applies these concepts to all Slavic peoples and had political significance during the recent Balkan Wars. Eurosianism was another expression of Russian authenticity developed principally by the Russian émigré community after 1917. This movement shares with the others a consciousness of Russia's unique character and mission. This theory characterises both European and Asian subjects as forming an organic United Eurasian people. All these movements are highly complex, beyond further analysis in this chapter. However pretentiously nationalistic and unworldly some of these philosophies may seem to be, the future success of the Russian Federation is crucial to global well-being and peace. The challenge for the whole population of the Russian Federation, whether non-religious, Orthodox, Muslim or other is to reach a pragmatic equilibrium involving a level of mutual toleration and respect among themselves which protects the common good.

The 1993 Constitution of the Russian Federation provides for freedom of belief. This was substantially modified by the 1997 Russian Federal Law on Freedom of Conscience and on Religious Associations which openly favours traditional religions – principally Orthodoxy, Islam and Buddhism.[8] There are signs that 'the security services were increasingly treating the leadership of some minority religious groups as security risks'.[9] The 1997 law represents a very significant accommodation of domestic Islam in Russia by the Moscow Patriarchate. Such an accommodation may be seen as politically realistic but it amounts to an abandonment of missionary work. It would have been anathema to the church before the 1917 Revolution.

Ethnic Russian demography is a major cause for concern, with a minimal birth rate and reducing life expectancy, particularly in the male population. The overall population is falling by half a million a year. Given the significant birth rate in the Muslim population, the ethnic Russian content is reducing even more rapidly than the headline statistics would indicate. President Putin has been voicing his grave concerns in this area.

Russian Muslim self-perception

In contrast to the ambitions of Tsars and the Russian Orthodox church, the conquered Muslim populations in the Russian empire have never given up the idea of converting the whole of Russia to Islam, thereby creating a genuine Islamic Russian *umma*. An Orthodox parish priest in Moscow complained that the Russian Muslims were trying to create a second Mecca when a large new mosque was finally built in Moscow servicing a growing Muslim population. Russian history, dating back to the Mongol invasions, has been pervaded with the need to contain the threat of Islamisation and Turkification. We perceive throughout Russian history, Tsarist, Communist and current, various initiatives designed to contain the threat of Islamisation and Turkification. The government has repeatedly sought to break up the formation of political blocks of Turkic peoples, e.g. by ensuring that Tatarstan and Baskirostan are treated as separate states.

Since *glasnost*, there has been a marked resurgence of Islam in the Russian Federation with considerable investment from Saudi Arabia and Egypt. The number of mosques has grown from virtual extinction to 7,000 in 2001. The 50 or more Muftiates have become politically significant.

As elsewhere in the Muslim world, there is a high birth rate. Various apocalyptic forecasts are made about its demographic impact. Studies indicate that the Muslim population, generally poorer and less well educated than ethnic Russians, is quite fractured, divided into ethnic and political groups. Such differences have been deliberately accentuated by Tsarist and Communist administrations.

The current main aim of domestic Islam is to get Islam recognised as the second religion of the Russian Federation on a par with Orthodoxy and no longer playing a secondary role. Beslan and other terrorist outrages and the continued uprising along the Southern Rim cannot help the achievement of this aim. The terrorists are claimed to have international links to Al Qaeda and are generally typified as *wahhabist* – a shorthand for this phenomenon. The aim of full recognition can only come about if Moscow comes to believe that a more formal recognition of the role of moderate Islam in Russia would help to isolate the Muslim extremists. This is unlikely at present.

Religion and state in Russia

Lawrence Uzzell has typified the church – state relationship in Russia as 'Religion on the leash'.[10] He claims that religious liberty has reached equilibrium after shrinking since the mid 1990s, particularly after the 1997 Law on Freedom of Conscience and Religious Associations referred to above, which favours so called 'traditional religions'. This equilibrium comes about as 'Putin has achieved everything he needs in church-state relations . . . as he has "believers on a leash"'.[11] Uzzell continues, 'It is inconceivable that a national leader of any major religious confession would energetically voice criticisms of the secular government's policies . . . that the Kremlin considers important'.[12] Putin is seeking to be seen to support the Moscow Patriarchate, attending public services and other events. The Federal Security Bureau (FSB) very recently announced the adoption of an Orthodox church in Moscow as its religious centre, surely a significant step in the process of recognising the Metropolitan Patriarchate.[13]

Compulsory registration of religious organisations has been a feature of Russia since Tsarist times. However, the registrations are not thought to reflect the demography of religious believers. Registration is an administrative process depending on local politics and can be whimsical. Up to 9,000 Muslim organisations may be unregistered; between 1,500 and 2,000 Pentecostal organisations are unregistered despite their efforts.[14]

Russian orthodoxy

Russian Orthodoxy fundamentally sees itself as a local as opposed to a universal church and has always done so. On its website,[15] it states that the Russian Orthodox church is a multinational, local (*pomiestnaia*), autocephalous church. In practice, this gives it a strong tendency to be a Russian Ethnic church. *The Guidelines for the Russian Orthodox Church's Attitude to Non-Orthodoxy* developed in 2000 by the Theological Commission of the Russian Orthodox church emphasises that 'the Russian Orthodox church does not equate itself to the Christian world in its entirety and rejects the notion that any Christian unity may exist beyond confessional boundaries'.[16] The document then states that the Russian Orthodox church should not cooperate with non-traditional churches in the Russian Federation, CIS or the Baltic States, which are all regarded as its 'canonical territory'.[17] Golovushkin describes the theories of the anti-liberal ideologies of the Metropolitan of St Petersburg and Ladoga (*Snytchev*), which denies the right of other denominations 'especially the Catholics to preach' in the canonical territory.

Throughout its history the Russian Orthodox church has seen conversion of non-Russians as a means of Russification – creating 'little Russians'. Il'Minsky and his followers struggled with conservative Orthodox church elements and with the concept of educating non-Russians in their native language in at least primary school level, as well as with the translation and delivery of the liturgy in non-Russian languages. Some excellent missionary work in this field was deliberately destroyed. Today, there is a strong tendency to deliver the liturgy in Church Slavonic – a language at least 1,000 years old and not exactly comprehensible to modern Russian youth. However, there is considerable support for the retention of Church Slavonic. This sacralisation of a past language may well be a sign of the urge felt since 1991 to hark back to an imagined 'golden' past. It is certainly a sign of the freezing of the religious evolutionary process that was well underway prior to 1917 and evidenced by the proceedings of the local council that took place at the time of the Revolution.

Russian Orthodoxy has lived through a horrendous attempt over seventy years to wipe it off the face of the earth. Progress since *glasnost* has been considerable. Overall, it claims 169 bishops and more that 27,000 parishes, 713 monasteries and numerous educational establishments.[18] This compares with 77,800 parishes in 1917 covering the Russian empire. Alexei Krindatch's detailed breakdown shows that about half the religious institutions are in the Russian Federation with a very significant proportion in Ukraine.[19] As outlined above, religious practice remains low but public confidence is high in the Russian Orthodox church, second only in confidence in the President.[20]

The author's brief experience in Kazan indicated well-attended Orthodox churches and a thriving seminary with some sixty students – many young.

A lasting impression is that the Moscow Patriarchate is not devoting that much attention to missionary activity. Krindatch comments, 'Protestant denominations in Russia pay much greater attention to systematic missionary activity than does the Russian Orthodox Church'.[21] The official website lists the missionary department under Archbishop John of Belgorod and Starooskol. Its main activities are internal mission to reclaim believers 'into the bosom of the church' and opposition to 'destructive cults'.

Domestic Islam

Islam is the second largest religion in the Federation. Estimates of numbers vary as many are based on ethnicity rather than declared belief. The general conclusion is that there are 12–20 million Muslims in the Federation.[22] The major cities have significant Muslim populations. There are large numbers of illegal immigrants in the Federation, many of whom may be at least nominally Muslim. There are thought to be about 7,000 mosques.[23] The Islamic population of Russia is not cohesive – it is made up of almost forty competitive ethnic groups with different languages, cultures and forms of religious practice. Muslims are in the majority in seven of the eighty-nine administrative provinces. Krindatch concludes that the 'declared aspiration for the unification of all Russian Muslims is overwhelmed by the disintegrative tendencies based not on religious but on ethnic tensions and the political ambitions of various Islamic leaders . . . No one single Islamic organisation or leader can speak on behalf of a majority of Russia's Muslims'.[24]

The Putin government has attempted to exercise ever more political control over the Russian Muslim communities, for example by fostering close relationships with the Muftiates. This has been extended into the field of education in which a unified teaching methodology is being applied in all the *medressahs* across Russia. This initiative is being fiercely resisted by parts of the Orthodox church and the Muslim community. Levels of religious practice vary considerably but, with the exceptions of Dagestan and Chechnya, are thought to be low.

Interfaith collaboration

While there appears to be little activity towards seeking mutual understanding across faiths on the lines of Vatican II at a religious level (*Nostra Aetate, Ecclesiam Suam,* et al.), there have been significant attempts at reaching mutual understanding at a semi-political and social level – generally in line with Kremlin policies. Shireen Hunter, in *Islam in Russia,* comments that there is frequently a divergence between Moscow and the local priests vis-à-vis Islam. She writes:

> While not relishing the rising profile of Islam, the central leadership [of the Church] . . . emphasizes the theme of inter-religious dialogue and cooperation to combat social ills.[25]

The Inter-Religious Council of Russia (IRCR) was created at the initiative of the Orthodox church with representatives of the four traditional religions. Its principal goal is to maintain an ongoing dialogue among the traditional religions and to 'jointly discuss the problems facing the contemporary Russian society in an attempt to develop a common position on them in order to testify in front of the people and government'.[26] The IRCR declaration of 10 September 1999 stated that its main task is to:

> Coordinate efforts by religious associations in internal and external peacemaking . . . The Council has not set as its task to promote rapprochement among religious teachings and doctrines, nor does it have any liturgical forms or theological positions of its own.

The IRCR is an affiliate member of the World Conference of Religions for Peace and is associated with the European Council of Religious Leaders/Religions for Peace (ECRL). The Russian Orthodox church has been 'strongly' associated with Religions for Peace for over thirty years. In addition, a new CIS Inter-Religious Council has been established. In a statement of 3 March 2004, the new council pledged itself to seek interethnic and interreligious peace as well as harmony and stability in society. The 10th anniversary of the IRCR was celebrated in June 2002 in the presence of the Patriarch Alexei II, Metropolitan Kirill and a wide range of senior representatives of Russia's traditional religions including the Supreme Mufti Talgat Tadjudin. Understandably, many of the discussions reported on their website concern the north caucasus.

There are a significant number of examples of the Russian Orthodox church (Metropolitan Patriarchate) taking the leadership in joint faith events. One of the most recent examples was the 9th World Russian People's Council on 10 March 2005, which included representatives of the Russian church outside Russia and the Old Believers as well as religious leaders of the Islamic, Jewish and Buddhist communities and several Christian Confessions on the occasion of the 60th anniversary of the Great Victory in the Great Patriotic War in 1945, where 'The participants unanimously acknowledged the great historical merit of the peoples in historical Russia for their victory over fascism'.[27] The 60th anniversary parades attended by President Bush and many other world leaders were designed to reinforce the special role of Russia.

47

Religious tolerance

While the top level political mechanisms described above have begun to function, largely in accordance with policies laid down in Moscow, the level of religious tolerance has not improved. Dimitry Golovushkin, a senior lecturer at the Herzen State Pedagogical University, St Petersburg, has described the recent trends.[28] He claims that:

> sociological surveys over the past ten years show that religious conflicts and religious fundamentalism . . . increasingly determine the atmosphere in Modern Russian society.[29]

He argues that while most ethnic Russians identify themselves as Orthodox, many of them are not believers. He typifies this as *external belief* which *assumes a nationalistic function* and *becomes an ideology*.[30] European cultures have achieved religious tolerance by the implementation of a policy of positive discrimination based on *solid national and supranational values*.[31]

The sad fact is the evidence of the low level of political culture and cultural pluralism, one of a whole series of factors that cause religious intolerance in Russian society.[32] 'Under the double pressure the western and Islamic worlds', the ambitions to realise a special form of union between church and state 'have mutated into a feeling of exclusiveness and isolation in the hostile environment'.[33] Golovushkin claims that religious freedom in Russia has been in retreat since 1994, when district and federal authorities, acting in the interests of the Russian Orthodox church, began to ignore the constitutional clauses which guaranteed religious freedom in accordance with the legislation of 1990 and the Constitution of 1993.[34] The concepts of Russian Orthodox canonical territory and attitudes to religious freedom and tolerance are taken up by the radical right wing of Russian Orthodoxy and are supported by a range of nationalist political parties including various Marxist and Communist groups. This is not to say that there are other groups both within Russian Orthodoxy and political groupings that support more liberal, less nationalistic views on religious tolerance, but it would appear at present that the more nationalist, exclusivist Russian Orthodox sentiment dominates.

Religious tolerance does not merely cover the relationships between the Russian Orthodox church and other forms of Christianity. It also relates to other religions in the Federation and the CIS, whether these are traditional religions as defined in the context of the 1997 Law on Freedom of Conscience and Religious Associations or other belief systems that fall outside its definitions. Russian Orthodoxy itself is split into several forms including the 'Old Believers'. Intra-Orthodox relationships have often been fraught.

Interreligious relationships on the ground do not reflect the high-level activities of the Inter-Religious Councils described above. Considerable tensions exist between the Muslim communities and others in various parts of the Federation, particularly when the local Muslim community wishes to erect a mosque.

Conclusion

Under President Putin, the sense of Russia's special mission has, if anything, strengthened. It is closely linked with a return to autocracy – President Putin claimed in an interview that autocracy is 'in the Russian genes'.[35] Moscow's political links with the west and Israel have changed radically since 9/11 despite the strains of the Balkan and Iraq wars. Putin's recent visit to Israel and the Middle East underlines this. Since the Second World War, the Soviet Union and the Russian Federation have tended to support the Arab Nations and Iran, most probably to counter western influence but possibly also in the somewhat naive belief that they would be able to spread their new belief system – Internationalism Socialism leading to Communism. However, since 9/11 this has changed.

With one million Russians in Israel (one sixth of the population) and significant trade links, Russia has supported Israel in one form or another since 1991, co-authoring the Roadmap Peace Plan. Putin pursues the War on Terror relentlessly. However, Moscow also maintains strong links with the Palestinians. President Mahmoud Abbas visited Moscow in January 2005. Coupled with his support for Iran and Syria, President Putin is seeking an influential role with both the Muslim nations and the Israelis.

In contrast, religious links have not really improved. The Moscow Patriarchate continues to seek to strengthen its position as the only church for ethnic Russians and Slavs, whether in the Federation, the CIS and elsewhere. Relationships with Roman Catholics remain tense. Recently, the situation with the Evangelical Lutheran church has taken a turn for the worst with the exclusion of Bishop Siegfried Springer.[36] This action was similar to the exclusion of a Catholic bishop in 2002.

All in all, Russian Orthodox self-confidence and insularity has, if anything, grown. The Moscow Patriarchate has edged ever closer to the state despite protestations by the Patriarch Alexei II to the contrary. Moscow has agreed to include lessons on the Orthodox culture in all state schools – this ruling has not gone unchallenged. Orthodox priests now serve as padres in many Russian army units. There is no sign of Muslim clerics being allowed to play such a role even though many of the soldiers are Muslim. The Muslims complain that pressure is put on their believers in the army to convert to Orthodoxy. The Orthodox counterclaim that there are attempts at forcible conversion of Russian soldiers captured by Muslim rebels. In one case, there is a popular call for the sanctification of a Russian soldier in Chechnya who was offered his life if he converted to Islam. On his refusal, he was decapitated.[37]

However, there are tensions at local level that vary from extreme around the Caucasus to moderately positive in regions such as Tatarstan. 9/11 has probably had far less direct effect on such local tensions than outrages such as the Moscow Theatre Siege and Beslan, which have served to harden local feelings. Moderation in Tatarstan provides a ray of hope that it may be possible to build a multicultural industrial society – indeed Tatarstan could be considered a possible model. Relationships between the Russian Orthodox archbishop in Kazan and the local Muslim community appear to be reasonably positive although the role of the Christian Tatars – the *Krestianin* – remains a bone of contention. One possible sign of hope lies in the interest being shown in the Russian Orthodox seminary in Kazan in the missionary and educational work of Il'Minsky in the nineteenth century.

The issue of proselytising remains highly controversial. The 1997 Law on Freedom of Conscience and Religious Associations implies an acceptance of the status quo among the recognised religions. However, the Muslims are actively recruiting ethnic Russians and others. There is no sense that any real effort by either the Russian Orthodox or the Muslims to begin to build a mutual interfaith understanding. The only ray of light would appear to be the St Andrew's Biblical Theological Institute, which has published serious studies on the opportunities for interfaith dialogue This institute is a result of Father Men's work and, sadly, is not mainstream Russian Orthodox. However, a delegation of senior Shia Muslim clerics met with the Moscow Patriarchate on four occasions. This is part of a broad initiative from the Shia Theological Centre in Qum which has included reciprocal visits between the Ampleforth Abbey in the UK and Qum in Iran.

There does not seem to be any coherent effort to develop a new form of mission within the Moscow Patriarchate of the Russian Orthodox church. True, there is a missionary department within the Patriarchate but I have not detected any significant activity in that area. The missionary challenge is immense. While the majority of Russians claim to be Orthodox, few have any idea of what it means. The population remains deeply secularised by Communism. Intermarriage was encouraged by the Communists. This has left a wide range of dilemmas in mixed religious marriages between Muslims and Orthodox. The Muslim approach to religious inculcation is better articulated and likely to win in any serious show down. Although the Orthodox approach to mission appears to be muted and defensive, there is no reason to believe that the Muslims are not proselytising aggressively right across the region making converts from ethnic Russians and others.

The 9/11 attack has had considerable effects at a political level in Russia and the CIS but only limited influence at local religious level. However, coupled with events in Moscow, Beslan, Madrid, London and other Islamist outrages, it has tended to reinforce the natural instincts of Russian Orthodoxy who continue to see themselves as the European bulwark against Islam as well as Arab and Turkic advances – a bulwark whose significance is not appreciated by the west!

The current assessment of the theological identity of the Russian Orthodox church would appear to be that the Metropolitan Patriarchate sees itself as an autonomous local church, not as a part of the universal expression of Christianity. There are few signs that the Moscow Patriarchate is seriously considering itself as a multi-ethnic church. The test case lies in how it treats the 300,000–400,000 *Kriashen* (baptised Tatars and other tribes) in and around Kazan. The signs are not particularly hopeful. This could well lead to conflict with other religious and ethnic groups. Indeed, there is significant evidence of increasing religious and racial intolerance.

There is little evidence of any serious missionary work apart from winning back the adherence and retaining the allegiance of ethnic Russians. The Moscow

Patriarchate has secured the nominal support of Putin's government for the history of Orthodox culture to be taught in Russian schools but this is being resisted in various quarters. While a broad range of seminaries has been set up, there is little evidence of religious education being widely implemented. Certainly the effort being put in by the Russian Orthodox church to the religious education of its flock compares poorly with the effort put in by the Muslims with *medressahs* and other Islamic education institutions.

There is a real danger that the ambition of the Russian Orthodox church to be arbiter of genuine Russian culture in the contemporary situation is not justified by the social realities on the ground in the Federation, bearing in mind the growth of Islam right across the Federation and the high level of secularisation of urban society. The apparent refusal of the Metropolitan Patriarchate and the more nationalist conservative elements in the church to abandon its primary ambition to be the ethnic church for native Russians effectively condemns the church to become a backwater in Russian history.

Some important issues need to be addressed by the domestic Muslim communities in the Federation. These include the search by domestic Islam in the Russian Federation to be recognised as the second state religion with equal status to Russian Orthodoxy. Such a recognition by the political and religious authorities and elites in the Federation would have profound implications, not least since in many of the semi-autonomous states that make up the Federation, Islam would be the dominant religion. Political recognition in such states could open the door to the introduction of shari'ah law. Although Islam has consistent written sources (Qur'an, Hadiths and shari'ah) supported by schools of jurisprudence (the majority of Muslims in Russia follow the *Hanafi* tradition), the Muslim communities have tended to be fragmented into tribal and other groups and have not so far been able to develop a coherent political presence. The two major groupings of muftis and political groups will need to find some measure of common cause in order to achieve this.

Despite the continuous terrorist incidents in the Caucasus and elsewhere, there is considerable hope in industrialised areas such as Kazan that moderate Islam can enjoy significant popular support. It is essential that such moderate movements are encouraged and assisted to resist the Islamist philosophies and practices being actively promoted at present. With a well-articulated system of education which far outclasses the Orthodox system, Islam in Russia is poised to make significant conversions among ethnic Russians and others.

The Russian Federation with its historical mix of different peoples, belief systems and cultures occupies a unique position in world affairs. The peaceful resolution of interreligious and interethnic issues in the Russian Federation would be of considerable significance globally. Importantly, it could provide an example for the resolution of similar engagements in other parts of the world.

Notes

1 Arnold, M., 'Dover beach', *The Poetry of Matthew Arnold – A Commentary*, (Oxford, Oxford University Press, 1940).

2 Kornoussova, B., 'Language policy and minority language planning in Russia: the case study of the Kalmyk Language', *Sociolinguistica international*, 1 (Noves SL., 2001).

3 Cited in Hunter, S. T., *Islam in Russia – The Politics of Identity and Security* (New York, M. E. Sharpe, 2004), p. 120, citing Malashenko, 'Islam in Russia: Notes of a Political Scientist', *Russian Social Science Review*, 41: 6 (November–December 2000), 64.

4 Egozaryan, V., International Relations Expert, Institute of Society Projects, Ekspert, RIA Novosti, cited in *Muslim News*, www.muslimnews.co.uk/news/news.php?article=9581 (accessed March 2005).

5 Estimates vary. Ravil Gaynutdin, Head of the Council of Muftis of Russia, in August 2005 claimed the figure to be 23 million ethnic Muslims, *Conflict Studies Research Centre, Russian Series 06/53*, p. 5.

6 Figures of religious practice vary somewhat but generally remain in low single figures. The research project 'Religion and values after the fall of Communism' (1991–99) showed that despite 82% claiming to be Orthodox, only 4% were 'real' practicing believers. Dimitry A. Golovushkin, Senior Lecturer, Chair of Religious Studies, A. I. Herzen State Pedagogical University, St Petersburg. *JSRI* (Spring 2004), www.dmitrygolovushkin-articol.htm (accessed March 2005).

7 Cited in Hunter, *Islam in Russia*, pp. 176ff. 'There is a broad consensus that Russia needs a new national identity' with differences about its precise nature. The consensus focuses on the 'Russian Experience' of the ethnic Russians and their culture. 'There can be no duality of cultures'. 'A Muslim culture cannot achieve equal status with Russian culture even in Muslim inhabited regions'. There are many types of Russian Nationalists: Christian, Solzhenitsyn and Aksiuchit, Communist (who appear to acknowledge the role of Orthodoxy), Zyugabov, geopolitical, Zhirinovsky and Dugin, Ultra groups and Reformists, Hunter describes each in some detail, pp. 176–91.

8 www.cesnur.org/testi/russia.htm.

9 International Religious Freedom Report, www.atheism.about.com/library/irf/irf03/blirf_russia.htm.

10 Uzzell. L. A., 'Russia: religion on a leash', www.orthodoxytoday.org/articles4/UzzellRussiaLeash.shtm (accessed March 2005), pp. 1–5.

11 Ibid., p. 1.

12 Ibid., p. 1.

13 *The Times* (Sept 2005).

14 International Religious Freedom Report 2003, http://atheism.about.com/library/irf/irf03/blirf_russia.htm (accessed March 2005).

15 www.mospat.ru/text/history/id/10.html (accessed March 2005).

16 Golovushkin, www.dmitrygolovushkin-articol.htm (accessed March 2005), p. 4.

17 Wikipedia updated Russian Orthodox Church (14 Janaury 2008).

18 The Russian Orthodox church website declares five clerical academies, thirty-three diocesan seminaries, forty-four diocesan schools, three Orthodox universities and other activities, www.mospat.ru (accessed March 2005).

19 Krindatch, A. D., 'Patterns of religious change in post-Soviet Russia: major trends from 1998 to 2003', *Religion, State & Society*, 32: 2 (2004), 115–36. This shows 9,515 Russian Orthodox parishes with 7995 priests (40% of overall Russian Orthodox total) in the Ukraine.

20 Ibid., p. 118. In a 2003 survey, the president enjoyed 81% rating followed by the church at 62% well ahead of the government and other institutions.
21 Krindatch, 'Patterns of religious change in post-Soviet Russia', p. 131.
22 Ibid., p. 123, citing Malashenko, 'Islam in Russia: notes of a political scientist', *Russian Social Science Review*, 41: 6 (November–December 2000), 58–9.
23 Ibid.
24 Ibid., p. 125.
25 Hunter, *Islam in Russia*, pp. 119–20.
26 Ibid., p. 119.
27 See website www.mospat.ru/text/e_news/id/8772.html (accessed March 2005).
28 Golovushkin, D. A., 'On the issue of religious education in modern Russia: national identity and religion', *JSRI*, 7 (Spring 2004), 101–10, www.hiphi.ubbclui. ro/JSRI/html%20version/index/no 7/dmitrygolovushkin-articol.htm (accessed March 2005).
29 Ibid., p. 1.
30 Ibid., p. 1.
31 Ibid., p. 2.
32 Ibid., p. 2.
33 Ibid., p. 3.
34 Ibid., p. 4.
35 *Pravda*, interview with Alexei II, 5 June 2002.
36 *Forum 18 News Summary* www.forum18.org (accessed April 2005).
37 *Daily Telegraph* (24/01/2004).

5

The Vatican, Islam and Muslim–Christian relations

Andrew Unsworth

The encounter between the Catholic church and Islam has a long history and has given rise to a well developed tradition of theological reflection.[1] Since the Second Vatican Council (1962–65)[2] relations between the two traditions have grown and intensified as the *global* encounter between Christianity and Islam has expanded. The Catholic church has engaged in a wide range of dialogical encounters with Islam on a number of significant issues, and at many different levels of engagement, such as: theological issues, religious freedom, the rights of the person, the rights of religious minorities and conflict resolution through religious exchange.

Paul VI (1963–78) and John Paul II (1978–2005) did more to promote better relations between Christians and Muslims than any other popes in history.[3] During the past forty years there has been an extensive diplomatic exchange between the Holy See and various states with majority Muslim populations, particularly during the influential pontificate of John Paul II. Many papal envoys are involved in this work and act on behalf of the Holy See in various parts of the world. The new pope, Benedict XVI, has indicated that he will pursue a similar policy.[4]

In this chapter I will outline briefly the history and development of the relationship between the Holy See and the Islamic world over the past half century. I will explain the role of the Roman Catholic church in contemporary Muslim–Christian relations, highlighting the key events of this period and explaining the teaching of the church and how the church, at an official level, has attempted to interpret and implement this teaching.[5]

What does the Catholic church teach about Islam?

During the pontificates of Paul VI and John Paul II many written documents and spoken addresses were produced which refer to Muslims and the Islamic faith. The major types of teaching documents produced by the Vatican are those from Ecumenical Councils, such as *Lumen Gentium*, *Nostra Aetate* and *Dignitatis Humanae*;[6] 'solemn' papal teachings, such as encyclicals and apostolic exhortations; and 'ordinary' papal teachings which are less definitive statements contained within homilies, papal letters and allocutions.[7] Teaching documents are also produced by Roman dicasteries, i.e. curial departments that assist the pope in the exercise of his universal pastoral and teaching ministry in the church.[8] The main dicastery dealing with issues of Christian–Muslim relations is the Pontifical Council for Interreligious Dialogue (PCID).

Robert Caspar, an expert advisor at Vatican II, reflects that when in 1965 the first sentence of *Nostra Aetate* art. 3 says: 'Upon the Moslems, too, the Church looks with esteem', it is significant in that it is, 'the first time in the history of the [Catholic] Church that the Magisterium, in solemn Council, advocates an attitude of esteem and of friendship towards Islam and the Muslims'.[9] In the text of the 'Dogmatic Constitution on the Church (*Lumen Gentium*)' promulgated on 21 November 1964 the Second Vatican Council taught that,

> the plan of salvation also includes those who acknowledge the Creator. In the first place among these there are the Moslems [Muslims], who, professing to hold the faith of Abraham, along with us adore the one and merciful God, who on the last day will judge mankind.[10]

In the 'Declaration on Non-Christian Religions (*Nostra Aetate*)' promulgated on 28 October 1965 we read:

> Upon the Moslems [Muslims], too, the Church looks with esteem. They adore one God, living and enduring, merciful and all-powerful, Maker of heaven and earth and Speaker to men. They strive to submit wholeheartedly even to His inscrutable decrees, just as did Abraham, with whom the Islamic faith is pleased to associate itself. Though they do not acknowledge Jesus as God, they revere Him as a prophet. They also honor Mary, His virgin mother; at times they call on her, too, with devotion. In addition they await the day of judgement when God will give each man his due after raising him up. Consequently, they prize the moral life, and give worship to God especially through prayer, almsgiving, and fasting.
>
> Although in the course of the centuries many quarrels and hostilities have arisen between Christians and Moslems, this most sacred Synod urges all to forget the past and to strive sincerely for mutual understanding. On behalf of all mankind, let them make common cause of safeguarding and fostering social justice, moral values, peace, and freedom.[11]

Lumen Gentium indicates that Islam is closest to Christianity and Judaism, because of its monotheism and in its reference to the patriarch Abraham. God's 'plan of salvation' therefore includes the Muslims in a mysterious and providential way. *Lumen Gentium* recognises that both religions worship the one true God. Robert Caspar suggests that: 'We [Catholics] cannot ever say again that we do not adore the same God, even if we call Him by different names'.[12] The hermeneutical implications of this assertion are complex and need careful clarification, however, Caspar's opinion corresponds with the official interpretation of the Catholic church.[13] The Council seemed to agree that Jews, Christians and Muslims, despite other differences of interpretation, are Abraham's 'spiritual heirs' in the order of faith.[14]

These themes are reiterated in *Nostra Aetate* which also contains a description of aspects of the 'Islamic faith'. Explicit reference to the Qur'an, to Muhammad and to the Hajj were omitted. The authors constructed the text of *Nostra Aetate* using phrases which were intended to convey a Muslim understanding of God's attributes.[15] No explicit reference is made to the Qur'an in the text of *Nostra Aetate*, nevertheless it is acknowledged that God is referred to by Muslims as a 'Speaker to men [humanity]'. According to Islam humanity ought to submit to these 'decrees'. The name 'Qur'an' means 'recitation'; a less accurate, but acceptable, translation may be 'a speech', and therefore the text can be seen to allude, albeit obliquely, to the Muslim belief in the Qur'anic revelation as authoritative divine speech.

The choice of the phrase 'submit wholeheartedly' is highly significant; the subtlety of its use in this context is often overlooked, in that the word 'Islam' itself literally means '(wholehearted) submission (to the will of God)'.[16] In the Qur'an 'Abraham' embodies this perfect submission to God's will. For Muslims Abraham is therefore a great *hanif* (Arabic – 'monotheist') and *mu'min* (Arabic – 'believer'), a 'father in faith, as a type and model of a heroic submission, with an active and confident faith'.[17] After other brief references to the Qur'anic view of Jesus and his mother Mary, and to those common doctrinal and moral values shared by Christianity and Islam, the second paragraph of *Nostra Aetate* 3 exhorts Christians and Muslims to move beyond past enmity, in order to overcome it, and the section ends with a consideration of theological issues and pragmatic considerations related to the question of religious freedom and the sharing of common objectives.

Lumen Gentium and *Nostra Aetate* presented a road-map for dialogue. In the context of the contemporary global encounter between Muslims and Christians diplomatic exchange is as important as 'theological' dialogue in the search for mutual understanding and world peace.

The Pontifical Council for Interreligious Dialogue

As the highest-ranking agency of the Holy See in the area of interreligious issues PCID promotes the study of religions and dialogue and has a special committee to deal with Islam. PCID receives delegations of Muslim dignitaries and scholars and sends its own staff abroad to act as members of official delegations and representatives of the Holy See. Its brief deals with 'religious questions' not 'socio-political issues'. It consults with Muslim scholars and has a special working group dedicated to the study of Islam and matters related to the worldwide Muslim–Christian dialogue. On 11 March 2006, PCID and the Pontifical Council for Culture were brought together into a formal relationship under the direction of Cardinal Paul Poupard. This arrangement was not a merger of the two offices as such. Cardinal Jean Tauran was appointed head of PCID in September 2007. In February 2006 the former head of PCID Archbishop Michael L. Fitzgerald (Missionary of Africa – White Father), an expert in Arabic and Islamic Studies, was appointed as Papal Nuncio to Egypt and the Arab League of twenty-two nations in order to focus on issues of a more explicitly socio-political nature.

In 1981 PCID prepared a revised version of *Guidelines for Dialogue between Christians and Muslims*. Commissioned by John Paul II and prepared by a team of Catholic scholars who were experts in Islamic Studies, this document facilitated theological reflection and encouraged best practice among Catholics engaged in dialogue with Muslims. The *Guidelines* are consistent with the 'mind' of the official church on the issues with which they deal. The contents of the *Guidelines* clarify or develop statements already made by the Magisterium of the church.[18]

Post-conciliar developments

The question about the status of 'Qur'anic revelation' in Catholic thought, the status of Muhammad and the Hajj (pilgrimage to Mecca) became especially important for Christian–Muslim dialogue in the post-conciliar period.

The Qur'an

Pope John Paul II referred to the Qur'an (Koran) on several occasions. Here I include two examples to demonstrate the development of a tradition within contemporary papal teaching of referring to the Qur'an. During a symposium on 'Holiness in Christianity and in Islam' on 9 May 1985 the pope said:

> Your holy Koran calls God 'Al-Quddus,' as in the verse: 'He is God, besides whom there is no other, the Sovereign, the Holy, the (source of) peace' (Koran 59, 23) . . . Thus, the Koran calls you up to uprightness (al-salah), to conscientious devotion (al-taqwa), to goodness (al-husn), and to virtue (al-birr), which is described as believing in God . . . being constant in prayer, keeping one's word, and being patient in times of suffering, hardship and violence (Koran 2, 177).[19]

The *Guidelines* make many references to the Qur'an. A profound appreciation for the Muslim faith is exemplified in the following paragraph:

> To Muslims the holy book constitutes the final, definitive and perfect revelation of previous books . . . Since it was directly revealed by God and sent down to earth in progressive sequences, the Qur'an possesses the uncreated character of the eternal Word . . . The classical interpretation is that the holy book is not simply inspired, for God alone is its author and the Prophet Muhammad merely transmitted it.[20]

Muhammad

Post-conciliar teaching is helpful in the way that it approaches the issue of Muhammad. It exhorts Catholics to,

> fully respect the deep affection which Muslims feel and manifest toward their Prophet . . . Christians should try to appreciate the authentic value of the life and work of the Prophet of Islam . . . They must renounce firmly 'all occasions where lack of respect has been shown, where incorrect statements in speech or in writing have been made, where unhelpful, even insulting, suggestions have been offered with reference to Muhammad, the venerated Prophet of Islam.' Instead of these negative judgements which came out of former concern for polemics and apologetics, Christians should assess in an objective way, and in consonance with their faith exactly what was the inspiration, the sincerity, and the faithfulness of the Prophet Muhammad . . . Christians will not require that Muslims recognize in Jesus all of the qualities which Christianity has conferred upon him . . . And, in like manner, a Muslim should not require that a Christian recognize in Muhammad all of the qualities that Islam has attributed

to him . . . they find in him evidence of certain mistakes and important misapprehensions. They also discern in him marks of prophethood.[21]

The Hajj

The *Guidelines* contain references to the Hajj:

> The annual participation of a multitude of pilgrims, ever growing larger, in the ceremonies of pilgrimage (Hajj) to Mecca is both a marvellous symbol and a tangible sign of the unity which brings Muslim men and women together . . . On pilgrimage Muslims transcend their ethnic, linguistic, economic and political diversity, because there 'believers are naught else but brothers,' as the Qur'an itself affirms (49:10).[22]

The *Guidelines* also explain the significance of Hajj for Muslims:

> The pilgrimage to Mecca takes them back to the sources of their faith and history, gives supranational dimensions to their religious experience, and, especially, prepares them for and leads them to the grace of contrition and forgiveness, through the various stages of a conversion to God.[23]

Muslim–Christian relations and religious freedom

The teaching of Vatican II on religious freedom is found in the 'Declaration on Religious Freedom (*Dignitatis Humanae*)', promulgated on 7 December 1965. The issue of religious freedom cannot be separated from related issues such as the rights of the person, the rights of religious minorities, and conflict resolution through religious exchange. This area of the life of the church involves effective diplomacy. The specific way in which the Holy See has developed relations with Muslim countries, communities and organisations worldwide has been crucial in protecting, and advocating on behalf of, those individual persons and communities around the world whose rights have be threatened or violated.

The Council had to deal with several unresolved matters in the life and teaching of the church in this area. It was recognised that the operative paradigm advocated by the church was no longer tenable within a changed historical context. The demands that twentieth-century modernity placed on the church had to be acknowledged, understood and responded to. This realisation was a response to the phenomenon of globalisation in a religious context in the sense that, for the first time, the bishops had a growing self-conscious awareness that they were members of what has been referred to as 'a world church'. There was a growing recognition of, and respect for, the dignity of non-Catholic Christians and the members of non-Christian religions.

At Vatican II issues were raised concerning the existence of political regimes that advocated the marginalisation and eradication of religious faith and practice. The church was concerned about the potential of totalitarianism of various types to threaten and subdue the rights of individuals and (religious) communities. There was also a desire to understand the newly developing human rights discourse from a Catholic philosophical and theological perspective, and a willingness to assist those who were working for the realisation of world peace, political stability, justice and the common good among the nations.[24]

Experts in this area had a developed sense that this newly emerging and multidimensional reality changed everything. Many of the bishops had an intuition of this too but needed to be guided through the issues in order to arrive at a considered opinion about the significance of the new world context and what exactly the response of the church ought to be.[25]

According to a Catholic understanding, the right to freedom of religion is intimately related to the dignity of the human person. The opening section of *Dignitatis Humanae* summarises its central teaching:

> A sense of the dignity of the human person has been impressing itself more and more deeply on the consciousness of contemporary man. And the demand is increasingly made that men should act on their own judgement, enjoying and making use of a responsible freedom, not driven by coercion but motivated by a sense of duty. The demand is also made that constitutional limits should be set to the powers of government, in order that there may be no encroachment on the rightful freedom of the person and of associations. This demand for freedom in human society chiefly regards the quest for the values proper to the human spirit. It regards in the first place, the free exercise of religion in society.[26]

The participation of the Catholic church in international relations has been highly significant since the Council, particularly with reference to the promotion of better Christian–Muslim relations. It must be remembered that the church has a concern for the legitimate rights and freedoms of all people, regardless of their religious faith or affiliation. John Paul II made this abundantly clear throughout his pontificate, especially when he addressed those who were involved in Christian–Muslim dialogue.

Arguably the most memorable address of this kind was that given by John Paul II in Casablanca, at the invitation of the Muslim ruler of Morocco, King Hasan II, in 1985. Within the context of the teaching of *Nostra Aetate* and *Dignitatis Humanae* the pope explored a joint Christian–Muslim vision of the rights of the person and of religious communities. He argued that common effort in this area could achieve the aspirations of all Christians and Muslims of good will to the establishment of mutual respect and understanding, as well as the promotion and defence of justice and peace:

> Christians and Muslims have many things in common, as believers and as human beings ... Everyone hopes to be respected for what he is in fact, and for what he conscientiously believes. We desire that all may reach the fullness of the divine truth, but no one can do that except through the free adherence of conscience, protected from exterior compulsions which would be unworthy of the free homage of reason and heart which is characteristic of human dignity. There is the true meaning of religious liberty ... Therefore, we must also *respect, love and help every human being*, because he is a creature of God ... Furthermore, this obedience to God and his love for man should lead us to respect man's rights. These rights are the expression of God's will and the demands of human nature such as it was created by God ... Therefore, respect and dialogue require reciprocity in all spheres, especially in that which concerns basic freedoms, more particularly religious freedom.[27]

Diplomatic exchange, the Holy See and Christian–Muslim relations

The Holy See has long enjoyed diplomatic relations with Muslim rulers and with countries containing majority Muslim populations. The Casablanca visit was one of the most significant meetings in the history of relations between Christianity and Islam. The visit showed that trust and good will could be achieved at the level of international religious diplomacy.

As early as the fourth and fifth centuries papal legates represented the interests of the popes. During the rise of the modern nation states in the sixteenth century, the papacy, as a spiritual and temporal power, was quick to adopt the most current practices in terms of the training of ambassadors for service in the courts of Europe.[28]

Cardinal Tauran has observed that, 'the Catholic Church is the only religious institution in the world to have access to diplomatic relations and to be very interested in international law'.[29] The Holy See currently enjoys full diplomatic relations with 174 countries worldwide. It has a variety of diplomatic relations with other international and regional intergovernmental organisations and bodies, most notably the United Nations Organisation (UNO), at which the Holy See is, out of choice, a 'permanent observer', rather than a 'full member', for reasons of neutrality. The Holy See has official relations with several non-governmental organisations (NGOs), as well as diplomatic relations with the European Union, the Arab League and the Palestinian Liberation Organisation.[30]

Several countries that have diplomatic relations with the Holy See are ruled by Muslim leaders or regimes whose members follow the Muslim religion, and which contain Muslim majority populations. However, the use of terms such as 'Islamic state' and 'Islamic ruler' is problematic; these terms suggest not only those states which contain a majority of people who adhere to Islam, i.e. where the Islamic religion has a significant social-cultural, and political influence, but also those states which seek to institute and enact a form of shari'ah law.[31]

In the late-twentieth century a number of states came under the influence of a variety of ideologies which have been described as 'Islamic Fundamentalist' or 'Radical Islamist'.[32] The proponents of these ideological positions, as much as they have gained political influence in states with a Muslim majority, have, on the whole, not been favourable to the rights of non-Muslim religious minorities. Some have also been responsible for funding terrorist atrocities, such as the 9/11 attacks on the USA, and for harbouring terrorists.[33] The religious rights of many Christians, and others, in such states have been severely threatened, and in some cases completely disregarded. The occurrence of religious persecution and the curtailment of religious liberties have done much to sour the Holy See's relations with these states. In his 'Address to the Bishops of Malaysia, Singapore and Brunei', 16 June 1990, John Paul II lamented the 'Islamisation' of Malaysia, which was threatening the rights of Christians;[34] and in the same month in his 'Letter to Asian Bishops', 23 June, 1990, he sadly reflected that:

[R]eligious intolerance [is] manifested in some Asian countries . . . certain governments in nations where there are many followers of Islam have assumed postures which seem not in keeping with that tolerance which is part of the venerable Islamic tradition.[35]

It is interesting to note the curt statement made by the pope on the opening of the largely Saudi-financed mosque in Rome, 21 June 1995, when, in no uncertain terms, he openly criticised the lack of 'reciprocity' in terms of the lack of religious rights for Christians in some Islamic states. On this occasion he left his hearers in no doubt that, although his comments did not mention any state in particular, they were most certainly levelled at Saudi Arabia:

> A grand mosque is being inaugurated today. This event is an eloquent sign of the religious freedom recognized here for every believer. And it is significant that in Rome, the centre of Christianity and the See of Peter's Successor, Muslims should have their own place to worship with full respect for their freedom of conscience. On a significant occasion like this, it is unfortunately necessary to point out that in some Islamic countries similar signs of the recognition of religious freedom are lacking. And yet the world, on the threshold of the third millennium, is waiting for these signs! Religious freedom has now become part of many international documents and is one of the pillars of contemporary society. While I am pleased that Muslims can gather in prayer in the new Roman mosque, I earnestly hope that the rights of Christians and of all believers freely to express their own faith will be recognized in every corner of the earth.[36]

In the recent promulgation of the Post-Synodal Apostolic Exhortation *Ecclesia in Europa*, 28 June 2003, the European bishops and the Holy Father felt it their duty to 'insist' on this principle of 'reciprocity' which ought to be evident in all such international encounters between Christians and Muslims.[37] Nevertheless, the Holy See has done much to make known the plight of Muslim populations, and to advocate on their behalf when their human and religious rights have been ignored. The role of the Holy See in protesting and advocating on the world stage, usually at sessions of the UN,[38] its high profile opposition to the Gulf War (1991)[39] and Iraq War (2003),[40] and its advocacy on behalf of Palestinian refugees,[41] are notable examples.

Conclusion

Since the Second Vatican Council there has been a positive reappraisal of the religious beliefs and practices of Muslims by the Catholic church. Although the Council 'adopted no theological position on Islam',[42] the assertion that Christians and Muslims worship/adore the same God has had profound theological significance for Muslim–Christian relations. This *theologoumenon* was not a consensus opinion among Catholic theologians before Vatican II; however, since the Council Catholic scholars working in the mainstream of Catholic theology have tended not to dispute this view. The *description* of the religion of Islam in the post-conciliar texts shows an impressive degree of sensitivity to the beliefs, values and practices of Muslims. Some of the omissions of the Council documents have also been addressed in various documents, notably the *Guidelines*.

The teachings of Vatican II, and the post-conciliar teachings, have yet to be fully 'received' by Catholics. A willingness to understand Islam and openness to practical engagement with Muslims is urgently required. Unfortunately church teachings and the action of the Holy See on behalf of the Catholic faithful can often be viewed as the sole responsibility of 'religious experts', i.e. theologians and the clergy. The example of John Paul II was an inspiration and a powerful witness to those involved in dialogue. The official teachings of the Catholic church deserve to be better understood and appreciated.

The Holy See still faces a number of challenges in the area of international religious diplomacy, especially with Muslim countries and states which observe forms of shari'ah law.[43] The annual published records of human and religious rights' abuses, especially in some Muslim countries, produced by *Aid to the Church in Need*, make sobering reading.[44] It is significant that Archbishop Michael Fitzgerald, a senior ranking Vatican expert on Islam, has been assigned by Pope Benedict XVI to the role of Papal Nuncio to Egypt and the Arab League in order to concentrate on socio-political issues, especially such issues as the call for Islamic 'reciprocity'.[45]

In terms of its involvement in the global Christian encounter with Islam at the level of international relations, the Holy See has done much to promote respect for the human person and religious freedom. Through its involvement in the UNO, and through bilateral and multilateral diplomatic relations with 174 countries, the Holy See has had a strong moral influence and is able to work very effectively towards the protection of the interests of those whose individual and collective rights are threatened. The Holy See has worked assiduously in its attempt to guarantee peace between the nations through its agencies and envoys in various regions of the world where conflict resolution is possible through religious exchange.

Notes

1 See Muhammed (SJ, Society of Jesus), Ovey N., *Muslim–Christian Relations: Past, Present, Future* (New York, Orbis, 1999).

2 I will also refer to the Council as 'Vatican II'.

3 A full analysis of their teachings can be found on the official website of the Holy See. I will make several references to such texts. Where no bibliographical reference is given, sources cited can be viewed at this website using the www.vatican.va search engine.

4 See Pope Benedict XVI, 'Address of His Holiness: meeting with representatives of some Muslim communities', Cologne, 20 August 2005.

5 It is important to note the distinction between the 'Holy See', 'the Vatican State', and the worldwide '(Roman) Catholic Church'. The term 'Holy See' refers explicitly to the pope, the Vatican Curia and other individuals and agencies who act as his representatives at an official level and who are designated as such. At the level of international law the 'Holy See' is recognised as a diplomatic entity which can be distinguished from the Vatican State, and more importantly, the (Roman) Catholic Church and its members taken as a whole.

6 See Rush, O., *Still Interpreting Vatican II: Some Hermeneutical Principles* (New York, Paulist Press, 2004).

7 Catholic theologians often refer to these teaching documents collectively as 'the Magisterium', although technically speaking those who produce the documents constitute the Magisterium. See Sullivan, F., *Creative Fidelity, Weighing and*

Interpreting Documents of the Magisterium (New York, Paulist Press, 1996), p. 1.

8 See Reese (SJ), J., *Inside the Vatican: The Politics and Organization of the Catholic Church* (Harvard, Harvard University Press, 1996).

9 Caspar, R., 'Islam according to Vatican II: On the tenth anniversary of *Nostra Aetate*', *Encounter: Documents for Muslim-Christian Understanding*, 21 (1976), p. 3. See also Georges C. Anawati's brief commentary, 'Excursus on Islam', Young, S. and E. (trans.) in Vorgrimler, H. (ed.), *Commentary on the Documents of Vatican II: Volume III* (London, Burns and Oates, 1969), pp. 151–4.

10 'Lumen Gentium', in Abbott (SJ), W. (ed.), *The Documents of Vatican II: With Notes by Catholic, Protestant and Orthodox Authorities* (Dublin/Melbourne, Geoffrey Chapman, 1967), p. 35.

11 'Nostra Aetate', in Abbott (ed.), *The Documents of Vatican II*, p. 663.

12 Caspar, 'Islam according to Vatican II', p. 3.

13 John Paul II focused on the theological significance of the expression '*together with us* (they adore the one merciful God)'. In his commentary on the Council, he seems to suggest that this expression 'seems not only to denote the fact that we are all monotheists, but also to imply that we have something in common where Revelation is concerned', Wojtyla, K., *Sources of Renewal: The Implementation of the Second Vatican Council*, trans. Falls, P. S. (London, Collins, 1980), p. 129.

14 Muhammed, *Muslim–Christian Relations*, p. 52.

15 See Caspar, 'Islam according to Vatican II', pp. 1–7. See Ovey Muhammed's brief comments in *Muslim–Christian Relations* which reiterate some of these observations, p. 60; see also Emilio Platti (OP, Order of Preachers) in, 'Islam: dialogue or confrontation?' (Manila, Centre for Contextualized Theology and Ethics, 2003), www.cteust.com/article2.htm, pp. 4–7.

16 Caspar, 'Islam according to Vatican II', p. 4.

17 Ibid., p. 5.

18 Pontifical Council for Interreligious Dialogue, *Guidelines for Dialogue Between Christians and Muslims: Prepared by Maurice Borrmans*, trans. Marston Speight, R. (New York, Paulist Press; English trans., The Missionary Society of St Paul the Apostle, 1990). Originally published in French as *Orientations pour un dialogue entre Chretiens et Musulmans* (Paris, Les Editions du Cerf, 1981).

19 Gioia, Francesco (ed.), *Interreligious Dialogue: The Official Training of the Catholic Church 1963–1995* (Boston, Pauline Books, 1997), p. 283.

20 PCID, *Guidelines*, p. 47.

21 PCID, *Guidelines*, pp. 57–8.

22 PCID, *Guidelines*, p. 19.

23 PCID, *Guidelines*, p. 62.

24 The influence of the *U.N. Universal Declaration of Human Rights*, 10 December 1948 (esp. article 18), the *U.N. International Covenant on Civil and Political Rights*, 16 December 1966 (esp. article 18), and human rights discourse generally has been very significant. The Catholic church's body of social teaching began with Leo XIII's encyclical *Rerum Novarum*, 1891. See also John XXIII's *Pacem in Terris*, 1963.

25 For a history and commentary on the text see Pavan, P., 'Declaration on Religious Freedom', in Vorgrimler, H. (ed.), *Commentary on the Documents of Vatican II: Volume IV* (New York/London, Herder and Herder/Burns and Oats, 1968), pp. 49–86.

26 'Declaration on religious freedom: on the rights of the person and of communities to social and civil freedom in matters religious', in Abbott (ed.), *The Documents of Vatican II*, p. 675; see also, the letter written by the pope addressed to European Heads of State: John Paul II, *The Freedom of Conscience and of Religion*, 1 September 1980; Rico (SJ), Herminio, *John Paul II and the Legacy of 'Dignitatis Humanae'* (Georgetown, Georgetown University Press, 2002).

27 'To the young Muslims of Morocco', Casablanca, 19 August 1985, in Gioia, *Interreligious*, pp. 297–305.

28 Archbishop Jean-Louis Tauran, 'On the theme "presence of the Holy See in the international organizations"', 22 April 2002, www.vatican_curia/secretariat_state/documents/rc_seg-st_doc_20020422, pp. 1–6.

29 Tauran, 'Holy See', p. 1; Vallier, I., 'The Roman Catholic Church: a transnational actor', in Keohane, R. O. and Nye, J. (eds), *Transnational Relations in World Politics* (Cambridge MA, Harvard University Press, 1972), pp. 129–52; Hehir, J. B., 'The Catholic church and the Middle East: policy and diplomacy', in Ellis, K. C. (ed.), *The Vatican, Islam, and the Middle East* (Syracuse, Syracuse University Press, 1987), pp. 109–24; Hanson, E. O., *The Catholic Church in World Politics* (New Jersey, Princeton University Press, 1987); Johnston, D. and Sampson, C., (eds), *Religion: The Missing Dimension of Statecraft* (Oxford, Oxford University Press, 1994); Kent, P. C. and Pollard, J. F. (eds), *Papal Diplomacy in the Modern Age* (Portsmouth, Greenwood, 1994).

30 'Bilateral and multilateral relations of the Holy See', www.vatican_curia/secretariat_state/documents/rc_seg-st_doc_20010123, pp. 1–6.

31 Exposito, J. L., *Islam and Politics* (Syracuse, Syracuse University Press, 4th edn, 1998); Thomas, S. M., *The Global Resurgence of Religion and the Transformation of International Relations: The Struggle for the Soul of the Twenty-First Century* (New York, Palgrave, 2005); Huntington, S. P., *The Clash of Civilizations and the Making of World Order* (Sydney, Simon and Schuster, 1997, 2002).

32 Some examples of the Holy See's concern about the rise of Fundamentalism can be found in John Paul II, 'Message for the World Day of Peace 1990', 8 December 1990; an 'Address to a Franciscan group involved in dialogue with Muslims', on 26 August 1995; The Post-Synodal Apostolic Exhortation *Ecclesia in Africa*, 14 September 1995; and in the Holy Father's 'Address to the 50th General Assembly of the United Nations', New York, 5 October 1995, www.vatican.va.

33 Some recent statements condemning terrorism: John Paul II, 'Address of the Holy Father to President Mubarak of Egypt', 24 February 2000; John Paul II, 'Address to the representatives of the world of culture, art and science', Kazakhstan, 24 September 2001; 'Intervention of the Holy See to the 24 Conference of European Ministers of Justice', Moscow, 4 October 2001; 'Statement of Mgr. Martino to the 56th Session of the General Assembly of the United Nations on Disarmament', New York, 15 October 2001; John Paul II, 'Message for the World Day of Peace 2002', 1 January 2002; 'Intervention of the Holy See to the 25th Conference of European Ministers of Justice', 9–10 October 2003; 'Day of Prayer for Peace in the World', Assisi, 24 January, 2002; 'To the G.B. Ambassador to the Holy See', Rome, 7 September 2002; 'To the Organization for Security and Co-operation in Europe', Varsavia, 11 September 2002, www.vatican.va.

34 Gioia, *Interreligious*, p. 436.

35 Gioia, *Interreligious*, p. 437. See also John Paul II, 'Address to the Diplomatic Corps', 13 January 1990, in *L'Osservatore Romano*, English Edition, 29 January 1990, p. 3.

36 *Islamochristiana*, 21 (1995), 176–7. See Willey, D., *God's Politician: John Paul at the Vatican* (London, Faber and Faber, 1993), pp. 93–112.

37 '*Ecclesia in Europa*: On Christ alive in His church the source of hope for Europe' (London, C.T.S., 2003), p. 44.

38 See John Paul II, 'Address to the 50th General Assembly of the United Nations Organization', New York, 5 October 1995. The pope also made a visit to the UN in order to address it on 2 October 1979, as did Paul VI before him.

39 See the 'Messages to His Excellency Saddam Hussein, President of Iraq and to His Excellency George Bush, President of the United States', 15 January 1991, in which the pope urged both leaders to stand down from the ensuing conflict. After the war had ended the pope personally wrote and signed the annual letter of greeting sent by the PCID to the world's Muslims to mark the Feast of *Id al-Fitr*: 'Message to the faithful of Islam at the end of the month of Ramadan', Rome, 3 April 1991, www.vatican.va.

40 See 'Statement of Cardinal Roger Etchegary, Special Envoy of John Paul II in Baghdad', 16 February 2003; 'Intervention of Mgr. Migliore at the Security Council of the United Nations on the Iraq issue', 19 February 2003; The 'Angelus' prayers were offered, by the pope, for peace, on the 2and 16 March, and on the 6 April 2003; 'Report by the Envoy of the Holy Father to Iraq, Mgr. Paul Josef Cordes in the aftermath of war', 2 June 2003, www.vatican.va.

41 See for example the pope's visit in order to address the residents of the Dheisheh Palestinian Refugee Camp, 22 March 2000, on his Jubilee Pilgrimage to the Holy Land, in *Insegnamenti di Giovanni Paulo II*, 23: 1 (2000), 414–16.

42 G.R.I.C, *The Challenge of the Scriptures: The Bible and the Qur'an*, trans. Brown, Stuart E. (New York, Orbis, 1989), p. 59.

43 *The Catholic Herald*, 'Editorial: the pope must speak: Benedict faces a major test of statesmanship', 18 November 2005.The recent murder of Fr Andrea Santoro (05/02/06) in Turkey in the wake of Muslim protests against the defamation of the Prophet Muhammad in a Danish publication has also raised further concerns for the welfare of Catholics, and others, in some Muslim countries. It should be noted that the Holy See was prompt in its condemnation of those who had provoked Muslims in this way. The Holy See also condemned the violence of those who, like Fr Santoro's killer, had used this unfortunate incident as a pretext for criminal behaviour against Christians. See *L'Osservatore Romano* (English Edition), 'Declaration of the Holy See press office – free to offend?', 8 February 2006, p. 8. Also Woodrow, A., 'Sacred and profane'; De Sondy, A., 'Truth behind the images'; Gearty, C., 'Limits to freedom'; and Bunting, M., 'Denmark's mask of tolerance slips', all in *The Tablet*, 11 February 2006, pp. 4–9.

44 Orban de Lengyelfalva, J. G. (ed.), *Violence Against Christians in the Year 2004* (Netherlands, Aid to the Church in Need, 2004).

45 *Catholic Herald*, 'Englishman first to go in curial shake-up', 24 February 2006, pp. 1 and 11. For a response to this news see Unsworth, A., 'Letter – no demotion', in the *Catholic Herald*, 3 March 2006, p. 11. For a more detailed discussion of some of the issues raised in this paper see Unsworth, A., 'John Paul II, Islam and the Christian–Muslim encounter', in O'Mahony, A., Peterburs, W. and Shomali, M. (eds), *Catholic-Shi'a Engagement: Faith and Reason in Theory and Practice* (London, Melisende, 2006), pp. 200–49.

6

Muslim–Christian relations in Egypt: challenges for the twenty-first century

Fiona McCallum

Egyptians – Muslims and Christians, are united under the Egyptian banner. (President Hosni Mubarak, June 2001)[1]

There is no difference between us at all. We are all Egyptians. (President Hosni Mubarak, January 2005)[2]

The Coptic Christian community in Egypt has long been proclaimed as an integral component of the country. The Copts are an indigenous group who are the ancestors of most Egyptians today. In fact, the term Copt is derived from the Greek *aigyptos* meaning Egyptian.[3] The debate over the size of the Coptic community causes controversy. According to government census figures, there are five to six million Copts, around 8% of the population.[4] However, church sources tend to cite 10%, expatriates 15–20% and academic research suggests 5–6%. In contrast, it is generally accepted that the Muslim community constitutes at least 90% of the population. The Christian community can be divided into three main denominations – Coptic Orthodox, Coptic Catholic and Coptic Protestant. As the vast majority of Egyptian Christians belong to the Coptic Orthodox church and there are few adherents without Egyptian heritage, it can be regarded as the Egyptian national church. The church in Egypt split from the universal church due to its rejection of the christological definition agreed at the Council of Chalcedon in 451. The persecution suffered under the pro-Chalcedon Byzantine empire ceased as a consequence of the Arab conquest in the seventh century. In time, the Coptic population declined, often due to mass conversion to Islam. Thus, it is generally accepted that by the mid-ninth century, they had become a minority in their own land.[5] Yet as illustrated above in the two quotes from speeches by the Egyptian President Hosni Mubarak, the notion of Egypt constituting two communities which combine to make one nation has remained strong regardless of the exact amount of Copts in present-day Egypt. This article seeks to explore the main developments in Muslim–Christian relations in Egypt since the twentieth century with particular emphasis on three issues that consistently hinder communal relations – church building, conversions and security. Recognising that the Coptic Orthodox church functions as the civil representative of the community, the strategies pursued by the church during the Mubarak years with regard to communal harmony, will be examined in order to provide an overview of contemporary Muslim–Christian relations and prospects for the future in Egypt.

Muslim–Christian relations in history

In general, the Coptic Orthodox church has tried to ensure peaceful relations with the Muslim majority. As Anthony O'Mahony states, living in an Islamic environment, the church 'has everything to fear and lose from religious conflict'.[6] Under centuries of Islamic rule, Christians as *ahl al-kitab* (people of the book) were considered *dhimmi* (covenanted people) who paid tax to the Muslim authorities in return for autonomy and religious freedom. Occasionally, Muslim backlash to the extensive presence of Copts in administrative positions would lead to communal tension, but apart from the rule of the eleventh-century Fatimid Caliph al-Hakim there have been few instances of mass persecution. The Ottoman authorities institutionalised the tradition of dealing with each Christian community as a group identified by their religious identity through the *millet* system which granted recognition of the patriarch as the spokesperson of the group. The weakness of the Ottoman empire from the mid-nineteenth century onwards provided an opportunity for Christians in Egypt to escape *dhimmi* status and become citizens of an independent Egypt. However, as Paul Sedra notes, this was not without risk. 'The advent of the notion of citizenship was a source of uncertainty and discomfort for the Coptic religious establishment and the community at large, as the control the *millet* system afforded the patriarch had long ensured communal security and stability'.[7] Communal relations were tense in the early twentieth century. During the British occupation of Egypt, the first Coptic prime minister was killed in 1910 by a Muslim nationalist. Many Copts believed that his religious identity was a key reason for his assassination.[8] A Coptic Congress was held in Assiut in 1910 calling for more representation, the end of discrimination and Sunday as a weekly holiday for Christians. This was followed by a Congress at Heliopolis held by Muslims in 1911 which rejected the demands of the previous meeting.[9]

The struggle for independence from Britain led to what is termed the Golden Age of communal relations in Egypt. Under the influence of Saad Zaghlul, the leader of the Wafd party, Muslims and Christians united to oppose colonial rule. Coptic members of the Wafd such as Makram Ebeid and Sinut Hanna were imprisoned by the British authorities and consequently were supported by Egyptians because of their loyalty to the nationalist cause. Their legal and foreign language skills also proved useful in negotiating with the British authorities. The Wafd movement offered hope to Christians in their pursuit of equality and political participation. The 1919 Revolution witnessed unprecedented cooperation between the two communities. A Coptic priest, Father Sergios, led a demonstration to al-Azhar against the exile of Zaghlul and was the first Christian to preach at this historic mosque.[10] Patriarch Kyrillos V advised against Copts accepting the post of prime minister which was being offered by the British as this was solely an attempt to divide the independence movement.[11] According to Carter, 'The Coptic reward for providing both leaders and followers to the movement was substantive incorporation into the post-independence political system'.[12] Coptic candidates were successful even in predominantly Muslim electoral districts and the cabinet usually contained two Coptic ministers.[13] The Coptic community was eager to be seen as Egyptian first and Christian second. Most rejected the use of quotas to ensure parliamentary representation and accepted Islam being proclaimed the official religion of the state. However, this proved to be a short period of communal cooperation. By the 1930s, the Islamist current had gained ground once more, especially with the founding of the influential Muslim Brotherhood in 1928.[14] Faced with this hostile environment, the Wafd began to decrease its commitments to Coptic equality. The number of Christian members diminished and it became difficult for Christian candidates to win parliamentary seats.[15] The failure of Copts to achieve lasting participation within the nationalist movement was complete when only seven Copts were elected under a Wafd–Muslim Brotherhood alliance in 1950.[16]

With the establishment of the Free Officers regime in 1952, there was little change in Muslim–Christian relations. Christian influence declined as a consequence of Nasser's nationalisation policies and the concentration of power in the military. However, they continued to be represented in the cabinet and parliament. Nasser enjoyed cordial relations with Patriarch Kyrillos VI who was able to obtain permission to build an agreed number of churches each year and a new patriarchal cathedral in Cairo.[17] Patriarch Kyrillos was instrumental in encouraging the development of the renewal process that commenced in the Coptic Orthodox church from the 1940s. Enjoying the fruits of the work started by the Sunday School movement, the church experienced a monastic revival which, in turn, helped revitalise the entire church and community.[18] During this period, the church focused on internal matters. Although this helped strengthen communal unity, it also served to distinguish the Copts from their Muslim compatriots, thus increasing their vulnerability to religious hostility. In the latter years of Nasser's presidency, the failings of the ruling ideology – pan-Arabism – became apparent. The quest for Arab unity had not been attained. The Egyptian regime, like other Arab nationalist governments, had also failed to deliver its political, economic and social promises. Finally, the Arab forces had been crushed in the 1967 Six Day War against Israel. Struggling to retain legitimacy, pan-Arabism gradually became replaced by its main rival – pan-Islamism. The Islamic revival which affected the entire region had a significant impact on communal relations in Egypt.

Muslim–Christian relations under Sadat

The presidency of Anwar Sadat represents a low point in Muslim–Christian relations in Egypt. Sadat was by no means anti-Christian. However, once in power, several factors combined to induce fraught church–state relations. Elected in 1970 after the death of Nasser, the immediate priority for Sadat was to secure his position. To counter Nasserist elements, he ordered the mass release of Islamist prisoners and tolerated their presence in universities and activities in the social sphere.[19] On a personal level, he adopted Islamic rhetoric in his speeches, and called himself 'The Believer President'.[20] The 1973 war against Israel was proclaimed a moral victory because, unlike the humiliation of the Six Day War, it was fought under the banner of Islam. One consequence of this Islamisation process was an increase in religious tensions.

This period also witnessed a significant change in the leadership of the Coptic Orthodox church. Patriarch Kyrillos VI accepted the *millet* system and concentrated on encouraging the church renewal movement. His successor Patriarch Shenouda III became the head of the church in 1971. He was the first member of the Sunday School reform movement to attain the highest position in the church. Aged only forty-seven when he became patriarch (relatively young for this office), he represented the new type of clergy. Nadia Ramsis Farah states that 'The new church leadership, well educated and more politicized than their predecessors, had a new perception of their role'.[21] Patriarch Shenouda believed that it was the duty of the church to represent the concerns of the community to the state. Under his dynamic leadership, several issues were raised including political participation and representation, religious extremism and intolerance and the problems of church building. The personality clash between Sadat and Patriarch Shenouda can also be seen as a factor for the strained church–state relations during this time.

The first major confrontation was directly linked to the difficulties over church building (see below for a full discussion on the relevant legislation). Muslim hostility to Coptic attempts to transform a Coptic-owned building into a church in al-Khanka in 1972 resulted in an attack on the church. Instead of appealing privately to the state authorities, Patriarch Shenouda sent a party of around 100 priests and 400 lay Copts to conduct mass on the ruined site.[22] This served to escalate the situation and led to the burning of Christian shops and homes. In response to this incident Sadat visited Patriarch Shenouda and, with the Sheikh of al-Azhar, condemned this violence. A parliamentary commission was established to examine the incident. However, its main recommendation – equal legislation for building places of worship – was not enacted.[23] The fundamental reason for this clash remained unsolved. Furthermore, Sadat was also furious at the assertive strategy adopted by Patriarch Shenouda.

The next major development was a concerted Coptic protest against a 1977 proposal to amend the constitution in order to introduce shari'ah law into the Egyptian legal system. This would affect Christians because the Islamic code for apostasy would be implemented. Christians who converted to Islam in order to obtain divorce or boost career prospects would no longer be able to return to the church.[24] Farah suggests that Patriarch Shenouda was willing to risk confrontation with Sadat in order to maintain the secular character of the Egyptian state. In this way, his actions can be interpreted as representing all Egyptians who did not wish to reside in an Islamic state, not just solely the Coptic community.[25] However, the main response from the Muslim community was resentment at what was perceived as Coptic interference in an issue that only affected Muslims. Patriarch Shenouda mobilised the community against these changes. Protesting that the new laws would violate their human rights, a Coptic Conference was held which demanded freedom of worship and government protection against militant attacks. It also called on the government to annul the Ottoman law relevant to church building, end discrimination and tackle extremism.[26] A five day collective fast served to highlight the problems facing the community.

There were also protests held by Coptic émigrés in the west, particularly in the United States. The strong reaction from the Coptic community must be seen in the context of frequent attacks on Copts, their property and churches. Eventually, the government abandoned the bill but this victory for Patriarch Shenouda was marred by increased violence against the Copts and inadequate state protection from these attacks.

The final confrontation between President Sadat and Patriarch Shenouda occurred over legislative changes as had happened in 1977. In 1980, the government again discussed a constitutional amendment that would make shari'ah law *the* principal source of legislation. Farah explains the significance of this legislation as the equality enjoyed by the Copts would no longer be constitutionally guaranteed but instead would be subject to state authorities.[27] Again, Patriarch Shenouda showed his public displeasure of this measure and also the failure of the government to prevent violence against the Copts. He cancelled the 1980 Easter celebrations and retired with the church hierarchy to a desert monastery.[28] This action was calculated to cause embarrassment as government representatives traditionally attended Easter celebrations to congratulate Patriarch Shenouda and the Coptic community. Sadat had also been humiliated during his trip to the United States. Coptic activists took out full page advertisements in influential newspapers and organised street demonstrations protesting about the situation facing the Copts and, more specifically, government inaction to protect them.[29]

This period witnessed an increased campaign against the Coptic reaction to the situation in Egypt. Sadat made several speeches that accused the patriarch of stirring sectarian strife. Sadat ascribed to the view that as president of Egypt, it fell to him alone to safeguard all Egyptians. The assertive policies undertaken by Patriarch Shenouda were interpreted as a challenge to his authority. Valognes suggests that Sadat was determined to halt this questioning of the position and power of the president by a religious minority.[30] He claimed that the patriarch was trying to become a political leader as well as a spiritual one. Various accusations were made including a conspiracy to establish a Coptic state in Upper Egypt, the acceptance of CIA funds and connections with the Lebanese Maronite Christian militias.[31] In such a climate, these claims severely damaged the integrity of Patriarch Shenouda in the eyes of many Muslims and gave credibility to rumours about Coptic conspiracies. Few in government circles seemed willing to accept that the assertive approach of the patriarch and the community could be due to the constant violence experienced by them. According to Watson, 'What the Copts regarded as legitimate defence of Coptic property and lives was regarded by Sadat's journalists as the rising militancy of the Copts in their response to the abhorrent militant Muslims'.[32] The final catalyst was the outbreak of communal violence in Zawya al-Hamra, a poor district of Cairo. Fourteen people were killed and over 100 wounded in riots which lasted several days.[33] Sadat used this conflict as justification for a crackdown on all opposition. While Islamists were the main targets, 150 Copts including eight bishops were also arrested.[34] Patriarch Shenouda was banished to a desert monastery in Wadi al-Natroun and in his absence, Sadat appointed a papal committee to administer church affairs.

Muslim–Christian relations in the immediate post-Sadat era

The assassination of Sadat ended this personality clash with Patriarch She-nouda. His successor Hosni Mubarak concentrated on combating the threat posed to the regime by the militant groups implicated in the death of Sadat. Patriarch Shenouda was not given permission to return to Cairo until Christmas 1985. This was partly due to the easing of communal tension and also the accep-tance that Patriarch Shenouda had retained allegiance from the community as the only legitimate leader of the Coptic Orthodox church. Violence against Copts still continued during the 1980s and 1990s. For example, churches and Christian property were destroyed in Abu Qurqus (Upper Egypt) in March 1990 while thirteen Christians and two Muslims who came to their aid were killed in an attack in Manshiat Nassir (also Upper Egypt) in May 1992.[35] A change in government strategy towards the militants occurred in the mid-1990s. This was primarily because these groups had increased their attacks on the security ser-vices and tourists. The economic impact of the 1997 Luxor massacre when fifty-eight tourists and four Egyptians were killed also alienated public support for these groups.[36] Government action mostly succeeded in crushing them and, consequently, militant attacks on Copts decreased massively.

With the decline of physical violence, communal relations have clearly improved from the turbulent Sadat years. The personality and policies followed by Mubarak have also been important. Hasan explains that unlike Sadat, Mubarak has not used the Coptic community as scapegoats or blamed communal clashes on Coptic conspiracies.[37] Although he has not prioritised the Coptic question, the mere absence of accusations of disloyalty was regarded as a vast improve-ment by the Coptic community. Under Mubarak, Egypt has experienced a gradual process of Islamisation. This is partly due to the promotion of official Islam to counter the influence of Islamic extremism. The Grand Imam of al-Azhar, Sheikh Mohamed Sayyid Tantawi, was appointed by the state and has publicly condemned religious extremists.[38] This Islamisation of society is also increasingly visible including an increase in attendance at prayers, Islamic dress and religious programming. Consequently, Muslim–Christian relations in the Mubarak era must be examined in the context of this religious revival.

The situation of the Coptic Orthodox church is also different from the Sadat era. Since his return from the desert, the approach of Patriarch Shenouda to church–state relations has become more recognisable within the traditional *millet* system. According to Hasan, there has been an awareness within the church leadership that the assertive policies described above did not solve the problems facing the community but instead antagonised both the authorities and wider society and demonstrated the vulnerability of the Copts. The fact that several influential church figures including reformists such as Bishops Samuel and Athanasios were willing to serve on the papal committee illustrated the divisions within the church over the policies pursued by the patriarch.[39] Many believed that the actions of the patriarch had increased the extent of the Muslim backlash during the 1970s. After the forced removal of Patriarch Shenouda to Wadi al-Natroun, Father Matta al-Maskeen, an influential monk, gave an inter-view to *Time* magazine suggesting that there was now more chance of peaceful relations between the church and the state.[40] Consequently, Patriarch Shenouda has concentrated on consolidating his authority within the church. Critics including Father Matta have been ostracised from decision-making. There has also been a huge increase in the number of bishops, most of whom can be regarded as protégés of the patriarch.[41] Patriarch Shenouda has adopted a more pragmatic approach to communal incidents. As both President Mubarak and the patriarch have acknowledged that they share the same enemy – Islamist extremism – he no longer calls for demonstrations after attacks on Christians as occurred during his first decade in office. In accordance with the *millet* system, the Coptic Orthodox patriarch enjoys prestige as the spokesman of the community to the state. Under Patriarch Shenouda, the renewal process has allowed the church to ensure its position as the focal point of the community. According to Dina al-Khawaga, the church leaders, 'take on the task of all the needs of the Copts, to centralize the ways in which they socialize, to compensate for their fragile status – as a minority – in Egyptian society, and to present them politically in the public sphere'.[42] Thus, an examination of Christian–Muslim relations in Egypt today is best served by focusing on the response of the Coptic Orthodox church to both tension and dialogue.

Church building

Many communal incidents, particularly those which lead to violence, can be related to a long-standing Coptic grievance – the laws governing church building. Under the Hamayouni Decree of 1856, government permission must be obtained before a church can be built legally. Furthermore, the regulations set out by the Ministry of Interior in 1934 impose conditions which must be satisfied in order to receive a building permit. These include an examination of the distance between the proposed site and surrounding mosques, the distance to the nearest church of the same denomination and the number of Christians in the area. The objections of local Muslim residents and businesses is also expected to be taken into consideration.[43] Presidential authorisation was also required for any repair work, both major and minor. In contrast, few restrictions were placed on the construction of mosques. The existence of two different sets of legal requirements for building places of worship would appear to counter the notion that both Muslims and Christians enjoy equal rights in Egypt.

The issues of church building and repairs are extremely important to the Coptic community. Due to population growth and rural to urban migration, existing churches are overcrowded. A substantial amount are dilapidated and in need of urgent repairs. Yet, it proved extremely difficult to obtain government permits. Only ten building permits and twenty-six repair licenses were granted to Coptic Orthodox churches between 1981 and 1990.[44] Applications often became mired in the administrative bureaucracy, resulting in several years passing until a decision was made. Yet during this time, mosques were often built near proposed sites for new churches, potentially making the application invalid according to the 1934 regulations. Due to these problems, unauthorised buildings have been used to hold church services. This tends to antagonise the local Muslim population who, in some cases, use physical force to halt these activities as occurred in the Khanka incident explored earlier. Official church buildings also tend to be extremely visible – sometimes including large towers and fluorescent crosses. This can significantly alter a neighbourhood and can be cited as one of the reasons for Muslim hostility to church building proposals.

Constant criticism of this inequality engraved into the legislation concerning church building led to a significant development in 1999. A presidential decree proclaimed that repairs of all places of worship would be covered by the 1976 Civil Construction Code. For the first time, mosques and churches were listed under the same category. Furthermore, presidential aides were able to authorise licences to build new churches. This decree had an impact on the amount of permits approved, e.g. twenty-three in 2001 and nine in 2002.[45] There was also appreciation, especially among Copts that the government had finally sought to address this key Coptic grievance. Yet, problems remained. The decision on applications could still take several years to be reached. Partly, this was due to the lack of priority given to these requests by the Ministry of Interior. Even once presidential permission was received, local authorities and the security services had the power to block construction. On a few occasions, the license to build a new church has been revoked after the existing building had been demolished. In 2001, President Mubarak ordered that two churches were to be rebuilt at the expense of the government after they were destroyed by local authorities.[46]

There has also been increased awareness that church building and the use of unauthorised buildings for services have proven to be one cause of communal violence. Some argue that Christians build a church without obtaining authorisation in the belief that once it is established, they will gain *de facto* recognition as the ruling authorities will be keen to avoid accusations of closing down churches. This serves to antagonise the local Muslim population, especially in Upper Egypt. In the first years of the twenty-first century, several clashes can be attributed to the controversial issue of church building. In July 2000, an attack in Giza province on a Christian farmer who was trying to build a church resulted in his death and the wounding of five others.[47] Four Christians were also injured when the village church of Beni Welmes was targeted in Minya province in February 2002.[48] In contrast to previous incidents, the government has tried to react quickly to limit communal unrest, particularly through participation in consecration services, which highlights that Christians are legally entitled to their own place of worship. The governor of Minya held a public reconciliation meeting with Muslims and Christians in Beni Welmes. The government also funded the reconstruction of the damaged church and the inauguration service was attended by the Secretary to the Patriarch Anba Youannes, the governor, security service officials, prominent politicians and Islamic figures.[49] Similarly, local authorities prevented a dispute over the transformation of a Coptic-owned library into a church from becoming a full-scale riot. However, five Copts were still injured in the clashes in Gaiza, a village near al-Ayyat in Upper Egypt.[50]

It is clear that a public place of worship takes on a 'sacred' quality which, in the case of churches, can cause tension between the communities. Another attempt to resolve this ongoing problem occurred in December 2005. A further presidential decree transferred the power to grant building permits to the regional governors. These must be addressed within one month and include detailed justification for any refusals.[51] If the above decree is fully implemented, it would be expected that Copts would be less likely to resort to establishing unauthorised churches to counter the overcrowding problem. However in some Muslim circles, there is a perception that the government has rewarded these illegal actions and granted too many concessions to the Coptic Orthodox church. From this discussion, it is clear that the resolution of this long-standing grievance is vital in ensuring lasting peaceful relations between the two communities. Yet, it is evident that individuals (on both sides) can still create obstacles concerning church building, thus increasing pressure on government policies which can generally be described as reactive rather than the prescriptive measures required to avoid unrest.

Conversion

Controversies surrounding reported conversions also cause communal tension. Both Muslims and Christians in Egypt face mass social pressure from their respective communities to maintain the faith they were given at birth. The deep feelings held about this issue means that in some circles a conversion is perceived as proving that one faith is superior to the other rather than reflecting the individual choice of one member of that religion. This helps to explain why conversions are often disputed and can adversely affect communal relations. In Egypt, there are no laws against converting to either faith. However, few Muslims convert, partly due to the social pressure mentioned above and partly as Christian evangelism is not encouraged neither by the authorities nor the predominantly Muslim society. Furthermore, those who do frequently move abroad and have little impact on the Christian community in Egypt.

In contrast, it is estimated that 10–15,000 Egyptian Christians convert to Islam each year. As throughout the centuries of Islamic rule, this is due to a combination of religious, economic and social reasons. Many of these converts are young women who often wish to marry Muslim men. This will have an adverse effect on the natural growth of the church as their children will be brought up as Muslims. Although Islamic law allows a Muslim man to marry a non-Muslim woman, a Christian cannot inherit from a Muslim. The inheritance laws and desire to be accepted by her husband's family can encourage such women to convert to Islam. Rumours concerning the kidnapping of young Coptic women are frequent.[52] However, little evidence has been gathered to give credence to these claims. Instead, the shame associated with conversion can be a factor in the decision of the family to declare a forced rather than voluntary conversion. These accusations can lead to Coptic demonstrations for the return of the women.

There is also a widespread perception among Copts that Islam – the official state religion – enjoys privileges which are denied to representatives of the Christian faith. Before the official process of conversion is complete, procedures must be followed including a meeting between the individual and a priest to discuss this decision. However, some Copts argue that this is not always implemented. Furthermore, Islamic missionary activities enjoy substantial resources and if not perhaps officially encouraged by the state, are certainly sanctioned in contrast to Christian attempts to evangelise among the Muslim population. The process for conversion to Islam can also be regarded as substantially easier than the opposite route, e.g. new identification cards with Muslim names are issued quickly. This belief that the state does not do enough to protect vulnerable Christians from campaigns to leave their faith, in contrast to its policies towards Christian proselytism, means that complaints are made to the hierarchy of the Coptic Orthodox church rather than state officials. To a certain extent, the church leaders have proved receptive to these pleas, aware that conversions to Islam obviously have a damaging effect on the church, both psychologically and in numerical terms. However, this increases the likelihood of clashes between the church and the ruling authorities and leaves it open to accusations of inter-ference in political affairs.

The most prominent example is the Wafaa Constantine affair which erupted in December 2004. The case attracted national attention due to the demonstra-tions which were held initially in the Beheira diocese and then in the grounds of the patriarchate in Cairo. The primary reason why this disputed conversion caused such furore was because the individual involved was not a teenager but instead a middle-aged woman who was the wife of a Coptic priest. Immediately, rumours were rife among the Coptic community that Wafaa Constantine had been abducted and forced to convert to Islam. Hundreds of demonstrators demanded that the state security authorities returned her to the church. Wider frustrations were voiced during the protests including dissatisfaction at govern-ment failure to stop so-called 'forced' conversions. Protestors clashed with police leading to injuries on both sides and the arrest of thirty-four Christians.[53] The situation was in danger of escalating further when Patriarch Shenouda retreated to the monastery in Wadi al-Natroun to illustrate his disappointment that Wafaa Constantine had not been returned as promised to church authorities. The symbolism of this measure cannot be overstated due to its connotations with the policies pursued by the patriarch during the turbulent Sadat years. The incident was resolved when Wafaa Constantine met with several bishops and stated that she had not converted to Islam and remained a member of the Coptic Orthodox church.

This event illustrates how easily disputed versions of conversions can lead to communal tension. The church response was particularly interesting. In an edition of *al-Keraza* (the official church magazine edited by Patriarch She-nouda), President Mubarak was praised for his efforts in attempting to resolve the issue. However, blame was attached to the strategies pursued by the police to quell the protests. Several photographs of wounded Copts including a priest were included in the article and accompanied by captions using emotive lan-guage.[54] Clearly, this is likely to reinforce the view that elements of the state authorities have not maintained their neutral role. Thus, the community is likely to continue to place its trust in the ability of the church hierarchy to represent its grievances to the relevant state authorities.

However, the resolution of this incident was criticised by some Egyptians who believed that the central authorities had conceded to the demands of Patriarch Shenouda. In this interpretation, the government colluded with the church to prevent an individual publicly declaring her true beliefs.[55] Not only did the pro-tests eventually succeed in gaining the return of Wafaa Constantine but the retirement of Patriarch Shenouda to the desert also ensured the release of those arrested at the patriarchate. Consequently, it is argued that at present, the church authorities have discovered a means successfully to obtain their desired outcome in the knowledge that the government is keen to defuse any situation that has the potential to create communal instability. It is also important to note that neither of these two interpretations appears to have considered the actual desire of Wafaa Constantine. In contemporary Egypt, conversion remains a public issue with huge implications for both communities. Consequently, any conversion attempt will be accompanied by simultaneous appeals to the government to either prevent 'forced' conversions or clamp down on the 'illegal' demands of the church. As pleasing one will frustrate the other, conversions are likely to challenge government policies and pose a continual threat to communal stability.

Violent incidents

Communal clashes have also proved a sporadic but persistent element of Muslim–Christian relations in Egypt. Since the government crackdown on militant groups from the mid-1990s onwards, that particular threat drastically declined. However, there have been several incidents, particularly in Upper Egypt, which in some cases have escalated into riots. One notable example is the violence which occurred in the village of al-Kush in January 2000. A dispute between a Christian shopkeeper and Muslim customer led to the deaths of twenty Christians and one Muslim as well as attacks on Christian homes and shops.[56] Communal relations in al-Kush were already tense after the murder of two Christians in 1998. Allegations of police brutality were presented in the international media as evidence of the persecution of the Coptic community. Many Muslims were outraged and blamed Copts, both in Egypt and abroad, for this portrayal.[57] Consequently, in 2000, the police were criticised for their failure to produce and implement contingency plans to deal with further incidents. Instead, the killings occurred over three days and spread to another village.

The aftermath of the al-Kush incident depicts the normal government response to communal violence. Reactive measures included holding a reconciliation meeting, funnelling funds into the village and changing its name to *al-Salaam* (peace).[58] Victims and attackers were not clearly distinguished and members of both communities were arrested. In the first trial of fifty-eight Muslims and thirty-eight Christians, ninety-two were acquitted. The retrial fared little better with only three convicted – one for killing the sole Muslim and two for the destruction of property.[59] Once again, such developments reinforce the perception that Coptic grievances are neither regarded as a priority by the government nor dealt with in the appropriate manner. Many Copts are dismayed that all communal issues are dealt with as security concerns. After the events at al-Kush, Patriarch Shenouda urged the government to resolve these issues rather than reverting to the traditional response of covering up problems.[60] The failure of the criminal trials led Youssef Sidhom, the editor of the Christian newspaper *Watani*, to state that this proved that Christian blood was worth little in Egypt and instead the only justice that Copts would obtain would be from God.[61] With few preventive measures undertaken by the government, there is a grave risk that any dispute can take on a religious dimension and escalate into communal clashes. As discussed earlier, several violent incidents can be traced to the complex issues surrounding church building. Thus, it would appear that without any significant change in government policies, sporadic outbreaks of communal violence will remain a feature of contemporary Egypt.

Communal violence of a different nature erupted in Alexandria in October 2005, demonstrating the varied challenges facing the Egyptian government in its attempt to ensure stability. At the centre of the dispute was a play performed two years earlier in a church in Muharram Bek, a poor district in Alexandria. Entitled *I Was Blind But Now I Can See*, the play featured a Christian convert to Islam who returned to his original faith after being asked to commit murder.[62] The distribution of DVDs of the play by unknown actors led to the story being published in the tabloid press in late 2005. Demonstrators congregated outside the church at the centre of the dispute demanding that Patriarch Shenouda give an explanation for this play which they claimed had insulted Islam. The police dispersed the crowds but no apology was forthcoming from the patriarch. A few days later, a young Muslim stabbed a Coptic nun and a man who came to her aid. Aware that the situation was extremely tense, the security forces surrounded the church and nearby mosque preventing worshippers attending Friday prayers. Violent protests left three dead and many injured (including police) as well as the destruction of many shops and cars. An article in *al-Keraza* blamed the violence on provocative media reports. As occurred in the Wafaa Constantine episode, dramatic language was used and all violence committed against Christian property was recorded.[63] The church leaders defended the play as targeting religious extremism rather than defaming Islam as charged by the protestors. This has led to criticism of the Coptic Orthodox church for portraying the community as victims when in fact it is argued that an explanation for the play may have contained the situation.[64] Some have also declared that it is further evidence of the ability of the church to manipulate the state authorities regarding communal incidents. In one sense, the government response replicates previous measures including issuing a joint statement by Patriarch Shenouda and Sheikh Tantawi urging Muslims and Christians to use dialogue rather than violence to solve problems.[65] However, there also appears to be some recognition that the recurring problems in Muslim–Christian relations can no longer be ignored. Non-governmental organisations sent fact-finding missions and the government-backed National Council for Human Rights formed a committee to discuss wider Muslim–Christian issues. Yet in conclusion, it is clear that in contemporary Egypt, communal problems are still prone to escalate into violent clashes.

Church response to Muslim–Christian relations in the Mubarak era

Due to its role as the civil representative of the community to the state, the strategies pursued by the Coptic Orthodox church in the Mubarak era can be interpreted as indicating the predominant view on the most effective means to respond to communal tension while safeguarding the survival and security of the community. Operating in an environment of relative communal stability marred by sporadic periods of tension, it is apparent that Patriarch Shenouda has adopted a more conciliatory and pragmatic approach in comparison to the Sadat years. There has been a return to the traditional *millet* system. In exchange for promoting loyalty to the regime, government interference in Coptic affairs has decreased. Hence, the patriarch has regained his position as spiritual and civil leader of the community. Describing the relations between the community, the patriarch and the president, Sedra states, 'Shenouda is dependent upon Mubarak, the church hierarchy is dependent upon Shenouda, and the Coptic community is dependent upon the hierarchy for social services and political leadership'.[66] Consequently in the Mubarak era, the church has prioritised internal concerns including the continued implementation of the renewal movement which is responsible for the vitality of the contemporary Coptic Orthodox church.

According to al-Khawaga, the Copts have chosen to be an 'exemplary religious minority' under the Mubarak presidency. Perhaps mindful of the problems experienced during the Sadat years, Patriarch Shenouda has been eager to praise President Mubarak. In a media interview in 2002, he stated that, 'Relations between Muslim and Coptic figures are excellent. President Mubarak is an enemy of all sorts of extremism, bigotry and discrimination'.[67] As has been seen in the incidents detailed above, the efforts of Mubarak to resolve each situation have been lauded and blame apportioned to elements of the bureaucracy or extremists. In general, the patriarch has stressed the need for a non-violent response from the community, urging that dialogue is the only means to find a long-lasting and just solution. Conciliatory measures undertaken by Mubarak have been met with public acclaim from Patriarch Shenouda. For example, each authorisation of a church building license is listed in *al-Keraza* and accompanied with a congratulatory message to the president.[68] Similarly, the patriarch rejoiced at the announcement in 2003 that 7 January – Coptic Orthodox Christmas – would become an annual official holiday for all Egyptians. This appreciation was shared by many in the Coptic community. For example, Youssef Sidhom said, 'What is particularly important in the president's announcement is that it gives Copts the sense that all citizens are treated equally, because their religious feasts are worthy of national recognition'.[69] Thus, the policies undertaken by Mubarak have reduced the sources of conflict between the church and state. Although there are no regular meetings between the two men and the Coptic question has still not been prioritised by the president, the absence of rhetorical attacks on the community as experienced under Sadat has convinced Patriarch Shenouda that the Mubarak regime represents the best option for the Copts at present. The Islamist current provides the main challenge to the existing Egyptian government. Its populist support was evident in the 2005 parliamentary elections when Muslim Brotherhood candidates running as independents won ninety seats even though their supporters were subject to harassment and there were several allegations of unfair practices.[70] Concern at the strength of the Muslim Brotherhood even before these elections helps explain the unprecedented support given by the church hierarchy to the nomination of Mubarak in the first ever directly elected presidential elections held in 2005. An article in *al-Keraza* urged its readers to vote for the incumbent due to his 'political wisdom, tolerance and experience'.[71] It is clear that a key element of church strategy towards Muslim–Christian relations has been to demonstrate support of and loyalty to the Mubarak regime.

The patriotic credentials of the Coptic community have also been emphasised in the post-1985 period. As detailed earlier, the image of the Copts had been tarnished by accusations of cooperation with foreign actors at the expense of the Egyptian national interest. Patriarch Shenouda has contributed to the national unity discourse favoured by the Egyptian elite, labelling both Muslims and Christians as 'sons of a single homeland'.[72] Hence, he does not consider the Copts as a minority group but instead part of the Egyptian nation. This opinion was made clear during the furore caused by the decision in 1994 to hold a Conference on Minorities which included a session on the Copts.[73] Patriarch Shenouda has also rejected any calls for foreign intervention to address problems faced by the Coptic community. 'We do not accept any foreign interference in our internal affairs, which we are solving in peace with the responsible persons in our country'.[74] The patriarch has given a lukewarm reaction to visiting delegations of the United States Congress International Religious Freedom Commission. He did not receive the delegation in 2005 and spoke with them only to 'correct false accounts' during the 2003 visit.[75] Such statements and actions can be regarded as a message to Coptic émigré groups who campaign in host countries for western influence to be used to force the Egyptian government to address Coptic grievances. Although these groups represent a minority of expatriates, their claims of persecution cause tension in Egypt. The ruling authorities have been quick to reject any foreign intervention, particularly from the United States. For example, Osama el-Baz, a political adviser to the Egyptian president, stressed that although the US is a valued ally, it 'should not rush to point a finger at domestic affairs such as the treatment of the Copts'.[76] Many Copts in Egypt are extremely aware of the repercussions that émigré campaigns could have on communal relations. A 1998 statement signed by over 2000 prominent Coptic figures bitterly attacked 'continued attempts made by enemy hostile forces in rumoring false claims of Coptic repression'.[77] It also accused the émigré activists of 'provoking lies on their own name and the name of Christians in Egypt so as to distort the image of the Egyptian government before the international community'.[78] There is danger that these activities will raise doubt about the loyalty of the Copts. This is illustrated by the fact that Copts in Egypt talk of their support for national unity, yet once they leave, some appear to 'bad mouth' the country. However, relations between the community and the activists would appear to be ambiguous. While there is recognition that there may be an adverse effect, some Copts argue that during crucial periods it is helpful to have people outside of the country willing to publicise the problems facing the community.

The loyalty of the Coptic community has also been enhanced by the firm commitment of Patriarch Shenouda to the Palestinian cause. The patriarch has banned pilgrimages to Jerusalem being performed by Copts. This will only be allowed once the holy city is under Arab control. Although some Copts persist in this pilgrimage, it is at the risk of excommunication from the church. Patriarch Shenouda has vowed that 'we will not enter Jerusalem except with our Muslim brethren'.[79] This strong stance against Zionism must also be viewed in the context of the ongoing struggle with the Egyptian Orthodox church over Deir as-Sultan, one of the holy places in Jerusalem. Since the nineteenth century, this site has been at the centre of a dispute over rightful ownership. Once Jerusalem came under Israeli control in 1967, the Ethiopians, with the support of the Israeli authorities, have held the keys for the property.[80] It is likely that this policy has influenced the general anti-Israeli stance held by the church leadership.

During the Mubarak presidency, there has also been an increased tendency from the Christian communities, Islamic religious establishment and government officials to promote interfaith dialogue at the institutional level. After the return of Patriarch Shenouda from Wadi al-Natroun in 1985, there was a strong awareness within the church hierarchy that the turbulence of the preceding years had severely damaged Muslim–Christian relations. Hence, the Committee of National Unity was established to obtain closer links with Muslim religious figures. Under the supervision of three of the protégés of the patriarch – Bishops Musa, Bula and Besanti – the committee invited prominent Muslims to lecture on Muslim–Christian relations in Egypt.[81] In the twenty-first century, these connections have now become institutionalised. Patriarch Shenouda and the Sheikh of al-Azhar, Sheikh Tantawi, appear to enjoy cordial relations. Both men are frequently invited to speak at the same conferences and lectures.[82] Joint statements have been issued to appeal for calm during tense periods such as al-Kush in 2000 and Alexandria in 2005. Patriarch Shenouda also attends Islamic conferences. In April 2004, he was present at the opening ceremony of the Islamic Affairs Supreme Council where he gave a speech entitled 'Tolerance in the Islamic Civilization' and used verses from the Qur'an and Hadiths.[83] This extensive knowledge of the religion of the other community greatly aids the success of such ventures. It is also common for religious dignitaries to visit each other on the occasion of religious festivals to offer congratulations, e.g. Christmas, Easter, Eid al-Fitr and Eid al-Adha. This increase in public meetings has not been confined solely to religious figures. The church hierarchy, especially Patriarch Shenouda, have regular meetings with regional governors and security officials. These all seek to restore goodwill not only between the Coptic community and the Islamic religious elite but also with the state.

One recent trend that can now almost be perceived as a tradition is the holding of interfaith *iftars* during Ramadan (the meal that breaks the Muslim fast during this holy month). Those hosted by the Coptic Orthodox church are held at various levels – at the patriarchate, dioceses and individual churches. Each year the patriarch invites prominent Muslim figures to a National Unity *iftar* banquet held in the Coptic Orthodox cathedral in Abbasiyya. In 2004, those sitting with the patriarch at the main table included the Sheikh of al-Azhar, the prime minister, the president of the assembly parliament, the president of the state council, the minister of religious endowments and several ex-prime ministers.[84] Similarly, Patriarch Shenouda, several bishops and influential laity figures are present at the annual National Unity *iftar* banquet hosted by the ministry of religious endowments. By publicly illustrating that the two religious leaders are granted the same privileges by the state, these measures reinforce the idea that the Egyptian nation is indeed made up of two religious communities. In an interview, Patriarch Shenouda commented that 'Muslims and Christians sit side by side in these dinners which gives a good impression and picture to the west about Egyptians and the good relations they have'.[85] While these activities can be taken as an indication of harmonious relations at the elite level, it is unclear what effect these have had on ordinary members of the respective communities. As explored earlier, many of the communal disputes arise from ignorance and suspicion of the other group. Furthermore, there is concern among some Copts that these efforts at promoting national unity had not brought tangible rewards and had little impact on the reality of Muslim–Christian relations. Again Youssef Sidhom writes, 'national unity feasts swell in number, while the proportion of problems solved steadily shrinks'.[86] Thus, national unity rhetoric may be strong but this practice has still to be transformed into genuine progress in Muslim–Christian relations.

Conclusion

From this discussion, it is apparent that the Coptic community under the leadership of the Coptic Orthodox church has tried to integrate into Egyptian society. At certain levels, this has been successful. Copts are certainly accepted as part of the Egyptian nation. However, there are still obstacles to be removed to ensure genuine communal harmony. Ansari notes that 'Most Egyptian writers insist that clashes between members of the two communities are aberrations in a society characterised by a long lasting harmony among its national components'.[87] Yet, it is the same unresolved underlying issues that are cited for the sporadic outbursts which occur, namely church building legislation, conversions and intolerance leading to violence. The Coptic Orthodox church also has a significant influence on the status of communal relations. As in the past, its role as defender of the community can lead to a situation of escalating violence. At present, the church and state authorities have respected the status quo. However, in the early twenty-first century, the national unity rhetoric appears to be struggling to cover the cracks in Christian–Muslim relations in Egypt. Until Coptic grievances are acknowledged and addressed by the Egyptian authorities, truly harmonious relations would appear to remain a distant prospect.

Notes

1 *Arabic News*, 'Moslems and Copts are sons of one homeland' (25 June 2001), www.arabicnews.com/ansub/Daily/Day/010625/2001062533.html (accessed 27 August 2003).
2 Al-Jazeera, 'Mubarak urges Christian–Muslim unity' (10 January 2005), www.aljazeerah/MubarakUrgesChristianMuslimUnity.html (accessed 17 January 2005).
3 Atiya, A. S., *A History of Eastern Christianity* (London, Methuen & Co Ltd, 1991), p. 16. See also O'Mahony, A., 'Coptic Christianity in modern Egypt', in Angold, M. (ed.), *The Cambridge History of Christianity: Vol. 5, Eastern Christianity* (Cambridge, Cambridge University Press, 2006), pp. 488–510.
4 Asad, C., *Geopolitique de l'Egypte* (Bruxelles, Editions Complexe, 2002), p. 54.
5 Roberson, R., *The Eastern Christian Churches: A Brief Survey* (Rome, Edizioni Orientalia Christiana, 1999), p. 28.
6 O'Mahony, A., 'The politics of religious renewal: Coptic Christianity in Egypt', in O'Mahony, A. (ed.) *Eastern Christianity: Studies in Modern History, Religion and Politics* (London, Melisende, 2004) p. 152; see also O'Mahony, A., 'Coptic

Orthodox thought in modern Egypt', in *One in Christ: A Catholic Ecumenical Review*, 40: 3 (2005), 16–52.

7 Sedra, P., 'Class cleavages and ethnic conflict: Coptic Christian communities in modern Egyptian politics', *Islam and Christian–Muslim Relations*, 10: 2 (1999), 224.

8 Nisan, M., *Minorities in the Middle East: A History of Struggle and Self-Expression* (London, McFarland & Company, 1991), p. 122

9 Tamura, A., 'Ethnic consciousness and its transformation in the course of nation-building: the Muslim and the Copt in Egypt 1906-1919,' *Muslim World*, 75: 2 (1985), 106.

10 Hasan, S. S., *Christians Versus Muslims in Modern Egypt: The Century-Long Struggle for Coptic Equality* (New York, Oxford University Press, 2003), p. 36.

11 Partrick, T. H., *Traditional Egyption Christianity: A History of the Coptic Orthodox Church* (Greensboro, Fisher Park Press, 1996), p. 149.

12 Carter, B. L., *The Copts in Egyptian Politics* (London, Croom Helm, 1986), p. 16.

13 Van Nispen tot Sevenaer, C., 'Changes in relations between Copts and Muslims (1952–1994) in the light of the historical experience', in van Doorn Harder, N. and Vogt, K. (eds), *Between Desert and City: The Coptic Orthodox Church Today* (Oslo, Institute for Comparative Research in Human Culture, 1997), p. 25.

14 Ibid., p. 26.

15 Hasan, *Christians Versus Muslims in Modern Egypt*, p. 52.

16 Carter, *The Copts in Egyptian Politics*, p. 276.

17 Watson, John H., *Among the Copts* (Brighton, Sussex Academic Press, 2000), p. 46.

18 For more information on the Coptic renewal process, see van Doorn Harder and Vogt, *Between Desert and City*.

19 Warburg, G., 'Islam and politics in Egypt: 1952–1980', *Middle Eastern Studies* 18: 2 (1982), 148.

20 Esposito, J. L., *The Islamic Threat: Myth or Reality* (Oxford, Oxford University Press, 1999), p. 95.

21 Farah, N. R., *Religious Strife in Egypt: Crisis and Ideological Conflict in the Seventies* (London, Gordon and Breach Publishers, 1986), p. 1.

22 Sedra, 'Class cleavages and ethnic conflict', p. 226.

23 Farah, *Religious Strife in Egypt*, p. 2.

24 Eibner, J. (ed.), *Christians in Egypt: Church Under Siege* (London, Institute for Religious Minorities in the Islamic World, 1993), p. 8.

25 Farah, *Religious Strife in Egypt*, p. 52.

26 Solihin, S. M., *Copts and Muslims in Egypt: A Study on Harmony and Hostility* (Leicester, The Islamic Foundation, 1991), p. 74.

27 Farah, *Religious Strife in Egypt*, p. 3.

28 Pennington, J. D., 'The Copts in modern Egypt', *Middle Eastern Studies*, 18: 2 (1982), 174.

29 Ayalon, A., 'Egypt's Coptic Pandora's box', in Bengio, O. and Ben-Dor, G. (eds), *Minorities and the State in the Arab World* (London, Lynne Reinner Publishers Inc, 1999), p. 58.

30 Valognes, J.-P., *Vie et mort des Chretiens d'Orient* (Paris, Fayard, 1994), p. 563.

31 Ansari, H., 'Sectarian conflict in Egypt and the political expediency of religion', *Middle East Journal*, 38: 3 (1984), 404.

32 Watson, *Among the Copts*, p. 96.

33 Asad, *Geopolitique de l'Egypte*, p. 58.

34 O'Mahony, 'The politics of religious renewal', p. 155.

35 Eibner, *Christians in Egypt*, pp. 23–4.

36 Springborg, R., 'Egypt: repression's toll', *Current History*, 97: 615 (1998), 32.

37 Hasan, *Christians Versus Muslims in Modern Egypt*, p. 116.

38 Barraclough, S., 'Al-Azhar: between the government and the Islamists', *Middle East Journal* 52: 2 (1998), 237.

38 Watson, *Among the Copts*, p. 102.

40 Watson, J., 'Hermits and hierarchs', in Thomas, D. and Amos, C. (eds), *A Faithful Presence: Essays for Kenneth Cragg* (London, Melisende, 2003), p. 280.

41 For an in-depth discussion of the centralisation process that has occurred under Patriarch Shenouda, see Hasan, *Christians Versus Muslims in Modern Egypt*, Part IV, pp. 123–66.

42 Al-Khawaga, D., 'The political dynamics of the Copts: giving the community an active role', in Pacini, A. (ed.), *Christian Communities in the Arab Middle East: The Challenge of the Future* (Oxford, Clarendon Press, 1998), p. 182.

43 O'Mahony, 'The politics of religious renewal', pp. 157–8.

44 Eibner, *Christians in Egypt*, p. 27.

45 US State Department Bureau of Democracy, Human Rights and Labor, *International Religious Freedom Report*, 2003, www.state.gov/g/drl/rls/lrf/2003/24448pf. htm (accessed 21 April 2004).

46 Ibid.

47 Ibid.

48 *BBC News*, 'Church bells lead to Egypt clashes' (10 February 2002), www.news. bbc.co.uk/1/hi/world/middle_east?1812730.stm (accessed 24 August 2003).

49 'Chronological review: intercommunal relations', *Proche-Orient Chretien*, 52: 4 (2002), 424.

50 *Al-Hayat*, 'Incident at village al-Ayyat, Upper Egypt' (9 November 2003).

51 *Middle East Online*, 'Mubarak eases restrictions on church building' (11 December 2005), www.copts.net/id-825 (accessed 11 December 2005).

52 See articles posted on Coptic expatriate sites such as US Copts Association, www. copts.com.

53 *BBC News*, 'Egyptian pope goes into seclusion' (20 December 2004), www.news. bbc.co.uk/1/hi/world/4110861.st (23 December 2004).

54 *Al-Keraza* (17 December 2004), www.copticpope.org/downloads/eng-keraza/ engkeraza31-12-2004.pdf (accessed 31 December 2004).

55 This argument is discussed in *Watani International*, 'The Coptic file' (13 March 2005), www.wataninet.com.articleid=502&lang=en (accessed 13 March 2005).

56 *Middle East International* 616, 'Egypt: communal killings' (14 January 2000), 17.

57 *The Economist*, 'Egypt's vulnerable Copts' (6 January 2000), www.economist. com/PrinterFriendly.cfm?Story_ID=271592 (accessed 25 August 2003).

58 *Al-Ahram Weekly*, 'The meanings of al-Kosheh' (3 February 2000) www.weekly. ahram.org.eg/2000/467/eg7.htm (accessed 25 August 2003).

59 Al-Ahram Weekly, 'Al Kosheh dossier reopened' (8 November 2001), www.weekly. ahram.org.eg/2001/559/eg6.htm (accessed 25 August 2003).

60 Al-Keraza, 'Coptic neomartyrs in the new millennium', Coptic Church Review, 21: 1 (2000), www.home.ptd.net/~yanney/coptic-neomartyrs.pdf (accessed 5 August 2003).

61 Watani International, 'Shock acquittals at El Kosheh' (9 March 2003).

62 Al-Ahram Weekly, 'Calm before the storm' (27 October 2005), www.weekly. ahram.org.eg/2005/766/eg7.htm (accessed 28 October 2005).

63 Al-Keraza (11 November 2005), www.copticpope.org/downloads/eng-keraza/ engkeraza11-11-2005.pdf (accessed 4 February 2006).

64 Al-Ahram Weekly, 'Too late for denials' (2 November 2005), www.weekly.ahram. org.eg/2005/767/eg11.htm (accessed 3 November 2005).

65 Al-Ahram Weekly, 'Calm before the storm' (27 October 2005), http://weekly. ahram.org.eg/print/2005/766/eg7.htm (accessed 28 October 2005).

66 Sedra, 'Class cleavages and ethnic conflict', p. 228.

67 Arabic News, 'Pope Shenouda highlights Egypt's religious tolerance' (31 May 2002), www.arabicnews.com/ansub/Daily/Day/020531/2002053135.html (accessed 27 August 2003).

68 Al-Keraza (5 August 2005), www.copticpope.org/downloads/eng-keraza/eng-keraza05-08-2005.pdf (accessed 17 November 2005).

69 Al-Ahram Weekly, 'A Christmas like no other' (2nd January 2003), www.weekly. ahram.org.eg/2003/619/li1.htm (accessed 10 January 2006).

70 The Economist, 'Not yet a democracy' (8 December 2005), www.economist.com/ displaystory.cfm?story_id=5280976 (accessed 10 December 2005).

71 Al-Keraza (22 July 2005), www.copticpope,org/downloads/eng-keraza/engker-aza22-07-2005 (accessed 10 January 2006).

72 Sedra, 'Class cleavages and ethnic conflict', p. 221.

73 Al-Gawhary, K., 'Copts in the Egyptian fabric', Middle East Report, 26: 3 (2000), 21.

74 Copticpope.org, 'His Holiness Pope Shenouda III's declaration concerning the events of el-Kosheh', www.copticpope.org/modules.php?name=Sections&op=vie warticle@artid=2 (accessed 5 August 2003).

75 Arabic News, 'Pope Shenouda to Akhbar al-Yom: Majority of Copts abroad support Mubarak' (31 March 2001), www.arabicnews.com/ansub/Daily/Day/ 010331/2001033143.html (accessed 27 August 2003).

76 Middle East Times, 'Egypt asks congress to leave the Copts alone' (1 March 1998), www.metimes.com/issue98-9/eg/copts.htm (accessed 5 September 2003).

77 Arabic News, 'On the Coptic issue in Egypt' (6 November 1998), www.arabicnews, com/ansub/Daily/Day/981106/1998110620.html (accessed 27 August 2003).

78 Ibid.

79 al-Ahram Weekly, 'Prized tolerance' (2 November 2000), www.weekly.ahram.org. eg/2000/506/eg3.htm (accessed 25 August 2003).

80 Meinardus, O. F., Christian Egypt: Faith and Life (Cairo, The American University in Cairo Press, 1970), pp. 464–5.

81 Hasan, Christians Versus Muslims in Modern Egypt, p. 116.

82 Al-Keraza (11 June 2004), www.copticpope.org/downloads/eng-keraza/engker-aza11-06-2004.pdf (accessed 5 July 2004).

83 Al-Keraza (7 May 2004), www.copticpope.org/downloads/eng-keraza/engker-aza07-05-2004.pdf (accessed 5 July 2004).

84 Al-Keraza (5 November 2004), www.copticpope.org/downloads/eng-keraza/ engkeraza05-11-2004.pdf (accessed 20 November 2004).

85 Al-Hayat, 'Investigations into al-Ayyat' (10 December 2003), translated from al-Hayat by Arab West Report, www.arabwestreport.info.

86 Watani International, 'Problems on hold' (21 November 2004), www.watani.com. eg/modules.php?name=News&file=article&sid=602 (accessed 21 November 2004).

87 Ansari, 'Sectarian conflict', p. 397.

7

Christians and Muslims in western Europe: from 'speechless co-existence' to shared citizenship?

Philip Lewis

The geographical focus of this chapter is western Europe, rather than those areas of Europe which were once part of the Ottoman empire with long established Muslim communities.[1] Western Europe has become in less than fifty years home to perhaps 13 million Muslims – the most significant religious change since the Reformation.[2] It would be wise but not practical to put 'Muslim' in inverted commas to leave open what exactly we mean by such a term. For some, Muslim-ness is mainly cultural, for others it is little more than an attribute of ethnic identity which can encompass a minimal involvement in religious rituals; for those who foreground Islam in their self-understanding it can take diverse expressions – mystic, missionary or militant. The term 'Christian', of course, once we move beyond sociological self-definitions, is equally complex. The Gallup International Millennium Survey found 'that 88 percent of western Europeans declare that they belong to a denomination, yet only 20 percent report that they attend services regularly apart from weddings and special occasions'.[3]

For many Europeans, minorities in their countries were often described in national and ethnic terms – Turks, Moroccans, Pakistanis – rather than as 'Muslim', until the shock of 9/11. Researchers routinely argue that less than 10% of Muslims 'belong to a Muslim or Islamic organization'.[4]

Muslim influences on western Europe – the retrieval of history

There have been multiple interactions – military, commercial and intellectual – between the Muslim world and Christian Europe for centuries. The Iberian peninsula which fell to Muslim armies in 718 could be characterised for much of its history, until its final reconquest with the fall of Granada in 1492, as a space of *convivencia*, the Spanish term for 'living side by side' of Christians, Muslims and Jews. While there was much intellectual and cultural exchange, we must avoid anachronism. This *convivencia* in medieval Spain, Sicily or the Crusader states was always 'tense, never relaxed . . . these were multicultural societies only in the severely limited sense that peoples of different culture shared the same territories'.[5]

As the Muslim hold on one part of Catholic Europe was weakening, at the same time in another, the Balkans, during the fourteenth century, it was being consolidated through Turkish conquest, at the expense largely of Orthodox Christianity. In 1453 Constantinople, the capital of the Byzantine empire for over a millennium and seat of eastern Christianity, fell to the Ottomans. For almost five centuries the Balkan states and south eastern Europe were part of this vast empire. Recent studies have begun to illuminate a long forgotten chapter of multiple exchanges with an Islamic world treated as an equal or the dominant partner.[6]

There are many unexpected episodes in this new field of historic inquiry, namely Muslim influences on western Europe. One recent study is a remarkable act of scholarly retrieval – *Islam in Britain: 1558–1685*.[7] Until this pioneer work, the intellectual, cultural and religious impact of the Ottoman empire and its North African regencies on Britain, between the accession of Elizabeth 1 until the death of Charles II, could be relegated to a footnote. In this study we learn of the fascination and fear inspired by the Ottoman empire. Istanbul was the biggest city in Europe, the centre of a multi-ethnic empire, admired for its religious tolerance and offering unrivalled possibilities for social mobility to converts. The balance of military power was evident in the fact that the British coastal towns were raided and shipping threatened almost with impunity by Turkish men-of-war.

In 1637 the Church of England established a process of penance and readmission for those who had converted to Islam while in captivity. In commercial and diplomatic treaties with the Ottomans, British monarchs had to concede that some of their subjects had converted to Islam and thus renounced allegiance to England. This was the context for references in contemporary drama and sermons to 'renegades'. Islam was even recruited as a rhetorical weapon in intra-Christian debates: a robust Ottoman religious Orthodoxy was commended by Anglican divines impatient of the acids of dissent; Islam's lack of a priesthood was commended by Puritans confronted by an oppressive Anglican hierarchy!

Particular debate surrounded the introduction in the mid-seventeenth century of the first coffee-house. Within a decade, the drinking of coffee had become so popular as to threaten . . . traditional ale! Known as the 'Mahometan berry' the debates around coffee touched on a range of issues, not least the question as to whether or not it enfeebled or heightened the sexual appetite. Was this a nefarious plot to undermine the fibre of Christian Englishmen?

A growing familiarity with the Muslim component in western history is of more than academic interest. It could begin to erode the notion that Islam is alien to the western intellectual and cultural tradition.

Demographic, economic and ethnic profile of the Muslim communities

The new Muslim presence in western Europe is the product of more recent history. Although there had been a trickle of Muslim migrants from India into Britain for 300 years with the founding of the East India Company, substantial Muslim migration only began in the late 1950s to the early 1970s to meet a growing labour shortage. Britain drew heavily on its ex-colonies, particularly Pakistan.

A similar pattern and chronology of migration can be traced for other ex-colonial powers. France looked to Algeria and Morocco. France and the Netherlands also drew on a further category of migrants, those Algerian and Moluccan soldiers who fought with the colonial armies and who also left with de-colonisation. Germany turned to Turkey after the Berlin wall went up in 1961 and traditional sources of labour in south west Europe had dried up.

A third stream of migrants tends to be refugees fleeing political oppression, whether Palestinian, Algerian, Bosnian, Kosovar, Iranian, Iraqi, Afghan, Somali, Turkish Cypriots and Tunisian. Such an incomplete list indicates something of the scale of the turmoil and political crises inflicting so much of the Muslim world which has intensified in the last twenty-five years. A fourth stream is better defined as sojourners, business people, students and diplomats.

While the Muslim communities across western Europe are necessarily multi-ethnic, in many countries one national group tends to predominate and shape the public profile of Islam. This is clear if we consider the three largest Muslim communities in western Europe: France 4.5 million (7% of the total population), Germany 3 million (more than 3%), UK 1.6 million (less than 3%). In each country the public image of Islam tends to be shaped by Algerians, Turks and Pakistanis respectively.

Such overall data gives little idea of the developing impact and visibility of Islam in western Europe. This presence is often confined to certain localities within a few major cities and characterised by a large and growing young community. Typical is Belgium. Already in 1989 there were about a quarter of a million Muslims or 2.5% of the population; however, in Brussels some 8% of the population was Muslim, including 23% of those under 20. In 1991 a quarter of all Pakistanis in Britain lived in two cities, Birmingham and Bradford; with the small Bangladeshi communities they together represented 8% and 11% of the population. In both cities they lived in a small number of inner city electoral wards: Birmingham in eight of forty-two wards; Bradford in seven of thirty wards. By 2001 the Muslim communities had grown to 14% and 16%, or 75,000 and 140,000 respectively. In Birmingham 25% of all children in schools are Muslim.

Most Muslims imported to do hard and often dirty jobs in labour intensive heavy industries were drawn from rural areas. The UK and Germany are typical in this regard: both drew on rural people who often came through a process of chain migration from certain villages in Azad Kashmir in Pakistan and Anatolia in Turkey. Most of those who came initially were men who intended to work for a few years then return home, to be replaced by a male relative. This 'myth of return' largely faded with the passage of restrictive immigration laws in the early 1960s in the UK and the early 1970s in France and the Netherlands.

A development cycle for Muslim communities in western Europe

We can broadly speak of the emergence of Muslim communities in the west moving typically through four phases. First, the pioneers; then 'chain migration' of generally unskilled male workers from a number of villages; followed by the migration of wives and children; finally, the emergence of a generation of Muslims born and educated in Europe. Each phase serves to enlarge the range of contacts and familiarity with western societies. During the second stage, the intention was for men to work for a few years and return to their country of origin, to be replaced by a relative who could continue sending remittances back. During this phase, the men often lived in multiple occupancy flats and houses; with the exception of the Algerians in France who spoke French and were already French citizens, most of the migrants elsewhere in western Europe saw no need to develop a good knowledge of the language and culture of their neighbours, sustained as they were by the myth of return.

The third phase is from reluctant sojourners to settlers. Reluctant, as we will see, since few had intended to leave their Muslim homelands for good, and there were few precedents within the Islamic tradition for Muslims choosing to leave the House of Islam – *Dar al-Islam* – for the non-Muslim world, historically described as the House of War – *Dar al-Harb*. During this third phase wives joined their husbands or a bride was sought from the homeland. With family consolidation, a network of institutions was developed to meet the religious and cultural needs of their families. This typically involved establishing places to worship – initially, a church might extend to them a use of a building, or a couple of houses or redundant commercial buildings would be acquired and converted into a mosque; then an imam would be sought, usually from the homeland, to teach the children the basics of Islam. During this third phase, Muslims had to develop the linguistic and social skills to interface with the municipal authority and key local institutions to make sure service provision was sensitive to their needs, whether in hospital, school or cemetery.

The third and fourth phases are, of course, overlapping. However, with the emergence of a generation of Muslims born and educated in the west, we see more Muslims being incorporated into public and civic society. There is an increase of Muslim councillors across Europe – for example, in 2001 some 200 in the UK, 130 in France and 120 in Belgium and Holland respectively; and an emergence of an Islamic civil society, with associations of Muslim lawyers, teachers and doctors. In centres of high Muslim settlement there is the consolidation of Muslim quarters with a whole range of goods and services provided by Muslim businessmen and professionals. In some countries there is a proliferation of private Muslim schools, as well as government funded Muslim schools. There are experiments in establishing Islamic seminaries – Britain has a network of twenty-five.[8] In Rotterdam a pioneer Islamic University has been created. In Brussels there is the emergence of Europe-wide Muslim legal and youth NGOs affiliated to the European Union.

All citizens are equal but some are more equal than others?

This four phase developmental cycle – from pioneer, sojourner, family consolidation to active citizen – is, of course, an ideal construct. Citizenship is a differential concept in the west and we need to explore the extent to which Muslims enjoy equal rights of citizenship. Also, such a schematised picture does not allow for the strong continuing links between Muslims in western Europe and their countries of origin.

In Europe, there have been three models developed for managing diversity:

1 The guestworker model, where migrants are seen to have a temporary presence (Germany). Historically, German nationhood was vested in the volk, an ethnic community, and citizenship based on descent.
2 The assimilation model, where migrants are seen to be permanent and considered as individuals enjoying full citizenship rights but expected to assimilate into majority culture (France).
3 The ethnic minority model, in which institutional space for the preservation of cultural specificity is allowed for migrant communities, who also enjoy full citizenship rights (UK).

The German model has been the least hospitable to extending citizenship rights to Muslims. The ethnic definition of citizenship, allied to the myth that Germany was not a country of immigration, inevitably left the millions of Turks in Germany in a sort of limbo, a situation that was congenial to the Turkish government, which wished to guarantee the continuing flow of remittances back to Turkey. This situation only changed with the new nationality law of 1999 which grants citizenship at birth to all children born in Germany, provided that at least one parent was born in Germany or arrived before the age of fourteen and holds a residence permit. Also dual citizenship would be tolerated, although not encouraged.

The French model of citizenship presupposes a strong centralised state which deals only with individual citizens. Others sorts of identification – regional, linguistic or religious – are tolerated so long as they do not impact in the public space, deemed to be Republican and secular. Thus Muslims in France can enjoy unimpeded citizenship rights. However, the price for such incorporation is to privatise religious commitment. Since Islam is a communal and public religion the struggle in France is over the extent to which the French state will allow such public expressions of Islam in the secular and public space. This, in part, was the reason for the 1989 crisis of the headscarf, where North African Muslim girls were not allowed to wear the *hijab* in the state school – the bearer of the Republican and secular ideology!

Historically, Muslims have found most ready acceptance for expression of their religious identity and full citizenship rights in the UK. The UK granted citizenship to Commonwealth migrants legally entering the country. It also allows more spaces for Muslim self-expression than most other European countries. As a state which comprises four nations, which has gradually made institutional space for denominational diversity since the Reformation, and which enjoys the relatively plastic category 'British' allowing some measure of multiple identities – British Jews – Britain has gradually extended to Muslims the same rights enjoyed by other faiths.

As importantly, Britain allows dual citizenship. Once again, Britain represents an exception. However, where dual citizenship is disallowed, this leaves immigrants in a dilemma, since they often forfeit inheritance rights once they the lose citizenship in their home country. A recent survey of Muslims in western Europe concluded that: 'In most countries, only 10–25 percent of the Muslim population can vote. There are two exceptions, the Netherlands . . . [and] Great Britain'.[9]

Making space for Muslims in Europe?

The incorporation of Muslims as equal citizens in Europe is a necessary but not sufficient condition of acceptance. Here the central issue is the extent to which institutional space is accorded to religion in public life.[10] Europe embodies three broad models of relationship between state and religion – cooperation between state and religion, the existence of a state religion and the separation between state and religion.

In Belgium, Germany, Italy and Spain all religions are officially recognised by law. The exact nature of this recognition varies: in Germany, notwithstanding the constitutional recognition of the principle of separation between state and religion and the state's neutrality in religious matters, the churches enjoy special rights as public corporations, thus giving legal authority to their social functions. The Spanish Constitution of 1978 established the separation of state and religions as well as guaranteeing religious freedom in 1980. However, Catholicism alone is cited in terms of cooperation between state and religion. While Islam has yet to enjoy the status of public incorporation in Germany – and with it the right to state funding of religious education in schools – the institutionalisation of Islam in Spain has occurred very quickly. A Spanish law in January 1992 gave official recognition to Islam via the Islamic Commission of Spain, which groups together most of the country's Muslim associations. The agreement grants financial and legal benefits, recognises religious marriages to be legally binding and introduces religious education in schools.

The existence of a state religion as in Britain and Denmark need not of itself disallow institutional space being made for Islam. This is clear from the British experience: because public and civic life is permeated with Christian influence it is proving increasingly hospitable to the religious concerns of Muslims. Theology departments have been extended to include religious studies. All new religious education syllabi used in state schools have to reflect the social fact of religious diversity. Because the state funds religious schools, which provide education for over 20% of all children, this category has been extended since 1998 to include a handful of Muslim schools. Any religious group can found a private school. There are now more than 100 Islamic private schools. In September 1999 the Prison Service appointed the first Muslim advisor and there is now a growing number of Muslim chaplains in prisons and hospitals. Public service broadcasting has always included explicit religious slots, which now include Muslim voices.

However, the existence of a state religion can hinder the equal treatment of Islamic needs. This has been documented recently with regard to the huge difficulties encountered by Danish Muslims in acquiring a state subsidised Muslim cemetery, difficulties exacerbated by the political success of a xenophobic and anti-Muslim party, the Danish People's Party.[11]

The formal separation of state and religion, where it is embedded in an ideological secularism, as in France, can discriminate against Islam. An anthropologist, John R. Bowen, has recently shown how French civil servants have stretched administrative rules to restrict naturalisation. He describes how they regard 'adherence to daily [Muslim] prayer[s] . . . as self-evident grounds of insufficient assimilation to French norms and grounds for disqualifying an applicant from obtaining French citizenship'.[12]

Muslims and identity politics in Europe

A Muslim academic, Tim Winter, who lectures in Islam in the theology faculty at Cambridge University and serves as a chaplain to Muslim students, has noted that Muslims broadly embody one of three expressions of Islam:

> Firstly, the 'time capsule' option often embedded in local ethnic particularities, which seeks to preserve the lexicon of faith from any redefinition . . . a 'liberal' option . . . which remains an elite option, despite the *de facto* popularity of attenuated and sentimental forms of 'Muslimness' . . . the third possibility is to redefine the language of religion to allow it to support identity politics. Religion has, of course, always had the marking of collective and individual identity as one of its functions . . . [However, this dimension has] been allowed to expand beyond its natural scope and limits . . . the result has often been a magnifica- tion of traditional polarities between the self and the other, enabled by the steady draining-way of religiously inspired assumptions concerning the univer- sality of notions of honour and decency.[13]

The roots of contemporary identity politics are complex. Modern society has eroded social hierarchies, where status and 'honour' were relatively fixed, in favour of the rhetoric of equality and human 'dignity'. In our post-Cold War world conflicts of class, ideology and political systems have gradually receded. In their place divisions based on group identities – cultural, ethnic and religious – have assumed a new significance. Democracies have ushered in what has use- fully been dubbed 'the politics of recognition', whereby a diversity of groups, cultures and special interests now clamour for equal status and recognition of their identity. With this plea for public recognition goes a demand for resources and representation in policy-making. Muslim identity politics follows in the wake of civil rights in the United States, gender and sexuality politics.[14]

The critical question is how to give public recognition to religious traditions without endorsing mutually exclusive visions of the good. One suggestion is that everyone should become 'bilingual': all must learn a public language of citizen- ship, while rooted in their respective secondary languages, cultivated in families, communities, associations. Religious traditions are understood as part of our 'moral ecology'. Various dangers are to be avoided:

1 If we recognise only the first public language, we in effect call for the disinte- gration of minorities.
2 If we recognise only secondary languages, we risk moving to a society of con- flicting ghettoes.
3 What is needed is a balance between the conflicting claims of the individual, the group and society as a whole.[15]

What is important is that the Muslim presence in the west has occurred at a time when western societies are hospitable to such debates. The term 'multicul- turalism' was coined to lever open space to accommodate the needs of religious and ethnic minorities. It has meant that integration of minorities does not have to inevitably mean what that term has denoted in France, namely assimilation. The creation of Muslim communities in the west has also given Muslims the freedom to express ethnic identities often suppressed in their countries of origin. Thus in France 'Algerian' actually encompasses large Berber communities; in Germany 'Turk' includes many Kurds; in Britain 'Pakistani' comprises a significant Kashmiri community. The freedom to express such ethnic identities can have curious expressions: in Birmingham three local councillors were returned who represent . . . a Kashmiri party!

A crisis in Muslim religious leadership in the west?

Thus far, the emphasis has been on the willingness of European societies to make space for Muslims, legally, institutionally and culturally. However, this begs the question of how Muslims themselves view their presence in the west. It is worth stressing the novelty of the situation in which many contemporary Muslims living as a minority in Europe find themselves. The majority – whether from North Africa, Turkey, Pakistan or the Middle East – migrated from countries where Islam was the dominant religious and cultural reality. The Sunni majority belong to a religious tradition which in its classical development took power for granted.

Qur'anic, Islamic juristic and historical material traditionally generated four options for Muslims in non-Muslim societies:

1 struggle to incorporate non-Muslim societies into *Dar al-Islam* (the domain of Islam);
2 *hijra* – migration – to *Dar al-Islam*;
3 isolation from non-Muslims;
4 engage in a pact with the non-Muslim state to ensure the religious freedom to perform basic religious obligations.

This last is the most promising model for Muslims in the west. Early Islamic history legitimised such an option, when the Prophet's followers fled persecution in Mecca and migrated to Abyssinia, a Christian country, between 615 and 622.[16]

If Muslims are successfully to negotiate their insertion into western societies much will turn on the quality and confidence of their religious leadership to enable a discerning Islamic engagement with wider society. At the moment, it is no exaggeration to speak of a crisis in religious leadership across the west. There are a number of reasons for this. Firstly, many western societies have been content to leave the provision of many imams to sending societies, e.g. the Turkish government has been allowed to fund and provide imams to Turkish communities whether in Denmark, France, Germany or Holland.[17] They only stay for a few years and then are replaced. This inevitably slows down the emergence in western Europe of indigenous Islamic seminaries.

Similarly, Saudi Arabia has funded many central mosques in capital cities across western Europe. Such funding means that key personnel in these mosques embody the Saudi tradition of *Salafi* Islam. Saudi Arabia was until the 1960s largely a closed society. The religious tradition developed from within such a closed society was literalist, puritanical and bitterly sectarian, intolerant of other interpretations of Islam, especially the more open and accommodatory traditions of Sufism to which most western European Muslims belong. In short, *Salafi* influence has exacerbated intra-Muslim sectarianism and its 'frequent use of the notion of *kuffar* (unbelievers, infidels) as a technique of moral othering [of Christians] . . . [can preclude] the possibility of coexistence premised on cultural pluralism and political civility'.[18]

Within the west, because large numbers of Muslims came from rural areas, they imported imams familiar with their social and cultural world. Such imams, even when well educated in the traditional Islamic sciences, usually had no western language and no more than a cursory acquaintance with western culture. Most were quite incapable of connecting with a new generation of Muslims, streetwise, socialised and educated in the west.

Among Muslims educated in the west, some are attracted to the Islamist traditions. The Islamists, for whom Islam is a system or political ideology, emerged in the 1920s and 1930s in India and in Egypt. In Europe, they have been at the forefront of creating an Islamic civil society sector – associations of Islamic lawyers, teachers and doctors. This is clear in France and in Britain.[19] Many are enabling just that pattern of engagement with wider society which is so necessary.

The radicalisation of Muslims in the west?

The spread of *Salafi* and radical Islamist groups, especially on college and university campuses, is partly a result of the failure of mainstream Sunni traditions to connect with young Muslims educated and socialised in western Europe. Ten years ago, the historian of the *Hizb at-Tahrir* movement already noted that many recruits in Britain were of South Asian ancestry:

> highly educated youth from factory-worker families. Compared with their parents and many organizations within British Islam, the party appears not only intellectually sophisticated, but also radical and highly political. This combination has enabled it to exploit the growing cultural chasm between such youth and their tradition-bound elders, and to tap into their feelings of alienation as they struggle to find a new identity against a background of their elders' traditional preoccupations with subcontinental politics and social norms.[20]

Professor Khaled Abou El Fadl, a distinguished Kuwaiti scholar of Islamic law, now working in the United States, has penned a damaging critique of *Salafi* Islam in the west in a widely reproduced article entitled '*Islam and* the theology of power'. In it he claims that political movements active in western Europe such as *Hizb at-Tahrir*, while influenced by national liberation and anti-colonial struggles, also draw on a *Salafi* theology which is at once 'puritan, supremacist and thoroughly opportunistic'.[21] It is this *Salafi* perspective which has been rendered accessible through massive Saudi funding. A recent study estimated that 'Saudi spending on religious causes abroad [is] between $2 billion and $3 billion per year since 1975 (comparing favourably with what was the annual Soviet propaganda budget of $1 billion), which has been spent on 1,500 mosques, 210 Islamic centres and dozens of Muslim academies and schools'.[22]

Throughout the 1990s, at the very time many western European states were cautiously seeking to accommodate Muslim-specific concerns, many young Muslims were becoming radicalised and angry. Bosnia and the continuing tragedy of Palestine are key moments in this process. The fact that European Muslims could be ethnically cleansed and savagely repressed, while European powers seemed content to remain on the sidelines or engage in ineffective interventions, fuelled the notion that Europe continued to harbour an ancient hatred of Muslims.

The USA's support for Israel and seeming indifference to the suffering of the Palestinians created disillusionment with instruments of international relations such as the UN. Why, it was repeatedly asked, did the west move energetically against Iraq for non-compliance of UN resolutions but look the other way when Israel did the same? Such a suspicion of anti-Muslim sentiment has to be seen in the wider context of two wars against Iraq, the bloody repression in Algeria, interventions in Afghanistan and Chechnya.

The catalogue of suffering seemed endless with the west either directly involved or supporting authoritarian Muslim regimes. This was happening at a time when Muslims were able to access information produced within the west by Muslims. Thus, Muslim identity politics increasingly 'thrives through romantic, global solidarities as wars and massacres in Palestine, Bosnia, Kosovo, the Gulf, Chechnya, Kashmir, India, and so on fill our newspapers and television screens and lead some young British-born Muslims to reinvent the concept of the *umma*, the global community of Muslims, as global victims'.[23] This can translate into either isolating Muslim communities from wider society – the *Salafi* option – or defining Muslim communities as in oppositional terms to western society, with democracy dismissed as part of *kuffar* (infidel) society, the route taken by *Hizb at-Tahrir*. Both are underpinned by a theology of intolerance and can generate a discourse of hate.[24]

If Muslims are to feel at home in the west, their legitimate worries about aspects of western foreign policy and the depictions of Muslims need to be heard and addressed. This was the burden of the Runnymede Trust report produced in London in 1997, *Islamophobia, a Challenge for Us All*. This does not mean ignoring extremist groups but does require a nuanced analysis of Islamism.

Since the events of 9/11 and the escalation of atrocities within Europe the danger is that Muslims will simply be seen as increasingly a security problem. This will feed into the Manichean discourse of political radicals and the *Salafis*. Draconian legislation sends out worrying messages. In the United States the Homeland Security Act and USA Patriot Act include the registration of visitors to the US drawn from a list of twenty Muslim or Arab countries. The British Anti-Terrorist Act 2001 allows imprisonment of those suspected of involvement in terrorist activities without trial for an indefinite period. In all, the consequences of 9/11 and 7/7 has been 'the exacerbation of the stigmatisation of Muslims, something effected by the linking of Islam, terrorism, and the socio-economic conditions of the European . . . inner city ghettos . . . [which can] result in the growth of a reactive and defensive use of Islam'.[25]

Muslim attitudes to Christians: a hall of mirrors?

The preoccupation of Muslims in Europe today is to establish themselves and their communities in a world which others have shaped at a time when Islam is often depicted as posing an essential threat to what their neighbours hold dear, whether democracy, religious freedom, human rights or gender equality. Muslims for their part respond by insisting that 'only Islam offers and promotes a real moral and ethical alternative to permissiveness, consumerism, hedonism, moral relativism and individualism associated with and promoted by the modern Western cultures'.[26]

Muslims face a bewildering range of tasks, practical, intellectual and institutional. These range from creating appropriate organisations which can bridge the ethnic and sectarian divisions within the Muslim communities so as to relate to the state; addressing Islamophobia; identifying practical strategies to address the emergence of a Muslim underclass in many western cities; developing an Islamic jurisprudence (*fiqh*) appropriate for minority status; networking groups of Muslim professionals within the legal, medical, political and educational/university system, to organising Islamic aid to help Muslim groups across the world, suffering from oppression and natural disasters.

In such a situation, the frank supersessionism written into the Islamic tradition *vis-à-vis* Christianity leaves little need or energy for 'curiosity' about 'the otherness of the other'.[27] Within self-consciously Islamic institutions and organisations in the west such a stance translates into one of four broad responses to Christianity. For most 'ulama, whether trained in or outside the west, Christianity is simply invisible, part of non-Muslim society often painted in lurid colours as irredeemably corrupt. Many imams embody a 'separatist' spirituality, warning their congregations against unnecessary interaction with '*mushrikun* and *kafirun* ("polytheists" and "unbelievers")', categories in which Christians are subsumed.[28]

Institutions committed to *da'wa* (invitation to Islam) often draw on and develop a rich anti-Christian polemical tradition.[29] International bodies which promote *da'wa*, such as the Mecca based Muslim World League, properly seek to defend the rights of Muslim minorities in Europe. However, once their rights have been secured in a given country, 'the second phase of the League's strategy is aimed at transforming the minority into a ruling majority through proselytization'.[30] Such a set of priorities leaves little space for genuine religious dialogue with Christians.

Radical Muslim groups have developed a rejectionist stance of all things western or Christian, for which the term 'occidentalism' has been coined.[31] Fortunately, this is not the whole story. As Muslims born, educated and embedded in communities whose future is in Europe generate a middle class and begin to be active in a range of professions including academia and journalism, so they join Muslim movements which can connect with wider society. Further, Muslim governments and transnational movements have no desire to be locked into some supposed clash of civilisations. There emerges an inchoate constituency willing to cooperate with churches, especially in addressing pressing social issues. The events of 9/11 have underlined the urgency for Muslims to build bridges with wider society, not least to counter a deepening Islamophobia. Such pragmatic engagement has the potential to generate a more informed and Islamically serious encounter with Christianity in its particularity and 'otherness'. This is true of Turkish groups affiliated to the Fethullah Gullen movement, Islamists attracted to the writings of Tariq Ramadan, as well as Sufi groups in Britain.[32]

Church responses at the international and national level

At an international level there are two key moments. In 1964 the Catholic church established the Secretariat for non-Christians – renamed the Pontifical Council for Inter-Religious Dialogue in 1989. This anticipated the positive teaching of the Vatican II declaration *Nostra Aetate*, which urged Christians and Muslims 'to strive sincerely for mutual understanding' and 'to make common cause of safeguarding and fostering social justice, moral values, peace and freedom'. In 1971 the World Council of Churches (WCC) set up a Sub-Unit for Dialogue with People of Living Faiths and Ideologies, which in 1991 was absorbed into the Office on Inter-Religious Relations.

Both institutions produced guidelines on interfaith relations – including Islam – as well as hosting seminars and conferences with Muslims on a regular basis. Their publications have been translated into many languages and encouraged a range of national initiatives, as well as Europe-wide developments. Among the plethora of initiatives taken with the support of the Vatican and the WCC two might be mentioned. The first is the Day of Prayer for World Peace organised by the Catholic lay movement Sant'Egidio (Saint Giles) on 27 October 27 1986, in Assisi, Italy. This was attended by Pope John Paul II and hundreds of religious leaders. Sant'Egidio, founded in Rome in 1968 to express Vatican II's commitment to ecumenical and interreligious dialogue and social concern, now has more than 18,000 members across the world. These commitments have further developed into a concern for peace making, not least in the Muslim world.

Illustrative of the concerns of the WCC are two Christian–Muslim colloquia convened by the Office on Interreligious Relations in 1992 and 1993. Fourteen scholars, evenly divided between Muslims and Christians, reflected on some of the most divisive issues in Christian–Muslim relations today, e.g. the nature of Islamic law and the extent to which it can accommodate religious diversity and social change; how 'secularism' is viewed within Christian and Muslim traditions; and divergent perceptions on the issue of human rights. The papers from these two colloquia have been published. An excellent introduction clarifies the fears and misconceptions both communities entertain about each other with regard to these issues. It is clear that Christian dialogue with Muslims on contentious issues, such as the shari'ah, can only progress in the context of an awareness of intra-Muslim debate.[33]

The Vatican and WCC sponsored events remind us of a number of important developments in Christian reflection on Islam. Firstly, since both faith traditions are international, issues cannot adequately be addressed at a national or even a regional level. Secondly, if Christian–Muslim dialogue is to engage the interest and imagination of more than a handful of activists it has to address contentious societal problems. As a previous chairperson of the WCC dialogue programme put it, Christian–Muslim dialogue 'cannot be limited anymore to being nice to one another'; although, there is still a place, of course, for 'overcoming misunderstandings, promoting mutual respect, exchanging experiences, looking for possibilities to cooperate'.[34] Thirdly, there is a place for long-term trust building across key institutions. In consultations both the Vatican and WCC have developed relations with international Muslim bodies such as the Organisation of the Islamic Conference and the Muslim World League, as well as with distinguished Muslim scholars.

Across western Europe, more and more national churches have designated individuals and committees to address Christian–Muslim relations, often drawing on personnel with missionary experience in the Muslim world, and supported by a growing number of Christian institutions producing a range of scholarly and popular literature. Among European countries the French Catholic church has the most developed relations with Muslims. In the early 1970s the Secretariat for Relations with Islam (SRI) was established in Paris. The Francophone world has generated high quality material produced by the Muslim–Christian Research Group (GRIC) which has been meeting for over twenty-five years. One of its early works has been translated into English under the title, *The Challenge of the Scriptures, The Bible and the Qur'an*.[35]

The French Episcopal Conference of Bishops authorised in 1999 an exemplary and accessible set of pastoral guidelines for relations between Catholics and Muslims in France. These sought, *inter alia*: to confront the fear of Islamic extremism by contextualising the phenomenon and locating it as a small minority within a complex and varied field of Islamic expression; to engage young people in relationships across both communities; to encourage Catholics living side by side with Muslims in deprived areas to challenge the social exclusion of and contempt for Muslims. Such pastoral guidelines are fed through a network of contact priests who have responsibility for relations with Muslims and inter-religious relations in some fifty French dioceses.

The more recent, German church engagement with Islam and Muslims provides a useful counter point to France. The Protestant churches established a Christian–Muslim working group in 1976 for interfaith dialogue, as well as a respected Christian–Muslim Documentation Centre in Frankfurt in 1978. Many German cities have church academies run by both Protestant and Catholic churches which have the public function as meeting places for discussion and debate. They organise workshops and summer schools on Islam. The churches, then, were among the 'first to perceive Turks as "Muslims" and, moreover, addressed them on equal terms as fellow religious beings'.[36] However, after a quarter of a century, these well-intentioned activities have been bedevilled by structural inequality:

Muslim participants never had the same rootedness in organisations as their Christian partners. At the outset, they were mostly young and had limited education. They knew little of theology, were even less experienced in dialogue and lacked the contextual knowledge necessary to become public actors in German society. In contrast, Christian participants, as a rule, were highly educated theologians, older and more experienced in dialogue, well placed within their organisations and equipped with intimate knowledge of the working s of German society. In other words, the churches' desire to communicate with Muslims confronted long-standing Christian institutions with the inexperienced representatives of nascent communities.[37]

This is not to belittle the solid body of informed knowledge about Muslims in Germany generated by these activities or the personal friendships made. However, such activities hardly touched the growing and localised Muslim communities in Germany or their Christian neighbours. When German policymakers and media woke up to the existence of the Hamburg cell which had produced key leaders of 9/11, even basic distinctions between Islam and Islamist, Arab and Turk were obscured in a moral panic which threatened to demonise all Muslims. It was not surprising that post 9/11, when the Catholic Bishops' Conference met, confirming the church's continuing responsibility 'to search for ways to enable true encounter', Cardinal Lehmann could summarise the relationships between the two faiths as 'speechless co-existence'.[38]

Across Europe groups of specialists who resource the churches meet in a variety of forums. An informal network of Christians, the Arras Group – named after the French city where it first met in 1980 – drawing from more than ten European countries, meets annually to exchange news and discuss particular aspects of Christian–Muslim relations. There is often overlap between its membership and that of the Islam in Europe Committee of CEC (Conference of European Churches) and CCEE (Council of European Bishops' Conferences) formed in 1987. During its present five year mandate it has produced a variety of material: documents on the vexed issue of interreligious prayer ('Christians and Muslims praying together?'); guidelines for dialogue ('Meeting Muslims?'); two letters addressed to the European churches sharing experiences around two issues ('The education of young Christians in a Pluralistic Europe' and 'The role of Churches in a plural society'). The committee has also promoted contacts with Muslims at a variety of conferences and venues including Tirana and Sarajevo.[39] A crucial issue which requires much more sustained theological reflection is the relationship in Christian terms between proclamation and dialogue, or in Islamic terms *da'wa* and dialogue.

Such activities can draw on an ever-increasing range of reliable publications – practical and academic: the oldest journal is *The Muslim World*, which started publication in 1911 in the USA; *Islamochristiana*, an annual publication produced in Rome, has been running for over a quarter of a century; *Islam and Christian-Muslim Relations* was started by the Centre for the Study of Islam and Christian–Muslim Relations (CSIC), University of Birmingham, almost twenty years ago and is now jointly published with the Center for Muslim–Christian Understanding, Georgetown University, Washington. CSIC has pioneered relations between Muslims and Christians since its foundation in 1976. Its particular strength is that from its inception it has been a genuinely collaborative venture involving Christians and Muslims at every level, teaching, organisation and students. Indeed, it now has a Muslim director.

To complete this review of the range and scope of organisational responses to the new Muslim presence, it is worth mentioning the increasing interest of governments in enabling a serious dialogue. In Austria the Foreign Minister Dr Alois Mock in 1993 and his successor Dr Wolfgang Schussel in 1997 convened through the agency of the Institute for Theology of Religions St Gabriel – a religious community near Vienna – two outstanding international Christian-Islamic conferences drawing on religious leaders, scholars and politicians from across the world. The transactions of both conferences have been published in German and English and provide a wealth of serious reflection and deserve to be better known. The first was entitled *Peace for Humanity, Principles, Problems and Perspectives of the Future as Seen by Muslims and Christians*; the second *One World for All, Foundations of a Socio-Political and Cultural Pluralism from Christian and Muslim Perspectives*. One particularly valuable feature of both publications is the inclusion of the frank discussion which followed key note addresses.[40]

In January 2002 the British prime minister inaugurated an annual, international seminar series involving twenty Christian and Muslim scholars hosted by the Archbishop of Canterbury at Lambeth Palace with the cooperation of Prince El Hassan bin Talal of Jordan. Academic papers and discussions of three of these seminars have already been published.[41]

Can the churches act as an antidote to religious nationalism?

Religious nationalism is a phenomenon sweeping the globe and is not peculiar to the Abrahamic religions.[42] An imagined Christianity is increasingly recruited by a resurgent political far-right across western Europe as part of its anti-Muslim rhetoric. Their appeal has to be situated within a context of rapid social and cultural change – wrought by globalisation, with its attendant economic insecurity – at a time when the nation state has been weakened by supranational and subnational regional politics, and therefore is often less able to deliver generous social welfare provision. In this situation, the stranger is often scapegoated, among whom the most visible tend to be Muslims.

This is clear in Scandinavia. The Danes, for example, have had little experience of religious and cultural diversity; 85% belong to the national Lutheran church, although only a small percentage worship regularly. Initially, at a time of full employment, immigrant labour was welcomed in the 1960s to enable economic growth. However, when the economic situation began to change in the 1970s immigrants began to be seen as economic competitors with the native Danish labour force. Moreover, as the Muslim presence increased – in 2000 some 150,000 or 2.7% – and became more visible, religious, ethnic and cultural otherness began to be problematised. This went hand in hand with increasingly negative media portrayals of Islam.

In this situation, politicians began to speak about Danish Christian culture threatened by Muslim culture. Culture became a portmanteau term to explain the problems Muslims had in integrating. This was a more congenial explanation than asking whether Danish society was structured in such a way as to discriminate, exclude and marginalise Muslims.[43] In the process, Islam and culture were essentialised as fixed and unchanging entities.

Fortunately, the churches have begun to respond to such challenges. Copenhagen has an innovative Islamic–Christian Study Centre involving Christians and

Muslims set up in the mid-1990s.[44] Recently the national church established a new forum for religious encounter with seven of the ten dioceses supporting it. Central to its programme is dialogue with Muslims. Such encounter will, it is hoped, challenge myths about Muslims in the country, since over 80% of Danes never meet a Muslim, given their concentration in a few urban areas.

The Danish situation simply focuses a number of issues facing the churches at large. Can they use their institutional influence to facilitate a conversation between the media and Danish Muslims, to enable a more nuanced representation of Islam and Muslim diversity to become visible and audible? Can religious education reflect the historic importance of Christianity, yet make space for the study of Islam? Can European history be studied to include the Muslim presence and intellectual and cultural influence on Europe?

Faith in the city?

A review of the new Muslim presence in Europe suggests in many places the gradual incorporation of Muslims in public and civic life with the emergence of a middle class. At the same time, there is the emergence of a Muslim underclass in many cities. The number of Muslims in prison has increased quite dramatically in the last decade in a number of European countries, most dramatically in France, where Muslims make up more than half of the male prison population.[45]

The issue of an emerging Muslim underclass in western European cities poses one of the sharpest challenges to the development of creative co-existence. Deprived communities are the most likely to look to the newcomer to blame. Muslim communities have grown exponentially in the last two decades, because they are predominantly young communities with aggregate family size considerably larger than the host community – although this changes across generations. Further, because Muslim settlement is heavily concentrated in a few cities and usually within Muslim quarters, many Muslims can live within an ethnic enclave; whether Turks in Berlin, Algerians in Lyons, Moroccans in Utrecht, Pakistanis in Bradford.

Often these same cities have experienced dramatic de-industrialisation with the collapse of those labour intensive heavy industries for which labour was imported in the 1960s and 1970s. This means that many elderly Muslims who lost their jobs are often unemployable, lacking the requisite linguistic and social skills. Thus, there is minimal interaction at work. Among their sons, educational underachievement and poor job prospects translates predictably into an escalating cycle of anti-social behaviour and crime.[46] This, then, reinforces Islamophobic sentiment in the wider society, although the causes have very little to do with Islam.[47]

Churches in these cities face the new challenge of sustaining a relevant presence in these Muslim quarters. If they pull out, then Muslims will be further encapsulated. Also, a key issue is the extent to which imams are being educated to connect confidently with their own young people and wider society. Here, there are some promising developments. Across western Europe, there is the beginning of the professionalisation of imams, as they move into spaces historically reserved for Christian clergy: chaplaincy in hospitals and prisons, as well as religious education teachers, whether in Holland or Britain. Here they are often collaborating with clergy and developing new social and intellectual skills. Such developments are vital for the health of European cities. At the moment, clergy who approach the imam in the mosque usually find people ill-equipped, linguistically or intellectually, to relate to them. This poses a massive barrier to developing healthy interreligious cooperation.

Clearly, the greatest challenge facing Muslims and Christians is to learn to share public and civic space, and seek together to shape it for the common good, a category familiar to Islamic jurisprudence. It is fitting to conclude this survey with reference to the launch of a national Christian–Muslim Forum (CMF) at Lambeth Palace in January 2006, where both the prime minister and its founding patron, the Archbishop of Canterbury, spoke.[48] The CMF is the fruit of a long gestation period of almost ten years and which involved a joint working party of Muslims and Christians who visited many cities in Britain with large Muslim communities. Here the views of local Muslims, Christians and policy-makers were canvassed to ascertain what sort of forum, if any, was needed to encourage, learn from and build on local initiatives. CMF includes all the major Christian denominations, as well as reflecting Muslim diversity. One major strength is that two of its three Muslim presidents are traditional Sunni 'ulama who have developed a range of new skills: one is a prison chaplain, the other has established a multipurpose Muslim community centre. Six pairs of Christian and a Muslim specialists have been chosen to resource six working parties concerned with: community and public affairs, education, youth, international relations, media and family. In the long term the hope is that such collaborative work will be rooted in showcasing and supporting local developments at city level. The future common good of many of our cities depends on such cooperation.

Notes

1 Albania, Bulgaria and the successor states of Yugoslavia – along with small Muslim communities in Hungary, Poland and Rumania – comprise 5.5 million Muslims. These areas tend to fall largely within the Orthodox Christian world, and have only recently emerged into the light of relative freedom after seventy years of communist oppression.
2 I have drawn these figures from two useful sources, Vertovec, S. and Peach, C. (eds), *Islam in Europe, the Politics of Religion and Community* (London, Macmillan Press, 1997) and Marechal, Brigitte (ed.), *A Guidebook on Islam and Muslims in the Wide Contemporary Europe* (French and English) (Louvain-La-Neuve, Bruylant-Academia, 2002).
3 Klausen, Jytte, *The Islamic Challenge, Politics and Religion in Western Europe* (Oxford, Oxford University Press, 2005), p. 139.
4 Ibid., p. 141. The quotation refers to a comprehensive Dutch study of Moroccan and Turkish Muslims in Holland.
5 Fletcher, Richard, *The Cross and the Crescent, Christianity and Islam from Muhammad to the Reformation* (London, Allen Lane, 2003), p. 116.
6 Two studies, in particular, are worth mentioning. Brotton, Jerry, *The Renaissance Bazaar, From the Silk Road to Michelangelo* (Oxford, Oxford University Press,

2002) and Colley, Linda, *Captives, Britain, Empire and the World 1600–1850* (London, Jonathan Cape, 2002).

7 Matar, Nabil, *Islam in Britain, 1558–1685* (Cambridge, Cambridge University Press, 1998).

8 See Birt, J. and Lewis, P., 'The pattern of Islamic reform in Britain: the Deobandis between intra-Muslim sectarianism and engagement with wider society', in Allievi, S. and van Bruinessesn, M. (eds), *Producing Islamic Knowledge in Western Europe* (London, I. B. Tauris, forthcoming).

9 See Klausen, *The Islamic Challenge*, p. 21.

10 The importance of church–state relations as a critical factor in accounting for the differential, incorporation of Muslim communities in western Europe has recently been argued by Fetzer, J. and Soper, J., *Muslims and the State in Britain, France, and Germany* (Cambridge, Cambridge University Press, 2005).

11 Klausen, *The Islamic Challenge*, pp. 109–13.

12 Ibid., p. 21.

13 Winter, T., 'Muslim loyalty and belonging: some reflections on the psychosocial background', in M. Seddon, *British Muslims, Loyalty and Belonging* (Leicester, Islamic Foundation, 2003), pp. 5–6.

14 See especially the classic text, Taylor, Charles, *Multiculturalism and 'The Politics of Recognition'* (Princeton, Princeton University Press, 1992).

15 See Sacks, Jonathan, *The Dignity of Difference* (London, Continuum, 2002), for a fine exploration of these issues.

16 These models draw on and develop a seminal article by Masud, M. K., 'Being Muslim in a non-Muslim polity: Three alternative models', *Journal of the Institute of Muslim Minority Affairs*, 10 (1989), 118–28.

17 See Pederson, Lars, *Newer Islamic Movements in Western Europe* (Aldershot, Ashgate, 1999).

18 Mandaville, Peter, 'Sufis and Salafis', in Heffner, Robert (ed.), *Remaking Muslim Politics*, (Princeton, Princeton University Press, 2005), p. 315. The bitter world-wide, sectarian struggle between Salafi and Sufi is accessibly covered in Sirriyeh, E., *Sufis and Anti-Sufis, the Defence, Rethinking and Rejection of Sufism in the Modern World* (Surrey, Curzon, 1999).

19 See Roald, Anne Sofie, *Women in Islam, The Western Experience* (London, Rout-ledge, 2001). Roald, a Norwegian convert to Islam, offers a fascinating window into Arab Islamists across western Europe and provides an illuminating insight into the nature of the *Salafi* tradition.

20 Taji-Farouki, Suha, A Fundamental Quest, Hizb al-Tahrir and the Search for the Islamic Caliphate (London, Grey Seal, 1996), pp. 177–8.

21 El Fadl, Khaled Abou, 'Islam and the theology of power', in Malik, Aftab Ahmad (ed.), *With God on Our Side, Politics & Theology of the War on Terrorism* (Bristol, Amal Press, 2005), p. 305.

22 Birt, Jonathan, 'Wahhabism in the United Kingdom: manifestations and reac-tions', in Al-Rashhed, Madawi (ed.), *Transnational Connections and the Arab Gulf* (London, Routledge, 2005), p. 169.

23 Modood, Tariq, *Multicultural Politics, Racism, Ethnicity and Muslims in Britain* (Edinburgh, Edinburgh University Press, 2005) p. 160.

24 See Cesari, Jocelyne, *When Islam and Democracy Meet: Muslims in Europe and the United States* (Basingstoke, Palgrave Macmillan, 2004), chapter five.

25 Cesari, J. and McLoughlin, S. (eds), *European Muslims and the Secular State* (Aldershot, Ashgate, 2005), p. 3.
26 Hassan, Riaz, *Faithlines, Muslim Conceptions of Islam and Society* (Karachi, Pakistan, Oxford University Press, 2002), p. 209.
27 Siddiqui, A., *Christian–Muslim Dialogue in the Twentieth Century* (London, Macmillan, 1997), p. 196.
28 Steenbrink, Karel, 'The small talk of Muslims and Christians in the Netherlands', in Waardenburg, Jacques (ed.), *Muslim–Christian Perceptions of Dialogue Today, Experiences and Expectations* (Leuven, Peters, 2000), p. 206.
29 See Lewis, P., 'Depictions of Christianity within British Islamic institutions', in Ridgeon, Lloyd (ed.), *Islamic Interpretations of Christianity* (Surrey, Curzon Press, 2001).
30 Breiner, B. F. and Troll, C. W., 'Christianity and Islam', in Esposito, J., *The Oxford Encyclopedia of the Modern Islamic World*, vol. 1 (Oxford, Oxford University Press, 1995), p. 284.
31 Ahmed, A., *Postmodernism and Islam: Predicament Promise* (London, Routledge, 1992), p. 177.
32 For Fethullah Gullen and Tariq Ramadan see Mandaville, 'Sufis and Salafis', pp. 316–20; Geaves, Ron, *The Sufis of Britain* (Cardiff, Cardiff Academic Press, 1999); Lewis, P., 'Imams, 'ulama and Sufis: providers of bridging social capital for British Pakistanis?', *Contemporary South Asia* (forthcoming).
33 For the role of Sant'Egidio see Appleby, R. Scott, *The Ambivalence of the Sacred, Religion, Violence and Reconciliation* (Oxford, Rowman & Littlefield, 2000), pp. 155–65. For the WCC colloquia see Mitri, Tarek (ed.), *Religion, Law and Society, A Christian–Muslim Discussion* (Geneva, WCC Publications, 1995).
34 Mulder, Dick, 'Developments in dialogue with Muslims: World Council of Churches', in Speelman, Ge, van Lin, Jan and Mulder, Dick (eds), *Muslims and Christians in Europe, Breaking New Ground, Essays in Honour of Jan Slomp* (Kampen, Kok, 1995), p. 160.
35 *The Challenge of the Scriptures* (New York, Orbis, 1989). The continuing work of the group and the challenges it faces is addressed in chapter six of Waardenburg, *Muslim–Christian Perceptions of Dialogue Today*.
36 Jonker, Gerdien, 'From "foreign workers" to "sleepers": the churches, the state and Germany's "discovery" of its Muslim population', in Cesari and McGloughlin, *European Muslims and the Secular State*, p. 115.
37 Ibid., p. 117.
38 Ibid., p. 120.
39 Much of this material is available on the internet at www.cec-kek.org. Speelman and Mulder's *Muslims and Christians in Europe* is a festschrift to Jan Slomp, the first chairman of the Islam in Europe Committee and contains useful material about the committee. For European developments also worth consulting is Penelope Johnstone and Jan Slomp, 'Islam and the churches in Europe: a Christian perspective', *Journal of Muslim Minority Affairs*, 18: 2 (1998), 355–63. For a comprehensive tour d'horizon of the range of recent Christian–Muslim activities see the concluding chapter, 'Dialogue or confrontation', in Goddard, H., *A History of Christian–Muslim Relations* (Edinburgh, Edinburgh University Press, 2000).
40 For the Austrian conferences see Bsteh, Andreas (ed.), *Peace for Humanity* (New Delhi, Vikas Publishing House, 1996); Bsteh, Andreas (ed.), *One World for All* (New Delhi, Vikas Publishing House, 1999), www.ubspd.com.

41 For the Lambeth papers see Ipgrave, M. (ed.), *The Road Ahead. A Christian–Muslim Dialogue* (2002); *Bearing the Word, Prophecy in Biblical and Qur'anic Perspective* (2003); *Scriptures in Dialogue, Christians and Muslims Studying the Bible and the Qur'an Together* (2004). All published by Church House Publishing, London.

42 See Juergensmeyer, Mark, *The New Cold War? Religious Nationalism Confronts the Secular State* (London, University of California Press, 1993).

43 For Denmark see the comments of Pedersen, Lars, *Newer Islamic Movements in Western Europe* (Aldershot, Ashgate, 1999), pp. 156–7.

44 I owe much of the information in this section to frequent email conversations with Rev. Dr Lissi Rasmussen, the Director of the Islamic-Christian Study Centre, Copenhagen.

45 This startling statistic was included in Dr Farhad Khosrokhavar's paper on Muslims in French prisons, delivered as a recent conference in London and reported in the February 2003 edition of *Dialogue*, produced by the Public Affairs Committee for Shi'a Muslims, Stone Hall, Chevening Road, London NW6 6TN.

46 In Britain, boys do less well than girls in education. The gap between boys and girls of Pakistani heritage is the widest of all groups.

47 In Britain, in seeking to understand the complex reasons for educational under-achievement of sections of Pakistani young men, two reasons among a complex of factors have been identified as touching on religion and culture. Many of these youngsters spend two hours a day, six days a week, for six to eight years, from six years old, in mosque schools after state school. Here they often learn the Qur'an by rote in Arabic without understanding it. Their teachers, imams often trained in Pakistan, operate with different pedagogical assumptions than those operative in European schools. This can leave them tired and with little time for school home work. The second factor has more to do with patriarchal rural culture, with localised studies suggesting that some 50% of marriages are contracted with relatives in rural Kashmir.

48 CMF has a website – www.christianmuslimforum.org – on which the inaugural speeches, including those by the archbishop and the prime minister can be read.

8

Varieties of Christian–Muslim encounter in Malaysia

Peter G. Riddell

Since its formation in 1963, Malaysia has become one of the most dynamic majority Muslim countries in the world, especially in terms of its attempts to develop into a modern, industrialised, pluralist society. Its present day population of around 24 million people is multifaith, with Muslims constituting around 60%, Buddhists 19%, Christians 9% and Hindus 6%.[1] However, it has not been all plain sailing for Malaysian governments and faith communities. The last quarter of the twentieth century was characterised by a struggle between the two main political groups in the majority Malay community, the United Malays National Organisation (UMNO) and the Islamic Party of Malaysia (PAS). The former, Muslim modernist in inclination, was strongly opposed to the more conservative PAS, which called for implementation of Islamic law and establishment of an Islamic state.[2]

Islamic resurgence and the end of an era, 1999–2003

The federal and state elections of 1999 marked a peak in the resurgence of Islam as a political force in Malaysia. There was a surge in support for PAS, with the party winning power in the state of Terengganu for the first time since 1962, supplementing its hold in the neighbouring state of Kelantan since 1990. In the 1999 elections support for the governing National Alliance (led by UMNO) fell from 70% to just over 50% of all Malay voters in peninsular Malaysia.[3] UMNO reportedly lost 2.9 million members in the years immediately preceding 1999.[4]

The PAS victory in two of Malaysia's thirteen states was quickly followed by diverse efforts to establish an Islamic society in Terengganu and Kelantan. The entertainment industry was dramatically reduced. Dress codes for women in government offices were implemented, with PAS leaders in Terengganu announcing in late 2003 that women in the state would not be allowed to wear mini-skirts or figure-hugging dresses.[5] Separate queues for men and women at supermarket check-outs were required and hotels in the two states were prohibited from selling alcohol. The response of the federal government to PAS Islamisation efforts in Terengganu was swift. The state government in Terengganu lost 'oil revenues worth between RM500 million and RM600 million annually after the federal government cut its royalty payment in the aftermath of the 1999 election', according to PAS Vice-President Mustaffa Ali. This was somewhat offset by 'tithes contributed by Muslims and Muslim-owned companies'.[6]

However, the stakes in the UMNO–PAS rivalry were increased when the PAS state government in Terengganu announced in 2002 its intention to implement strict Islamic codes of punishment for serious crimes. This followed PAS efforts to do the same in Kelantan in 1993. Stern opposition to these PAS initiatives came from the federal government, an alliance of some fourteen parties but dominated by UMNO. This latter party has always been willing to support a measured implementation of Islamic law in the private domain for Muslims, such as concerning marriage, divorce and inheritance. Indeed, Dr Mahathir Mohammad, prime minister from 1982–2003, promoted an UMNO-led programme of Islamisation, also involving the establishment of Islamic financial institutions, educational bodies and media programming.

However, UMNO opposed the introduction of Islamic codes of crime and punishment. The party was successful in blocking these PAS efforts, as responsibility for this area of law lay within federal, not state jurisdiction. The bottom line was that the UMNO-led Malaysian government was intractably opposed to what it considered PAS's 'throwback' approach of returning to ancient pristine society. UMNO vigorously resisted PAS's call for the institution of Islamic law. However, it expressed its opposition in Islamic terminology wherever possible, thus creating the impression of a clash of Islamisations.

The collapse in support for UMNO among the Muslim Malay population in the 1999 elections precipitated an upping of the UMNO Islamisation ante in terms of both rhetoric and policy in an attempt to regain lost support. For example, the Muslim Scholars Association (MSA) targeted media comment which they considered derogatory to Islam or Muhammad. The MSA campaign reached the National Islamic Affairs Committee chaired by Dr Mahathir. The result was a federal government decision in mid-April 2002 to implement existing but little used laws which stipulate that anyone found guilty of insulting Islam would be fined and/or jailed.[7]

Malaysia – an Islamic state?

The anti-PAS vitriol by UMNO was strong. Prime Minister Mahathir accused PAS of being a traitor to the Malay heritage and to Islam because of its downgrading of academic excellence, commenting, 'such people are the reason why Muslim countries are always left behind in development'.[8] But UMNO attempts to undermine PAS support was not restricted to name-calling. In October 2001, Dr Mahathir stated that calls for Malaysia to become an Islamic state were redundant, as it was already one.[9] In support of this declaration, the Malaysian federal government issued a booklet entitled *Malaysia adalah sebuah Negara Islam* (*Malaysia Is an Islamic State*). Though the English language version was later withdrawn from circulation because of the resulting furore among religious minorities, the Malay language version continued to be available. As observed by University of Malaya scholar Patricia Martinez, 'the overwhelming reason for the prime minister's announcement of Malaysia as an Islamic state was as another salvo in the battle for the legitimacy of Islam between his party in the ruling coalition, and the Islamic opposition party, PAS'.[10]

Christian responses

Though the UMNO-led programme of Islamisation was more benign than PAS Islamisation plans, it was nevertheless also of concern to the 40% non-Muslim minority of Malaysia, including Christians. Indeed, many non-Muslim Malaysians regarded the competing approaches to Islamisation as two sides of the same coin.[11]

Perceptions of discrimination

Specific aspects of the spiralling Islamisation rhetoric and policy-making exacerbated a sense of exclusion among Malaysian Christians. The ongoing government directive forbidding the use of the term Allah by non-Muslims, dating as far back as 1989, continued to cause resentment among Malaysian Christians. Prominent Malaysian evangelical Ng Kam Weng commented that 'as long as the ban is still in place, we are on the wrong side of the law'.[12] Brother Anthony Rogers of the Malaysian Catholic church commented on the motive behind the government policy in the following terms: 'These measures banning use of Allah and the Indonesian Bible reflect a culture of insecurity on the part of the Malays rather than a direct preoccupation with Christian doctrine'.[13] The earlier banning of the Indonesian Bible was echoed in April 2003 when the Malaysian government banned the *Bub Kudus*, the Bible in the Iban language. The Ibans, numbering around 550,000, constitute almost one third of the population of the Malaysian state of Sarawak. The Bible was first translated into Iban in 1988, and at the time of its banning was into its 8th edition, with 5,000 copies printed every five years by the Bible Society of Malaysia. The banning caused expressions of protest from various quarters. The Archbishop of Kuching, Peter Chung, complained that no explanation had been given for the decision. Some Muslims spoke out as well. For example, Malaysian Bar Council President Kuthubul Zaman Bukhari criticised the ban, saying that it 'infringes on the right to freedom of religion'.[14] In the wake of such protests, the ban was lifted in the same month that it was announced. Nevertheless, it reminded Christians that their use of their sacred text was subject to the vagaries of government policy.

Other pressures from the Malay Muslim community made Christians feel as if they were being targeted during the period 1999–2003. For example, Christian videos and DVDs about the life of Christ attracted complaints from the Malay language tabloid *Harian Metro*, as they were on sale in public shopping malls and, according to *Harian Metro*, this could 'adversely affect the faith of Muslims that are weak in their religion's teachings'.[15]

A sense of exclusion was also felt in the schools sector. Private non-Muslim schools had gradually been integrated with the state education system during the latter years of the twentieth century. This led to a predominance of Muslim teaching staff and administrators in formerly Christian schools. While Muslim students at these schools were required to study Islamic Studies, non-Muslim students were not able to study their own faiths but were instead offered a subject entitled Moral Education, widely unpopular and described by one writer as 'the most maligned subject in the school curriculum'.[16]

The issue of apostasy continued to be a bone of contention between governments, both federal and state, and religious minorities which had advocated on behalf of certain individuals wishing to convert away from Islam. In a letter to the Malaysian Consultative Council of Buddhists, Christians, Hindus and Sikhs (MCCBCHS) of 4 June 2002, Director of the National Department of Registration, Datuk Azizan Ayob, said that the change of a Muslim name to a non-Muslim name and vice versa must be supported with a letter from the Islamic department or the relevant state shari'ah court.[17] Hence changing faith between Islam and other faiths would depend on the approval of Islamic authorities, an unlikely scenario given Islamic law's entrenched opposition to Muslims renouncing Islam.

Although issues such as the above were causes for concern and discomfort for many Christians, physical threat was not frequently present. Nevertheless, isolated instances of violence against Christian communities were reported in the period 1999–2003 during which Islamic resurgence was at its peak. On 21 July 2001, the Marthoma Christian Community Center, in the city of Sungei Petani, was set on fire with damage estimated at £55,000. Police attributed responsibility to the Kumpulan Militan Malaysia (KMM, Malaysian Militant Group), an Islamist group suspected of being connected with al-Qaeda.[18] Furthermore, October 2001 witnessed further attacks on churches. A Molotov cocktail was thrown through the window of St Philips church in southern Johor; Christ the King church in Sungai Petani had windows smashed and chairs burnt; and Christ Community Centre church in Subang Jaya was completely destroyed by fire.[19]

Such attacks were infrequent and not considered to be connected with government policy. However, a greater cause of discontent among Christians was the long-held perception that church construction was impeded by government, whether federal or state. For example, by 1992 the ratio of mosques to Muslim worshippers was 1:800 in Johor and Perak, whereas the ratio of non-Muslim places of worship to worshippers was 1:4,000 in Johor and 1:5,000 in Perak.[20] A decade later at the peak of Islamic resurgence the situation had not changed. Nor did Islamic political leaders show sympathy with Christian concerns. Abdul Hadi Awang, chief minister of the state of Terengganu and president of PAS was asked why the state government had not approved an application to build a new Catholic church in Kuala Terengganu. He replied that the chapel belonging to a local convent currently used for Catholic worship was sufficient for the church's requirements, adding:

> To build a new church, with a tall steeple and *lambang* [symbol or cross], in a public place would be a sensitive issue . . . They [the church] have to consider the sensitivities of the community around them. They have a place of worship now; we think it is adequate. We would allow them to build a *dewan* [hall], but not a prominent steeple. It's for their own safety.[21]

Strategic responses

Christians were far from inactive in responding to the climate of Islamic rivalry around them in the period 1999–2003. One hurdle which Christians faced was the problem of internal disunity. Rev. Dr D. Lakshman of St Aidan's Anglican church of Bahau commented: 'The fact that churches are unable to recognize each other's baptism only shows the extent of disunity that still exist[s] among Christians'.[22] Fr Philip Thomas and Dr John Gurusamy indicated that Christian divisions along ethnic lines were 'still a problem within the mainline Protestant churches'.[23]

Nevertheless, there are signs that ethnic divisions are breaking down within the Malaysian churches. Prominent evangelical Ng Kam Weng commented in interview that 'ethnic divisions within the church are diminishing as a factor in church life. For example, many Indians from the minority within the Christian community hold leadership positions. This is never a topic of discussion. Islamisation has brought Christians together'.[24] Brother Augustine Julian of the Malaysian Catholic church agrees, saying: 'This is not an issue today among Catholics. Catholic churches are now well integrated'.[25]

A key device for overcoming divisions among the churches on ethnic and denominational lines has been the formation of the Christian Federation of Malaysia (CFM). Since its inception in 1986, this umbrella body, which groups the Catholic Church of Malaysia, the Council of Churches of Malaysia and the National Evangelical Christian Fellowship (NECF), has had six major assemblies. These gatherings, together with smaller meetings springing out of the CFM structure, have provided an opportunity for Christians of diverse denominational grouping to share concerns and plan joint action. Ng Kam Weng comments that 'the CFM has generated goodwill between different Christian groups over the years. It provides a very good platform to deal with the Government and largely has a positive record of action'.[26] Brother Anthony Rogers, however, suggests that CFM successes have been uneven: 'CFM has achieved something in bringing Christians together in practising their rights. But in terms of working more closely together for the larger issues in Malaysia – social, economic, cultural (e.g. charity, secularism) – the CFM has not been effective in uniting Christians'.[27]

The increased rhetoric regarding the Islamic state concept, both by PAS and in Prime Minister Mahathir's declaration of October 2001 that Malaysia was already an Islamic state, triggered increasing reactions from the Malaysian Christian community. Speaking at a public forum in January 2002, Ng Kam Weng responded to PAS claims that non-Muslims oppose implementation of shari'ah law simply because they don't understand it, saying:

> PAS politicians are being disingenuous . . . The fact is non-Muslims are more concerned about the fundamental issue of citizenship rights . . . the issue that most troubles non-Muslims . . . is, whether PAS's Islamic state effectively disenfranchises non-Muslims from the legal system.

He drew out of Islamic law the concept of dhimmitude, seeing it as a subordinate role assigned to non-Muslims under Islamic legal theory, and threw down the gauntlet to PAS, calling on the party to declare 'decisively that it will not implement the *dhimmi* system and that all citizens will be accorded equal rights and legal status'.[28] In a similar vein, the *Catholic Asian News* called for a national referendum to decide whether an Islamic state or secular state was the preferred model of Malaysians.[29]

On 18 July 2002, following the passing of the Shari'ah Criminal Offences (Hudud and Qisas) Bill by the Terengganu Legislative Assembly, the CFM issued a press release which affirmed the thrust of the secular state argument by stating

'The CFM believes and upholds the secular and democratic system of governance inspired by the social contract of our country's founding fathers'.[30] Nevertheless, such Christian challenges to the principal actors in the intra-Muslim struggle were worded with care in order to avoid inflaming the situation. In the wake of the 11 September 2001 terrorist attacks on American targets, the NECF issued a press release, dissociating radical extremism from Islam and declaring: 'the global struggle against terrorism is not a conflict with Islam'. At the same time, the statement warned about the local scene: 'in the Malaysian context, religious extremism has a significant bearing on our multicultural, multi-ethnic and multireligious society. What happened in the United States should give us a new urgency and perspective in evaluating the radical religious movements, which sow seeds of religious militancy in the country'.[31]

In a pastoral response to the 9/11 attacks intended for its Christian constituency, NECF was at pains to distinguish between Islamic radicalism and Malaysian government authorities:

> The leadership of NECF Malaysia recognises that the attacks are, indeed, the culmination of unchecked evil whose ugly face of terror has been allowed to spread its wings through global terror networks. Local militants identified by our Government recently have also evidenced this terror – seemingly aroused and bred by hate feelings.[32]

Brother Anthony Rogers added his voice of moderation on behalf of the Catholic church:

> Christians should not just negatively condemn [the Federal Government] and PAS. Rather they should positively consider how they can contribute to an improvement of the Kingdom (of God on Earth). The ideal society in Malaysia is a state which recognises religious pluralism.[33]

Ng Kam Weng summed up Christian perceptions of the impact of the struggle between the federal government and PAS in the following terms:

> Christians conceive that the UMNO policies open the way for PAS. The bureaucracy has been Islamically empowered, and is assuming its own momentum beyond the control of the Barisan Government. UMNO is now seeing this effect of the Islamisation policies and is trying to back-pedal, as it now realises that PAS is gaining through the Federal Government's Islam policies.[34]

Engagement by Christians with Islamic authorities and communities has not limited itself to lobbying on issues to do with rights. Interfaith dialogue assumed increasing importance during the period 1999–2003, as Christians sought ways to build good working relationships with Muslim compatriots. The Catholic church of Malaysia has encountered considerable success in interfaith dialogue activities, with particular parishes, such as the St Francis Xavier Parish in Kuala Lumpur, playing a leading role. Catholic groups explored diverse approaches to dialogue, as summed up by Jojo M. Fung, a Malaysian Jesuit priest and researcher:

> The dialogue of life is an initial yet essential step among the other three types of dialogue: dialogue of action, dialogue of religious experience and dialogue of theological exchange.[35]

Small group dialogues organised at the parish level have been supplemented by higher level interactions. For example, the Catholic Church of Malaysia initiated a Day of Prayer for Peace on 24 January 2002, in the wake of the 9/11 attacks and the Mahathir statement on the Islamic state which had caused such concern among religious minorities. The event was attended by heads of all the major religions in Malaysia, and was designed to coincide with an interfaith day of prayer held at Assisi in Italy under the pope's auspices.[36]

In another effort at dialogue, Muslim writers were sometimes invited to contribute to Christian periodicals. For example, Dr Amir Farid Isahak, the Muslim Chairman of the Interfaith Spiritual Fellowship (INSAF), contributed an article to the *Catholic Asian News*, in which he called for dialogue and suggested that the guidelines for dialogue should be Sincerity, Trust, Objectivity, Multiperspective Knowledge, Wisdom, and Gracious Conduct, adding that 'one should never try to prove one's own religion is superior nor bring down other religions'.[37]

From Mahathir to Badawi

Dr Mahathir retired as prime minister in October 2003, after twenty-two years at the helm of Malaysia. He was replaced by Abdullah Ahmad Badawi, who came to the position with significant credentials as an Islamic scholar. However, he was something of an unknown quantity as a national leader. Many commentators questioned his ability to stem the seemingly irresistible surge of support for PAS among the Malays.

In his first three months as prime minister, Badawi prioritised policy in both secular and religious matters. He first launched a campaign against corruption, and authorised the arrest of several leading public figures, including a former minister in the Mahathir cabinet, Perwaja Steel ex-chief Eric Chia.[38] He also scaled back several grandiose building projects which had been conceived under the previous administration, such as a controversial railway mega-project. He even authorised investigations into allegations of police brutality, corruption and inefficiency. These measures served as a shot across the bows for those within UMNO who expected Badawi to be simply a clone of Mahathir.

Badawi's attention was also directed to religious affairs. He led mass prayers during the fasting month of Ramadan in 2003, thereby signalling his intention to challenge the claims of PAS leaders to speak for Malay Muslims in spiritual matters.

2004 general elections and the decline of PAS

When federal and state elections were announced for 21 March 2004, PAS leaders moved quickly to introduce Islamic rhetoric to the campaign. PAS spiritual leader Nik Abdul Aziz Nik Mat declared that those who voted for PAS would earn a place in heaven. In response, Prime Minister Badawi spoke in measured tones on 8 March at a political gathering in Seremban, saying 'we can't promise heaven. It is up to God. We can only work to become good Muslims'. His predecessor, ever ready to debate with his erstwhile opponents in PAS, responded to the PAS promise of paradise to those who voted for it by quipping 'Who has been there to verify this?'[39]

At the same time, Badawi launched his vision of *Islam Hadhari* as a counter to the PAS dream of an Islamic state. For Badawi, Islam would be equated with forward-looking development and progress, rather than a backward-looking shari'ah state.[40] Furthermore, he preached a vision of Malaysia for all Malaysians, regardless of race or religion. He spoke the language of inclusivism in articulating his vision:

> I want the Muslims to go back to the basics. The religion of Islam is a religion that promotes peace. The religion of Islam is . . . not against modernity. It's not against progress . . . Islam is a religion that provides you with a strong imperative to do well and to live at peace with the non-Muslims and to be able to work together on the basis of mutual respect and recognition of rights: of their rights as well as our rights.[41]

So the choice was left to Malaysia's 10 million voters to determine whether the surge in support for PAS's purist vision seen in 1999 would be carried further. International interest in the elections was intense, given the prominence of radical Islamic conservatism in the context of the 9/11 attacks, the War on Terror, and terrorist bombings in Bali and Madrid in previous years. In the event, the PAS engine ran dramatically out of steam. The state of Terengganu was swept from their grasp, with the party only retaining four of the 32 state parliamentary seats. Even in Kelantan, the UMNO-led coalition almost won, with a desperate PAS victory being declared by the barest of margins only after a recount.

Nationally, the governing coalition won 198 of the 219 seats. PAS only retained seven of the twenty-seven seats it held in the previous parliament. This was a sweet victory for both Abdullah Badawi as prime minister and for his coalition government, which had been so shaken after the 1999 results. It also brought considerable relief to Malaysia's non-Muslim minority. Furthermore, this result in Malaysia served to encourage Muslim governments elsewhere which faced conservative Islamist opponents who called for the creation of shari'ah states. The Badawi-led victory provided support for those Muslims who claimed that Islam need not be characterised by harsh penal codes and belligerent and gratuitous anti-western rhetoric.

Causes for optimism or concern?

At the time of writing, Prime Minister Badawi had been in post for two years. A range of features of this period suggests that the tensions experienced in the interfaith arena from 1999–2003 have somewhat reduced. The Badawi administration introduced a new national service programme in his first year in office. In 2004, 85,000 young Malay, Chinese and Indian citizens joined together in a three month training programme intended to lead to greater interethnic and interreligious harmony. Such ethnic intermixing also automatically meant interaction between faiths. This experimental programme was reinforced by the establishment in October 2004 of a National Unity Council designed to better unite the races.

There were also signs of increased public recognition of non-Muslim events. The World Council of Churches Faith and Order Commission met in Kuala Lumpur in August 2004, with sessions given a level of coverage in the government-run media 'that normally attends national elections or the latest developments in the *Malaysian Idol* competition'.[42] It would be difficult to conceive of such a situation in other Muslim majority countries such as Iran, Saudi Arabia, Pakistan and even Egypt.

Prime Minister Badawi gave a presentation at the meeting, praising the event as an example of necessary Christian–Muslim dialogue and taking the opportunity to express criticism of his PAS opponents in oblique terms:

> Many people practice their faith in absolutist terms . . . They refuse to take into account the modern world in which we live. They refuse to understand that so much of religious teaching is shaped by the context of the society in which it originated. For those who are rigid, dogmatic and absolutist, it does not matter whether you are in the tenth or 21st century, you must live according to the literal teachings of your religion.[43]

In the same month Badawi delivered an address at the General Assembly of the Islamic Da'wa Council of South East Asia. In this speech he called for new fatwas to guide Muslims in the modern world, again showing his commitment to promoting a twenty-first-century reformist vision of Islam.

Badawi's leadership style differs from that of Dr Mahathir in key respects. He does not adopt the hectoring, anti-western stance of Mahathir, preferring to speak in a more measured, less passionate and less belligerent manner. Overall he projects a more inclusive profile, which has provided some encouragement to religious minorities after the period from 1999–2003 when some minority members felt under siege. Badawi's more optimistic, open mood has been reflected in other voices as well. At the September 2004 UMNO General Assembly, UMNO Youth Chief Hishamuddin Hussein called for a review of the New Economic Policy (NEP), which had been originally designed in the early 1970s as an affirmative action instrument to address Malay economic disadvantage. Hussein argued that the NEP had achieved its main goals, and was now contributing to a 'widening gap in income, equity and property ownership and a digital divide among the races', with the non-Malays being the losers.[44] Such a statement from a prominent member of UMNO, based on minority rights advocacy, reflected the winds of change blowing through Malaysia's largest political party.

Indeed, the influence of Badawi's rhetoric was felt in the wider Muslim world as well. A meeting of Organisation of Islamic Conference (OIC) member states in Pakistan from 28–29 May 2005 embraced the ideals of the Islam Hadhari philosophy promoted by Prime Minister Badawi as the way forward for OIC members.[45]

Questions remain

Nevertheless, such a positive assessment of the first two years of the Badawi administration should be balanced by a consideration of some important questions which cause continuing disquiet among some sections of the religious minority communities.

The first relates to the Islam Hadhari vision of Prime Minister Badawi. On the one hand, this vision arouses opposition from conservative Muslims, who regard it as a sell-out. On the other hand, some among the religious minorities see it as a new front for increased Islamisation. Indeed, the ten principles of Islam Hadhari seem sufficiently vague as to allow diverse possibilities for interpretation and implementation. The principles are as follows:

1 faith and piety in Allah;
2 a just and trustworthy government;
3 a free and independent people;
4 a mastery of knowledge;
5 a balanced and comprehensive economic development;
6 a good quality of life;
7 protection of the rights of minority groups and women;
8 cultural and moral integrity;
9 safeguarding the environment; and
10 strong defences.[46]

Questions which Christians might ask are, for example, does the first principle allow Christians the right to once again use the term Allah in their worship and religious writing? More broadly, does the first principle assume an Islamic understanding of faith and piety, and how is it to be implemented? Furthermore, in relation to the seventh principle, the term 'protection of the rights of minorities' can be understood in various ways. Is it to mean 'protection' in the sense that *dhimmis* were protected under Islamic law, or will it allow religious minorities full and equal access to the instruments of power in the state of Malaysia?

Indeed, some developments since Badawi became prime minister seem to run counter to the spirit and letter of Islam Hadhari. For example, there have been cases of censorship by the Malaysian government of a type which seem to target religious minorities. So Muslims were barred from watching the film *The Passion of the Christ* (2004), which was so popular in the west. Very few theatres were permitted to show the film, and identity cards specifying religion were checked on entry.[47] Teresa Kok of the mainly Chinese Democratic Action Party posed the following question which cuts to the core of the Islam Hadhari principles:

> Isn't this regulation against the spirit of a multiracial society where mutual understanding of each other's belief and religion is most needed to promote unity among the people in the country?[48]

In a similar case of censorship appearing to target Christianity, even the animated movie *Prince of Egypt* was banned because it was seen as not sufficiently Islamic in its depiction of Moses.[49]

Bannings did not stop with films, however. As Christmas approached in 2004, there were media reports of a request within government to ban the mention of Jesus at the public Christmas celebration at Petaling Jaya on December 25. These celebrations were to be held in the presence of King Syed Sirajuddin and Prime Minister Abdullah Badawi. The proposed banning was reportedly designed 'to protect Muslim sensibilities'.[50] A public outcry from the Christian community resulted in this proposal being discarded, with hymns mentioning Jesus being included in celebrations.[51] But again the fact that such proposals are even floated must contribute to feelings of uncertainty among the Christian minority *vis-à-vis* the sincerity of the Islam Hadhari philosophy.

Book bannings also picked up pace during 2005.[52] Those books targeted include works by Muslims which aroused the ire of government. For example, copies of PAS leader Abdul Hadi Awang's *Hadharah Islamiyyah bukan Islam Hadhari* (*Islamic Civilization, Not Civilized Islam*) were confiscated by government officials in various locations because of its challenge to the concept of *Islam Hadhari*. Some of the books banned were by Christian authors, who were considered as producing works which were 'detrimental to public order'. These included Karen Armstrong's *A History of God*, a comparative study of monotheistic faiths, and *The Cross and the Crescent* by Phil Parshall, a prominent American missionary among Muslims.

In fact, the culture of banning in Malaysia is fed by both government and opposition parties. PAS leaders have been active in seeking to ban the popular *Malaysian Idol* pop singing contest, which is modelled on the British *Pop Idol* contest.[53] However, it should be noted that such action to defend moral virtues often targets Muslims and lets non-Muslims off lightly. For example, a raid by the federal territory's Islamic department on Zouks nightclub in Kuala Lumpur in early 2005 led to Muslims being transported to the local police station and detained overnight while non-Muslims were allowed to party on. Some of the Muslims involved faced prosecution for indecent behaviour, while others were required to receive counselling to learn 'true Islam'.[54] Such action is taken in the federal territory under the Shari'ah Criminal Offences (Federal Territories) Act of 1997. Section 19(1) of this Act prohibits alcoholic consumption by Muslims, while Section 29 states that 'Any person who, contrary to Islamic law, acts or behaves in an indecent manner in any public place shall be guilty of an offense'.[55] Muslims found guilty under Section 29 most commonly pay a fine of less than RM1000 (£143) after pleading guilty.[56]

The contrast between the spirit of openness to diverse religious expression contained within the Islam Hadhari principles and government attempts to proscribe certain religious activities extends to religious fringe groups as well. For example, the Sky Kingdom, a minor interfaith sect based in the state of Terengganu, claims to allow members to continue to belong to any faith, including Islam, and promotes a message of love and tolerance. The group was raided by police in July 2005, and twenty-one people were arrested, including some former Muslims.[57]

That particular incident impacts on the apostasy issue, which continues to arouse minority concerns. In a case which attracted much media attention since the Badawi administration took office, four converts to Christianity from Islam launched a legal challenge to have freedom to practise the faith of their choice. The case reached the federal court, which dismissed the appeal after taking nine months of deliberations. Mr Daud Mamat, sixty-two, Ms Kamariah Ali, fifty-one, her late husband Mohamad Ya and Mr Mad Yacob Ismail, sixty-two, had all renounced Islam in 1998, and initially served twenty months in jail for 'deviant practices inconsistent with Islamic teachings'. They were instructed to attend repentance classes but refused, which was deemed as contempt of the shari'ah court and led to another three years in prison in 2000.[58] The federal court decision represented the end of the legal road for them.

Minority concerns with such decisions have largely fallen on deaf ears among Muslim authorities. For example, respected academic Professor Shad Saleem Faruqi plays the 'Christian mission = colonialism' card to rationalise Malaysian government refusal to extend the same right to change faith to Muslims as is enjoyed by non-Muslims: 'Christianity's link with the merchants, missionaries and military of the colonial era is still fresh in many minds. The disproportionately strong support that Christian missionary activities receive from abroad also arouses fear and resentment'.[59]

Professor Faruqi explains the outcome of the Daud Mamat case in writing: 'A Muslim cannot escape the jurisdiction of the *shari'ah* court by a unilateral act of renunciation. The *shari'ah* court continues to have jurisdiction till the issue of status is determined at law . . . The issue of whether an individual is an apostate or not was one of Islamic law and not civil law'.[60]

Eloquent argumentation cannot hide the fact that in such a situation, individual Muslims are at the mercy of an unsympathetic system, and have the cards stacked against them. Time will tell whether the seeming openness of the Islam Hadhari principles can overcome such evident discrimination against Muslims who wish to change their faith.

In another somewhat different case which caused concern to Malaysian religious minorities, non-Muslim mother of two Shamala Sathyyaseelan took legal action against her estranged Muslim husband after he had the children converted to Islam without her consent.[61] She won the support of Malaysia's Catholic bishops in this case, which ultimately went as far as Malaysia's High Court. But in turn that body referred the matter to the shari'ah court for final resolution. This decision gave immediate advantage to the father, as under Islamic law a Muslim parent in a mixed-marriage has rights over the children in case of divorce. This case clearly highlights the problem of having a dual legal system.

Finally, the Islamic state debate continues to fester, and poses challenges for the Badawi administration as it tries to emerge from the tensions of the 1999–2003 period. In June 2004, Lim Kit Siang of the opposition Democratic Action Party took advantage of the new political climate to declare that Dr Mahathir's pronouncement in October 2001 that Malaysia was an Islamic state was incorrect. He asserted that Malaysia was in fact a democratic secular country. Rather than engaging with Kit Siang's comment, Malay leaders responded that he should not be making such comments. According to Deputy Prime Minister Datuk Seri Mohd Najob Run Razak: 'it is not proper to make it an issue just because Malaysia is an Islamic country'.[62] This issue of debate clearly has some considerable distance to run.

Conclusion

The Islamisation train is still clearly very much on track in Malaysia, though there are signs that the Badawi administration is seeking to keep it in check.

This train is no doubt fuelled by external events, such as 9/11 and the War on Terror, as well as the internal Malaysian circumstances discussed in previous pages. Muslim self-identity in Malaysia is clearly a priority for many Muslims, as indicated by Ahmad Nadzer Idris, a Malaysian businessman, who comments as follows on import-export issues: 'Since September 11, Muslims want Muslim products. They're diverting their center of reference back to their Muslim brothers'.[63]

Malaysian Christians have clearly felt considerable easing of pressure since the demise of PAS in the elections of 2004 and the onset of the Badawi administration with its more nuanced rhetoric. However, it will take some time for Prime Minister Badawi to overcome the damage to interfaith relations which resulted from the Islamisation struggle under his predecessor. In the words of Ng Kam Weng, 'Dr Mahathir created a Frankenstein in the form of the Islamisation process. It will take a strong man to control this Frankenstein'.[64]

The key question is whether Badawi is the man to control the Frankenstein of Islamisation? Lawrence Andrew, editor of the *Catholic Herald*, has his doubts, commenting that 'I think [Badawi] has forces around him who may curtail his openness'.[65] Only time will tell.

Notes

1 'Malaysia census shows minorities dwindling', *Straits Times Interactive* (8 November 2001).

2 For a discussion of Malaysia's Islamic history between 1957 and 1999, see Riddell, Peter G., 'Islamization and partial shari'a in Malaysia', in Marshall, Paul (ed.), *Radical Islam's Rules: The Worldwide Spread of Extreme Shari'a Law* (Lanham, New York & Oxford, Rowman & Littlefield, 2005), pp. 135–60.

3 Jayasankaran, S. 'Mahatir reaches out', *Far Eastern Economic Review* (1 February 2001).

4 *Harakah Daily* (23 June 2001), www.202.157.186.6/Jun/L23jun2001_3.shtml (accessed 30 April 2005).

5 'No mini-skirts please, we're Malaysian', *Reuters* (5 January 2004).

6 Osman, Salim, 'High stakes in Terengganu', *Straits Times Interactive* (11 March 2004).

7 'Malaysia to enforce ban on articles insulting Islam', *Reuters* (15 April 2002).

8 *The Star* (24 June 2001), www.thestar.com.my/news/story.asp?file=/2001/6/24/nation/2403umba&sec=nation (accessed 30 April 2005).

9 'Malaysia seeks views from Cairo on Islamic state', *MSNBC News/Reuters* (24 October 2001).

10 Martinez, Patricia, 'Is it always Islam versus civil society?', in Nathan, K. S. and Kamali, Mohammad Hashim (eds), *Islam in Southeast Asia: Political, Social and Strategic Challenges for the 21st Century* (Singapore, Institute of Southeast Asian Studies, 2005), p. 151.

11 For a discussion of Christian–Muslim relations in Malaysia prior to 1999, see Riddell, Peter G., 'Islamisation, civil society and religious minorities in Malaysia', in Nathan and Kamali (eds), *Islam in Southeast Asia*, pp. 168–72.

12 Ng Kam Weng in interview with the author, Kairos Research Centre, Petaling Jaya, 6 September 2002.

13 Brother Anthony Rogers in interview with the author, National Office for Human Development, Kuala Lumpur, 29 August 2002.

14 Kuppusamy, Baradan, 'Bible ban alarms Sarawak tribes', *South China Morning Post* (18 April 2003).

15 'Objections to image of Jesus', *Catholic Asian News* (March 2002), 5. In contrast, I saw anti-Christian polemical works by Ahmed Deedat on full display in many Kuala Lumpur bookshops around the same time.

16 D'Cruz, Percy, 'Moral education syllabus revamp', *Herald, the Catholic Weekly* (8 September 2002), 3.

17 Lim, Julie, 'Changing details in identity card not easy for converts', *Herald, the Catholic Weekly* (30 June 2002), 19.

18 'Malaysia: fourth church burnt in weeks', *The Barnabas Fund* (1 November 2001), www.barnabasfund.org/News/Archive/Malaysia/Malaysia-20011101.htm; 'Churches torched by Islamic extremists in Malaysia in reaction against war in Afghanistan', www.hrwf.net/html/malaysia2001.html#Churchestorchedby,

19 'Opposition party condemns attacks on churches', *Yahoo! Asia –News* (23 October 2001).

20 Quoted in Nam, Ng Kiok, 'Islam in Malaysia', in Rajashekar, J. P. and Wilson, H.S., *Islam in Asia: Perspectives for Christian–Muslim Encounter* (Geneva, Lutheran World Federation, 1992), p. 100.

21 Netto, Anil, 'Malaysia: PAS winning few hearts so far', *Asia Times Online* (6 March 2004).

22 Shastri, Herman, 'Our baptism is great sign of our unity in Christ', *Berita CC*, (Jan–Mar 2002), 11.

23 Fr Philip Thomas and Dr John Gurusamy in interview with the author, Syrian Orthodox Church, Kuala Lumpur, 30 August 2002.

24 Weng, 6 September 2002.

25 Brother Augustine Julian in interview with the author, Xavier Hall, Petaling Jaya, 30 August 2002.

26 Weng, 6 September 2002.

27 Rogers, 29 August 2002.

28 Weng, Ng Kam, 'Pluralist democracy of Islamic state', paper presented at Kairos Public Forum, Kairos Research Centre, Kuala Lumpur, 10 January 2002, 1–2.

29 'Editorial', *Catholic Asian News* (March 2002), 2.

30 Christian Federation of Malaysia press release (18 July 2002).

31 Press release, www.necf.org.my/html/press_release_27sept2001_f.htm (27 September 2001, accessed 20 May 2002).

32 'NECF Malaysia's pastoral response to the current world crisis', www.necf.org. my/html/WTCcrisis_f.htm (27 September 2001, accessed 20 May 2002).

33 Rogers, 29 August 2002.

34 Weng, 6 September 2002.

35 Fung (SJ), Jojo M., 'Dialogue of life at the margin', *Catholic Asian News* (August 2002), 15–16.

36 'Supplement', *Herald, the Catholic Weekly* (17 March 2002).

37 Isahak, Amir Farid, 'Guidelines for dialogue', *Catholic Asian News* (August 2002), 6–8.

38 'Abdullah's tactics confound opposition', *The Straits Times Interactive* (9 March 2004).

39 Tisdall, Simon, 'Malaysia's prosperity keeps Islamic fundamentalists at bay', *The Guardian* (7 June 2005).

40 'Abdullah's tactics'.

41 Prime Minister Badawi, in interview with Zia Sardar, *The Battle for Islam*, broadcast on BBC2 on 5 September 2005.

42 Heim, S. Mark, 'A different kind of Islamic state: Malaysian model', *The Christian Century*, 121: 20 (October 5, 2004), 30.

43 Heim, 'A different kind of Islamic state', 31.

44 'It's time to review Malay agenda: UMNO youth chief', *The Straits Times Interactive* (28 September 2004).

45 Macan-Markar, Marwaan, 'Islamic push for Malaysian moderation', *Asia Times Online* (7 June 2005).

46 Sulong, Wong, 'Islam Hadhari the way forward', *The Star* (6 May 2005), www.thestar.com.my/news/liStasp?file=/2005/5/6/nation/10876555&sec=nation (accessed 30 April 2005).

47 Goodenough, Patrick, 'Malaysia won't allow Muslims to see Gibson's "The Passion"', CNSNews.Com (28 July 2004).

48 Ibid.

49 Ibid.

50 Gatsiounis, Ioannis, 'Bid to ban Jesus', *Asia Times* (23 December 2004).

51 'Jesus back in Christmas carols', *AsiaNews.it* (24 December 2004).

52 Netto, Anil, 'Reading into Malaysia's book ban', *Asia Times Online* (6 May 2005).

53 'Malaysia's opposition party PAS wants 'Malaysian Idol' scrapped', *Radio Singapore International, Newsline* (23 July 2004).

54 Kuppusamy, Baradan, 'Islamic law' called "indecently" vague, *Asia Times Online* (10 February 2005).

55 Ibid.

56 Ibid.

57 Kent, Jonathan, 'Malaysia sect detainees test law', *BBC News* (24 August 2005).

58 'Four who renounced Islam lose appeal in top court', *Straits Times Interactive* (22 July 2004).

59 Faruqi, Shad Saleem, 'The Malaysian constitution, the Islamic state, and Hudud laws', in Nathan and Kamali, *Islam in Southeast Asia*, p. 260.

60 Faruqi, 'The Malaysian constitution', p. 263.

61 'Shades of Islamic state worry bishops in Malaysia', *ZENIT* ZE04090908 (9 September 2004).

62 'Not proper for Kit Siang to question Islamic country, Najob says', *Utusan Online* (11 June 11 2004).

63 Gatsiounis, Ioannis, 'Halal, Malaysia's next sacred cow', *Asia Times* (June 2004).

64 Weng, 6 September 2002.

65 Goodenough, 'Malaysia won't Allow Muslims to see Gibson's "The Passion"'.

9

Christian–Muslim relations in the Philippines: between conflict, reconciliation and dialogue

Rocco Viviano

Although blessed with natural riches and a climate which could constitute the basis for economic self-sufficiency, Mindanao, the southern region of the Philippines, is also wounded by an ongoing conflict, generally perceived as a religious conflict, which hinders development and keeps many Mindanaoans in a state of poverty and, above all, insecurity.

In the year 2003 the highest number of deaths in Mindanao was caused by war and its consequences.[1] As a response to the Davao bombings on 4 March and on 2 April 2003, which killed 38 people and injured 189, President Macapagal-Arroyo declared the city under a state of 'lawless violence' and ordered police and military intervention.[2] Despite the absence of direct evidence, the attacks were attributed to the Abu Sayyaf rebel group, and up to now the only indisputable truth is that these episodes belong within the same frame: the conflict between government and Moro rebel organisations.[3] More episodes of violence followed: fifteen civilians were killed and several others wounded in the MILF (Moro Islamic Liberation Front) attack on the town of Maigo, Lanao del Norte, on 24 April. On the following 4 May, it was the turn of Siocon, Zamboanga del Norte, where twenty-eight people lost their lives in a clash between rebels and the government military.[4] As a result the government–MILF peace talks scheduled for the 9–11 May in Malaysia were called off by the president.[5]

The ceasefire agreement of 18 July 2003 between the government and the MILF seemed promising for peace in Mindanao.[6] At present, peace talks are ongoing and no major incidents have occurred since. It would be naive, however, to think of the problem as solved.

The Mindanao conflict is just an example showing how important it is in our time that reflection on interreligious dialogue combines academic endeavour and the need for mutual understanding and reconciliation among people. Globalisation has changed the nature of the interaction between cultures and religions: communities and individuals struggle to negotiate between local and global identities, and an increase in local conflicts can be witnessed worldwide.[7] The Philippine conflict calls Christians to reflect on and engage in constructive interfaith relations amid an urgent need for reconciliation and peace. It is not sufficient to condemn those who are considered directly responsible for the violence: the MILF and Abu Sayyaf rebels are only symptoms of a deeper problem whose roots must be identified and addressed for an adequate and effective response.

This chapter considers how during the past four decades, the Catholic church in the Philippines has become increasingly aware of the complexity of the problem, and how it has approached interreligious engagement with the Muslim community. The historical roots of the conflict are examined for a better appreciation of the progress made with regard to the Catholic–Muslim encounter in the Philippines after Vatican II. Then some elements are highlighted which emerge from the ongoing dialogue and reveal the possible direction for the church in the Philippines to continue such engagement towards peace in the country, based on relationships of greater trust and friendship, within which it is possible to learn from one another's faith experience and commitment.

The roots of the conflict: the background to Christian–Muslim relations in the Philippines

The relationship between Christians and Muslims in contemporary Philippines is the result of historical, geographical, social and economic factors. A brief look at the encounter in past and recent history will provide an important basis to understand the present situation more clearly.

Christianity and the Catholic church in the Philippines
The Philippines is often described as 'the only Christian Country in Asia' because of its majority Christian population.[8] This is the result of the past four centuries of the country's history, particularly marked by the Spanish colonisation. The Catholic church arrived in the Philippines with the Spaniards and was formally established when the diocese of Manila was created, as suffragan to Mexico (6 February 1579). Its first bishop was the Spanish Franciscan Domingo Salazar. After sixteen years, the diocese of Manila was raised to archdiocese, and three new dioceses were created as suffragan to it (Nueva Caceres, Nueva Segovia and Cebú). In 1910 the diocese of Lingayen started, by separation of twenty-six parishes from Manila. Others began similarly: San Fernando (1948), Imus and Malolos (1961) and Antipolo (1983). More recently the diocese of Manila was divided again resulting in the creation of the dioceses of Novaliches and Parañaque (7 December 2002), Cubao, Kalookan and Pasig (28 June 2003).

The southern part of the archipelago, where the Muslim presence is mainly concentrated, remained under the jurisdiction of the bishop of Cebú until the diocese of Jaro was created in 1865. The church started developing in Mindanao-Sulu with the institution of the diocese of Zamboanga in 1910, comprising the island of Mindanao and the Sulu archipelago. The dioceses of Cagayan de Oro and Surigao were formed before the Second World War, while before the end of Vatican II a number of prelatures were constituted and Jolo was made first an Apostolic Prefecture (1953) and then a Vicariate (1958). More jurisdictions were instituted after the council, including the Marawi Prefecture (1974).

This brief overview shows that, although Christianity reached the southern Philippines around 1565, the Catholic church has been structuring itself up until recent times, particularly in the Mindanao-Sulu area where it is relatively young.[9] In the year 1991, the Catholic church in the Philippines celebrated its Second

Plenary Council, which represents an important development in the church's process of self-understanding, including with regard to interreligious relations.[10]

Islam in the Philippines

Muslims in the contemporary Philippines

According to the Catholic missionary Sebastiano D'Ambra, the Philippines constitute an exceptional case in the history of Islamic expansion, whereby in a particular country a large majority has become a small minority.[11] According to the year 2000 official census on religious preference Muslims make up only 5% of the entire population of the Philippine Republic (about 80 million), alongside 92.6% Christians (81% Catholics and 11.6% Protestants), 0.08% Buddhists, 1.7% followers of indigenous and other religions and 0.5% with no religious affiliation.[12] Some Muslim scholars, however, argue that 'census takers seriously undercounted the number of Muslims because of security concerns in Mindanao . . . preventing them from conducting accurate counts outside the urban areas'. Therefore some claim that the Filipino Muslim community amounts to 8–12% of the population.[13] The majority of Muslims (94%) are concentrated in the western and southern area of Mindanao, in the Sulu archipelago, and in the southern part of Palawan.[14] Muslims constitute the majority in five provinces: Maguindanao, Lanao del Sur, Basilan, Sulu and Tawi-Tawi,[15] but large communities can be found elsewhere in Mindanao and also in Metro-Manila (Luzon).[16] Thirteen ethnic groups generally associate themselves with the Muslim religion.[17] Among these groups, the Maranao, Maguindanao and Tausug make up 76% of the Muslim population; the Sama, Yakan, Sanguil and Badjao constitute 21%, while the residue six groupings constitute the remnant 3%.[18] Protestant missionary and scholar Peter Gowing observed, however, that '2.2 million Filipinos who embrace Islam are not a minority' if considered as part of the South East Asian region, which is the most densely Muslim-populated area of the world. Muslim Filipinos are aware of being part of this majority, having more in common with the Muslim Malays of Indonesia and Malaysia (in terms of religion, culture and of historical, political and economic relationships) than with the Christian Malay majority of the Philippines.[19]

Arrival of Islam in South East Asia and in the Philippines

The process of Islamisation of the Philippine archipelago cannot therefore be studied in isolation, but needs to be considered against the background of the spread of Islam across South East Asia.[20] Oscar Evangelista defines trade as the 'dynamic force' in 'the courtly centres and coastal principalities' of South East Asia at the time of the arrival of Islam. According to him it is possible to trace the presence of Arab traders in that region back to the fifth century. In the thirteenth century, however, the southern area of the Philippines (along with Central and East Java, Bali and the Moluccas) became an important centre for Arab Muslim trade.[21]

Islam came to South East Asia from the sub-Indian continent gradually, especially in areas strongly influenced by Hindu and Buddhist traditions. Evangelista identifies diverse factors to explain Islam's success in rooting itself in the region: firstly, it seems that Sufism favoured Islam's acceptance by local populations, on account of its capacity for integrating elements of other religious traditions, as well as with a more direct and emotional approach to spirituality. The second factor was political, as loyalty to the Islamic world constituted a possible political alternative to Hindu Majapahit and Buddhist Siam. Finally, at the time of European colonial expansion, acceptance of Islam was possibly a reaction against attempts to introduce Christianity into the region.[22]

A Muslim settlement in the Sulu Archipelago probably started at the end of the thirteenth century by foreign traders who intermarried with members of the local ruling families, and possibly assumed some political importance. The *tarsilas*[23] mention *Tuan Masha'ika* and *Tuan Maqbalu* as the important figures of this period. The possible arrival of Sufi missionaries (*makhdumin*) in the late fourteenth century also encouraged the local population's acceptance of Islam. A second Muslim wave came from Sumatra in the early fifteenth century. By the mid-fifteenth century the sultanate of *Sharif ul-Hashim* was established and Islam spread inland. By the early sixteenth century, thanks to increased contacts with Malaysia, Sulu became part of the wider *Dar al-Islam* in South East Asia. From Sulu, Islam moved to Mindanao, which became the springboard for further expansion in the Philippine archipelago. Towards the end of the sixteenth century, connection with Sulu and the Moluccas, especially through marriage alliances, contributed to deepen the process of Islamisation, also favoured by the reaction to Spanish attempts to extend their sovereignty and Christianity to Mindanao. Towards the end of the sixteenth century, Islam was beginning to impose its rule in the Manila area, but the arrival of the Spaniards interrupted the process. The expansion of Islam in the southern Philippines was relatively slow. Its adoption, however, by part of the local population influenced their sense of identity and cohesion.[24]

Muslim–Christian relations in the Philippines in history

First encounter: the Spanish period (1565–1898)
Centuries of interaction between Christians and Muslims in the Philippines have shaped the attitudes which characterise present day engagement.[25]

The first historical encounter between Muslims and Christians in the Philippines occurred with the arrival of the Spanish in the early sixteenth century. Although Ferdinand Magellan reached the archipelago in 1521, Spanish hegemony in the newly discovered territories started with Miguel Lopez Legazpi in 1565.[26] The aims of the Spanish expedition were threefold: to find a channel of communication with the Orient, then controlled by the Portuguese; to establish a platform for new commercial and missionary activities with China and Japan; and the Christianisation of local populations.[27]

According to Carmen Abubakar, the fact that the encounter between Filipino Islam and Christianity was mediated by Spanish Catholicism determined the 'tone and style' of the meeting. Still vivid in the minds of the Spanish *conquistadores* was the memory of the Moorish occupation of Spain ending with the Fall of Granada in 1492. When they realised that the newly discovered territories were inhabited by people who shared the same religion of their old Moorish enemy, they approached them feeling that they were involved in a new stage of 'the struggle fought between Christianity and Islam several hundred years before during the Crusades (eleventh to the thirteenth centuries) and during the *Reconquista* in Spain itself (twelfth to the fifteenth centuries)'.[28]

The confrontation between the Moros, as the Filipino Muslims were called by the *conquistadores* on account of their religious connection to the Moors, and the Spaniards, who were identified with Christianity, fostered distrust, which was soon extended to the Christianised Filipinos of the northern islands, as they were involved in fighting the Muslim Filipinos on behalf of the Spanish colonisers during the three-century long Moro Wars. This constituted the beginning of 'the alienation that came to characterise Muslim–Christian relations' in the Philippines.[29]

Resistance to the Spanish invasion was fierce: in fact while the Spaniards succeeded in driving the Muslims away from Luzon and Visayas, they never succeeded in controlling the Muslims of Mindanao and Sulu.[30]

The scars left by the Moro Wars are still visible today. To subjugate the Moros, forcing them into Catholicism, the Spanish pursued the destruction and depopulation of Muslim villages, destroyed their commercial maritime activities by capturing and burning their sea craft, and rendered their islands uninhabitable, by cutting and burning their coconut and fruit trees. Moreover, many Moros were deported to Luzon and forced to convert to Catholicism. The response of the Moros was equally fearful: warriors would attack and destroy the villages of locals who had become Christians, and sell hundreds of them on the slave market of the East Indies.

The Spanish Catholics viewed Islam as a false religion from which the Moros had to be delivered,[31] while the Muslims fought to preserve their religion, way of life, land, their freedom and independence.[32]

American rule and the Commonwealth (1898–1946)
With the Treaty of Paris (1898), Spain ceded the Philippines to the USA. The Americans initially adopted a policy of non-imposition, and seemed to be aware of the differences and deep-rooted hostility between the Christianised Filipinos of the north and the Muslims of the south.[33] After succeeding in breaking Muslim resistance through military intervention, they adopted a 'politics of attraction', 'designed to uplift the Muslims politically and economically' and integrate them into the Philippine nation.[34] A period of calm followed the treaty signed by General Bates and the Sultan of Sulu on 20 August 1899.

However, while government's efforts were aimed at bringing both communities to cooperation for their mutual benefit, American officials saw Mindanao as the 'land of promise'. Settlers from other islands, mainly Christians from Luzon and the Visayas, were introduced in what the Moros considered their ancestral land. They soon felt that this policy of migration was aimed at taking control of their area, and perceived 'integration' as the imposition of a Christian government and the destruction of their cultural and religious identity.

According to Majul, when the Commonwealth period was inaugurated in 1935, as a transition period towards Philippine independence, the Muslim Filipinos were 'handed over to Christian Filipinos to be governed'.[35] The transfer of settlers in Mindanao was accelerated, and towns with Christian majorities appeared in traditionally Muslim areas. Following the old Spanish and American pattern, Christian Filipino officials regarded the Moros as inferior and as 'wards to be educated in a superior culture'.[36] Similarly, the church looked at Mindanao-Sulu as an area for proselytising. In response, Muslims harboured the same feelings of distrust and hostility of the past.

Independence: the first stage (1946–1968)
Independence was granted on 4 July 1946 and the Republic of the Philippines was born. Despite previous requests on the part of the Muslim Filipinos for their territories either to remain under American rule or to be granted independence as a separate state, the southern islands were incorporated into the new Filipino jurisdiction.[37] Muslim Filipinos had long feared this as sanctioning the destruction of their own identity and culture. The sense of alienation already experienced under American rule deepened.[38] As they had done with previous foreign rulers, they also resisted the Filipino government.

During the first period of the Republic, the crucial issues were the question of the land (as part and parcel of the government's policy of integration) and the gradual development of the idea of Moro secession from the Republic (as a Muslim Filipino response to that policy).

In 1954, responding to Muslim insurgencies over the issue of the land, the government resolved to investigate the problem. The outcome was that Muslims did not identify themselves as Filipinos, nor feel part of the nation.[39] Unfortunately, the Commission for National Integration, created in 1957, failed because of the government's lack of support,[40] and also because of Moro fear that integration would bring about the dissolution of their identity and way of life.[41] They still wished to be part of the Muslim Malay-Indonesian world.

In 1955 about 200 Muslim Filipinos were granted scholarships for education at al-Azhar University in Cairo, as part of the programme sponsored by Egyptian President Nasser.[42] This generated a movement of intellectual Muslim Filipinos which favoured the crystallisation of the Moro identity, and enhanced the long nourished quest for self-determination and independence of the *bansa Moro*.[43] Although it was perceived as an isolated episode, it was significant that in 1961, Ombra Amilbangsa from Sulu presented a bill in congress asking for the creation of an independent Republic of Sulu. This was followed by the short-lived Hajal Ouh revolutionary movement for the independence of Sulu, Basilan and Zamboanga, ending with the death of its founder at the beginning of the insurrection.[44]

Christian–Muslim relations in the Philippines since 1968
After the March 1968 massacre, when several Muslim recruits were killed within the military base of Jabidah, *datu*[45] Matalam of Cotabato announced the birth of the Muslim Independence Movement (MIM), for the creation of the independent Republic of Mindanao and Sulu.[46] Conflict was now open; violent clashes followed, from mid-1970 through 1971, between the Christian armed group of the *Ilagas* and their Muslim counterparts, the *Blackshirts* and the *Barracudas*.

The climate of violence offered President Marcos the opportunity to declare martial law, in September 1972. Consequent action aimed at disarming Muslims provoked clashes with the army. Against this background the Moro National Liberation Front (MNLF), led by Nur Misuari, came into prominence. The MNLF considered the government insensitive to the Muslims and threatening their religion, culture and institutions, and saw political separation as the only solution.[47]

Soon the MNLF earned the support of the Council of Ministers of the Islamic Conference, which favoured their negotiations with the Filipino government. The process led to the Tripoli Agreement, in 1976, in which the two factions reached a compromise: the MNLF shifting its objective from secession to autonomy, and the government granting autonomy to the Muslim areas of the Republic. The shift in the MNLF objectives caused the less moderate fringes of the movement to form the Moro Islamic Liberation Front, officially announced in 1984 by Salamat Hashim, former collaborator of Misuari and leader of the new movement until his death on 13 July 2003. The MILF put emphasis on Islam and regarded itself as a religious movement, while considering the MNLF as secular.[48]

Unfortunately the Tripoli Agreement was only partially implemented: while the cease-fire was observed immediately, it soon became evident that the government had no intention of honouring the other commitments.[49] Marcos unilaterally announced the formation of the Autonomous Regions IX and XII, and called for a referendum regarding their structure.

To prove the sincerity of its intentions, the government implemented projects to benefit Muslim Filipinos.[50] Many Muslims, and particularly the MNLF, regarded the government's steps as palliatives seeking international publicity rather than the welfare of Muslim Filipinos.

In 1986, Marcos's removal from power created a 'breathing space' amid Christian–Muslim tensions. New President Aquino met Misuari, seeking a solution to the problems and the Jeddah Accord was signed in January 1987. Unfortunately this too yielded no meaningful result.[51] Following other attempts, the Congress held a plebiscite over the issue of autonomy: on 19 November 1989 only four provinces out of thirteen voted to be part of the Autonomous Region in Muslim Mindanao (ARMM). The National Unification Commission (NUC),[52] formed by President Ramos in June 1992, resumed negotiations with the MNLF, and in September 1996 the final accord on the implementation of the Tripoli Agreement was signed.[53]

The NUC also attempted negotiations with the MILF. Talks were held in August and September 1996. An initial accord was signed on 7 January 1997 to cease hostilities and carry out further negotiations. Despite the continuing hostilities between the MILF and the government military, peace talks continued and formal negotiations began on 25 October 1999. Hostilities persisted and violence escalated. On 17 March 2000 the military attacked MILF's main camp at Abubakar, as well as others, during the so-called 'all-out war' launched by the then President Joseph Estrada. In response, Salamat Hashim called for a jihad against the Philippine government.

Another protagonist on the scene of Christian–Muslim engagement in the Philippines is the Abu Sayyaf group. Reportedly, it started in 1991 and came into prominence in 1995 with a raid on the predominantly Christian town of Ipil, in Zamboanga del Sur. The group was founded by an Islamist, Abdurajak Janjalani, who had trained with radical groups in Egypt and studied in Libya, returning to the Philippines with an agenda for establishing an independent Muslim state.

Abu Sayyaf, which means 'bearer of the sword', believe that the only way to save Islam from succumbing to materialism is to eliminate any western influence; they also assert that co-existence with unbelievers is not an option for Muslims. The group, which allegedly is connected with the wider fundamentalist movement within Islam and with other terrorist groups, is involved in notorious kidnapping for ransom, and uses violence to achieve its goals. Abu Sayyaf opposes both MNLF and MILF. The fact that it functions in small autonomous units rather than as a whole, makes negotiations more difficult. Although Janjalani was killed in a confrontation with the police on 18 December 1998, the activities of the group have continued.[54]

Given the complexity of the situation, which is the inevitable consequence of how the relationship began and developed, talk about Christian–Muslim relations in present day Philippines cannot be limited to the religious sphere, but necessarily involves the socio-political dimension.

Responses to the conflict: Christian–Muslim encounters

Since the Second Vatican Council, the Catholic church in the Philippines has deepened its awareness of the presence of Islam and the importance of Christian–Muslim dialogue, and has responded to the conflict at a twofold level: that of the official teaching and that of the praxis. At the level of teaching, John Paul II has certainly given a significant contribution. Particularly significant are his message to the Muslim Filipinos delivered during his first pastoral visit in 1981,[55] and the addresses to the Philippine bishops.[56]

The teachings of the Catholic Bishops' Conference of the Philippines (CBCP) show a twofold gradual shift with regard to interreligious dialogue, Islam, the Muslim Filipino minority and their demands for self-determination.[57] The first shift is from equating 'Filipino' and 'Christian' to realising that the Filipino nation is a culturally and religiously pluralistic society. The second regards the notion of dialogue: shifting from the idea of 'negotiations aimed at ending conflicts' to the idea of 'engagement for building a culture of peace'. Significant contributions to a deeper awareness on the importance of dialogue come from the Second Plenary Council of the Philippines (1991) and the Catechism of the Catholic church in the Philippines (1997).[58]

At the experiential level the church has promoted numerous initiatives towards a solution to the violent conflict, which, since the 1970s, in the southern Philippines has claimed about 125,000 lives.[59] Religious congregations have played a very important role in promoting a spirit of mutual understanding between Christians and Muslims in Mindanao. Particularly significant has been the contribution of the Oblates of Mary Immaculate (in the dioceses of Cotabato and Jolo), especially through education towards peace and dialogue. Their *Notre Dame Schools* have provided quality education to Christians and Muslims alike in full respect of each person's faith, fostering mutual esteem and trust. The Claretians have played a similar role in the diocese of Isabela (Basilan).[60]

The work of Bishop Bienvenido Tudtud must be mentioned.[61] He was the first leader of the Prelature of St Mary in Marawi, which was created when Pope Paul VI expressed his desire that the church in Mindanao should engage in a specific 'ministry of reconciliation' between Christian and Muslims.[62] At the ecumenical level, the role of Peter Gowing, of the Dansalan Research Centre in Marawi, has been outstanding. One fruit of the ecumenical co-operation in Marawi is the Joint Catholic–Protestant Consultation on Christian Presence among Muslims that took place on 24–27 July 1978. The participants addressed a 'Communication' to both Christians and Muslims.[63] In the year 1990, the CBCP created a Commission for Interreligious Dialogue to promote interreligious engagement in the light of Vatican II and more recent documents of the church, to support and connect existing initiatives, and to keep contact with the Pontifical Council for Interreligious Dialogue. Among many initiatives and institutions for dialogue and peace, the Silsilah Dialogue Movement and the Bishops-'Ulama Conference have made a significant contribution to Christian–Muslim dialogue and to the peace-building process. Both started at a local level and have rapidly become important points of reference at the national level.

The Silsilah Movement

Beginning and aims
Rooted in the missionary experience of Sebastiano D'Ambra, a member of the PIME,[64] the Silsilah Dialogue Movement started on 9 May 1984, in Zamboanga City, to foster deeper understanding between Christians and Muslims. It seeks to bring people from both communities together to share the richness of their respective faiths and cooperate in the building of durable peace in Mindanao. The 'Silsilah Vision Statement' describes the spirit of the movement:

> In the name of God, the source and fountain of dialogue, Silsilah envisions a life-in-dialogue for all Muslims, Christians and peoples of other living faiths in respect, trust and love for one another and moving together towards a common experience of harmony, solidarity and peace.[65]

When Fr D'Ambra arrived in the Philippines in 1977, the Moro struggle in Mindanao was raging. The way Muslims and Christians approached one another because of deeply prejudiced mutual images profoundly touched Fr D'Ambra, who resolved to commit his life to the cause of reconciliation through dialogue between the two communities.[66]

After immersing himself in the local language, culture and problems, he shared the simple life of a small community of Muslims. The Silsilah Movement sprang from a 'spiritual experience' that D'Ambra describes in these words:

> God was talking through my new Muslim friends, saying to me in the deepest part of my spirit that: 'He, the Lord, is the fountain and source of dialogue ... That ... changed my life and gave me the courage to take a lot of risks, and later, to start the Silsilah Dialogue Movement.[67]

The Sufis employ the term Silsilah to describe their link of unity with Allah. The Silsilah Movement is founded on the conviction that it is possible for every person to rediscover the Silsilah that links them to God, whatever one's religious beliefs. This is possible because God initiates and sustains a dialogue with the entire humanity. God 'reveals' his love for humanity in different ways (i.e. faiths). His style of dialogue, however, is always the same, and the Silsilah Movement intends to be a response to God's dialogue.[68]

The Silsilah Movement is meant to be the 'common house and family' for people of all faiths,[69] where, in the spirit of Silsilah, all are encouraged to deepen their understanding of God's dialogue with them: Muslims are encouraged to re-appropriate the significance of the 'great jihad', the struggle for the purification of the heart, and Christians are encouraged to deepen their understanding of the Beatitudes.[70]

'Culture of dialogue' and 'life-in-dialogue'

The purpose of the Silsilah Movement is 'to promote a culture of dialogue', which implies 'life-in-dialogue with God, with oneself, with others and with creation', rooted in one's experience of faith.[71] A 'spirituality of dialogue' is required, on the one hand, to sustain a process of personal transformation according to the values of one's own faith; on the other hand, to encourage individuals to join hands in a process of social transformation, according to common ethics founded on shared religious values.[72]

Thus the culture of dialogue contributes to transforming conflicts into peaceful situations 'where all persons are respected in their human and spiritual aspirations as creatures of God and part of the same human family'.[73] The Silsilah Vision strongly emphasises the connection between dialogue and peace.

The promotion of the culture of dialogue is an answer to God's call for unity in diversity in the midst of today's pluralistic world. Its aim is to encourage people of different cultures and faiths to 'learn from the beauty and uniqueness of other cultures and religions, and see in them the signs of God's dialogue with humanity and . . . creation'.[74] In this sense the culture of dialogue constitutes the wider framework for interreligious engagement.

Life-in-dialogue is not only the visible expression of the 'culture of dialogue', but also the concrete means for promoting it. According to the Silsilah Vision, the first requirement for dialogue of life, with the 'religious other' in particular, is 'sincerity of heart' rooted in an act of faith. In fact, in the context of the southern Philippines, where the 'religious other' is often perceived as the enemy and a threat, it takes a leap of faith to believe that 'in the heart of each person there is always a "corner" of openness and kindness ready to start a sincere dialogue'.[75]

Secondly, life-in-dialogue signifies a serious commitment to solidarity, paying attention to the less privileged of society and giving voice to their aspirations for the respect of their dignity and rights. Those who commit themselves to this lifestyle of dialogue, become themselves 'living dialogues' providing mediations between sectors of society.[76]

Thirdly, life-in-dialogue means commitment to promoting the culture of dialogue through education and formation. The process of education starts in the family, trying to reach all the structures of society, to 'change the trend of egoism in the world, forming people who understand the importance to relate with brothers and sisters, members of the same family created by God'.[77]

Development and activities

The Silsilah Movement started as a 'small group of Muslim and Christian friends praying and reflecting together on their mission of dialogue'[78] and has developed through a wide range of activities and initiatives. The Silsilah Centre was opened in Zamboanga City in 1986. It hosted permanent exhibits on the culture of dialogue and peace, provided a venue for conferences, lectures and meetings, as well as a place for prayer and meditation for people of all faiths, Christians and Muslims in particular. The Centre also issues the *Silsilah Bulletin* and other publications,[79] and has developed programmes aimed at forming people of dialogue. The most important education program is the Silsilah Summer Course on Muslim–Christian Dialogue, offering intensive courses on Islam, Christianity and interreligious relations. It includes the opportunity for Christians to experience life with Muslim families and for Muslims to live with Christian families, as part of their experience of interreligious engagement.[80] Silsilah courses are also included in the programmes for the formation of candidates to the priesthood in the seminaries of Mindanao.[81]

Harmony Village, inaugurated outside Zamboanga City in 1990, includes the Oasis of Dialogue, which is a training and formation centre, and the Silsilah Institute (since 1999).[82] An Oasis of Prayer/Interfaith-Ashram was opened in Silang, Cavite, in 1997, providing a place for silence, meditation and prayer according to the 'spirituality of Silsilah'.[83] The Silsilah Movement also contributed to the constitution of the Movement of Muslim–Christian Dialogue, begun in 1992 in the Diliman Campus of the University of the Philippines, Manila, as a forum on Muslim–Christian dialogue.

A primary school was opened in a predominantly Muslim village, on the idea that the culture of dialogue in the community can be effectively promoted beginning with the youngest generations.[84]

The Silsilah prayer takes place every Saturday at 3pm, when Christians and Muslims gather to pray and share their faith experiences. Prayer starts with the recitation of the *Al-Fatiah* by a Muslim, Qur'anic and Biblical readings follow, and then the *Our Father* is recited by a Christian. Then the participants share their personal experiences of interreligious engagement in the light of their faiths.[85]

More recently, in December 2004, the movement formally expanded from Zamboanga to other towns and cities of Mindanao, as well as to the Philippine capital, through the Silsilah Forums. These are constituted by people, both Christians and Muslims, who commit themselves to work together to improve Christian–Muslim understanding and relations in their respective places, in the spirit of Silsilah. The forums have coordinators who meet regularly in Zamboanga for training and to coordinate their activities with the movement.

Silsilah spirituality also inspired the constitution of the Emmaus community, in 1987, composed of Catholic women who devote themselves to Muslim–Christian dialogue. They are committed to a shared life of prayer and work among the destitute Christians and Muslims of Santa Catalina, a very poor area of Zamboanga City,[86] focusing on the Eucharist as the source of dialogue and fostering friendly relationships among people of different creeds.

The Silsilah Movement has had its share of difficulties. From the beginning, Fr D'Ambra encountered opposition and mistrust from both Christians and Muslims, as well as from government authority.[87] The greatest test, however, was the killing of Fr Salvatore Carzedda, close friend and cooperator of Fr D'Ambra, on 20 May 1992. It is thought that he was murdered because of his commitment to Christian–Muslim dialogue.[88]

The Bishops-'Ulama Conference

Origins

Over the past ten years, the Bishops-'Ulama Forum (BUF, recently renamed Bishops-'Ulama Conference, BUC) has played an important role in cementing Muslim–Christian relations in the Philippines.[89] It is composed of the Catholic Bishops of Mindanao, the Muslim religious leaders of the 'Ulama League of the Philippines, and the bishops of the National Council of Churches of the Philippines (NCCP).

The formula 'In the service of peace and development in Mindanao',[90] which opens every BUC statement, illustrates that in the spirit of interreligious dialogue BUC members are constantly committed to peace and better Christian–Muslim understanding in the southern Philippines.

In 1992–93 the National Unification Commission[91] brought different religious leaders together to reflect on the ongoing conflict in Mindanao and identify its causes.[92] After the Abu Sayyaf attack on the town of Ipil in April 1995, the government of the Philippines sponsored a series of meetings in different cities of Mindanao resulting in a 'Mindanao Agenda for Peace and Development'.[93]

In this context five Catholic bishops and ten Muslim 'ulama met in July 1996 at the Ateneo de Manila University to consider the prospects of peace. This paved the way for the First Bishops-'Ulama Forum Dialogue, which took place in Cebú City on 26th November of that year.[94]

The BUC has since developed into a more structured organisation: in May 1997 (Third Dialogue) the bishops of the NCCP were invited to become part of the forum; a Tripartite Commission was created to monitor areas of concern and implement the decisions of the forum; a joint secretariat was also created to assist the commission.

Ethos and objectives

The Bishops-'Ulama Conference represents the response of religious leaders to the conflict in the southern Philippines. It started as a 'corrective' to the peace process, as both the Catholic bishops and Muslim leaders felt that the socio-economic and political effort for durable and constructive peace has to be grounded on the Philippine cultural and religious traditions. The BUC intends to provide this missing component, without which many peace efforts have proved ineffective.[95]

The starting point of dialogue is 'the spiritual bases for peace in their respective traditions, grounded in the belief in one God, a common origin, and a common destiny for all'.[96] Dialogue within the BUC takes place mainly at the level of common action, and aims at bringing commitment to interfaith relations, peace and development to the grassroots.

Activities and fruits

Since 1996, the BUC has been meeting regularly to work for interreligious dialogue and peace,[97] and has gradually taken a more definite identity and role in the Mindanao peace process through continuous attention to the events and receptivity to the most urgent challenges.

The BUC has promoted dialogue forums at a regional level, to address local issues.[98] A seminar-workshop was held in April 1998 to advance dialogue locally. It has also encouraged the creation of a network to coordinate the activities of such centres and of other organisations working for the same purpose.[99]

Together with its peace partners (which include Catholic Relief Services and UNICEF), the BUC conducts community-based workshops to promote a culture of peace, and cooperates with schools encouraging the introduction of peace education into their syllabuses. All of these activities aim at promoting mutual understanding among Christians, Muslims and *Lumads*.[100]

Prompted by the BUC, the First Mindanao Imam-Priests Conference took place in Davao City from 1 to 4 December 1998. Various imam-priest meetings have followed since throughout Mindanao, enabling local religious ministers to know one another and practice Christian–Muslim dialogue locally.[101] In February 1999, the BUC launched its newsletter, *Bitiara*, and in May of the same year the Mindanao Week of Peace celebration was approved, to promote the convergence of all peace initiatives in Mindanao. It was held from 25 November to 1 December of that year under the title, 'Healing the Past and Building the Future'. Since August 1999, the BUC has supported the 'Zones of Peace', an initiative taken by the people with the support of the church, NGOs, local officials and the Government Peace Commission, to create spaces where weapons are banned in order to protect peace.[102]

The BUC has significantly contributed to the peace process in Mindanao, especially as it has gradually gained a position of mediation between the Government and the MILF. Along this line, the BUC contributed to the important agreement of 18 July 2003 between the government and the MILF.[103] The BUC is of great significance for Christian–Muslim dialogue and reconciliation, as it offers the image of Christian and Muslim religious leaders working together in friendship. This gives them authority to denounce any actions against human rights and dignity.

The Catholic church and the Muslim community in the Philippines: an assessment of the encounter

Why is Christian–Muslim encounter necessary at all in the Philippines? What are the major hindrances to constructive engagement? How is the Catholic church responding to the challenge? And what are the elements, emerging from the experience of interreligious dialogue, which seem promising for future developments? An assessment of the ongoing engagement must take these questions into consideration.

Reasons for Christian–Muslim engagement in the Philippines

Since Vatican II the Catholic church has increasingly acknowledged interreligious dialogue as integral to its identity and mission. However, in the specific case of the Philippines, there are also specific reasons that make such engagement particularly urgent.

In the first place the Catholic church in the Philippines must be considered within the framework of Asian Christianity and Catholicity. This has immediate ecclesiological and missiological implications. In fact the Federation of Asian Bishops' Conferences (FABC) has strongly emphasised Asia's multicultural and multireligious heritage as essential to the self-understanding of the church in Asia and its specific mission.[104] Secondly, in the specific context of the Philippines, what makes interfaith encounter, and Christian–Muslim relations in particular, immediately urgent is the need for reconciliation and peace in response to ongoing violent conflict. This, however, needs some clarifications, as there are two possible risks. On the one hand there is the danger of reducing, at least *de facto*, interreligious dialogue merely to 'negotiations towards peaceful agreement' and to confine it to the sphere of social justice. This would not do justice to Catholic theological understanding of and teaching on interreligious dialogue as an integral dimension of the life of the church. The risk is that one aspect, namely the 'dialogue of common action', prevails over other forms of interfaith dialogue, particularly *theological engagement* and *religious experience*.[105] On the other hand, there is the risk of forgetting that 'higher' levels of interfaith engagement require certain preconditions in order to be reached. In the Philippine context a necessary precondition is a peaceful environment freed from fear of the *other*. This requires a slow and painstaking process of reconciliation, beginning from the grassroots. Work for peace and reconciliation is aimed at phasing out fear and mistrust to make space for respect, mutual esteem and reciprocal enrichment. In this sense commitment to reconciliation is an integral part of work for dialogue. This is what the Philippines needs and what the church in the Philippines needs to address now.

Obstacles to the encounter

Contrasting standpoints
It has been argued that the conflict in the southern Philippines is not a religious conflict.[106] However, while it is true that it is not possible to reduce the causes of the conflict to the religious differences between Christians and Muslims,[107] it is also true that an adequate approach to the problem cannot underestimate the religious element. An objective reading requires the complexity of the issue to be acknowledged and dealt with from a broader perspective that takes into account diverse factors.

The contemporary conflict in Mindanao is profoundly rooted in the history of Christian–Muslim encounter in the Philippine Archipelago during the past four and a half centuries. In his speech to the Muslim Filipinos in Davao, John Paul II also spoke about the influence of the past on the present status of Philippine society.[108] But in what sense does history condition the present?

The events of history have certainly nurtured mutual feelings of fear and mistrust, widening the gap between the two major faith communities of the Philippines. However, it must be stressed that the tension between Christianity and Islam pre-existed their historical encounter in the Philippines, and it is important to be aware that the roots of the clash are to be ultimately found in that original 'irreconcilable' difference.

When analysing the reasons for Christian–Muslim misunderstanding in the Philippines, Peter Gowing has used the expression 'of different minds', to illustrate the deeply contrasting 'visions' that underpin the attitudes of the two faith communities.[109] According to Gowing it is possible to discern the contrast at five different levels. In the first place, although recognising the inadequacy of shorthand, he characterises the Muslim–Christian contrast as the 'Age of Faith versus the Age of Politics', highlighting the difference between the Christian and the Muslim visions of politics and faith and, in particular, of the way these interact.

Secondly, Gowing suggests that the contrast regards Filipino identity, as Christians tend to emphasise a common Filipino character, while Muslims tend to emphasise difference.

The third contrast consists in special privileges versus human rights. Where the Muslims maintain that it is a question of human rights to have their own code of personal laws modelled on their belief, Christians regard it as a special privilege whereby certain Filipino citizens are exempted from the obligations of national law.

The fourth divergence concerns the notion of development. The divergence between Christian and Muslim perceptions of development in the Philippines has been a source of misunderstanding. Often, Christians have wondered why Muslims seemed to reject their offer of a better standard of life, while Muslims have seen it as a trap aimed at annihilating their identity through absorption into the Christian mainstream.[110]

This relates to the fifth point of misunderstanding, which involves the concept of integration. While from the Filipino Christian standpoint, integration does not exclude the right and freedom to practice one's own religion,[111] Muslims often perceive it as a fatal threat to their Islamic identity.[112] Gowing suggests that the use of different terminology (e.g. 'orchestration') might provide a way of conveying the notion of unity-in-diversity.[113]

Gowing's account gives an idea of how easily misunderstanding can occur if the two profoundly divergent standpoints come into contact without the corrective of mutual clarification. In particular, if left unattended, contrasting standpoints may favour the perpetuation of images of the other based on prejudice and fears rather than on mutual knowledge and trust. Often the Moro image still conditions Christian views of Muslims, while some Muslims still see Christians as invaders, land-grabbers and a threat to their Islamic identity.[114]

Internal struggles

Muslim–Christian encounter in the Philippines is also hindered by differing agendas: in general, the Christian community seeks integration, while the Muslims pursue self-determination. The respective aims determine different struggles within each community.

Since the 1970s the Catholic church in the Philippines has struggled to appropriate the new outlook inaugurated by Vatican II. During the past thirteen years efforts have been especially significant in the struggle to acknowledge the necessity of dialogue.

There is an ongoing struggle within the Catholic community to make space for the Muslim community.[115] There are opposing forces within the church which deserve serious attention as they manifest yet another struggle: the struggle to come to terms with the memory of past wounds received from elements of the Muslim community, the pain of which makes it difficult to forgive and forget.[116]

Muslims are struggling too. They share the same struggle to overcome the memory of past clashes and suffering at the hands of Christians. Some Muslims also share in the struggle for integration into the Philippine nations (for example, the compromise between the MNLF and the government in 1976 and, more recently, the agreement with the MILF). Some elements of the Muslim community are struggling against being integrated into the *bansa* Filipino. At various levels, Filipino Muslims see the Islamic community of South East Asia as their pivot and pole of attraction. In some cases the sense of belonging to *Dar al-Islam* is much stronger than Philippine identity, and this constitutes a significant obstacle to the encounter, particularly when it takes the shape of violent confrontation, as in the case of the Abu Sayyaf.

An ongoing dialogue

Culture of peace and dialogue

Following Vatican II, the Catholic church in the Philippines has made remarkable efforts towards Christian–Muslim encounter. There have been a large number of initiatives at various levels, of which the Silsilah Movement and the Bishops-'Ulama Forum are two significant examples.

In response to the conflict, efforts towards dialogue have taken a specific direction, whereby for the church in the Philippines to work for Christian–Muslim dialogue is closely related to a commitment to peace. On the whole, dialogue is promoted by encouraging a 'culture of peace and dialogue' and by giving priority to *dialogue of life* (e.g. the Silsilah Movement) and *common action* (e.g. the BUC).

The culture of peace is being promoted through education and cooperation on issues of social justice.[117] It seems, however, that two aspects are becoming increasingly important for the encounter: history and the basic ecclesial communities.

History revisited

Given the importance of the past for contemporary Christian–Muslim relations in the Philippines, interreligious engagement demands that the history of the encounter between the two faith communities (and the different worlds they represent) be approached from new perspectives.

On the one hand, for the sake of objectivity and completeness, it is necessary that history be rewritten taking into account not just the mainstream perspective of Christian Filipinos, but also the Moro point of view, as well as that of the *Lumads*.[118] On the other hand, it is also necessary to question interpretations of history which perpetuate commonplaces. For LaRousse, for example, the idea that 'the Spanish held a blind animosity for all Muslims', should be considered alongside cases of Spanish-Muslim cooperation. Similarly, the idea that before 1521 the Muslim community was unanimous against any external 'attempt at colonisation' and that all problems came with the Spanish needs to be reconsidered in the light of existing conflicts among different ethnic groups.[119]

An effort to liberate history from the burden of ideological interpretations can favour the recognition of the role of each ethnic group and community in the formation of the nation, and allow for better mutual appreciation. To some extent, such effort could also throw light on the history preceding the arrival of both Islam and Christianity, and thus help the Filipinos to retrieve common roots and identify elements of a common narrative in support of a Filipino national identity.[120]

A more objective reading of history, however, could at least partially favour the 'embracing of memories',[121] forgiveness of past mutually inflicted wounds and more trusting relationships. In this regard accounts of positive relations and experiences of dialogue and cooperation between Christians and Muslims should become part of Philippine history.[122] In this sense Bishop Tudtud insisted that the church should contribute to bringing about 'a series of happy events that will be remembered during the years to come in contradistinction to the ... unhappy events' of the past.[123]

Basic ecclesial communities and basic dialogue communities

The church in the Philippines insists that interreligious dialogue is a task of each local church. In particular, 'basic ecclesial communities' (BECs) can provide one effective way of promoting interreligious dialogue at the grassroots.

The encyclical *Redemptoris Missio* describes basic ecclesial communities as:

> Groups of Christians who, at the level of the family or in a similarly restricted setting, come together for prayer, Scripture reading, catechesis, and discussion on human and ecclesial problems with a view to a common commitment. [They] are a sign of vitality within the church, an instrument of formation and evangelisation, and a solid starting point for a new society based on a 'civilization of love'.[124]

BECs represent a place for shared responsibility and commitment, and a 'source of new ministries'.[125] Their model is the early Christian communities, gathered to listen to God's Word, to celebrate the Eucharist, and to share according to the needs of each member (see Acts 2: 42–7). The Second Plenary Council of the Philippines saw the BECs as a 'great hope for the Church in the Philippines', on account of their 'potential for evangelisation'.[126]

These communities constitute a space where interreligious dialogue can take place at the most basic level and make a difference to the life of the people. In 1999 the Archdiocese of Cotabato, Mindanao, launched a programme for interreligious dialogue, centred on BECs,[127] where particular emphasis is put on the sharing of experiences of life with Muslim neighbours. This experience seems to suggest that through the BECs the culture of peace and dialogue can be effectively promoted among Catholics and thus contribute to the process of reconciliation between Filipino Christians and Muslims.

According to LaRousse, BECs can potentially stimulate the formation of 'Basic Human Communities of Christians and Muslims', taking Christian–Muslim dialogue a step further. Towards the end of the 1980s the Silsilah Movement was considering the possibility of creating such 'Basic Dialogue Communities'[128] as a potential context for Christians and Muslims to rethink their relations, history and identities in the light of the encounter with the other.[129] Today, after twenty years the experiment seems to have given some fruits and could become a point of reference for similar attempts in Mindanao and in the Philippines as well as elsewhere.

Conclusion

The complexity of the situation of Christian–Muslim relations in Mindanao does not allow for easy answers and solutions to the ongoing conflict in the Philippines. The local Catholic church is aware that the response to the situation is ultimately a question of response to Islam, and indeed the church's struggle to make space for the Muslim community shows that the challenge is being taken quite seriously.

It is important, however, that two irreducible tensions be accepted as part and parcel of the church's specific mission in the Philippines. One is between dialogue and proclamation, and the other between Christianity and Islam. How is the church in the Philippines seeking to integrate interreligious dialogue with its particular mission? This precedes the question of Christian–Muslim relations. On the one hand the church's mission is universal in its very nature: firstly, it has the responsibility to be, among humanity, the 'sign and sacrament'[130] of the salvation offered by God through Christ (through witness and proclamation); secondly, to represent humanity's aspirations to God (through intercession). On the other hand, God's offer of salvation through the Paschal Mystery reaches all human beings through their consciences, cultures and religions, 'in ways known only to God'.[131]

The problem is how to maintain the cosmic dimension of the church's mission while allowing that religions may have a purpose in God's plan; how to integrate faithfulness to the missionary mandate ('go, proclaim, baptise'), while learning from other religions (i.e. how can 'Tradition' be enriched by 'traditions'?).

These theological questions take up a concrete character in any particular context like the Philippines, where the encounter between Christianity and Islam occurs in the encounter of people. How is this particular church trying to acknowledge the importance of the Muslim community for its life and mission, without diluting its missionary thrust?

Regarding the second tension, it is not enough for the church to do its best. Effective and constructive interreligious engagement requires a two-sided commitment: dialogue will function only with the clear will on both sides to make it work. The situation in the Philippines demands that not only the Christian but also the Muslim community take responsibility and take up the challenge posed by the very existence of the other. Both parties are expected to declare their commitment to a constructive relationship, whereby each community may be enriched by the other without losing its own identity. This requires the will to come together and 'negotiate the common space',[132] to grow together as integral parts of a single nation.

Perhaps it cannot yet be taken for granted that the national unity of the Philippine Republic is as important a concern from either side. Perhaps it is necessary to invite the Muslim community to say openly how high a priority this is for them. Fortunately, the BUC and Silsilah Movement – among many other initiatives – show that such bilateral commitment is possible, both at the level of leadership and at the grassroots.

For interfaith dialogue to be durable and effective it cannot be reduced to a mere strategy for conflict resolution; its theological urgency and validity must be acknowledged. Persevering in 'the twofold struggle' (dialogue-mission; Christianity-Islam), and trying to work more 'with' rather than 'for' Muslims, the Catholic church in the Philippines can function as leaven: it can be a stimulus for all Filipinos to seek authentic and constructive dialogue, aimed not just at reconciliation and peace, but also at mutual help to grow in their respective cultural and religious identities.

Notes

1 Arquilas, Carolyne O., 'War caused the most number of deaths; vigilantes too', *Mindanews Archive* (5 January 2004), www.mindanews.com/2004/01/04nws-passages.html (accessed 19 May 2006).

2 See Zamora, F. B., 'State of "lawless violence" declared in Davao', *Philippine Daily Inquirer* (2 April 2003). Canuday, Jowel F., Gallardo, Froilan and Parreno-Martinez, Anette, '15 killed, 44 injured in Davao seaport bombing', *Mindanews Archive* (3 April 2003), www.mindanews.com/2003/04/02nws-bomb.html (accessed 19 May 2006).

3 Since the time of Spanish colonisation, the term *moro* refers to Filipino Muslims.

4 See 'Twenty-two dead in attack on Zamboanga del Norte town', *Philippine Daily Inquirer* (4 May 2003). 'Government troops in massive hunt for MILF rebels', *Philippine Daily Inquirer* (5 May 2003).

5 See 'Malaysia hopes RP government, MILF resume peace talks', *Philippine Daily Inquirer* (6 May 2003).

6 'Church mediates a cease-fire in southern Philippines, *Zenit* (21 July 2003), www.zenit.org (accessed 21 July 2003); 'MILF chief to head peace talks with government', *Philippine Daily Inquirer* (19 July 2003).

7 Schreiter, Robert, 'Reconciliation. Looking towards mission in the 21st century', lecture delivered at the Missionary Institute of London, 21 March 2002.

8 Gowing, Peter G., 'The Muslim Filipino minority', *Crescent in the East* (Atlantic Highlands, NJ, Humanities Press, 1982), p. 211.

9 LaRousse, William, *A Local Church Living for Dialogue. Muslim–Christian Relations in Mindanao-Sulu (Philippines), 1965–2000* (Rome, Pontifical Gregorian University, 2001), p. 19.

10 See Secretariat of the Second Plenary Council of the Philippines & Catholic Bishops' Conference of the Philippines, *Acts and Decrees of the Second Plenary Council of the Philippines. 20 January–17 February 1991* (Manila, Catholic Bishops' Conference of the Philippines, 1992).

11 D'Ambra, Sebastiano, 'Christian–Muslim relations in the Philippines', *Islamochristiana*, 20 (1994), 180.

12 See US Department of State – Bureau of Democracy, Human Rights and Labour, Philippines. *International Religious Freedom Report 2003*, www.state.gov/g/drl/rls/irf/2003/24318.htm (accessed 8 August 2004).

13 Ibid.

14 LaRousse, *A Local Church Living for Dialogue*, pp. 12–13.

15 Gowing, 'The Muslim Filipino minority', p. 211.

16 See US Department of State – Bureau of Democracy, Human Rights and Labour, Philippines. *International Religious Freedom Report 2003*.

17 See D'Ambra, 'Christian–Muslim relations in the Philippines', p. 180.

18 LaRousse, *A Local Church Living for Dialogue*, pp. 15–16.

19 Ibid. See also Riddell, Peter, *Islam and the Malay-Indonesian World* (London, C. Hurst & Co., 2000).

20 Abubakar, Carmen, 'Islam in the Philippines – the Moro problem', in Engineer, Asghar Ali (ed.), *Islam in Asia* (Lahore, Vanguard Books, 1986), p. 41; Oscar Evangelista, 'Some aspects of the history of Islam in Southeast Asia', in Gowing, Peter G. (ed.), *Understanding Islam and Muslims in the Philippines* (Quezon City, New Day, 1988), p. 16. Nicelli, Paolo, *The First Islamisation of the Philippines* (Zamboanga City, Silsilah Publications, 2003), pp. 15–16.

21 Evangelista, 'Some aspects of the history of Islam in Southeast Asia', p. 17.

22 Ibid., pp. 18–21.

23 The word *tarsila* is the Philippine adaptation of the Arabic Silsilah, and among other meanings, designates a genealogical account to trace the chain (Silsilah) of succession back to a mythical or religious leader. See Madale, Nagasura T., 'The Hejra towards Muslim-Christian dialogue: problems and options', in Madale, Nagasura T., *Essays on Peace and Development in Southern Philippines* (Cagayan de Oro City, Capitol Institute for Research and Extension, 1999).

24 Majul, Cesar Adib, *Muslims in the Philippines* (Quezon City, University of the Philippines Press, 1999), p. 84; Abubakar, 'Islam in the Philippines', p. 44.

25 Majul, Cesar Adib, 'Muslims and Christians in the Philippines', Ellis, Kail C. (ed.), *The Vatican, Islam and the Middle East* (Syracuse, NY, Syracuse University Press, 1987), p. 310.

26 D'Ambra, 'Christian–Muslim relations in the Philippines', p. 182.

27 Gowing, Peter G., *Islands Under the Cross. The Story of the Church in the Philippines* (Manila, National Council of Churches in the Philippines, 1967), pp. 16–17.

28 Abubakar, 'Islam in the Philippines', p. 45.

29 Ibid., pp. 48–9.

30 See Diamond, Michael J. and Gowing, Peter G., *Islam and Muslims. Some Basic Information* (Quezon City, New Day, 1981), p. 77.

31 Majul, 'Muslims and Christians in the Philippines', pp. 312–13.

32 Yam, William L., 'Islam in the Philippines', in Pullapilly, Cyriac K. (ed.), *Islam in the Contemporary World* (Notre-Dame, Indiana, Cross Roads Books, 1980), pp. 360–1.

33 Majul, 'Muslims and Christians in the Philippines', p. 315.

34 Diamond and Gowing, *Islam and Muslims. Some Basic Information*, p. 78.

35 Majul, 'Muslims and Christians in the Philippines', p. 312.

36 Ibid., p. 317.

37 Ibid., p. 318.

38 Abubakar, 'Islam in the Philippines', p. 56.

39 LaRousse, *A Local Church Living for Dialogue*, p. 123.

40 Ibid., pp. 123–4.

41 Abubakar, 'Islam in the Philippines', p. 61.

42 LaRousse, A Local Church Living for Dialogue, p. 125.
43 In Filipino, the term *bansa* denotes the concept of nation and community.
44 LaRousse, A Local Church Living for Dialogue, p. 127.
45 *Datu is* the Muslim Filipino traditional community leader.
46 On the issue of Islamic separatism in the southern Philippines, see Gutierrez, Eric U., *Rebels, Warlords and Ulama, A Reader on Muslim Separatism and the War in Southern Philippines* (Quezon City, Institute for Popular Democracy, 2000).
47 Majul, 'Muslims and Christians in the Philippines', p. 321.
48 LaRousse, *A Local Church Living for Dialogue*, pp. 160–1
49 D'Ambra, 'Christian–Muslim relations in the Philippines', p. 188.
50 In October 1976 the Agency for the Development and Assistance of Muslims in the Philippines was created; in February 1977, a code was presented reflecting the *Shari'ah*, and the *Shari'ah* court was established; in April 1977, the Manila mosque was completed; in February 1978, the Philippine Pilgrimage Authority was launched; in July 1978, the Commission for Islamic Affairs was set up; in June 1980 an international conference was held in Manila on the 600th anniversary of Islam in the Philippines and the fourteenth century of Hijra. (See Gowing, Peter G., 'Christian–Muslim dialogue in the Philippines, 1976–1981', *South East Asia Journal of Theology*, 23: 1 (1982), 38–40).
51 D'Ambra, 'Christian–Muslim relations in the Philippines', p. 191.
52 The NUC was set up as an advisory body to the peace process, on the basis of consultations with various sectors of society. (See 'Profiles', Mindanao State University's Research and Development Centre, *Compromising on Autonomy: Mindanao in Transition*, Accord Series, 2nd Edition, August 2003 (also available at www.c-r.org/accord/min/accord6/index.shtml (accessed 20th May 2006)).
53 LaRousse, *A Local Church Living for Dialogue*, pp. 171–8.
54 For a detailed profile of the MNLF, MILF and Abu Sayyaf, and their activities, see Chalk, Peter, 'Militant Islamic extremism in the southern Philippines', Isaacson, Jason F. and Rubenstein, Colin Lewis (eds), *Islam in Asia: Changing Political Realities* (New Brunswick, NJ, Transaction Publishers, 2002), pp. 187–222. Chalk argues that by 'implementing a sustained program for socio-economic growth and development' the government of the Philippines could remove the civilian support-base to the MILF and Abu Sayyaf, thus removing their very *raison d'être* (ibid., p. 211–12).
55 John Paul II et al., '20 February: Davao Airport: meeting with the representatives of the Muslim community', *Bulletin Secretariatus Pro Non-Christianis*, 46 (1981), pp. 6–11. The Muslim leaders, Mohammad Ali Dimaporo (for the Maranao), Simeon A. Datumarong (for the Maguindanao) and Albert-Ulama Tugung (for the Tausug), expressed their gratitude for the pope's visit and highlighted its importance for the Muslim Filipinos.
56 John Paul II, 'To the bishops of the Philippines on their *Ad limina* visit', Rome 12 October 1985, Gioia, no. 478; John Paul II, 'To the bishops of the Philippines on their *Ad limina* visit', Rome 30 November 1990, Gioia, no. 696; See John Paul II, 'To the bishops of the Philippines on their *Ad limina* visit', 27 September 1996, *Bulletin Pro Dialogo*, 95 (1997), pp. 175–7; John Paul II, 'Address to the bishops of the Philippines on their *Ad limina* visit', Part 1, 25 September 2003; Part 2, 9 October 2003; Part 3, 30 October 2003, available at www.vatican.va/holy_father/john_paul_ii/speeches/2003 (accessed 22 August 2004).

57 CBCP, 'Reconciliation today' (27 November 1983), Catholic Bishops' Conference of the Philippines, *Pastoral Letters 1945–1995*, ed/ Quitorio, Pedro C. (Manila, Peimon Press, 1996), p. 574. See LaRousse, *A Local Church Living for Dialogue*, pp. 432–33. CBCP, 'An urgent appeal for peace in Mindanao' (6 July 2000), cbcponline.org (accessed 12 June 2003).
58 LaRousse, William, 'Is dialogue possible?', *Landas*, 16: 2 (2002), 274. For a detailed account of all initiatives, sponsored by both the government and other agencies, both at a national and local level, see Fitzgerald, Michael, 'Christian–Muslim dialogue in South-East Asia', *Islamochristiana*, 2 (1976), 171–85 (with regard to the period 1962–76) and Gowing, 'Christian–Muslim dialogue in the Philippines, 1976–1981', 37–48 (covering the years 1976–81).
59 LaRousse, *A Local Church Living for Dialogue*, pp. 446–50.
60 Ibid., pp. 450–2.
61 See Ziselsberger SVD, George, *The Vision of Dialogue of Bishop Bienvenido Tudtud* (Zamboanga City, Silsilah Publications, 1990); Prelature of St Mary in Marawi, *Dialogue of Life and Faith: Selected Writings of Bishop Bienvenido Tudtud* (Quezon City, Claretian Publications, 1988).
62 LaRousse, *A Local Church Living for Dialogue*, pp. 467–71.
63 Dansalan College and Prelature of Marawi, 'Joint Catholic-Protestant consultation on Christian presence among Muslim Filipinos: communication', *Occasional Bulletin of Missionary Research*, 3 (January 1979), 31–2.
64 The Pontificio Istituto per le Missioni Estere (Pontifical Institute for Foreign Missions) is a Society of Apostolic Life for the Mission, founded in Italy in 1850.
65 Silsilah Dialogue Movement, 'Silsilah vision. The spirituality of life-in-dialogue', www.silsilahdialogue.org (accessed 24 June 2003).
66 D'Ambra, Sebastiano, 'Silsilah growth. From a personal experience to the movement's experience', www.silsilahdialogue.org (accessed 24 June 2003).
67 Ibid.
68 Silsilah Dialogue Movement, 'Silsilah vision'.
69 D'Ambra, 'Silsilah growth'.
70 Silsilah Dialogue Movement, 'Silsilah vision'.
71 Silsilah Dialogue Movement, 'Culture of dialogue', www.silsilahdialogue.org (accessed 24 June 2003).
72 Ibid.
73 Ibid.
74 Ibid.
75 Ibid.
76 Ibid.
77 Ibid.
78 D'Ambra, 'Christian–Muslim relations in the Philippines', p. 203.
79 LaRousse, A Local Church Living for Dialogue, p. 501.
80 Ibid.
81 Ibid., pp. 503–4.
82 Ibid.
83 Ibid., p. 502.
84 Ibid.
85 Ibid.
86 D'Ambra, 'Christian–Muslim relations in the Philippines', p. 203.

87 D'Ambra, 'Silsilah growth'.

88 D'Ambra, 'Christian–Muslim relations in the Philippines', pp. 203–4. Silsilah Dialogue Movement, 'Padayon', www.silsilahdialogue.org (accessed 24 June 2003).

89 For a detailed description and analysis of the BUF, see Sebastiano D'Ambra, *Building a Culture of Dialogue: Bishops-Ulama Forum Experience*, doctoral dissertation, Notre Dame University, Cotabato City (October 2000); in particular pp. 90–141.

90 See Bishops-Ulama Forum, 'Statements', ibid., pp. 177–204.

91 Kalinaw Mindanaw, 'Primer on the Bishop-Ulama Forum', www.mindanao.com/kalinaw/buf/primer.htm (accessed 12 July 2003).

92 Ibid.

93 Ibid.

94 LaRousse, *A Local Church Living for Dialogue*, pp. 480 and 482.

95 Mindanaw, 'Primer on the Bishop-Ulama Forum'.

96 Ibid.

97 See LaRousse, *A Local Church Living for Dialogue*, pp. 482–7.

98 Mindanaw, 'Primer on the Bishop-Ulama Forum'.

99 LaRousse, *A Local Church Living for Dialogue*, p. 487.

100 Ibid., p. 487–8.

101 Ibid., p. 489–90.

102 Ibid., p. 508–9.

103 See 'Church mediates a cease-fire in southern Philippines', *Zenit* (21 July 2003), www.zenit.org/english/news.html (accessed 21 July 2003).

104 FABC, 'Evangelisation in modern Asia', Statement and Recommendations of the First Plenary Assembly, nos. 9–18. See also FABC, 'Prayer, the life of the church of Asia', Statement and Recommendations of the Second Plenary Assembly, nos. 30–6. John Paul II spoke of the special missionary vocation of the church in the Philippines as 'to bear witness to the Gospel in the heart of Asia' (John Paul II, 'Discourse to the Bishops of the Philippines on *Ad limina* Visit' *Bulletin Pro Dialogo*, 95(1997), pp. 175–6.

105 Pontifical Council for Interreligious Dialogue and Congregation for Evangelization of Peoples, *Dialogue and Proclamation*, Rome (19 May 1991), no. 42.

106 See D'Ambra, 'Christian–Muslim relations in the Philippines', p. 195.

107 See present study.

108 John Paul II, 'To the representatives of Muslims in the Philippines', Francesco Gioia, *Interreligious Dialogue. The Official Teaching of the Catholic Church (1963–1995)* 365 (Boston, Pauline Books and Media, 1997).

109 Gowing, Peter, G., 'Of different minds. Christian and Muslim ways of looking at their relations in the Philippines', *International Review of Mission*, 67 (1978), 74–85.

110 See ibid., pp. 75–7. Gowing argues that, because of mounting secularisation, 'Philippine Christian society . . . tends to see the world in secular-political terms', while in recent times Filipino Muslims 'have become even more self-consciously committed to ordering their lives around the teachings and practices of Islam'. This is not to say that the Christian way of life is detached from Christian faith and that only the Muslim way of life is profoundly religious; rather it is to say that there seems to be more self-consciousness about that link on the part of Filipino Muslims.

142

111 Gowing, 'Of different minds', p. 83.
112 'No law shall be made respecting an establishment of religion, or prohibiting the free exercise thereof. The free exercise and enjoyment of religious profession and worship, without discrimination or preference, shall forever be allowed. No religious test shall be required for the exercise of civil or political rights' (*Constitution of the Republic of the Philippines*, 1987, art. III, sec. 5).
113 Gowing, 'Of different minds', p. 84.
114 Jose' Ante, 'Christian–Muslim relations in the Philippines', *Encounter*, 214 (April 1995), p. 3; Gowing, Peter G., *Mosque and Moro. A Study of Muslims in the Philippines* (Manila, Philippine Federation of Christian Churches, 1964), p. 30.
115 See LaRousse, *A Local Church Living for Dialogue*, p. 526; D'Ambra, 'Silsilah growth'; also see D'Ambra, Sebastiano, *Life in Dialogue* (Zamboanga City, Silsilah Publications, 1991), pp. 76–7.
116 LaRousse, *A Local Church Living for Dialogue*, p. 527.
117 D'Ambra, Sebastiano, 'Towards a culture of dialogue in the Philippines. Muslim-Christian intercultural communication in Mindanao', *Journal of Dharma*, 24: 3 (1999), 290–8. Also see De Castro, 'Is dialogue possible? A response', *Landas*, 16: 2 (2000), 306–7.
118 LaRousse, 'Is dialogue possible?', pp. 287–8.
119 LaRousse, *A Local Church Living for Dialogue*, pp. 523–424.
120 Eric Casiño argues that an anthropological approach to difference could provide an important basis for unity between Christian and Muslim Filipinos. (Eric Casiño, 'The anthropology of Christianity and Islam in the Philippines: a bipolar approach to diversity', in Gowing, *Understanding Islam and Muslims in the Philippines*, pp. 36–45). On the same line, Paolo Nicelli argues that despite differences due to religious affiliations, there exist a 'Filipino identity', and 'it is possible to identify some common traits which are part of the character of the different people of the Philippines and this can help us to understand who really are the Filipinos'. (Paolo Nicelli, *The First Islamisation of the Philippines* (Zamboanga City, Silsilah Publications, 2003), pp. 26–34.)
121 Curaming, Lilian, 'Is dialogue possible? A response', *Landas*, 16: 2 (2002), 299–300.
122 LaRousse, *A Local Church Living for Dialogue*, p. 523.
123 Bienvenido Tudtud, *Dialogue of Life*, quoted LaRousse, *A Local Church Living for Dialogue*, p. 469.
124 John Paul II, Redemptoris Missio, Encyclical Letter on the permanent validity of the church's missionary mandate, Rome (7 December 1990), no. 51.
125 Ibid.
126 Secretariat of the Second Plenary Council of the Philippines and Catholic Bishops' Conference of the Philippines, *Acts and Decrees of the Second Plenary Council of the Philippines. 20 January–17 February 1991* (Manila, Catholic Bishops' Conference of the Philippines, 1992), nos. 137–40.
127 LaRousse, 'Is dialogue possible?', p. 286.
128 D'Ambra, *Life in Dialogue*, pp. 109–11.
129 LaRousse, 'Is dialogue possible?', pp. 286–7.
130 Second Vatican Council, *Lumen Gentium*, no. 1.
131 Second Vatican Council, *Gaudium et Spes*, no. 22.
132 See Barnes, Michael, *Theology and the Dialogue of Religions* (Cambridge, Cambridge University Press, 2002), pp. 230–54.

10

Islam and Christian–Muslim encounters in Australia

Anthony H. Johns

Australia is increasingly a plural society. It is gradually, if uneasily, learning to accept differences of pigmentation, dress, language and religion as part of the natural diversity of our world. Its population of 19 million includes almost half a million Muslims,[1] making Islam the largest religious denomination in Australia after Christianity. These Muslims are diverse ethnically, multilayered socially and educationally, widely dispersed geographically, so any generalisation is fraught with paradox. As Bilal Cleland remarks, nowhere are to be found Muslims from so many different parts of the world – in all from sixty-eight different ethnic and linguistic groups – as in Australia, except in Mecca at the festival of the Hajj.[2]

There is then nothing monolithic about the Muslim presence in Australia. Rather there is a variety of views and emphases in the life of these communities, and in the attitudes of individual faith leaders. This chapter attempts to examine not so much Islamic life and activities in Australia, as how Muslims respond to the challenges they face in a non-Muslim land, and Christians to them.

In levels of density, the distribution of Muslims ranges from sparse, the occasional individual or family, to areas in which they have a critical mass of significance, to political parties at local, state or even national level, even in areas where they do not enjoy majority status. The level of practice and individual commitment to religion and community among them is equally wide-ranging – from those who regard themselves simply as cultural Muslims, to those who practice their religion at various levels of faithfulness, to the very few who find in Islam an ideology of revolution. Yet it is difficult to conceive anywhere of a minority so statistically miniscule, with such a high national profile, which is perceived almost exclusively through the lens of international events in which for the most part they have no part, and over which they have no control.

There are variations in Muslims' relationships with each other, in the spiritual and ideological emphases of their leaders, in the relationship with the wider Australian community, which is itself increasingly variegated, their relations with their countries of origin, either through family members remaining in the 'old country', or through alignment or otherwise with the political policies of the old home, or response to government pressures from it.

There have been significant contacts between the territories of north and northwest Australia. Some Muslims, from the sixteenth century on, were fishermen from the southern Celebes, collecting *beche de mer*; others, rather later, were Muslim Malay pearl divers, after the discovery of pearls and pearl shell in the area of Broome in 1870. If these are not taken into account, a rough timeline of Muslim settlement in Australia can be established with four dates. The first is 1866, the year in which 124 camels and 34 Afghan herders arrived in the island continent. They had been brought to assist in transport across and exploration of the desert interior of the country. They came, not because they were Muslims, but because they could handle camels. Their arrival nevertheless marked a new stage in the entry of Islam into Australian history, even though there was little realisation at the time that they were the forerunners of what was to become a new faith community in a new nation. They came, largely on a short-term basis, to serve the economic needs of the separate colonies that constituted Australia at that time. Even so, culturally they left memorials of their presence and their religion. These included mosques, the oldest of which was built in 1889 near Adelaide and is still in use. Another, built in 1891, was at Broken Hill in New South Wales, and is now a museum maintained by the Broken Hill Historical Society. The remains of others can be seen on the old route to the north east between Adelaide and Brisbane. A few devotional books belonging to them still survive, containing collections of Arabic prayers and invocations, bound in rough leather to protect their pages from the dust and grit of the desert. In addition, in Alice Springs (central Australia), there are street names that attest their one-time presence: Mahomet Street and Khalick Street, and a school called the Charlie Sadadeen School. The trans-Australian railway is known as the Ghan – an abbreviation of Afghan, commemorating the transport system across arid central Australia managed by the Afghans in 1879. A living link with these Afghans survived until 1962, when one of them, who arrived in 1885, died at the age of 106.[3] And a descendant of one of the north Indian families who followed in their wake, Hanifa Deen, has given a vivid account of them in her book, *Caravanserai – Journey Among Australian Muslims*.[4]

There was little growth in the Muslim population for the next ninety years. The White Australia Policy introduced on Federation in 1901 largely excluded Asians and almost by definition Muslims, from entering Australia. Although there had been a slight relaxation in its application during the 1920s which allowed a number of family reunions for Indians who had followed the Afghans into Australia prior to Federation, the policy acted as an effective brake on the development of Muslim communities in Australia. Nevertheless, during the same period, groups of Albanian Muslims, being European in physiognomy, were able to enter the country. In the 1940s there was the migration on a small scale of Turkish-Cypriot Muslims, facilitated by the fact that they had British passports. Numbers, however, remained small, and went almost unnoticed until the second date in our time line, 1950.

This was the year in which Australia's engagement with the new nations to its north at a diplomatic level gradually began to make an impact on a wider public. This was due to the growing, although largely transitory, presence of individual Asians in the country, comprising diplomats, and increasing numbers of students coming to Australia and New Zealand under the Colombo Plan, many of whom were Muslims from Malaysia and Indonesia. As a result peoples hitherto unknown found their way into the Australian ken.

It was also during the 1950s that a number of Asians with professional qualifications were granted Certificates of Exemption from the dictation test to enter Australia to take up professional appointments. They included academics, among whom were Muslims, two of them appointed to university posts to teach the languages and cultures of Asia. This was a result of an initiative of the then Menzies government to extend the scope of the traditional parameter of the humanities in Australian universities, by making available in university curricula courses devoted to the languages and cultures of Australia's Asian neighbours. Thus middle-class Muslim intellectuals began to find a place in, and make their mark as significant members of, the Australian professional and educational elites.

A climax of these developments was the building of the Canberra mosque, an initiative of the embassies of Muslim countries. It was opened on 26 January 1960/27 Rajab 1379 H., the feast of the Mi'raj, by the then Indonesian Ambassador, A.Y. Helmi, to meet the religious needs and serve as a sign of the presence of a Muslim community in the national capital. By definition almost, it served a community of significant social standing in the Australian Capital Territory (ACT).

The third date on the time line is 1968. This was the year in which a migration agreement was signed with Turkey, the first such agreement to be signed with a non-European state. It was designed to bring Turkish working-class migrants to Australia. They were to come, it should be emphasised, not as in Germany as guest workers, but as migrants with prospective rights of citizenship. There were 186 in the first cohort to arrive. They landed at Sydney airport in November 1968, and were dispersed in automotive assembly lines, clothing and textile factories. Between 1968 and 1971, over 10,000 of them were to emigrate from Turkey. They came to meet Australia's labour needs in an expanding economy. That they were Muslims was fortuitous. There was little realisation at the time that their arrival was to extend the faith community first brought to Australia by the Afghans, a hundred years earlier. However, there was a group of descendants of that small, older community of Muslims at the airport to give them a ceremonial welcome as brothers, seeing in their arrival a link with the arrival of the Afghan Muslims a century before.

There was a double edged symbolism in this arrival. It was poignantly significant to the descendants of the Afghans. Yet it also resonated with Australian memories of the ANZAC defeat by the Turks at Gallipoli in 1915, in the light of which their welcome as new Australians had an almost poetic irony.

There is a further irony implicit in their arrival. Just as it was an Australian need that brought the Afghans to Australia a hundred years earlier, it was likewise an Australian need for labour, after the traditional sources of migrants in western Europe had dried up, that brought Turks to Australian factory floors. And this circumstance left them vulnerable to unemployment in the periods of economic recession that were to come. It meant that now there were two levels of Muslim presence in Australia. A small but educated elite that could meet with older Australians on equal terms, and command respect at a professional level, and a much larger and growing working class which faced problems of a different nature.

The fourth timeline is the formal abolition of the White Australia Policy in 1972. This opened the way for many diverse peoples, Muslims among them, to make their home in Australia. It reflects a radical shift in Australia's immigration policies and, as a result, the beginning of a change in its self-perception as a monocultural to a pluralist, multicultural society. The significance of this for the extension of the Muslim population is reflected in census statistics. In 1947 there were no Muslims included in the Australian population. Their presence is first recorded in 1971, when they constituted 0.2% of the population. In 1986 they were 0.5%, in 1991 0.9%, in 1996 1.1% and in 2001 1.5%. The individuals these statistics represent are not evenly distributed: 50% of Australia's Muslims are in Sydney, 32% in Melbourne. The remainder are distributed between Perth, Brisbane, Adelaide, Canberra and Hobart. Only 4.3% are outside these major centres of population.

The majority of these Muslims are Lebanese and Turks. The remainder come from a variety of ethnic backgrounds, their distribution often *pari passu* with the outbreak of conflicts and instability in various parts of the world: the Arab-Israeli war of 1967 and the continuing Palestinian tragedy, the war in Cyprus in 1974, the secession of East Pakistan from Pakistan to become Bangladesh in 1975, and the outbreak of civil war in Lebanon in 1975 (by 1981 Australia had received about 16,500 Lebanese-born Muslims, who today form the largest group within the Australian Muslim community), the Russian invasion of Afghanistan in 1976, the Islamic revolution in Iran in 1979, and the continuing sequence of breakdowns of order in the Balkans (between 1991 and 1995 Australia accepted 14,000 Bosnian refugees).

More recent waves of migrants include refugees from Somalia, Afghanistan and, between 1997 and 2001, numbers of Muslim boat people from the Middle East reached Australia, some of them highly qualified professionals. Hundreds are currently detained waiting for a decision on their refugee status. In short, there is a constant engagement between world events and the movement of peoples to Australia.

All migrants to a country with a largely unrelated culture face problems of adjustment and adaptation. Some are common to all 'third-world' migrants: the trauma of leaving home, family, language, social structure, familiar climate and religious environment, the culture shock encountered on arriving in a new country, with a language few of them know. For Muslims in particular, the great cycle of annual celebrations that mark the progress of the Muslim year were virtually unknown in their new country. They moved from an environment in which their religion carried authority, was part of the air they breathed, and was a given in every day discourse, and family and interpersonal relationships, to one in which it had no status. There, if misfortune struck, if a death occurred, everyone around them knew what was required, and how to respond. In the new environment, even to find a place to perform the ablutions and to pray at work was difficult (especially for women). They were 'ethnics' and their cultural values went unrecognised.

The sexual freedom they observed in Australia confirmed for many their fears of the moral danger in the new environment, and heightened the sense of a need for security behind the defensive walls of their own ethno-religious community.

Participation in social life outside these walls was difficult. A rigorous interpretation of the Qur'anic prohibition of alcohol forbade even attendance at functions at which alcohol was served; this combined with concerns as to whether food served was *halal* limited the possibility of social mixing with workmates on the factory floor, or 'drinking together' in 'the local'. Thus participation in social occasions such as the celebration of a football victory and even the celebration of Christmas and Easter as secular holidays to be shared with other Australians was closed to them.

These circumstances led to a reliance on ethnic identity to provide a comfort zone. It is part of the nature of Islamic societies that religious commitment is expressed through strong regional and cultural forms which result from a fusion between the universal forms and doctrines of Islam and local beliefs and lifestyles. It cannot be over-emphasised that ethnic identity is an important element in the self-perception of Muslims in Australia, communities tending to perceive and identify themselves as much by language and ethnic origin as by the profession of Islam.

Within these ethnic sub-divisions too, however, Islam had the means to transform groups of individuals into communities. They include the discipline of the daily ritual prayers, the Fast of Ramadan and the family and community celebrations of the festival marking its conclusion, and equally the celebration of the festival of the Hajj, with its strong universalistic dimension. All have a strong centripetal function, providing instruments by which they could either govern themselves, or establish a definable place for themselves within a non-Muslim state. To these may be added family and ethnic, *madhhab* and sometimes *tariqa* (Sufi Brotherhood) networks. (There are Sufis among Australian Muslims, and an Australian Centre for Sufism was established in Sydney in 1999.) All these factors, imbued with the spirituality of the Qur'an and Hadith, and the authority of the law under the guidance of the ulama, combined to create the motivation to establish centres of learning and worship, schools and mosques. All served to define and sustain a sense of corporate identity. Once these existed, however sparse the external supports available, a familiar environment was assured for later arrivals who otherwise would have found no language community, no relatives, no friends, and scant facilities for the expression and practice of their faith and its transmission to a new generation.

A small group of Muslims meeting in a single room for prayers and Qur'an classes easily became a nucleus from which a mosque could grow. And a mosque once established serves as a centre for worship, and the expression, interpretation, inculcation and celebration of Muslim belief and practice, and serves as a community reference point, providing a means for self-identification in the new homeland.

Gary Bouma in *Mosques and Muslim Settlement in Australia* tells of fifty-seven mosques in Australia. Two already referred to – one near Adelaide and the other in Broken Hill – are over a hundred years old. The Canberra mosque, also already mentioned, was opened in January 1960. The first mosque in Sydney was built in the late 1960s, and in Sydney and New South Wales today there are upwards of twenty mosques, the majority of them built since 1968. Of these, the largest and for some the most beautiful, is the Imam Ali mosque at Lakemba. Another major mosque is the King Faisal mosque, built by the Islamic Society of New South Wales, and yet another the imposing Gallipoli mosque at the suburb of Auburn, founded by the Turkish Islamic Society, and inaugurated in 1999.

In Melbourne there are more than twenty-five mosques. The largest, in the suburb of Preston, like a number of others includes an administrative section, class-rooms, library and catering area. There are mosques in all the other capital cities each with its own story to tell, and others continue to be built. These mosques are largely the result of the initiative of local ethnic communities, in some cases supported by governments or NGOs of their respective homelands, in others by the Kingdom of Saudi Arabia, anxious to extend its own Hanbali school of Islamic praxis. It extended to the provision of imams, and of education facilities for Muslim children. Fortuitously, that is to say during the 1970s and early 1980s, this coincided with the explosion of oil prices, and so-called petro-dollars for charitable projects from the Arab countries were plentiful, and the various Muslim communities took full advantage of these opportunities.

Much of Islamic religious education is carried out at an informal level, at home or in the mosque. There are, however, continuing efforts to establish Islamic schools in the mainstream education systems of the states in which they are located, along with Arabic and Islamic Religious Instruction, thereby providing a secular education within an Islamic environment. Thanks to Australian government (Commonwealth and state) support for community-based schooling first won for the Catholic school system in the 1960s, in the 1980s Muslims were able to begin the establishment of primary and secondary schools.

There are now a number of Islamic schools teaching the final two years of secondary education, some of them including languages such as Turkish in their curricula, and well-established ones such as the King Khalid Islamic College in Melbourne, the Malik Fahd Islamic School in Sydney, and the Islamic College of Perth, provide a high quality education measured by the level of university entrance achieved – a striking example of upward social mobility in the second generation of Muslim migrants. Today there are twenty-three Islamic schools, with a student population of around 10,000 (see Appendix at chapter end).

There are also a variety of institutions designed to train Muslims in their religion, and educate the general public, such as the Foundation of Islamic Studies and Information at Arncliffe in Sydney. In addition to these, there is a cornucopia of Islamic associations that have mushroomed in all the states and territories of Australia, to meet concerns of various kinds. Some appeal primarily to a specific ethnic group, of say Turks or Egyptians, others to a wider constituency.

There are those which among their other activities organise travel groups to Mecca to perform the 'Umra or the Hajj pilgrimage. The itinerary for these journeys may include as a side trip a visit to the Aqsa mosque on the Temple Mount in Jerusalem. There are yet others that concern themselves with the moon-sighting necessary to establish the beginning and end of the fasting month,[5] and others concerned to ensure that *halal* food is readily available. An example of the success of this concern is to be seen in Brunswick, an inner-city, working-class suburb of Melbourne with Turkish clubs, restaurants, coffee houses and bakeries, all *halal*.[6] They also discuss issues of dress, and questions such as whether it is obligatory for women to wear a head-scarf. There are friendship organisations, such as is the El Sadeaq (*sic*) Society based in Melbourne. This has a community centre and small mosque for its mainly Egyptian members. It functions as a surrogate family, embracing Egyptians of all ages, and is dedicated to serving their religious, educational, recreational and social needs, which neither state nor society provide. There are others such as an Arabic Speaking Welfare Workers Association, the Federation of Islamic Youth, and yet others dedicated to social welfare, community support and matters of community concern throughout the various Muslim communities. Among them is the Canberra Islamic Centre founded in December 1993. There are a number of convert support groups.

In addition, there are a number of women's organisations, such as the Arab Women's Solidarity Foundation, and various Women's Friendship and Support Groups, which organise courses and lectures to assist women in problems they face living in Australia. Among these, of special importance is Muslim Women's National Network of Australia, which publishes a newsletter distributed to sixteen women's organisations in New South Wales, and six in the other states and territories. These organisations have memberships ranging from 20 to 300.[7]

The organisations in the various states are represented at state councils, and the state councils at the federal level have been represented since the 1970s by the Australian Federation of Islamic Councils (AFIC), an umbrella organisation for all Australian Muslim organisations that wished to have formal association with it. The Federation has been funded by support from the local communities, from oil-rich Muslim countries, by revenue generated through the issuing of *halal* certificates indicating that animals had been slaughtered for consumption as food according to the correct rituals, and as its capital resources increased, from its own investments. Utilising these funds, AFIC has been able to provide funds to support the varied activities of the Muslim community, both at local and national levels, and make contributions towards the building of new mosques, providing prayer facilities, the appointment of imams, and arranging educational facilities for Muslim children. It has weathered the storm caused in the late 1980s by the temporary decline in world oil prices and the subsequent reduction in petrol dollars available for the propagation of Islam worldwide, thanks to the buffer provided by the generous support in the previous decade, in particular from the kingdom of Saudi Arabia.

Some of these organisations, such as the moon-sighting committee, are single issue, others are wider ranging in their ambit, and have broader concerns. They differ widely in character, some are conservative and exclusivist, others open and inclusive. Taken together, they represent a cross-section of cultural, social, political, community and intellectual concerns, in part the response of Muslims of different ethnic backgrounds to their now minority status, and in part the response to a perception of the challenges of a rapidly changing world.

The imam of the Canberra mosque,[8] for example, offers a leadership that could be regarded as conservative and exclusivist. Because of a large transitory component, he is not able to generalise about the ethnic mix. He sees this exclusiveness as a safeguard to the integrity of the community. The observance of dietary rules should not be limited to abstinence from pork or pork products.

His regards it as improper that Muslims participate in functions where alcohol is served, even if they themselves do not drink. Likewise it is inappropriate for Muslims to enter a church building, even as guests at a wedding or mourners at a funeral. Whenever possible, Muslims should provide their own community services, and not accept those provided by a secular government. He does not take part in interfaith dialogue. He will, however, speak to leaders of other faith communities if requested to give information about Islam and is always ready to welcome groups coming to the mosque to learn about Islam. He is also always ready to visit local hospitals to tend to the spiritual needs of Muslim patients.

Notwithstanding this exclusivism, there is a warmth and kindness and genuine human concern in his manner, and the mosque and its environs have a cordial, welcoming atmosphere. Clearly, he is motivated by a concern that the community needs support and protection in a markedly secular environment.

The Muslim community in Canberra according to the 2001 census is now 3,487, or 1.2% of the population, far larger than when the mosque was designed and built in 1960, thus there are inevitably other options for the realisation of Islamic ritual, and it is self-evident that his reading of Islam is not universally accepted. Particular ethnic communities that have a critical mass make their own arrangements. The Indonesian community, for example, has its own religious programme: for Friday prayers, for *tarawih* devotions during the Fasting Month and for the public prayers on the occasion of the two festivals. There is an Indonesian community Religious Study Circle which meets monthly for a meal followed by the night prayer and a lecture, sometimes with guest speakers coming from Indonesia. There are other organisations and independent centres in Canberra for a realisation of Islamic ritual. This pluralism within the Islamic communities cannot be over-emphasised.

A different style of leadership is presented by the Gallipoli mosque in Auburn, a suburb of Sydney.[9] It serves a large and vigorous, mainly Turkish community, the congregation at the Friday Juma' prayer being over 2000. It is associated with the New South Wales Turkish Islamic Centre, an organisation that is outward looking, and aims to play a community role on equal terms with other strategic groupings in the wider Australian community. Its leadership represents the second generation of Turkish residents in Australia, fluent in English, and as Mr Osalp, one of its directors, puts it, they are concerned to look outwards and share in the non-Turkish and non-Islamic life around them.

The antecedents of the Gallipoli mosque go back to 1977, when Turkish migrants established the Qur'an Course of the Auburn Islamic Cultural Centre, as the seed out of which the mosque grew. The mosque itself was inaugurated on 28 November 1999. The occasion was one rich in symbolism as an indication of the acceptance both of the Turkish community in their new home, and the establishment of Islam as a religion in and of Australia. The name chosen for it, the Gallipoli mosque, has a special resonance in Australia. It is a name that has had a key role in the development of an Australian national consciousness and sense of identity, evoking the memory of the military encounter between Australians and Turks in 1915. Historically, this encounter took place in the geopolitical context of the First World War. But it has wider resonances. At one level the conflict was political, between Britain, France and their allies, and Germany.

At another it was interracial, between Anglo-Celts and the Turkic peoples of Central Asia. But at yet another, though not often construed in these terms, it was between Australian soldiers by and large Christians, and Turkish soldiers defending their homeland, by and large Muslims.

The symbolism was clearly present in the ceremony itself: in the performance of the Turkish and Australian national anthems, in the recitation of verses from the Qur'an, followed by a rendering in English, and in the mix of guests and speakers representing senior members of the Turkish local and diplomatic communities, and of the state of New South Wales and the Australian Commonwealth government. But a climactic moment was marked by the speech of the state president of the New South Wales branch of the Returned Services League, in which he gave a generous welcome to this non-Anglo-Celtic community to Australia, and to the building of a centre for worship by members of the faith community of Islam declaring Australia its home.

It holds open days to introduce the general community to the mosque and to Muslims, and circulates a newsletter. Mr Osalp and the centre regard interreligious contacts as important for all communities, and regularly visits and talks with the clergy of Christian denominations. Within the last three years they took the initiative to found the Affinity Intercultural Foundation precisely for the purpose of such dialogue, inspired by the writings and thought Fethullah Gulen, one of the first in Turkey to take interfaith dialogue seriously, who met the Orthodox Patriarch Bartholomeus, and had an audience with Pope John Paul II.[10]

The Canberra Islamic Centre has already been mentioned. It is distinctive in its organisation, goals and achievements, and one to which Australian converts have made an important contribution. It thus offers a significant model for the indigenisation of Islam in Australia.[11] The membership is currently around 1,200, of whom about fifty are actively associated with various sub-committees. According to the 2001 *Census of Population and Housing* the Muslim population of Canberra is 3,487, although this may be an underestimate. In any case the proportion of membership the centre has achieved is impressive.

It was established to provide a venue for social and cultural activities appropriate to an Islamic lifestyle, and to liaise on behalf of Muslims with the Australian government and Muslim community. It is not a mosque, although it has ample prayer facilities, and does not compete with the Canberra mosque. The ACT (Australian Capital Territory) government recognised it as a community organisation and granted it a prime site of land of 16,000 sq. metres on which an exquisitely designed complex of buildings has been erected. It was formally opened in 2003.

Among the centre's goals is to provide an environment in which all ethnicities can feel comfortable but in which none is dominant. Given the ethnic diversity of its membership, instead of giving Arabic a central position, it recognises five languages, English, Turkish, French, Urdu and Arabic. It gives 'parity of esteem' to minor variations in ritual observance, such as those between Sunni and Shi'a, among the various traditions of Islam. Women have equal rights in its organisation, and may be elected to the executive council. The question as to whether women should 'cover', is regarded as a matter for the individual conscience.

Among its achievements is the establishment of an Australian National Islamic Library, already containing many thousand volumes. The project was launched by the then governor general in 1997, and was opened in 2003. Its resources are available to all with an interest in Islamic life and culture. It received support from wide sections of the ACT community, including in 2004 the gift from the Dominican Order of a valuable Islamic Studies collection of books assembled by the late Fr L. P. Fitzgerald OP, an internationally respected scholar of Islam in his own right, and a pioneer of Christian–Muslim dialogue in Australia. Like the Auburn Turkish Cultural Centre, it includes a vigorous programme of interreligious dialogue in its activities. It is self-funding, and for this purpose is registered as a charity, and is the first Islamic institution in Australia to which donations are tax deductible, and makes use of the services of the ACT electoral office in running its elections, thereby establishing its place and claiming its legitimacy within a civil society.

The centre is concerned with the problems of youth in the community. These are of the same kind as afflicts the broader community: drugs, under-age drinking, premarital sex and unplanned pregnancies. It responds to them as misguided attempts by young people to discover themselves in an environment without the traditional mechanisms of support, trying to find their feet in a new country.

It works with refugees from as far afield as Iraq, Eritrea and Indonesia. It provides them with moral support, and makes accessible to them information about the legal avenues accessible to them, while declining to coach individuals in the preparation of their cases for acceptance as refugees.

It circulates a well-presented monthly newsletter via the internet, which keeps members in touch with its activities. It includes interesting and often courageous articles, in the April 2000 issue reprinting an essay by an English convert to Islam, complaining about the suspicion with which he was often treated when attending a mosque, and the petty matters of detail on which he was questioned to assess whether or not he was a sincere Muslim, leading him to expostulate: Islam, Yes! Muslims, No![12]

The centre has made itself a respected institution on the Canberra scene, and as it grows, its membership of diverse backgrounds is evolving culturally in two ways: firstly, by the gradual but continuing acculturation of its members in an Australian environment, and secondly by new blood brought into the organisation by converts. While no figures are given, these converts are largely Anglo-Celts, Chinese and East Europeans. There are very few aboriginals. Of interest is that a large proportion of converts are women.

When the first Turkish migrants arrived in Australia in 1968, there was little knowledge, let alone appreciation, of Islam as a civilisation and culture in the country. The inherited image in western folklore of Islam as a religion of violence and the sword lingered on, as indeed it still does.

When migrants had come almost exclusively from Europe, the government had regarded their assimilation into the Australian community as it then was, as a matter of course. After the migration agreement with Turkey in 1968, and the official abolition of the White Australia Policy in 1972, there was a conscious shift from this policy of 'assimilationism' to one that accepted 'multiculturalism' as a national goal. There was a recognition at government level of the contribution diverse cultural traditions could make to a country now becoming home to diverse peoples, and the value of providing them the means to retain their traditions while developing their cultural identities as Australians.

Thus the end of the decade saw in place a number of publicly funded institutions designed to support this multicultural ideal: a Department of Multicultural Affairs, research projects on settlement in Australia, the establishment of the Special Broadcasting Service to broadcast programmes in the languages of all the major ethnic communities on radio and television, an Adult Migrant Education Programme, and further facilities for migrants, including translation services and English classes. All these facilitated the development of Muslim communities. This was not mere window dressing. The Preston mosque in Melbourne was opened in 1976 by the assistant secretary general of the World Muslim League in the presence of a personal representative of the then prime minister Malcolm Fraser, the leader of the opposition, then Gough Whitlam, and local religious leaders, including the Catholic Archbishop of Melbourne. In other words there was government, civic and church representation at the event at the highest level. It shows how within eight years of the signing of the migration agreement with Turkey, and six years after the abolition of the White Australia Policy, Islam had been recognised as a faith community significant in the development of Australia as a nation, and at an official, macro-level, was welcomed by government, the older established religions in the country, and the community at large. At a symbolic level, the inclusion of a recitation of the Qur'an among religious readings at the inauguration of the new parliament house in 1988 is a further example of recognition given to Islam.

In the late 1950s, a recognition of the relevance of Asia to an understanding of Australia's place in the world and the general education of its citizenry led to a phased introduction of the study of Asian languages and cultures into the education system, at first at the tertiary level. By 1968, university courses in the cultures and histories of Asia had an established place in the curricula of most Australian universities, and in 1971, the Australian National University was host to the 28th International Congress of Orientalists. At the same time, religious studies as a discipline devoted to the study of world religions also began to make its way into the education system, bringing with it inevitably a better understanding of Islam, and other world religions that were now finding a place in Australia. There followed the introduction of courses presenting the spiritual, intellectual and jurisprudential traditions of Islam, and the rich and varied realisations of Islamic culture in South and South East Asia. Unfortunately, with changing academic fashions, emphasis in recent years has tended more to political and social issues of immediate concern rather than to the richness and variety of Islamic humanism and its scriptural roots.

The ecumenical movement, especially after Vatican II, played a role. As Catholics, Protestants and Jews learned to have a positive relationship with each other, they also began to develop a positive response to the challenge of the truth claims of faith communities that had developed outside the largely European tradition to which they belonged, although this was not the case with a number of Pentecostal and Evangelical Christian traditions. Indeed, faith-leaders of the mainstream religious traditions in Australia often showed a pastoral concern in educating their flocks about the positive values of Islam, and the respect due to Muslims. They, and concerned laity, organised conferences and seminars at which Christians and Muslims could meet with and speak to each other.

A pioneering example, and the first of its kind to be held in Australia, was a conference on Islam and Christianity held at Mannix College, Monash University in 1979, addressed by local Muslim and Christian academics and visiting scholars from Egypt and Saudi Arabia. Such meetings have continued at state, national and international level since then, one of the most recent being held at Melbourne University in January 2004, an antipodean counterpart to the St Catherine's Conference, 'Christians and Muslims in the Commonwealth: A Dynamic role in the future', held at Cumberland Lodge, Windsor, in 2004.

Other institutions have sponsored similar programmes, and there is an abundance of networks and newsletters that serve to keep members of the various communities in touch, notable among them being *Bridges*, the newsletter of the Christian–Muslim Network, organised by the Sydney-based Columban Centre for Christian–Muslim Relations. In 2006, the Australian Catholic University established at its Canberra campus a semester course leading to a graduate certificate in interfaith relations, and in 2007, at its Melbourne campus, appointed a Turkish Muslim scholar to the newly established Fethullah Gulen Chair for the study of Islam and Muslim–Catholic relations.

The goal of these activities has been to share understanding and appreciation, to understand the quality of faith in Islam, to see Muslims as fellow pilgrims on a common journey, and to move beyond the 'us' and 'them' attitudes to other religions (and ethnicities) of earlier years. It is reciprocated by a number of Muslim community organisations, such as the Affinity Intercultural Foundation mentioned earlier. Thus over the past thirty years, there has been progress in the achievement of a wider, positive awareness of the changing profile of the ethnic and cultural composition of the nation.

Nevertheless, unresolved tensions and ambiguities remain and are widespread and, at a subliminal level, there remains a widespread dislike and distrust of Muslims, often overtly expressed by the promptings of the 'shock-jocks' of talk-back radio. It is as though the inherited image of Islam remains for many a template that accommodates every unsympathetic perception of and encounter with Muslims, the attractiveness of the template is enhanced by the fact that it provides a useful reductive identification of the other. There is a widespread if ill-defined sense that visible signs of commitment to Islam, particularly by 'ethnics', is aggressive in nature, and that a woman's wearing of the veil is an ostentatious intrusion of religious (and *ispso facto* a foreign ethnic) identity into public life.

Among the expressions of this hostility is the reluctance of many local councils to give approval to the building of mosques or buildings for use by Muslims. The rationalisations include fears of the inconvenience worshippers might cause to the flow of traffic, or the disturbance to the tranquillity of the early morning hours by the dawn call to prayer, or since 9/11 that they may provide a breeding ground for terrorists.

Unfortunately little that is positive concerning the Muslim world outside Australia has made headlines in Australia over the past thirty years, and the basic template seems validated. If anything, the situation has deteriorated. Examples are numerous: the Iranian Islamic Revolution of 1979, the social and cultural barbarism of the Taliban in Afghanistan; the death sentence decreed against Salman Rushdie in 1989 for his novel *The Satanic Verses*, as a result of which a number of individuals associated with the distribution and translation of the book into foreign languages have been murdered. Closer to home there has been the interreligious violence in eastern Indonesia, the mass demonstrations in the capital Jakarta with political leaders calling for an Islamic revolution, and the orchestrated bombing of churches across Indonesia on Christmas Eve in 2000.

Political commentators, even in the quality press, such as it is, report and comment on such incidents in such a way as to exacerbate such feelings, high-lighting the perception that violence is endemic in Islam. It gave prominence to speeches by Indonesian political figures demanding an Islamic Revolution, accompanied by illustrations show groups of frenzied Muslim men, with bared teeth and faces contorted with rage carrying banners with slogans 'Tolerance Is Nonsense, Slaughter Christians' and the like.[13] In reporting this incident Greg Sheridan, Foreign Editor of *The Australian*, reacting to the success of the Islamic party PAS in the 1999 Malaysian elections, self-consciously echoes the opening of the Communist Manifesto, writing, 'There is a fire burning in South East Asia, and that fire is Islam',[14] though later adding the qualification, 'Islam in Malaysia is a much gentler creed than it is in much of the Middle East'. Another article of his appears under the banner headline, 'Extremely worrying symptoms: beware the Islamic dominoes'.[15] His terminology is reminiscent of that of the cold war, and reflects a common view, even if it is not his, that Islam is the new enemy of the west after the collapse of Marxism. He also appears to endorse simplistic and misleading categories of analysis, such as that between a gentle, adaptive South East Asian Islam, and an authentic, rigorous and intolerant Middle Eastern Islam, and between 'moderate' and 'extremist' Islam.

It is interesting that the only substantive, appreciative comment on Islamic affairs to appear in the daily press recently is a report on Islamic finance, under the headline, 'Goodwill banking – Arab Bank is about to put a whole new spin on borrowing',[16] and having noted that Islamic banking is widely used by Malaysia and Indonesia, Australia's two main trading partners, concludes, 'There is a tremendous amount of goodwill towards Islamic banking'.

It was not at first realised in Australia that the violence in east Indonesian (and the southern Philippines) was part of, or at least associated with, the emer-gence of Islamism as a worldwide, radical ideology of violence. This ideology is represented in Indonesia by al-Jama'atu'l-Islamiyya (widely known by its acronym JI), an organisation founded in 1993 which regards Australia as a component of the South East Asian zone of a restored Caliphate.

In February 1998, Osama bin Laden announced a *fatwa* calling for the killing of Americans and their allies as an individual duty (*fard 'ayn*) for every Muslim who can do it in every country in which it is possible to do it. This *fatwa* lit the fuse which led to explosions of terrorist violence in Indonesia, among them the attacks on thirty-eight churches across Indonesia on Christmas Eve 2000, and elsewhere in the world. There followed the awesome destruction of the twin towers in New York on 9/11; the suicide bomber attack on two night clubs in Bali in October 2002, as a result of which over eighty Australians were killed; the attack on the Australian Embassy in Jakarta in September 2004, and a second Bali bombing in October 2005, in which more Australians were killed. The bombings in London in July 2005 had a particularly malign effect on perceptions of Islam in Australia. In the first place because a number of the victims were known to Australians, in the second because they had been perpetrated by second generation British Muslims of Asian descent, British educated, who spoke English fluently and fitted no identifiable terrorist profile.

Despite these contretemps, the seminars, conferences, dialogue meetings and the like to establish mutual respect between Muslims and other members of the community continued. Nevertheless, distrust was heightened, especially with the jailing of two Anglo-Australian converts to Islam, one of them charged with conspiring to blow up the Israeli Embassy, and the continuing saga of another Australian convert captured in Afghanistan and held in Guantanamo Bay. These events provided fresh fodder for the talk-back shock-jocks, and the correspondence columns of the press continue to be coloured by highly charged anti-Muslim letters. At least two member of the national parliament demanded that the wearing of the *burqa* be banned, because it could be used to conceal explosives. One former senior public servant went so far as to suggest the formation of a Queen Isabella Society to exclude and even expel Muslims from Australia. The situation has not been helped by a handful of maverick Muslim self-styled leaders who deny the involvement of Muslims in 9/11, and publicly attribute it to Israel and the CIA.

This distrust of Muslims and fear of terrorists became a factor in Australian politics at the 2001 general election. From 1998 there had been increasing numbers of refugees from Iraq, Afghanistan and Iran. Having reached Indonesia by air, they attempted to complete the journey by barely seaworthy boats. They included women and children. In December 2001, thus after 9/11, a merchant ship, the *Tampa* picked up some refugees whose boat had foundered. It was diverted from mainland Australia, and the refugees it had saved were disembarked and interned in various island locations. The image this created of a political leader acting decisively to exclude from Australia potential terrorists in the guise of refugees had a decisive effect on the outcome of the election.

From 2001, security has increasingly become a concern of government policy, a concern directed almost exclusively towards Muslims. The situation became more highly charged when, in 2003, Australia joined the coalition of the willing in the invasion of Iraq. This was opposed by a significant proportion of the Australian population on various grounds. Some Muslims opposed this invasion on the same grounds as the general population. Others opposed it because it was perceived as an attack on Muslims, and saw themselves inevitably exposed to any backlash resulting from it.

The perception of Islam as a problem is being addressed in various ways and at different levels. There have been major conferences sponsored by universities and other non-government institutions to explore the problems of established societies facing the challenge of high profile migrant minorities, what they perceive as their role in a new environment, and what they claim as their rights. A major international conference organised by two universities (Deakin and

Melbourne), 'Islam, human security and xenophobia', held on 25–26 November 2005, discussed the issues that now have a high profile in Australia's perception of itself. Another international conference, held in Canberra a few months earlier, was entitled 'Civil society, religion and global governance: paradigms of power and persuasion'. University courses on religion are turning their attention to the discovery and encouragement of 'liberal' Islam, and are bringing to Australia for further study a number of staff members of religious training institutes in Indonesia, deemed to be inculcating 'liberal' Islam, to study in Australia for higher degrees. As a complement to this the Australian government has made plans to offer financial support to religious institutions teaching moderate Islam. Aiming to provide a model of interreligious harmony, in December 2004 the Australian minister for foreign affairs and trade, Alexander Downer, led a multifaith delegation from Australia to promote dialogue and mutual understanding. Muslim members of the delegation, however, were carefully vetted, and Downer attempted, unsuccessfully, to include in the conference a political counter-terrorism agenda.

In a number of ways, the government has attempted to take control of what it regards as the situation. One is by the introduction of rigorous anti-terror sedition laws passed by parliament towards the end of 2005 permitting phone taps and other modes of surveillance, and authorising the detention of suspects with their names and the charges against them suppressed.[17]

At the same time the government attempted to engage with leaders of Muslim communities. Thus in August 2005, the prime minister convened a summit of fourteen selected Muslim leaders (individuals deemed to be non-extremist), to urge that they reject any perverted interpretation of Islam that tolerates terror. It was also proposed that a register of imams be established, and that imams be required to have a knowledge of English.

In much the same manner, but with a sensitivity lacking in the approach of the national government, the chief minister of the ACT in December 2005 appointed a seven member Muslim advisory. His remarks, although addressed primarily to his constituency, pinpoints precisely the problem now facing Muslims in Australia: 'It is a matter of great concern that some Canberrans, on the basis solely of their faith, are perhaps being made to feel as though they should exert themselves in a way other Canberrans need not, to prove they were loyal and law-abiding'.

In a reciprocal gesture from the Muslim community, the attorney general, Philip Ruddock, was invited to give a speech on the Eid al-Adha (10 January 2006) at Sydney's largest mosque before a congregation of 10,000. Insensitive to the spiritual meaning of the festival, and to the courtesy of a guest due to his host, he told them of their responsibility 'to uphold the laws of this country'. The patronising tone of his remarks did not go unnoticed. Subsequently Keysar Trad, founder of the Islamic Friendship Association of Australia, claimed that Mr Ruddock's remarks revealed an underlying 'contempt' for Muslims, adding, 'He doesn't have as much respect for Australians of a Muslim background as he should'.[18] It is difficult not to see in Ruddock's phrasing a trace of the subliminal sense of Muslims as the ethnic and the other referred to earlier. It is a deep-seated, even though often unconscious attitude of many Australians to Muslims, and a serious obstacle to an understanding and acceptance of the place of Muslims in Australia, and of their acceptance of their role and their rights in a new country.

The Muslim communities in the country are under many pressures, in part ethnic, in part social, in part religious. Like other faith communities, they face the challenge of living in a plural changing world in which little is constant. Since there is in Australia no large and stable community supported by instrumentalities of government behind which to shelter, they are mercilessly exposed to a variety of confrontations, in many cases ethnic identity provides the only solace.

This is what lies in part behind the violence between Muslim Lebanese and Anglo-Australian street gangs on the Sydney beach of Cronulla on 11 December 2005. The previous Sunday there had been a minor skirmish between Lebanese youths and life savers. On the 11 December Anglo-Australians organised revenge attacks on the Lebanese. SMS messages announced 'national Leb and wog bashing day'. Placards, displaying a knowledge of Muslim sensitivities, bore slogans such as 'Love '[Cro]nulla, fuck Allah' and 'Muhammad is a camel raper'. Any individual of Middle Eastern appearance was pursued and beaten, and women's *hijabs* torn off. Essentially the event was a territorial dispute between white trash and unemployed second generation Lebanese youth from Lebanese ghettos in suburbs surrounding Cronulla. However, the religious insults gave the event a wider resonance. The evening saw Lebanese revenge attacks on Anglo-Australian individuals, cars and property. Rumours were spread that the Lakemba mosque was going to be attacked, a church hall burned down, and churches vandalised. Some Lebanese preachers had after all been denouncing the near nakedness of Australian women on the beach, and saying that they were inviting rape.

It is difficult to assess the depth and distribution of the tensions on either side that led to this outbreak of violence. It is clear, however, that as far as Muslims were involved, it concerned only Lebanese of a particular age group, social class and location. There is no suggestion of it being an expression of pan-Islamic feelings across Australia, or even Sydney. Yet talk-back radio and letters to the press attributed the root cause of the riot to Islam and Muslims. In fact it highlighted one of the problems facing Muslims in Australia: the dominance of ethnic organisations in Muslim community structures. It is one of the problems Muslims recognise and are facing, and is addressed in the press at a high level by Muslims with professional standing, writing for the national press in a discourse that commands respect. Irfan Yusuf, a Sydney lawyer, addresses the problem Muslims create for themselves and their community when they place ethnicity on a par with their being Muslims. Recently, he wrote an article for the *Sydney Morning Herald*[19] with the opening line, 'Something is rotten in the state of Australian Islam'. He pointed out, by way of example, that the Lebanese Moslems' Association that manages the Lakemba mosque refuses full membership and voting rights to anyone ineligible to hold a Lebanese passport. He added that the Muslim League of New South Wales that manages the Green Valley mosque allows only persons of Fijian-Indian origin to belong to its committee. It follows that in very many cases imams are brought in from overseas who often do not know English, and are unfamiliar with Australian conditions, who present an understanding of Islam that is irrelevant to young people, which drives them either to radical preachers or to abandon religion altogether. He calls for Australian Muslims at a grass roots level to take back control of their mosque societies from the governing ethnic cliques, away from overseas and largely irrelevant imams. 'The caravan moves on . . .'

Appendix: Islamic schools

	1982–89	1990–95	1996–2000	Student numbers	% primary
Australian Capital Territory	0	0	0		
New South Wales	3	1	6	4,000	65
Queensland	0	1	0	250	100
South Australia	0	0	1	100	100
Tasmania	0	0	0	0	
Victoria	2	2	3	3,000	65
Western Australia	1	2	1	1,900	65
Total (2000)	6	6	11	9,250	

This information and the table are given in Johns, Anthony H. and Saeed, Abdullah, 'Muslims in Austraslia: the building of a community' in Haddad, Yvonne Yazbeck and Smith, Jane I. (eds), *Muslim Minorities in the West Visible and Invisible* (Walnut Creek, Lanham, New York, Oxford, Altamira Press, 2002), pp. 195–216.

Notes

1 According to the 2001 *Census of Population and Housing* there are 281,600 Muslims in Australia. This is 1.5% of the total population (but 3.4% of the population of Sydney, and 2.6% of the population of Melbourne, though reaching 10% of the population in some suburban concentrations of population). There are reasons, based on figures for mosque attendance, membership of organisations, and other methods of assessment, for regarding 400,000 as a closer estimate.
2 In a personal document giving an account of his conversion to Islam.
3 Fitzgerald, Laurence P., 'Christians and Muslims in Australia', *Islamochristiana*, 10 (1984), 163.
4 Deen, Hanifa, *Caravanserai – Journey Among Australian Muslims* (Melbourne, Allen and Unwin, 1995).
5 Deen, *Caravansarai*, p. 63.
6 Deen, *Caravansarai*, p. 15.
7 On the basis of information supplied to me by Mrs Aziza Abdel Halim, president of the network and deputy chair, Regional Islamic Da'wah Council of Southeast Asia and the Pacific Women's Movement.

8 The views presented are of Mr Mohamed Suwayti, by birth a Palestinian from near Hebron, imam of the Canberra mosque, based on an interview on 14 May 2000.

9 This information was supplied by Mr Mehmet Osalp, the director for non-Turkish and non-Muslim relations at the NSW Turkish Islamic Centre associated with the Gallipoli mosque at Auburn, in a telephone conversation on 5 June 2000.

10 An inspiring presentation of Fethullah's Gulen thought is given in Unal, Ali and Williams, Alphonse, *Fethullah Gulen Advocate of Dialogue* (Virginia, The Fountain, 2000).

11 This information was supplied by Mr. Asmi Wood, who spoke of the organisation with me in an interview on 20 January 2000.

12 *CIC Newsletter* (April 2000).

13 *Canberra Times* (8 January 2005), p. 11

14 *The Weekend Australian* (19–20 February 2000), p. 30.

15 *The Australian* (19 May 2000), p. 11.

16 *The Australian* (7 April 2000), p. 34.

17 *Australian Financial Review* (18 January 2006) reports that charges against nine men on terrorism charges in Sydney were complex, and the delay in receiving the brief from the crown was because phone records and the results of surveillance were still being examined.

18 *The Australian* (11 January 2006), p. 4.

19 *Sydney Morning Herald* (29 December 2005), p. 11.

11

Christianity and Islam in Syria: island of religious tolerance?

Emma Loosley

In an ever-shrinking world Syria remains something of an anomaly. While television viewers are used to having the latest events beamed straight into their homes and assume that few places on earth remain unknown, Syria remains remarkably mysterious.[1] News reports on events in Damascus are invariably sent from Amman, Tel Aviv or Jerusalem. On rare occasions they are filed from Beirut and this all goes to create a mystique; Damascus at the beginning of the twenty-first century remains in public perception as a dangerous, closed society, that is somehow perceived to exert a malign influence over its neighbours and, naturally enough, over its own inhabitants.

So why are we so ignorant about what is only, after all, a small country in the Eastern Mediterranean?

Naturally the misconceptions and strong emotional responses generated by the mention of Syria, or the Syrian Arab Republic to give the country its official title, are due to its location in the heart of one of the most unstable regions in the world. Sharing borders with Turkey, Iraq, Jordan, Israel and Lebanon means that Syria has been directly or indirectly involved in conflict throughout the entire twentieth century and the repercussions of 9/11 ensured that these conflicts would continue. Political instability or complete lawlessness at different times in Lebanon, Israel and Iraq, political weakness in Jordan and religious and ethnic persecution in Turkey have all affected Syrian domestic politics, even before unrest in Syria itself has been considered. Largely due to Syrian opposition to Israel and Israel's close political tie with the USA, Syria has been dubbed a pariah state and is effectively isolated from the global community. Comparisons are made between the Ba'ath Party of Syria and the Ba'athist regime of Saddam Hussein in Iraq, but how much do we really know about Syria? More importantly in the context of this chapter, how does the Syrian government view religion and freedom of religious expression in a region torn apart by ostensibly religious issues?

As so little is generally known about Syria, it is probably a good idea to begin with some facts. The Syrian Arab Republic has been ruled since 1963 by the Ba'ath Party, an Arab socialist political movement that split to provide rival interpretations of the party in Syria and Iraq. Since 1970 the Syrian party has been headed by the Al-Assad family, first by Hafez Al-Assad and then, since his death in 2000, by his son Bashar Al-Assad. This means that the country is a one-party state and other political movements are suppressed by the ruling regime, which essentially amounts to a clique of loyalists around the Al-Assad family. While this makes the situation appear black and white to outsiders, who take the view that lack of political freedom leads directly to an oppressed populace, the Syrians themselves hold a variety of views on their political system and many of these opinions are far from negative. Perhaps surprisingly, the majority of favourable comments concern religion; Syria has many religious minorities and all of them cite the stable internal situation in Syria under the Ba'ath Party as the reason why they are largely supportive of the current regime.

Exact figures are difficult to come by, not least because a few of the *bedu* and villagers in some remoter settlements have a *laissez faire* attitude to registering exact details of births and deaths, but recent estimates put the population of Syria at around 18.5 million people. In common with most of the developing world this is an essentially youthful society with 37.4%[2] aged fourteen years old or younger. What is most interesting is how the population breaks into different religious affiliations. Estimates suggest that the Sunni Muslim majority account for 70–74% of the population with the remainder comprising Alawites, Druze, Ismailis, Christians, Yazidis and an extremely small number of Jews. Of these groups the Alawites are the most numerous comprising 12%[3] and the others make up the remainder. As the ruling Al-Assad family are Alawite, this group wields a disproportionate amount of power within the country. Which leaves us with the question of the Christians; in the late 1990s the Christian population of Syria was generally quoted as being 12–15%. External figures today put this figure at 10–12%, but Christian leaders within the country privately suggest the reality is nearer 8–9%.

With the Alawites in charge, Sunni Islamic extremism is kept in check by an often brutal government response. The facts of the assault on the city of Hama in 1982 to quell an uprising of the Muslim Brotherhood have never been truly established, but the centre of the city was destroyed and the death toll went into thousands. Since 1982 the Muslim Brothers have been a relatively minor fact of life in Syria. Attacks are not widely publicised even within the country and are often only discovered by accident, for example in the late 1990s an intercity bus from Damascus to Aleppo was blown up as it left the Damascus bus depot. In Syrian Orthodox Christian circles in Aleppo this was known as they had lost a member of the congregation, but only those who knew a victim were aware of the incident. Most people are indifferent to the local television news channels and newspapers and prefer to receive their news through the age-old method – word of mouth. Very few incidents reach the international press and if they do, they are interpreted very differently by foreign observers. For example, just before Easter 2004 the international press reported widespread civil unrest in Hassake, in the far north-east of Syria. In the UK this was reported as Muslim–Christian clashes with a number of fatalities. In Syria the Christian population of Aleppo (who have many relatives and friends in Hassake) reported that the problem was a Sunni Arab–Kurdish dispute that had begun at a football match and spilled out on to the streets for several days afterwards. They reported that there were deaths, but relatively few (less than ten) and that the whole situation had been triggered by a sudden influx of Kurds caused by the war in Iraq. This had led to an imbalance in the local Sunni-Christian-Kurdish ethnic and religious mix and sparked the riots.

Who are the Alawites?

The Alawites are a Shi'ite sect who have traditionally lived in the mountains that abut the Syrian coast. Today they are spread over two countries, as the French government ceded the Hatay (the region round Antakya, ancient Antioch) to Turkey in the build up to the Second World War in an attempt to secure Turkish neutrality in the coming conflict. This means that even today the majority of the Hatay is inhabited by Alawites and Arabic-speaking Greek Orthodox Christians (known as *Rum* Orthodox in Arabic) who live peaceably together and complain of their lack of religious freedoms under the Turkish government.[4] The two communities are also linked by their shared language, Arabic, which means that they are handicapped in Turkish society by not speaking or writing Turkish.

Of course in Syria their situation is totally different. As the ruling family comes from the Alawite community, all Alawites have a stake in protecting the status quo and many families with blood or friendship ties to the Al-Assad family gain financially or socially from these familial and clan networks that are still a central part of Arab society. Their beliefs also make them particularly well-suited as neighbours for the Christian communities that inhabit the same mountains. The Alawites eschew formal worship in congregational mosques and espouse private prayers at the shrines of venerable Sheikhs. As these Sheikhs often include Old Testament or Christian figures, it is not unusual to see both Christians and Alawites praying at the same tombs in Syria. One example is a late-antique tomb at ancient Cyrrhus in the north west of Syria. The site is now called Nebi Uri as the tomb is locally regarded as the burial place of the Old Testament Prophet Uriah. In this case the Christians do not see the shrine as a place of pilgrimage, but it is an example of how many of these Sheikhs are often pre-Islamic holy men adopted by the Alawites.

This more informal mode of worship means that there are no mosques in Alawite villages and by extension no formal preaching by an imam every Friday. Without this there is no rigid Muslim doctrinal stance set up in direct opposition to a church within the same village and possible tensions are avoided. Only one problem remains and this is the intractable Christian–Muslim social issue of intermarriage, which will be addressed later in this chapter. Of course this radically different form of worship is due to the fact that the Alawites are a long way from traditionally Sunni Orthodoxy, so much so that some Sunni have even questioned whether the Alawites are actually really Muslims at all. However what is clear is that they are Muslim and, like the other Muslim minorities in Syria, the Druze and Ismailis, they are Shi'ite Muslims. Because of this Syria is in a minority in the Islamic world. Although a secular state, Syria is ruled by a family that follow a branch of Shi'ite Islam and only one state in the world is officially Shi'ite: The Islamic Republic of Iran. This can cause problems when dealing with other Arab Muslim states as they are all without exception Sunni states. It also explains Syria's growing friendship with Iran and its somewhat ambivalent relationship with Iraq, where under Saddam Hussein the Shi'a majority were victimised by the Sunni ruling elite. Having said this, the Syrian model of Shi'ite rule under the Al-Assad family and the Ba'ath Party relies on the complicity of other religious minorities to keep them in power. This means that it depends too much on Christian support to limit Christian freedoms, as has happened in Iran since 1979 or is likely to happen now to Iraqi Christians.

The challenges facing Syrian Christians

Given this relative freedom, why is the Christian population of Syria declining? Is this due to internal or external factors? Most importantly of all, is this decline in any respect linked to living in a society with a Muslim majority and does this necessitate a formal Christian response to their Muslim fellow countrymen? Naturally these are extremely complex issues and a variety of factors have been identified among the Christian community as to why their numbers are shrinking, but surprisingly few relate directly to religious factors. The first reason is an issue that currently affects most of the western world: falling birth rates. Most Christians in Syria dwell in urban areas and follow a profession. As a consequence of this they place great emphasis on education and all Christian families, from the poorest to the wealthiest, have aspirations for their children to become doctors or engineers. Naturally this puts a financial strain on families as, not only must they support student offspring, but they lose the income that a child could bring into the home having completed the minimum school attendance by their early teens. For the Christians, as for middle-class Muslims, the answer has been to have smaller families. Unlike the Muslims, this is a movement that has permeated all levels of Christian society so that large Christian families are now rare outside a few village communities. One reason that the Christian population appears to be declining is simply that they are having fewer children than their Muslim counterparts. Which leads us on seamlessly to the next factor: transferable skills in short supply in western societies, for example the shortage of junior house doctors and general practitioners in the UK, means that educated urbanites find it much easier to emigrate to the west. On a points system doctors and engineers discover that it is relatively easy to find employment opportunities in Europe, Northern America or Australasia. Since 9/11 this situation has accelerated in the Christian community, where it is commonly believed that Christians are more likely to be successful in visa applications than Muslims. Whether or not there is any truth in this is difficult to discern, but this does not stop rumours regularly circulating that Christians will gain easy access to Canada, New Zealand or some other Christian society.[5]

This leads us to the next reason for the shrinking Christian population in Syria: economic stagnation. With the few trade agreements Syria held with the outside world severely curtailed since 9/11, the Ba'ath Party had sought a *rapprochement* with its counterpart in neighbouring Iraq. Contracts from Saddam Hussein's government were bringing employment to Syria until the Iraq War. Now only Iran will enter into trade agreements with Syria and so a static economy and unemployment fuel an exodus of skilled people from all religions and levels of society. But if birth control, education and emigration are all seen as factors affecting the Christian population of Syria, we cannot deny that these factors will also cause an impact among the Muslims, both the Sunni majority and the various Shi'a minorities. Which leads us finally to the heart of the matter: are there any issues facing the Christians in contemporary Syria that are provoked by their presence in a Muslim majority country and, perhaps more importantly, what are their responses to this?

Perhaps the largest impediment to closer relations is the Syrian legal system. Surprisingly it is the freedom that this system gives to religious groups that causes serious social divisions. While criminal law remains the responsibility of the state, matters pertaining to family law are entirely in the hands of the relevant religious authorities. For example, this means, for Christians, that divorces and any resulting decisions about maintenance and child-raising are in the hands of the ecclesiastical courts. The reality of this fact is that divorce is extremely rare among Christians and strongly taboo. Divorcées in particular are left social outcasts as the blame is usually attached to the female, whatever the causes of the marriage breakdown. This affects Christian–Muslim relations more than any other factor in Syrian society, because to marry a Muslim places an individual outside the remit of the ecclesiastical courts and effectively severs them from the Christian community entirely. Any Christian woman marrying a Muslim may keep her religion, but her children are deemed Muslim and it is accepted that she must now abide by Muslim codes of law. A Christian man must convert if he wishes to marry a Muslim woman and it is this that keeps the two communities apart. While many Muslims are more than happy to be friends with Christians, Christians with young or unmarried children are generally wary of friendship because they do not want their children to form an emotional attachment with a Muslim.

What appears a Romeo and Juliet situation to the west can be a life or death decision in Syria, where a young Muslim wanting to convert to Christianity for a relationship or otherwise, could find themselves with a death sentence hanging over their head – not from any civil or religious authority but from the shame felt by their extended family. For a young Christian marrying a Muslim, the result is not death but usually a lifelong exile from family and friends. While some women, for it is usually women who are in this situation, manage to remain in touch with their family, many others find themselves completely isolated from their origins and never fully accepted into their new families. Unfortunately the problems are passed on to the next generation and many children of these mixed marriages find themselves culturally confused. A number find themselves drawn to their mother's faith but are unable to practice it. They are often also drawn to Christian members of the opposite sex who will remain deliberately distant because they do not want to marry a Muslim, even if the person in question is Muslim on paper only.[6]

Attitudes to Christianity in Syrian society

As may be inferred from above, Christians are widely viewed as well-educated and valuable members of society, hence their general desirability as marriage partners. This regard for Christians as people disciplined by their community into a high moral standard has led to a widespread acceptance of their wider role in the country as a whole. Christians hold high government offices in areas such as the ministries of tourism and culture and are ubiquitous in all areas of public life, with the notable exception of military matters, which are still held in a stranglehold by the Alawite elite. This regard means that Christians are treated as mainstream members of society. Christian children are educated with their Muslim counterparts at mixed primary schools and single-sex secondary schools. The curricula are the same with the exception of religious education, when the students are separated to be taught the Bible or the Qur'an as appropriate.

For Syrians one measure of acceptance is how often their affairs are reported on the state-owned news channels. In 1997 Hafez Al-Assad received the whole Syrian Orthodox synod, headed by His Holiness Patriarch Ignatius Zakka I Iwas, at the presidential palace and the whole event was televised. This was seen as a great honour and public endorsement of the Syrian Orthodox church at the highest level. The pilgrimage of His Holiness Pope John Paul II to Damascus in May 2001 dominated the country with blanket coverage in the local media. When the Pontiff was the first pope to enter a mosque, by accepting an invitation from the Syrian Grand Mufti to visit the Umayyad mosque in Damascus, the whole populace was captivated.[7]

Within Christian circles there are naturally different views as to how they are perceived by the Muslim majority of the country. Most Christians are perceptive enough to point out that although they live harmoniously with the various Muslim minorities – the Alawites, Ismailis and Druze – relations with the Sunni are another matter. While relations are good with the Sunni authorities, many Christians are suspicious of the Sunni majority. They accept that the Al-Assad government has kept power by favouring religious minorities and they are aware that if the Ba'ath Party fell, as in Iraq, the Christians would become the targets of Muslim extremists.

Therefore the situation is on a knife-edge, something all Christians in Syria are uncomfortably conscious of. As long as the Ba'ath Party and the Al-Assad family remain in power Christians have religious freedom to regulate their domestic affairs, may wear what they want, ring bells, have processions and generally worship freely. The price of this is to support the political status quo. If the regime falls, then all Syrians feel the best case scenario would be a Lebanese-style civil war. The worst case would be to emulate Iraq.

Syrian Christian views on politics and religion

Naturally there are as many political opinions as there are Christians in Syria and they cover a wide spectrum. There are also a variety of opinions held on Christianity, as in Syria religion is worn in the same way that an ethnic minority seeks to have a badge of identity in the west. A Christian may well be an atheist; in Syria being Christian signals a kind of ethnic belonging as much as being part of a faith. For a number of working-class Christians there are complaints against the government for the poor economic state of the country but no more consideration of the political situation than that. In Aleppo, the most Christian of all Syrian cities, it is surprising to find a number of well-educated middle-class professionals supporting the Ba'ath Party. When questioned they all state that they would rather have curtailed political freedom and stability than democracy and a war, as in their neighbours, Lebanon and Iraq. Many Christians in the north of Syria are descended from refugees from contemporary Turkey and they also point out that the secular state in Syria is a benign ruler as far as Christians are concerned when compared with Turkish persecution of not just the Armenians in the 1915 genocide, but all Christians up until and including the present day.

While this attitude appears to be a majority view there are dissenters who argue that maintaining the current situation means an unacceptable loss of political freedom. This group of intellectuals is where Christians and Muslims come closest in their aims and aspirations for the future and people involved in these issues are often the most open to interaction with others of different faiths. In fact throughout Syrian society it seems that the more educated and wealthier classes are more open to dialogue with other religions than the poorer, unskilled members of society who revert to ancient prejudices, on both sides of the religious divide, to justify their place in the world. In this Syria is no different from any other country, but if as mentioned above, there are people of both faiths prepared to engage with each other, what does this mean for Syrian Christians? Most significantly the question is whether these Christian–Muslim dialogues are the fruit of a coherently planned strategy or remain individual initiatives of limited efficacy.

Christian initiatives for dialogue

It must first be noted that with the Christian population of Syria as divided by sectarian issues as their Muslim counterparts, it is impossible for us to view Christian overtures towards their Muslim fellow countrymen as one concerted action. Rather there are a series of different projects undertaken by different Christian groups at a variety of levels of engagement. Some seek to gain political links, while others work towards closer cultural and social relations. While some of these initiatives are viewed positively by the ecclesiastical authorities, others are viewed in a more negative light and it must be stressed that Middle Eastern Christians who are very open minded in all other respects often still baulk at the idea of closer relations with their Muslim neighbours.

The first, and perhaps most obvious, strategy to promote better Christian–Muslim relations is to try and disseminate more information on both faiths to the populace. While religious discussion programmes on Qur'anic questions are common throughout the Middle East, in Syria it is not uncommon to have a mufti and a bishop debating a moral or ethical question on a state-sponsored talk show. The Syrian Orthodox Metropolitan of Aleppo, H. E. Mar Grigorios Yohanna Ibrahim, is a regular fixture on these shows and his personal acquaintance with the Syrian president, observer status at the UN and links to the World Council of Churches and various Catholic organisations, mean that his lead is taken seriously by other ecclesiastical figures in Syria. In fact the success of his public dialogues is such that in 2004 he was invited to lecture on Christianity on Saudi Arabian television, in the first such invitation offered to a Christian.[8] These initiatives reached a new level in 2005 when the Grand Mufti of Aleppo was appointed Grand Mufti of Syria on the death of the previous incumbent. Because of the friendship between the Metropolitan and the mufti they have now established a two-week training course for priests and imams, where the clerics are encouraged to develop homilies that can be delivered in both the church and the mosque.[9] This kind of work does stimulate debate and raise wider awareness of a number of issues, it is also extremely politically significant, but it is difficult to claim that this type of initiative has any lasting effect on mainstream Syrian society. Within the Syrian Orthodox community in Aleppo people are proud of their bishop, but largely unwilling to follow his example and engage in dialogue with Muslims. He is seen as an excellent politician and leader, but dialogue is not seen as a necessary element of daily life.

As this seems to be a common perception, how can this attitude be changed? One way is leadership at local levels. Community authority figures such as local imams and priests can lead the way by visiting each other at festival times and acknowledging the celebrations and tragedies of the parallel religious community. This is in fact a situation that is beginning in some communities in Syria where there is the presence of a shrine common to both faiths. Within the country a number of Christian shrines have been adopted by Muslims and an acknowledgement of this fact goes a long way to encouraging closer community relationships; in some cases, such as the shrine of Our Lady of Saidnaya, there is a tacit acknowledgment that both Christian and Muslim women thought barren have conceived after a pilgrimage to the site. The dual faiths of pilgrims are acknowledged but not discussed. At other shrines the dual identity of the object of veneration is openly accepted and two interpretations of the same holy person survive alongside each other. An excellent example of this is the Monastery of Mar Elian esh-Sharqi (St Julian of the East) in Qaryatayn in the Syrian desert between Homs and Palmyra. Mar Elian is also referred to as Mar Elian esh-Sheikh (St Julian the old man) by the Christians, but he is called Sheikh Ibrahim Hauri by the Muslims. *Khouri* being an Arabic word for priest, the corruption to *Hauri* seems to be a tacit Muslim acknowledgement of the Christian origin of the shrine. In fact this dual worship goes back until at least the fifteenth century according to the evidence of an inscription over the monastery entrance signed by the local emir.[10] While this historical information is interesting, what is more relevant today is the way that the villagers treat the dual identity of this personage. Firstly, all villagers are very quick to declare that he is 'their' saint or sheikh. This is perceived as a village identity transcending religious affiliation and this sense of village unity over and above religious divisions is reinforced every 9 September, the annual feast day of the saint, when both Christians and Muslims attend a special mass celebrated by the diocesan bishop which is followed by an oration on Mar Elian/Sheikh Ibrahim by the village mufti. While this is an excellent example of an aspect of the sacred transcending the religious divide to create a festival valid for all the inhabitants of a village, cases such as this are relatively rare and, as spontaneous outpourings of reverence for a particular holy man, cannot be used as a model to foster closer relations in other situations. The initiative here is unplanned and heartfelt but it is not an example that can be followed by other communities and it does not go so far that it breaks down the social boundaries that exist between the two religions within the community.

So if educational campaigns by religious leaders and community movements are only partially successful in stimulating a deeper level of interaction between Christians and Muslims, rather than simply maintaining a peaceful co-existence based on voluntary social segregation, is it possible to overcome Christian reservations about Muslim religious law and foster deep friendships across the divide? Obviously the answer to this must be yes. There are circles in Aleppo, and almost certainly in other cities, where this open, religiously mixed friendship is so commonplace that it is not considered extraordinary. These circles are largely drawn from the mercantile and professional classes where money has brought people into contact and financial contacts have led to friendship. These groups all function according to a particular dynamic; firstly, there are the all-male friendship groups that meet for coffee, gambling evenings or cruising the night clubs, where the friendship group is kept away from familial surroundings and as a 'boys night out' side-steps any uncomfortable issues raised by a mixed-sex gathering. Secondly, there are circles formed by married couples who regularly visit each other's houses and eat in restaurants together. Here the social codes are observed by talking of children but never letting the children, even adult children, into the circle unless they are safely married within the parents' religion.

Having taken into account individuals' initiatives, spontaneous community interaction and simple friendship, are there any large-scale projects in Syria that currently seek to bring Christians and Muslims closer together? The answer lies with a new monastic movement that, although founded in Syria, now seeks a model for Christian witness in Muslim majority countries that can be exported across the world.

In the steps of Massignon[11]

Louis Massignon (1883–1962) has exerted a strong influence on many western Christian scholars who have sought a deeper understanding of Islam. Having credited the strengthening of his own Christian faith to the mystical dimension of his studies of al-Husayn ibn Mansur al-Hallaj (858–922CE), a mediaeval Sufi mystic, Massignon went on to espouse a path of dialogue concentrating on the Abrahamitic origins of the three great monotheistic faiths.

While many have been influenced by Massignon's ideas, a religious community in Syria was founded in 1991 to try and implement his ideas for a monastic life dedicated to the cause of Muslim–Christian dialogue. The Community of al-Khalil takes its name from the Islamic name for Abraham, 'The Friend [of God]', although it is colloquially known as the Community of Deir Mar Musa after the monastery where the order was founded.[12] The whole project stems from the vocation of one Jesuit, Fr Paolo Dall'Oglio, who was inspired by the works of Massignon to found a community with a calling to embrace Christian–Islamic dialogue. The life of this community follows the usual monastic vows of poverty, chastity and obedience but the members also take an extra undertaking to provide 'Abrahamitic hospitality' to all who visit or request shelter at the monastery. In particular they seek to reach out to the local, predominantly Muslim, society in an attempt to foster reciprocal social links and projects that will benefit the whole region. To this end the community has arranged regular meetings with the shepherds and goatherds that frequent the mountains around the monastery in order to explain the process of desertification and the need to rotate herds – particularly the goats, who rip up foliage by the roots. The area has now been named a national park and is the centre of an agro-biodiversity project and annual meetings of all stakeholders mean that the local herders are kept informed of progress and now understand the need to preserve the environment if their way of life is to continue. Increased visitors to the nearest town, An-Nabk, 18 kilometres from the monastery, has led to a growth in trade for local restaurants and taxi and bus drivers. The interest in the site has also led to a civic renewal of the town centre that was largely destroyed in the late 1980s by catastrophic flash-flooding. As local people have become more aware of their heritage, and that the monastery projects can bring prosperity to the region, it has become usual for large numbers of villagers including the village mufti and other imams to visit the monastery on Fridays to discuss village matters with Fr Paolo.

As word of the Community of Al-Khalil has spread Fr Paolo and other members of the community, which is a foundation for both sexes, have been invited to engage with people involved in religious and social programmes throughout Syria and in the wider region. This includes Fr Paolo giving the homily at the Shi'a shrine of Sitt Zeinab on the feast of Imam Ali and regularly speaking at the Abu Noor (Sunni) Islamic University, while Sister Huda attended a meeting for Middle Eastern women of all faiths in Cyprus to discuss future directions for collaboration and to debate issues that affected them all. This led to a lasting friendship with the daughter-in-law of the late grand mufti of Syria and has paved the way for a female discussion on belief, as women have previously been overlooked in matters of dialogue in the Middle East. A mixed community allows men and women to debate issues in a neutral space at the monastery where no allegations of sexual impropriety can stain the honour of female delegates (a matter as serious in Syria for Christian girls as for Muslim ones).

The reputation of the community has spread to the international stage with a series of articles and documentaries, largely aimed at Italian and Francophone audiences. Italians, French and Swiss have proved particularly receptive to the message and many young French visitors say that they feel at ease in Deir Mar Musa as they can equate it with their religious experiences at Taizé. Although a very different movement, the Community of Al-Khalil is a young community and its message seems particularly attractive to young people from their teens until their thirties. Many who come within the orbit of the community in their youth continue to work for it as unofficial ambassadors even if they do not feel they have a monastic vocation, in fact this growing number of 'friends' has prompted a recent proposal to establish a lay-order to supplement the work of the core monastic order.

The monastic constitutions for the creation of the Community of Al-Khalil were presented to the Vatican after the community received the personal blessing of Pope John Paul II during his visit to Damascus in May 2001. They were accepted last year and the community now runs a local parish as well as Deir Mar Musa. If vocations allow there are plans to expand to Iran and Pakistan in the future.

Conclusion

It is an irony that it is the Ba'athist regime reviled by much of the western world that allows religious pluralism to flourish in Syria. In a region that has been torn apart time and again on the pretext of religion, the Syrians in general acknowledge that this is a rare achievement. In fact they are quick to point out that the government is always ready to intervene on the side of the minority. Several summers ago the (largely Sunni) *bedu* made raids on the Druze town of Shabha in the south of the country, looting property and killing several Druze who tried to defend their possessions. The army swiftly intervened to protect the Druze and my Christian friends all repeated this story as evidence of why they felt secure in Syria. Very few emigrations are due to political reasons outside of privileged urban intellectual society. The most common factor, in fact almost the only reason for emigration among Christians, is the stagnating Syrian economy and the desire for a materially higher standard of living. The fact that the standard of living rises only in the material sense must be highlighted here, as in terms of leisure time and social activities most Syrians have a lifestyle that the majority of western society would envy. They work very few hours compared to their European counterparts and their familial and social networks mean that most families rarely have an evening without some activity planned. Apart from the financial situation most Christians confess that the only thing that would make them consider moving is, in the words of George Bush, regime change. Many were anxious about the transfer of power from Hafez Al-Assad to Bashar Al-Assad in 2000, but when the handover was smooth these worries disappeared. A Lebanese Maronite friend married to a Syrian *Rum* (Greek) Orthodox Christian refuses to move back home to Lebanon from Aleppo, reasoning that even now she does not feel that Beirut is a stable enough environment for their four children. She would rather they had less money in Syria and feel safe, than have wealth and be at risk of political instability in Lebanon. Her personal preference, after her experience of the Lebanese civil war, is for a stable one-party state rather than a fragile democracy that cannot guarantee safety.

This really leads us to the heart of the matter. As highlighted in the introduction, many people know very little about Syria and their assumptions are often based on flawed information. Armed with a lack of reliable data on the Syrian Arabic Republic it is all too easy to assume that people in Syria share a common worldview with western society. The reality of life in a country surrounded by other states that persecute religious minorities, are engaged in civil war or have just emerged from civil war, is very different. In such a situation stability is precious and if this comes with religious freedom attached then this is an extremely positive situation. Obviously not all Christians feel this way and it is always the educated urban elite who are heard on the international stage. They are the group most likely to be politically active and oppose the regime, but it is as well to remember that they are only a small voice and cannot be said to represent the majority of Christians. Many friends, bishops, teachers and an architect among them, have explained to me at length what they see as the benefits of the current political system in Syria and it is important to give them a voice, rather than simply to pander to western sensibilities and condemn a way of thinking that is unfamiliar to us.

Notes

1 To date little has yet been written on the state of interreligious encounters in Syria. This situation is complicated by the denominational peculiarities of the

country whereby it is home to a multiplicity of both Christian and Islamic groups. This chapter is intended as an introduction to the subject and a basis on which to develop further discussion. For background see the two studies by Elizabeth Picard, although dated they are still of value, 'La Syrie de 1946 à 1979', in Picard, *La Syrie d'aujourd'hui* (Paris, Éditions du CNRS, 1980), pp. 143–84; 'Y a-t-il un problème communautaire en Syrie?', *Maghreb-Machrek*, 87 (1980), 7–21.

2 Figure from www.cafe-syria.com. See also Seurat, Michel, 'Les populations, l'État et la societé', in *La Syrie d'aujourd'hui* (Paris, Éditions du CNRS, 1980), pp. 87–141; and Wieland, Carsten, *Syria at Bay: Secularism, Islamism and 'Pax Americana'* (London, Hurst & Co., 2006).

3 Figure from www.state.gov. On the Alawite disposition see Firro, Kais M., 'The 'Alawi in modern Syria: from Nusayriya to Islam via 'Alawiya', *Der Islam*, 82: 1 (2005), 1–31 and for a general overview, Hinnebusch, Raymond A., 'Syria', in Hunter, Shireen T. (ed.), *The Politics of Islamic Revivalism: Diversity and Unity* (Bloomington, Indiana University Press, 1989), pp. 39–56. New voices are emerging in Syrian Islam see Weismann, Itzchak, 'Sa'id Hawwa and Islamic revivalism in Ba'thist Syria', *Studia Islamica*, 85 (1997), 131–54; 'Sa'id Hawwa: the making of a radical Muslim thinker in modern Syria', *Middle Eastern Studies*, 29: 4 (1993), 601–23.

4 This is based on a stay with a Christian family in the Christian-Alawite town of Semandağ, south of Antakya. The visit was in 1997 and the community was dying due to a lack of young men. All families sent their sons away before military service as they claimed that Alawite and Christian conscripts were sent to dangerous postings in the east to fight a civil war against the Kurds.

5 These were opinions regularly expressed in my presence from 1997 onwards and Christians strongly believe 9/11 has led to more freedom for Syrian-born Christians at the expense of their Muslim fellow countrymen.

6 This information has been gathered by running an archaeological project over a number of years in the Syrian desert. Local workers of both religions were thrown together with (largely female) students studying in Damascus and the politics of the flirtations eluded me until a worker explained who was Christian, who was Muslim, and why some of the flirtations were doomed from the start.

7 As an aside it is interesting to note that whilst the world was interpreting the political and religious repercussions of this visit, Syrian Christians were more interested in the fact that the pope was not asked to remove his slippers before entering the mosque. For them, Catholic or Orthodox, this was the most important fact because of the respect they felt it showed to a Christian leader. This was reported to me by a monk present at the event who witnessed the pope entering the mosque wearing embroidered slippers. On Syriac Christianity see O'Mahony, Anthony, 'Syriac Christianity in the modern Middle East', in Angold, Michael (ed.), *The Cambridge History of Christianity: Vol. 5, Eastern Christianity* (Cambridge, Cambridge University Press, 2006), pp. 511–35.

8 Personal communication with H. E. Mar Grigorios Yohanna Ibrahim. Syria is also a zone of ecumenical dialogue between the Christian churches, see Ibrahim, Gregorius Yohanna, 'Healing and reconciliation: Roman Catholic-Syrian Orthodox dialogue', *One in Christ: A Catholic Ecumenical Review*, 40: 4 (2005), 39–48.

9 Information from Dr Aziz Abdul Nour, UK Representative of Moran Mar Ignatius Zakka I Iwas, Syrian Orthodox Patriarch of Antioch and all the East.

10 For the details of this inscription see Kaufhold, H., 'Notizen über das Moseskloster bei Nabk und das Julianskloster bei Qaryatain in Syrien', *Oriens Christianus*, 79 (1995), 48–119.

11 See Unsworth, A., 'The Vatican, Islam and Muslim-Christian relations', in this volume. For a discussion of Massignon's influence on the Catholic Church and thinkers see also the studies by O'Mahony, Anthony, 'Our common fidelity to Abraham is what divides': Christianity and Islam in the life and thought of Louis Massignon', O'Mahony, Anthony and Bowe OSB, Peter (eds), *Catholics in Inter-religious Dialogue: Studies in Monasticism, Theology and Spirituality* (Leominster, Gracewing, 2006), pp. 151–90; '*Le pélerin de Jérusalem*: Louis Massignon, Palestinian Christians, Islam and the State of Israel', in O'Mahony, Anthony (ed.), *Palestinian Christians: Religion, Politics and Society* (London, Melisende, 1999, pp. 166–89; 'Mysticism, politics, dialogue: Catholic encounters with Shi'a Islam in the life and work of Louis Massignon', in O'Mahony, Anthony, Peterburs OSB, Wulstan and Shomali, Mohammad Ali (eds), *Catholics and Shi'a in Dialogue: Studies in Theology and Spirituality* (London, Melisende, 2004), pp. 134–84; 'Louis Massignon, the Seven Sleepers of Ephesus and the Christian–Muslim pilgrimage at Vieux-Marché, Brittany', in Bartholomew, Craig and Hughes, Fred (eds), *Explorations in a Christian Theology of Pilgrimage* (Aldershot, Ashgate, 2004), pp. 126–48; and Dall'Oglio (SJ), Paolo, 'Massignon and jihad, through De Foucauld, al-Hallaj and Gandhi' in *Faith, Power and Violence*, ed. Donahue SJ, J. J. and Troll SJ, C.W., *Orientalia Christiana Analecta*, 258 (1998), 103–14.

12 Deir Mar Musa al-Habashi translates as the monastery of St Moses the Abyssinian or Ethiopian. See also Loosley, E. and Dall'Oglio, P., 'La communauté d'al-Khalil: une communauté monastique au service du dialogue islamo-chrétien', *Proche-orient Chrétien*, 54 (2004), 117–28.

12

Christianity, Shi'a Islam and Muslim–Christian encounter in Iran

Anthony O'Mahony

Christianity in Persian history and culture

Christianity in Persia has a very ancient history, and as early as the second century the religion was well established there.[1] About twenty bishoprics were established by about the third century,[2] and the Persian church even sent missionaries of its own from Iran to distant countries of the Far East and China.[3] References to Christianity can be found in Persian literature from the earliest period. Christian beliefs and institutions are frequently mentioned in various genres, and many works contain allusions to legends of Christian saints, martyrs and ascetics.[4]

The Church of the East,[5] which was the predominant expression of Christianity, according to S. Gerö accepted the imposition of Arab rule with little understanding of what it meant. There is evidence for the early levying of taxation, which soon was felt to be burdensome, but there is no reason to regard this tax as the sign of imposition of full communal *dhimmi* status. The 'disestablishment' of Mazdean religion gave renewed impulse to the ongoing conversion of Zoroastrians. The general atmosphere of tolerance is evident, in contrast to the rigid interpretation of the *dhimma* in the Abbasid period. The boundaries may have been more flexible between the several religious groups in the seventh century than one would think; there was more than just the familiar one-way traffic of Christians converting in droves to Islam.[6]

The 'concordat' between the episcopate of the Church of the East and the Persian imperial authority, illustrated in the synodal acts of the fifth and sixth centuries, was not followed by the appearance of a 'Persian Constantine', who would have converted the Sasanian empire to Christianity.[7] At the time of the Arab conquest the Christian leaders no longer felt, it seems, that the church was bound to the Sasanian imperial system. Impressed by the ease and rapidity of the Arab conquest they made their submission to the new order, which initially at least was characterised by a degree of *laissez faire*.[8] There was a myopic lack of comprehension of Islam as a new aggressive religious movement that sought political rights and dominant power. Despite the noteworthy beginning of large-scale missionary enterprise around this time,[9] the Church of the East did not take advantage of the spell of relative freedom in the seventh and early eight centuries to consolidate its gains. Rather one can see the appearance of a certain communal exhaustion after intense internal jurisdiction and confessional struggles in the late Sasanian times. The way was being prepared for the imposition of inferior, marginal *dhimmi* status as determined by the Islamic rulers. The Christians did come to realise that it made a great deal of difference, in the long run, which master they served, but by then they had really no choice at all in the matter. This proved that the fate and fortune of the Church of the East was tied up for better or worse with the Sasanian state since at least the early fifth century.[10]

The long historical, religious and cultural relationship of Persia and Christianity has created a strong presence of Christian imagery in Persian poetry and Sufi literature. A considerable number of works touching on, sometimes directly treating, the topics of Christianity in Iranian Islam already exist.[11] Contact with Islam is not, however, the only source for knowledge of Christian beliefs, institutions, behaviour and vocabulary mirrored in Persian culture. Christianity had a long history in pre-Islamic Persia.[12] In addition, Qamar Ariyân suggests that contacts with contemporary Christians living in Persia, Muslim propaganda and disputation with Christian theologians, and even indirect influence from Gnostic and Manichean sources during the last two centuries of the Sasanian empire and the early centuries of Islam, all had an impact. Memories of Christian activity in pre-Islamic Persia were an important factor shaping the understanding of Christian customs and institutions expressed in the Persian literature of the Islamic period.[13]

New possibilities for the evaluation of Christianity in Iran took place under the Il-Khanid rulers of Persia (1256–1336) before Gazan Khan (1295–1304), who were not Muslims. They and their officials established links with both eastern and western Christians, and Christian rulers in Asia Minor and Europe cherished hopes of an alliance with them against Islam. Most research suggests that during this period few traces of animosity against Christians can be found in the Persian literature of the time. Leonard Lewishon has suggested that during the later half of the thirteenth century a Muslim Sufi perspective on religious diversity developed which was often more 'inclusivistic and ecumenically minded'. By medieval times in general and the Mongol period in particular in Persia (1256–1336), attitudes of contempt towards Christians and Jews were often gradually replaced, among the Sufis at least, by one of 'ecumenical tolerance', although this change in attitude among mystics seems to have been, partially at least, politically motivated. Insofar as the Mongols' reign in the thirteenth-century Persia, Lewishon states:

> In the wider Turco-Indo-Persian cultural sphere, modes of interreligious understanding which developed during the Mongol period profoundly affected the interpretation of Christianity in Persianate *belles lettres* and theosophy down to the end of the seventeenth century – such that even today one still finds poets and writers who advocate the type of esoteric Christianity or interiorised Christianity in an Islamic Sufi garb . . . The fact that the religious promiscuity of Persian society in the thirteenth–fourteenth century Mongol Persia bears much similarity to the amorphous diversity of the multi-religious culture of today's post-modern society.[14]

However, Isabel Stümpel-Hatami informs us that the image of Christianity in Persian thought has been more determined by Iranian encounter with western Christianity, than by Shi'a Islam's relationship with the indigenous Oriental Christian communities – the Church of the East and Armenian Christianity. Persian publications on Christianity discuss mainly its development in the west while they contain only brief remarks about the existence of eastern churches. 'The response to Christianity from within Iran has been determined by several factors. The manifold activities of occidental Christian missionaries through educational and medical assistance in schools, hospitals and bookshops and media did not prosper without provoking deep concern, reaction and protest of the Shi'a Muslim religious class. For some the more the Christian mission was organized, the more it appeared to them like an ever-growing network of conspiracy'.[15]

Along the same lines, the Iranian Jewish scholar Sorour S. Souroudi on the poetry of Muhammad Riza Shafi'i (M. Sirishk) employs Jesus' crucifixion and his miracles allegorically to create a false messiah who symbolises the oppressive attitude of the Christian west towards the Islamic east: 'Lined up as beggars / We reaped with the sickle of each Crescent / Multiple harvests of poverty and hunger / In the miracle fields of this uncrucified Jesus. O messiah of plunder, of hate! O artificial messiah! Where is the rain to wash off your face. The false images, the shadows of deceit'.[16]

While Riza Shafi'i deploys the Jesus motif in a negative form, it does in fact represent a changed poetic form. During the early part of the twentieth century classical Islamic motifs, myths and legends began to lose their prominent position in the Persian literary canon. The intense nationalistic sentiments, especially after the Constitutional Revolution (1906–11), expressed during that period resulted in the partial revival of ancient Iranian myths and legends that had, to different degrees, fallen into disfavour during the classical period due to Islamic influence.[17] Souroudi confirms that among the poetic figures of Persian classical poetry that have retained their appeal, even for the modernist poet, Jesus is the most outstanding. The personality and presence of Jesus is understood and interpreted in new ways which previously had not been found in the classical canon. For example, Jesus' image as a persecuted man who bore his burden with love and who did not give up his belief even at the cost of his life, which he sacrificed for others does not on the whole receive much attention in Islamic writing in general. Jesus is portrayed in the New Testament as a spiritual shepherd or leader who bears the burden of public responsibility. All his words and acts, including the fact that he did not oppose crucifixion were aimed at saving others. This main characteristic appeals to some modern poets who also feel the burden of public responsibilities. Again introduced by Souroudi, Mâhdi Akhavân Sâlis (M. Omid) writes: 'As my enemy's desire, a lonely soul, and the pen on my back, a cross. Has fate mistaken me for Mary's Jesus?'.[18]

Judging by these poems, it seems that not only Jesus' image, but also the poet's self-image and his relation with his surroundings have changed since the classical period; and it is this later change the new image of Jesus reflects. This represents a historical rupture and a new dimension to how Shi'a Islamic and Iranian thought in Iran understands and relates to Christianity.[19]

A reflection on Christianity in the modern era by the influential Iranian Shi'a thinker is given by Ali Shari'ati (1933–1977), one of the main precursors to the Islamic revolution, who had spent some years in Paris were he met a range of Catholic thinkers, particularly Louis Massignon (1883–1962),[20] who deeply contributed to his religious and political thought.

> Through Massignon, Shariati was exposed to a radical Catholic journal named *Esprit*. Founded by Emmanuel Mounier, a socially committed Catholic, *Esprit* in the early 1960s supported a number of left-wing causes, particularly national liberation struggles in the Third World. It carried articles on Cuba, Algeria, Arab nationalism, economic, underdevelopment, and contemporary communion – especially the different varieties of Marxist thought. Its authors included Massignon, Michel Foucault, Corbin, Fanon, radical Catholics, and Marxists such as Lukacs, Jacques Berque and Henri Lefebvre. Moreover, *Esprit* in these years ran frequent articles on Christian-Marxist dialogue, on Left Catholicism, on Jaure's religious socialism, and on Christ's 'revolutionary, egalitarian teachings'. Despite the influence of Massignon and *Esprit*, Shariati later scrupulously avoided any mention of radical Catholicism. To have done so would have weakened his claim that Shiism was the only world religion that espoused social justice, economic reality and political revolution.[21]

However, it is in Shari'ati's writings that we find some outstanding and original reflections on Christianity:

> It is Mary, who made that dry and haughty Yahweh descend from his throne, he who was indifferent in his omnipotence, who was enthroned with his angels and who stamped on creation like a ruined village, and from time to time used to throw a look of pity in its direction, it was she who made him come to earth, made him tender and tame on Earth. He who was accessible to no one was made incarnate in the sinless and good face of his Jesus. Yes! So wasn't Jesus God! It was Mary who made God come to Earth and fashioned him in the image of a man and it is Caesar who put him on the cross and nailed his four limbs to it. But it was still the work of Mary: it was she who made God descend to Earth and made him go up from the Earth into the heavens of the gibbet and that time God ascended from his gibbet into the heaven of his solitude [. . .] But thanks to this descent and ascent, in his essence some very important transformations happened . . . Because Christ is the Holy Spirit and the Word of God, is the pure blood of God that had been nailed to the cross, and he had done all this to save the spirit of man from original sin and he saw that peace and reconciliation and charity and love, on earth, have stretched their wings and that hearts have been raised from their rottenness, their hate, their jealousy, their ugliness and their baseness'.[22]

The politics of Christian presence

Modern history has placed the Christian communities in the contested borderlands between Iran and its neighbour states situated in conflicts not of its making and beyond their control. The border in the sixteenth and seventeenth centuries between the emerging Shi'a power in Iran and the 'sunni' Ottoman empire change hands constantly. Christians living mainly in those disputed areas suffered from those ceaseless wars that accelerate their withdrawal towards the northern mountains. The Christian communities disappeared from Baghdad, Tabriz, Nisibis, cradle of the Church of the East, and from Maragha, where the Catholicos is based, at the end of thirteenth century.

Shah Abbâs (1588–1629) turned to the Armenian and Georgian Christians to modernise his army and rule the provinces of his empire.[23] After conquering Armenia the Shah displaced and transferred large groups of Christians to Iran. Armenian communities were now located in large urban centres, in particular Isfahan. They quickly took control of the great trade from India to Europe and were granted a quasi monopoly of the silk trade.[24] The 'New Julfa' quarter and monastery became an influential centre of Armenian culture.[25] Persia opened up to the European world and sent a series of missions to the Papacy and European states.[26] The Latin missionaries, Augustinians, Capuchins, Carmelites, Dominicans, and Jesuits arrived in Persia and engaged in religious exchange.[27] The Christian encounter with Islam rulers could be a deadly political affair which could end in religious martyrdom. The Georgian Queen Kétévan, who was killed in Shiraz in 1624, is considered one such Christian. Her martyrdom was widely seen at the time as a Christian witness and has recently been acknowledged as an 'ecumenical event'.[28]

In 1828, the Turkmentchai treaty put an end to the Russia–Persia war; Christians settled in the most remote disputed fringes of the country continued to suffer from conflict between Iran and its neighbours. The treaty authorised the emigration to Russia of all the Armenians from Persia. Thirty-five thousand Armenians from Azerbaijan left the country. As for their brothers from the central part of the country, now isolated and weakened, they suffered from the unstable situation and from the religious tensions brought by the war. Towards the middle of the nineteenth century, the Armenian community in New Julfa was in economic and demographic decline. The surrounding Armenian villages lost half of their population between 1856 and 1872. The other main Christian community, the Church of the East and the Chaldean church, with approximately 45,000 members, was based in western Azerbaijan, in the plain that runs from the lake Urmiah to the Ottoman border.[29]

After the Second World War cold war politics created further displacement of Christians and new difficulties emerged: the Soviet forces stayed in Azerbaijan and Kurdistan where they provoked separatist movements. In early 1946, an independent Kurdish republic was proclaimed in Mahabad, south of Lake Urmiah. At the same time, a state was formed in Iranian Azerbaijan. The Assyrian and Chaldean Christians, most of them native to these regions, were divided between their allegiance to the central state and pressure from the separatists. The Armenians welcomed the repatriation campaign of the Soviet Armenian government, but it stopped suddenly in 1947, leaving thousands totally distraught, as they had sold all their possessions to prepare for their departure.[30] In the following years, the political situation in Iran remained unstable. The new Shah, Muhammad Reza, came into conflict with the nationalist movement nurtured on hostility to western presence. It erupted into open conflict and the Shah, threatened by a popular uprising, was forced to leave the country in 1953;

however, the army, helped by the United States, allowed him to return to Tehran a few days later.

Transformed by this event, Muhammad Reza from then on played a more important part in the affairs of state. The regime was semi-parliamentary from 1963 onwards, and evolved into an authoritarian monarchy. But at the same time reforms aiming at rapidly modernising Iranian society were implemented. Known as 'the white revolution' they deeply offended the Islamic religious establishment, whose material interests suffered from the agrarian reform and whose ascendancy over society was threatened by measures such as literacy, the emancipation of women, and the westernisation of society. The Shah underestimated the capacity of religious circles to exploit the situation against him. As the years passed, he became more isolated, obsessively pursuing his dream of making Iran a great regional power. The Islamic revolution brought to an end his regime in 1979.

The thirty-seven years of the reign of Muhammad Reza were good years for the Christians and other minorities in Iran, principally due to the impartiality of the state towards the dominant religion. An atmosphere of relative 'religious freedom' prevailed – the minorities experienced religious emancipation as they never had before. The Shah devoted himself to erasing discrimination and putting in place the elements for a legal status for religious communities that had never really existed in Iran. The law in 1943 codified the personal status of non-Muslims. Despite the 1906 constitution,[31] which reserved political functions for Muslims, Christians had been represented in most of the governments as vice-ministers (it was usual practice that in Islamic states only Muslims could be ministers). Christians, Jews and Zoroastrians had a parliamentary representation more than proportionate to their number. The protection of the state was given to non-Muslim places of worship, while the foreign Christian congregations and missions maintained a schools network. Furthermore, developments in education and for the promotion of the rights of women eased the social pressure of Islam, which in turn lead to a greater acceptance of religious minorities by the rest of the population. But this policy was conducted in a spirit of enlightened despotism without trying to obtain the support of the people concerned. Discredited as the policy of Shah, after the Islamic Revolution this period of emancipation and tolerance towards non-Muslim religious communities paradoxically has been seen by some scholars as undermining the situation of the Christians and other minorities, who were blamed by Islamic groups for allowing themselves to be protected by the regime.

The place of the Christians in Islamic Iran has never been satisfactorily defined.[32] The Shi'ite tradition for a large part has ignored the regime for 'the people of the book' as defined in Muslim tradition.[33] The Persian empire did not follow the Ottoman *millet* system in creating a definitive organisation for religious minorities.[34] The presence of other religious 'nations' apart from the Islamic one as political entities inside the Iranian state would have supposed Christian communities large enough with a powerful ecclesiastical hierarchy, as in the Ottoman empire, which was not the case in Iran. Shi'ism does not consider all the religions of Iran to have equality. Thus the fate of the Christians in Iran has been to suffer the same discriminations and difficulties as the rest of the majority Shi'a population but Christians could not benefit from the protection of official status. In practice, Christians lived apart, in rural areas with difficult access or in reserved quarters of the towns. They had no other guarantee than tolerance – often quite changing – from their Muslim environment and the protection of the monarchs, such as the personal guarantee by Muhammad Reza's regime. The modernisation of the country and the nationalist movement had not eased their integration in Iran. Religion, language and culture distinguished Armenians, Assyrians and Chaldeans from other Iranians. Anti-western sentiment was easily extended to the native Christians because of their role as cultural and political intermediaries between Iranian society and the west.

With the establishment of the Islamic Republic the status of Christians has become the one of a religious minority organised and under the authority of the state. After half a century of slow emancipation they now have *dhimmi* status.[35] One of the few positive aspects of this situation is that the Christian community, even with its restrictions and constraints, now benefits from constitutional recognition. The cruel persecutions suffered by the non-recognised minorities, such as the Baha'is underline *a contrario* the importance of this.

Christians have representation in parliament, as do the Jewish and Zoroastrian communities, with three seats including two for the Armenians and one for Assyrian-Chaldeans, that is to say more than their population would normally require. The 1943 law defining the personal status of non-Muslims has been maintained and even reinforced. Tribunals in each religious community decide on questions relating to personal status with canon law. Their decisions are granted executive force by the public authority.[36]

Since the Islamic Revolution the churches have suffered from a 'low level' of permanent insecurity which has encouraged emigration especially of the young. Interestingly, unlike in Iraq, there has been a weak response to a vocation in the priesthood; this is no doubt due to the lack of public and religious space given to non-Shi'a Muslim communities.[37] The Armenian church has had to rely on clergy from Lebanon and Syria, while the Assyrian and Chaldean churches have called on their co-religionists of Iraq. The disorganisation, which followed the departure of foreign missions, especially as the principal providers of education in support of local Christianity, left the communities vulnerable. There is fear among Christians in Iran that their distinctive religious and cultural identity might disappear under the weight of modern history and contemporary political forces. There is also the question of a unified Christian front, which is difficult to achieve as the Armenians and the Assyrians and Chaldeans are doctrinally very different and often live in separate regions, although there is a significant common presence in Teheran. The ecumenism is still limited to formal relationships between ecclesiastical dignitaries. Due to size and position in society the significant theological revival in Iraq (at least until 2003) has not been possible in contemporary Iran.[38]

The preservation of Armenian and Syriac identity was provided, before the revolution, by the existence of a network of religious schools (approximately sixty primary and secondary Christian schools with 25,000 students) and cultural associations offering language courses. They have since been confronted by a theocratic state which controls the religious instruction and which seeks to promote Persian rather than minority languages and cultures. Muslim directors have been appointed and the ministry of Islamic direction must approve schoolbooks. It is often the case that the generation taught in Persian has problems understanding the liturgy and catechism in Syriac. Under the monarchy, some Syriac literary activity had been able to develop, such as journals and books; however, this cultural and intellectual revival quickly declined during the Islamic Republic.[39]

Christianity in modern Iran

The Armenian presence in Iran, approximately 130,000, some 60,000 have left since 1979, constitutes one of the most important Armenian communities of the Middle East diaspora, if not the most important, considering the rapid decline of the Armenian community in Lebanon.[40] The largest concentrations of Armenians in Iran are the 100,000 in Tehran, 10,000 in Isfahan, their historical centre, and 2000 in Tabriz. A small number of Armenians still live in rural areas, northwest of Isfahan and in Iranian Azerbaijan. Many of the wealthiest Armenians left during the revolution, those who remain are well represented in the liberal and technical professions or in the traditional sectors of trade and craft industry. Political orientation is generally 'Armenian nationalist', which is accepted without difficulty by the Iranian government because this can be used in its relations with Turkey and with the modern Armenian state.

The Armenian church is divided between three dioceses, Isfahan, Tabriz and Tehran.[41] The head of the Tehran diocese is an archbishop who acts as chief of the Armenian community. Each diocese has a mixed diocesan council with clerical and lay membership. The Armenian church in Iran until 1945 had been under the authority of the Catholicos of Ejmiatsin, but given the control exercised in Armenia by Soviet power, the church became part of the jurisdiction of the Catholicos of Sis (Cilicia), based in Antelias in Lebanon which during the cold war period was considered as pro-western. There is a small Armenian Catholic community with its origins in the seventeenth century, and Protestant churches exist dating from the nineteenth century onwards.[42]

The Armenians have sought to accommodate themselves to the Islamic state, for example, immediately after the revolution the Catholicos of Sis, the former bishop of Isfahan went to Iran to meet Ayatollah Khomeini. Back in Tehran in 1993 to celebrate Christmas, he went and meditated at the Imam Khomeini mausoleum. During the Iran–Iraq war (1980–88) mobilisation of Christians took place with Armenian fighters paying a blood tribute on the battlefields; the Christians of Iraq were required to do the same.[43]

The relationships between the Armenian community and the Islamic Republic should not, however, be idealised. The Islamic government born from the revolution is too deeply convinced of Muslim superiority and its ideology is too rigid to allow Christianity to flourish. While Armenian schools are allowed, there are measures which restrict Christian instruction, and an obligation to use Islamic materials, especially in regard to the Qur'anic understanding of Christianity, that bear no relation to Christian doctrinal authenticity and truth. Armenian Christian identity has been able to deepen and bloom against a history of displacement and genocide. This has required an 'enculturation' in a unique religious and political environment, a Shi'a Islamic state. For the Armenian Christian community to flourish it will require all its resources for survival to sustain a presence, which will be for the benefit for all in Iranian society and culture.

The second Christian community in terms of size (20–25,000) and importance is the Assyrian Church of the East and the Chaldean Catholic church with its historical centre in western Azerbaijan in the region of Lake Urmiah.[44] The Syriac Christian presence dates from the movement of members of the Church of the East from Mesopotamia towards the northern mountains, after the Mongol invasion. As with their co-religionists in the Hakkari (now in the modern Turkish Republic), this region from the later part of the nineteenth century became the centre of struggle for influence between Ottomans, British and Russians. The latter succeeded for a while to attract members the Assyrian and Chaldean communities to their church thanks to a Russian Orthodox mission sent in 1898.[45] Against this trend of ecclesial fragmentation the Assyrian community sought to create the foundations of cultural and political unity.[46] During the First World War conflict between the Turkish and Russian forces who occupied the Urmiah region lead the Assyrian and Chaldean communities to a disaster: many of them chose in 1915 to take refuge in Russia while the others, in 1918 were forced to flee southwards to seek the protection of the British authorities in Iran and then Iraq. These Syriac Christians only partially recovered from this displacement, settling in the Urmiah region or in Tehran. The other alternative for the community has been to seek a future elsewhere and they have immigrated in large numbers.[47]

The Assyrian and Chaldean communalities of Iran are divided between two main families, three if one considers the small Protestant minority: the Church of the East under the Catholicos Mar Denkha IV, and the Chaldean Catholics whose patriarch is located in Baghdad, Emmanuel Delly III.[48] While the two churches have a similar liturgy and belong to the same Syriac Christian culture, there are still slight differences between them. The majority of Assyrians of the Church of the East are descendants from Christian populations of the mountain, who are themselves subdivided in two groups: those who were living in Azerbaijan from time immemorial and those who took refuge in 1915, originating from the Turkish Hakkari. On the contrary the Chaldean Catholics come mainly from the plains, either Mesopotamia (south of Kurdistan) or the region of Shah-pour (ex-Salmas), in Iranian Azerbaijan. The two communities do not speak the same Syriac dialect and have a somewhat 'different collective psychology'.[49] The Church of the East are mountain people with an independent spirit and their church acts as guardian of the Assyrian national tradition. The Chaldean Catholics are from an agricultural background and have not experienced to the same degree the traumatic history of massacre and displacement.[50] During the Iran-Iraq war they, like the Armenians, found themselves recruited into the Iranian army in the fight against Iraq and no doubt in certain circumstances their brother Christians of Iraq.[51]

Relations between the Chaldean church and the state have suffered because its hierarchy is based in Iraq; while the Catholicos of the Church of the East had been until recent times based in Iran. The monarchist government used its Assyrian minority to bolster its foreign policy with regard to Iraq. After the 1975 rapprochement on that border, the Assyrians of Iran found their activities, particularly regarding the acquisition of a homeland, more restricted. However, under the monarchy the Assyrians benefited from the lack of sectarian strife that in the past had plagued their relationship with their Muslim neighbours.[52] For this reason, many openly and loudly supported the Shah. His approaching removal seemed to many of them a threat to the existence of the community. They feared both retaliation for the support they had given him in the past, plus second-class status under a theocratic state. Patriarch Mar Dinka IV had the great misfortune to assume office just as the Iran–Iraq war began; partly as a result he settled reluctantly in Chicago separated from his church and people in the Middle East.[53]

In contemporary Iran there are also very small numbers of other eastern Christianities: Arab Orthodox or Russian Orthodox communities. There is an Episcopalian (Anglican) church of Iran, which forms one of the four dioceses of the Anglican church in the Middle East, founded in the nineteenth century thanks to the efforts of the church missionary society. Its headquarters are in Isfahan and its bishop, since 1961, is a Persian. It suffered a great deal after the revolution when it lost all its property and institutions. Members of this church have experienced martyrdom.[54] The creation of Latin Episcopal structures in Iran dates from the seventeenth century, with the Latin archdiocese of Isfahan. Until the revolution the Catholic community ran an impressive and prestigious educational and welfare network, but none of this remains *in situ*. However, there continues an active diplomatic and scholarly exchange between the Vatican, the Catholic church and the Shi'a state.[55] There is also a large, but largely unrecorded, number of Iranian converts to Christianity in Iran and especially in the diaspora, which might number tens of thousands of members.

Conclusion

Christianity in Iran has an ancient lineage. Christianity has experienced significant historical changes that have to some degree defined its minority status and position in relation to Persian culture and religion. The modern era has witnessed its revival and decline, and its fight for survival. The Christian presence in Iran is in a unique position, acting as it does as the only local interface between Shi'a Islam and its state, which has often been locked in conflict with the west and its neighbours, and the Christian world. Christianity in Iran is important to both Christianity and Islam and while its continuing presence will be challenged, its significance will not be diminished.

Notes

1 For a general historical survey of Christianity in Persia or Islamic Iran see Waterfield, R. E., *Christians in Persia* (London, George Allen & Unwin, 1973); Bugnini, A., *La Chiese en Iran* (Rome, Ed. Vencenziane, 1981).

2 Asmussen, J. P., 'Das Christentum in Iran und sein Verhältnis zur Zoroastrismus', *Studia Theologica*, 16 (1962), 1–22; 'Christians in Iran', *Cambridge History of Iran*, 3: 2 (1983), 924–48.

3 Tajadod, N., *Les Porteurs de lumière: péripéties de l'église chrétienne de Perse du IIIe au VIIe siècle* (Paris, Plon, 1996).

4 For an overview of the subject see: Russell, J. R., 'Christianity in pre-Islamic Persia: literary sources', *The Encyclopedia Iranica*, 5: 5 (1991), 523–8. For Islamic sources see Dammen McAuliffe, J., 'Persian exegetical evaluation of the *Ahl al-Kitâb*', *The Muslim World*, 73: 2 (1983), 87–105.

5 Brock, S., 'L'Église de l'Orient dans l'Empire sassanide jusqu'au vie siècle et son absence aux conciles de l'Empire romain', *Istina*, 40 (1995), 25–43.

6 Gerö, S., 'Only a change of masters? The Christians of Iran and the Muslim conquest', *Transition Periods in Iranian History, Cahiers de Studia Iranica*, 5 (1987), 47.

7 Chaumont, M.-L., 'Le christianisation de l'Émpire iranien, des origines aux grandes persecutions du IV e siècle', *Corpus Scriptorum Christianorum Orientalium*, 499 (1988), 16–198.

8 The standard history of the period is Labourt, J., *Le Christianisme dans l'empire perse sous la dynastie Sassanide (224–632)* (Paris, V. Lecoffre, 1904), which, according to James R. Russell, 'closed his classic account of the Muslim conquest with his influential statement that the Christian either showed a neutrality favourable to the invaders or at least did practically nothing to help the Persians, this passivity continued a pattern of behaviour the Aramaeans of Mesopotamia who had been dominated and exploited by the stronger for over a millennium', Russell, 'Christianity in pre-Islamic Persia', 524.

9 Fiey, J.-M., 'L'expansion de l'Église de Perse', *Istina*, 40 (1995), 149–56.

10 Gerö, 'Only a change of masters?', 48; and Gerö, S., 'Christians in the Sassanid empire: a case of divided loyalties', *Studies in Church History*, 18 (1982), 1–19.

11 Foremost among which may be mentioned is by the Anglican bishop in Iran, Hassan B. Dihqâni-Taftî, *Masîh wa Masîhiyyat nazd-I Irâniyân, I: Sayr-I ijmâlì dar târìkh; II: Dar Shi'r fârsì dawrân-I sabk-I kukan; III: Dar nazm wa nathr wa hunar-I mu'âsì* (London, Suhrâb, 1992–94).

12 A significant voice here is the work of Jewish Egyptian Dominican scholar Père Jean P. de Menasce (OP) on the Mazdean account of Judaism, Christianity and Islam which has highlighted this interreligious encounter in Iran. Monnot (OP), Guy, *Père de Menasce et l'Islam, Jean de Menasce (1902–1973)* Textes réunis par Michel Dousse et Jean-Michel Roessli (Fribourg (Suisse), Bibliothéque cantonale et universitaire, 1998), pp. 185–91. A further dimension to this encounter is the scholarship and poetry of an English Dominican scholar of Islam in Persia – Iran see O'Mahony, Anthony, 'Cyprian Rice, op., l'Islam chiite et la mission dominicaine en Perse-Iran, 1933–1934', *Mémoire dominicaine: Les Dominicains et les mondes musulmans*, 15 (2001), 217–25.

13 Qamar Ariyân, *Chihrah-yi masîh dar adabiyât-I fârsî* (Tehran, Intishârât-I mu'în, 1990). See also the synopsis of these findings by the same author, 'Christian influences in Persian literature', *Encyclopedia Iranica*, 5 (1991), 539–42. See also the critique by Richard, Y., 'Le Visage du Christ dans la poésie persane', *Marana Tha* (Paris-Téhéran), 29 (1993), 26–7.

14 Lewishon, L., 'The esoteric Christianity of Islam: interiorisation of Christian imagery in medieval Persian Sufi poetry', in Ridgeon, L. (ed.), *Islamic Interpretations of Christianity* (Richmond, Curzon, 2001), pp. 127–56, p. 133.

15 Stümpel-Hatami, I., 'Christianity as described by Persian Muslims', in Waardenburg, J. (ed.), *Muslim Perceptions of Other Religions: A Historical Survey* (Oxford, Oxford University Press, 1999), pp. 227–39. A full exposition is given in her *Das Christentum aus der Sicht zeitgenössischer iranischer Autorn: Eine Untersuchung religionskundlicher Publikationen in persischer sprache* (Berlin, Klaus Schwarz, 1996). See also the general overview by O'Mahony, A., 'The image of Jesus and Christianity in Shi'a Islam and modern Iranian thought', in Thomas, D. with Amos, C. (eds), *A Faithful Presence: Essays for Kenneth Cragg* (London, Melisende, 2003), pp. 256–73.

16 Shafi'i, M. R., *Dar Kucha-bâghhâ-yi Naishâpur* (Tehran, 1970) quoted in Souroudi, S. S., 'On Jesus' image in modern Persian poetry', *The Muslim World*, 69: 4 (1979), 221–8, p. 227.

17 Souroudi, S. S., 'Poet and revolution: the impact of the Iranian constitutional revolution on the literary and social outlook of the poet', *Iranian Studies*, 12 (1979), 3–41, 239–73.

18 Mâhdi Akhavân Sâlis (M. Omid): *Pa'iz dar Zindân* (Tehran, Rowzan, 1969), p. 52, in Souroudi, 'On Jesus' image in modern Persian poetry', p. 224.

19 Leirvik, O., 'Jesus in Shi'ite tradition', in *Images of Jesus Christ in Islam*, Uppsala, *Studia Missionalia Upsaliensia*, 76 (1999), 76–80.

20 O'Mahony, A., 'Mysticism, politics, dialogue: Catholic encounters with Shi'a Islam in the life and work of Louis Massignon', in O'Mahony, A., Peterburs, W. and Shomali, M. A. (eds), *Catholics and Shi'a in Dialogue: Studies in Theology and Spirituality* (London, Melisende, 2004), pp. 134–84; 'Mysticism and politics: Louis Massignon, Shi'a Islam, Iran and 'Ali Shari'ati – a Muslim-Christian encounter', *University Lectures in Islamic Studies*, 2 (1998), 113–34.

21 Abrahamian, E., *Radical Islam: The Iranian Mojahedin* (London, I. B. Tauris, 1989), p. 108.

22 The passages quoted here are taken from an article by Richard, Y., 'Lettre à mes amis d'Iran sur Dibâtch et Shari'ati', *La Croix l'événement* (3 août 1994), 13 and are taken from the two final volumes (33/1 et 33/2) of Shari'ati's *Œuvres completes*, Vol. 1, pp. 49–50 and Vol. 2, pp. 718–19.

23 Forand, P. G., 'Accounts of western travellers concerning the role of Armenians and Georgians in sixteenth century Iran', *The Muslim World*, 65 (1975), 264–78.

24 McCabe, I. B., *The Shah's Silk for Europe's Silver: The Eurasian Trade of the Julfa Armenians in Safavid Iran and India (1530–1750)* (Leuven, Peeters, 1999).

25 Ghougassian, V. S., *The Emergence of the Armenian Diocese of New Julfa in the Seventeenth Century* (Leuven, Peeters, 1998).

26 Alonso, C., 'Una embajada de Clemente VIII a Persia (1600–1609)', *Archivum Historiae Pontificiae*, 34 (1996), 7–126.

27 Richard, F., 'Catholicisme et Islam Chiite au "Grand Siècle": Autour de quelques documents concernant les Missions catholiques en Perse au XVII ème siécle', *Euntes Docete*, 33 (1980), 339–403.

28 Gulbenkian, R., 'Relation vérítable du glorieux martyre de la reine Kétévan de Géorgie', *Bedi Kartlisa*, 40 (1982), 31–97; Flannery, J., 'The martyrdom of Queen Ketevan in seventeenth century Iran: an episode in relations between the Georgian church and Rome', *Sobornost/Eastern Churches Review*, 27: 1 (2005), 8–25.

29 Hellot, F., 'Les Assyriens de Perse au XIXe siècle', *Dabireh*, 3 (1988), 161–85.
30 Mouradian, C. S., 'L'Immigration des arméniens de al diaspora vers la R.S.S. d'Armenie 1946–1962', *Cahiers du monde russe et sovietique*, 20 (1979), 79–110.
31 Tsadik, D., 'The legal status of religious minorities: Imânî Shi'i law and Iran's constitutional revolution', *Islamic Law and Society*, 10: 3 (2003), 376–408; Bordor, D., 'A comparative overview of the Iranian constitutions of 1906–07 and 1979', *Iran and the Caucasus*, 10: 2 (2006), 263–86.
32 Savoury, R. M., 'Relations between the Safavid state and its non-Muslim minorities', *Islam and Christian–Muslim Relations*, 14: 4 (2003), 435–58.
33 Ahl al-kitab was used by Muslim tradition to designate non-Muslims who had a revealed scripture which Muslims only partially recognised and could gain 'Qur'anic rights based upon paying a "poll-tax" (jizya)'. Friedmann, Y., 'Classification of unbelievers in Sunni law and tradition', *Jerusalem Studies in Arabic and Islam*, 22 (1998), 163–95.
34 See the remarks by Nenad Moacanin on Islam and the Ottoman system, 'Some remarks on the supposed Muslim tolerance towards *Dhimmis*', *Südost Forschungen*, 48 (1989), 209–15.
35 As a sign of their submission to the Islamic authority they were obliged to pay tribute and special taxes, in particular *Jizyah* and the *Kharaj*. The doctors of Islam law tended to draw quite distinct boundaries between Muslims and non-Muslims, and to interpret the subjection of *dhimmis* to Islamic authority as a justification for discriminatory and humiliating measures imposed upon them. Noth, A., 'Möglichkeiten und Grenzen islamischer Toleranz', *Saeculum*, 29 (1978), 190–204; 'Abgrenzungsprobleme zwischen Muslimen und Nicht-Muslimen: die Bedingungen "Umars (as-surut al-'umariyya)" unter anderem Aspekt gelsen', *Jerusalem Studies in Arabic and Islam*, 9 (1987), 290–315.
36 On the position of Christian communities under the Islamic Republic see Sanasarian, E., *Religious Minorities in Iran* (Cambridge, Cambridge University Press, 2000), pp. 73–105.
37 O'Mahony, A., 'Christianity in modern Iraq', *International Journal for the Study of the Christian Church*, 4: 2 (2004), 121–42.
38 Brock, S., 'The Syriac churches in ecumenical dialogue on Christology,' in O'Mahony, A. (ed.), *Eastern Christianity: Studies in Modern History, Religion and Politics* (London, Melisende, 2004), pp. 44–65; O'Mahony, A., 'The Chaldean Catholic church: the politics of church–state relations in modern Iraq', *The Heythrop Journal*, 45: 4 (2004), 435–50.
39 Carney, D., 'Le Chrétientés de la République Islamique', *Les Cahiers de L'Orient*, 48 (1997), 85–91.
40 Sanjian, A., 'The Armenian minority experience in the modern Arab world', *Bulletin of the Royal Institute for Interfaith Studies*, 3: 1 (2001).
41 Tchilingirian, H., 'The Catholicos and the hierarchical Sees of the Armenian church', in O'Mahony (ed.), *Eastern Christianity*, pp. 140–59.
42 Whooley, J., 'The Armenian Catholic church: a study in history and ecclesiology', *The Heythrop Journal*, 45: 4 (2004), 416–34.
43 Petrosian, V., 'Assyrians in Iraq', *Iran and the Caucasus*, 10: 1 (2006), 113–47.
44 De Mauroy, H., *Les Assyro-chaldéens l'Iran d'aujourd'hui* (Paris, Publications du department de géographie de l'université de Paris-Sorbonne, no. 6, 1978); and for a general description, O'Mahony, A., 'Syriac Christianity in the modern Middle East', in Angold, M. (ed) *The Cambridge History of Christianity, Vol. 5:*

Eastern Christianity (Cambridge, Cambridge University Press, 2006), pp. 511–35.

45 Suttner, E. Chr., 'Die Union der sogenannten Nestorianer aus der Gegand von Urmia (Persien) mit der Russischen Orthodoxen Kirche', *Ostkirchliche Studien*, 44 (1995), 33–40.

46 Naby, E., 'The Assyrians of Iran: reunification of a "millat", 1906–1914', *International Journal of Middle East Studies*, 8 (1977), 237–49.

47 De Mauroy, H., 'Mouvements de population dans la communauté assyro-chadéenne en Iran', *Revue de Géographie de Lyon*, 43: 3 (1968), 333–56.

48 Patriarch Delly knows Iran well as he had on a number of occasions gone to comfort and pray with the number of Iraqi Christian prisoners of war, who might be considered some of the most forgotten of all, still held since the ending of the Gulf War, see O'Mahony, A., 'Life and death of a patriarch: Mar Rouphael I Bidwid, Patriarch of Babylon and the Chaldean Catholic church in Iraq', *Sobornost/Eastern Churches Review*, 27: 1 (2005), 26–46.

49 Valognes, J.-P., 'Les Chrétiens d'Iran', in Valognes, *Vie et mort des chrétiens d'Orient*, pp. 767–95, p. 785.

50 de Coutois, S., Aurora V. (trans), *The Forgotten Genocide: Eastern Christians, the Last Arameans* (New York, Gorgias Press, 2004); Alichoran, J., 'Du genocide à la diaspora: les Assyro-chaldéens au XX éme siècle', *Istina*, 39 (1994), 363–98.

51 According to Joseph Jacoub, 40,000 Iraqi Christians died in Iran–Iraq war 'The Christians in Iraq: a historical perspective', *Journal of the Assyrian Academic Society*, 5: 2 (1991), 32.

52 Schwartz, R. M., *The Structure of Christian–Muslim Relations in Contemporary Iran* (Halifax, Nova Scotia, Saint Mary's University, 1985).

53 Baum, W. and Winkler, D. W., *The Church of the East: A Concise History* (London, Routledge Curzon, 2003), pp. 135–57.

54 Deqâni-Tafti, H. B., *The Unfolding Design of My World: A Pilgrim in Exile* (Norwich, The Canterbury Press, 2000).

55 Bill, J. A. and Williams, J. A., *Roman Catholics and Shi'i Muslims: Prayer, Passion and Politics* (Chapel Hill, London, The University of North Carolina Press, 2002).

13

Christian–Muslim encounters in South Africa

Chris Clohessy

This chapter attempts to trace the genesis, rooting and history of Islam in South Africa, with special reference to the area known as the Western Cape, where the majority of Muslims now live. It also tries to examine the spirit of resistance that characterised South African Islam in the post-1960s period and the resurgence of this spirit after the first democratic elections in 1994. As will be seen, the Islamisation of South Africa, and the South African Islam that resulted, was based upon five definite determining marks or characteristics, which have moulded and shaped the religion in this region until the present day.

Despite the democratic elections and the end of apartheid,[1] it is difficult to look at the history of South Africa, and at the Islamisation of that country, without categorising people in terms of colour. This is the unfortunate legacy of the South African situation, but is also part of the dynamic that has forged the history of the country. In trying, therefore, to articulate the nature of South African Islam, the question of colour and racial classification will be one of the points of reference, and is used purely to clarify certain issues.

It should also be noted that there is a dearth of information concerning South African Islam. This is due partly to the repression of the apartheid years: silenced by history, the Muslim community in South Africa is only now, in the context of democracy, finding a voice and an identity. Finally, this short chapter is an historical sketch and as such does not do justice to the vitality, vibrancy and rich multicultural heritage of Islam in South Africa and South African Islam.

Context

'The loss of cultural roots can be a profoundly disturbing experience and even in our own day it can produce an aggressive, defiant religiosity as a means of asserting the beleaguered self'.[2] Perhaps these words from Karen Armstrong most aptly describe the situation of South African Islam, which has rooted itself among a particular people and in a unique socio-political context. But Islam in South Africa has been nurtured and shaped not only by a particular political context, nor alone by the social grouping in which it took root. From the very beginning, the history of its own arrival and growth, and of the country it had come to, has profoundly shaped and characterised Islam until the present day.

In reality, not only Islam in South Africa, but more especially South African Islam is the product of a whole range of social, cultural, political and historical factors which, from its very genesis in the country have determined its growth and acceptance.

There are perhaps five distinguishing marks or characteristics, factors which have shaped Islam from the first moments of its arrival and which have played a determining role in the way Islam developed and took root. It is these five traits which must be borne in mind in any reading of Islamic history in South Africa, since they can be traced from the very beginning and have determined the nature of contemporary Muslim society in that country. These traits might be enumerated as follows:

1 The very first Muslims, the 'forefathers' of the present Islamic community, arrived in South Africa as slaves and political prisoners. As such, they were the victims of the Dutch colonial policy. Islam in South Africa is primarily a result of colonialism, in stark contrast to Christianity, which has always been viewed as the religion of the state, and of the powerful.

2 From the very beginning, racial classification forced boundaries, unknown in and contrary to the concept of the *umma*. From the very beginning therefore, Islam found its integrity severely assaulted by the representatives of white, Protestant colonial power, and was forced into novel ways of maintaining the *umma*.

3 The immediate religious oppression, restrictions and hardships made Islam, from the very outset, the 'monotheism of the dispossessed'[3] and produced a spirit of resistance, often dormant but ever-present, which would mould later years of defiance and struggle.

4 From its beginnings, Islam offered the socially and economically marginalised slaves a secure status and a distinct identity. To a great extent, this is still the case today within the so-called 'coloured' population, the descendants of the first slaves and the racial grouping in which Islam continues to find its most popular welcome and support. It is within the context of this racial grouping that a defiant religiosity and spirit of resistance is most clearly seen today.

5 Finally, the 'fathers' of Islamisation in South Africa have been the traders and Muslims of strongly Sufi tendencies. In this, the Islamisation of South Africa is not unlike that of other parts of Africa. But the historical context into which Islam was born, as well as the varying cultures, religions and backgrounds of the first slave communities (notably at the Cape), forced the first Muslims to find innovative ways of forming an *umma* and has led to syncretism and 'acculturation' which has given Islam, especially in the Cape, a unique and distinct flavour.

It is in the light of these five distinguishing characteristics that the history of South African Islam should be read. They provide not only the context, but also offer insight into the nature of contemporary Islam in that country. They can be distinctly detected, woven into the story of the South African Muslim community, and have quite clearly shaped and determined the Islamisation of the country.

Genesis

The first moments of Islam in South Africa are shrouded in a fair amount of obscurity and historical discrepancy. Besides a small community originating from Zanzibar and settling in the area of Natal, the majority of South African Muslims can trace their roots to Indonesia, Malaysia and India. These first Muslims entered South Africa at various times and in different places, and it is these arrivals that are the subject of historical debate. The following historical opinions have been posited:

1 1694 saw the arrival of Sheikh Yusuf of Macassar,[4] a Sufi and a follower of the theology of al-Ash'ari. Born in Macassar in South Sulawesi in Indonesia, and of noble descent, Sheikh Yusuf was exiled to the Cape after being held for ten years in the Castle of Colombo in Ceylon, Sri Lanka. This incarceration and exile resulted from his resistance and protracted guerrilla warfare against the Dutch in the Bantam in Java in 1683. Fighting on the side of Sultan Ageng Tartayassa under great odds and hardships, he kept the Dutch imperialist designs in check for almost a year, finally surrendering on the promise of relief for his captured followers and a pardon for himself. Incarcerated in Ceylon, he continued to engineer resistance against the Dutch until, in the interests of Dutch security, he was exiled to the Cape of Good Hope, arriving in April 1694. He and forty-nine followers were settled on a farm called Zandvliet, fifty-seven kilometres from Cape Town (a distance which, it was hoped, would isolate him from the Indonesian slave community in Cape Town). In fact, his settlement later became a sanctuary for escaped slaves.[5] While his banishment to the Cape is seen by some as the beginnings of the liberation movement, and while he is hailed as 'the father of Islam in South Africa', it is clear that there were already Muslims in the Cape prior to his arrival.

2 1652 witnessed the arrival of Jan van Riebeeck: historians posit that without doubt there were Malaysian Muslim slaves in the party of this first Dutch colonialist.

3 Other historians hold that in 1693 a runaway Muslim slave (Ibrâhîm) arrived at the Cape: but I have been able to find little data to place this on a firm historical footing.

4 In 1658 a group of 'Mardyckers' ('free' Muslims employed as soldiers to protect the Dutch colonial settlements) arrived at the Cape.

Two points are important. The first is that for certain Islam entered South Africa in the first decade of the Dutch colonial presence. The second concerns the question of the 'strands of identity' which would play a major role in the shaping of South African Islam. These strands, which would weave a distinct and colourful Muslim community, have been classified as follows:

1 The first strand: c. 1667, the entry of slaves from one or other island of the Indonesian archipelago, as well as from Malaysia, Sri Lanka and Ceylon. These Muslims were converts of the Arab traders from the eighth century onwards.

2 The second strand: c. 1694, the entry of later Muslim political exiles, including Sheikh Yusuf and Sheikh Madura, the Rajah of Tambora, who died in 1754 on

191

Robben Island, the prison which would later hold Nelson Mandela. These were, for the most part, Muslims of academic leanings and Sufi tendencies.

3 The third strand: c. 1860, the entry of Muslim labourers from India.

4 The fourth strand: c. 1860s–1870s, the arrival of traders from North India who settled in Natal (south east coast) and Guateng (the interior, originally called the 'Transvaal'). These traders, together with the Sufi's, played a crucial role in the Islamisation of South Africa. But there is a discrepancy between historians as to how many of them were Muslim: Sonn holds that they were a minority,[6] while Hiskett posits that Muslims were in the majority.[7]

5 The fifth strand: c. 1873, witnessed the arrival of over 100 families from Zanzibar, who settled in Natal.

With these various arrivals came immediate racial classification, which was to play a vital role in later South African history, but which assaulted the integrity of the Muslim concept of the *umma*. The Indonesians were classed as 'coloured' and the Indians as 'Asian'. The families from Zanzibar appeared to have caused some difficulty: technically, they were 'black' Africans, but for some reason (probably the fact that they were Muslims), they were classified as 'Asian' and hence they lived, were educated and made a life for themselves in strictly Asian areas.

Certainly, the primary Islamisation of South Africa was the result of Dutch colonial policy and the contiguous slave trade. Later, the traders and Sufi's would, as in other parts of Africa, play a major role. But the very first Muslims arrived chained in the holds of oppressor's ships, slaves and political prisoners, destined to be classified in racial terms and oppressed by religious persecution and social marginalisation. This is the heritage of South African Islam, the foundation on which it has been built. Both the arrival of the first Muslims as victims of white, Protestant colonial policy, and their racial classification under the auspices of the same policy, have moulded the way Islam would be practiced in South Africa.

It is in the light of these first beginnings that we must turn our attention to the rooting of Islam in the country, and a process of Islamisation that continued against almost impossible odds.

Roots

From the very start, Islam, already burdened by it social status (or lack thereof) and the indignity of racial classification, faced restrictions, persecution and hardship. In spite of this, and of various counter-measures by the Dutch colonial authorities, it grew steadily and rooted itself firmly. What is clear is that from the very beginning there was a 'spirit of resistance', often dormant but ever-present, which has, at least after the 1960s, manifested itself yet again in contemporary South African Islam.

Between 1657 and 1804 it was a criminal offence, punishable by death, to practice or propagate Islam publicly (the minutiae of the law even forbade circumcision). The so-called 'Statutes of India' were a set of laws imposed and aimed at the restriction of Islamic religious practice in the Batavian empire (i.e. all Dutch colonies):

1 No-one shall trouble the Ambionese (Mardyckers) about their religion or annoy them: so long as they do not practice in public or venture to propagate it among Christians or heathens. Offenders to be punished with death, but should there be among them those who had been drawn to God to become Christian, they are not to be prevented or hindered from joining Christian churches.

2 No public or private meetings of these people (the Muslims) should be held in the town of Batavia and its provinces – the priest being liable to be put in chains until further orders.[8]

A form of religious freedom would only be established in 1804 with the arrival of the British, the new colonial power in South Africa. There was, admittedly, a slight relaxation at the end of the eighteenth century. A Muslim school was established in 1793 and a mosque, built by the slaves and exiles, in 1797 (around this time also the first copy of the Qur'an was copied by a prisoner on Robben Island). But early Islam was rooted in restriction and censorship with its first, slave-built, visible manifestations arising over 100 years after the arrival of the religion.

As a result of the restrictions, the earliest Muslim community was to develop innovative religious associations based primarily on its South Asian Sufi practices. Since these first Muslims came from various regions of the world, there arose a diversity of cultures and practices in the roots, especially of the Cape Muslims, which would later be manifested in a variety of ways. Furthermore, the first Muslims were slaves, housed in common slave lodgings with others, from various cultural and religious backgrounds. This encounter led to an 'acculturation' as Muslims imbibed cultural traits from their fellow slaves (mostly Christian and Hindu). Again, this would be manifested later by various syncretic Muslim practices, most of which have died out. All religious worship and education was 'home based' and secret, so that there were many private forms of Islamic manifestation. Only the Dutch Reformed Protestant church was tolerated, and outside of this, no religion (including Catholicism and other forms of Christianity) was to be exercised, taught or propagated, either publicly or privately. Despite this, there was a rapid rate of growth and conversion among the non-Muslim slaves. In embracing this new faith the slaves, while 'gaining' socially with a new identity, retained many of their own customs and traditions, adding to the distinct strands of syncretism in early South African Islam, in a situation that was largely cut-off and isolated from outside Islamic contacts.

If Islamic history worldwide identified traders and Sufi masters as two important agents in the root and spread of Islam, then South African Islam is no exception to this. In the arrival of traders from north India were the seeds of the Islam now rooted on the Natal coast and in the Gauteng interior. In the case of South Africa, the most prominent agents in the rooting of Islam, not only as a religion but also as a form of resistance against colonialism, were the Sufi's who arrived here mainly as captives and exiles. Prominent among these were Sheikh Yusuf of Macassar, *Qadi* 'Abd al-Salam of Tidore (known later as 'Tuan Guru' – 'Mr Teacher') and Shah Gulam Muhammad Habibi. These, and others, played a prominent role, especially in education that was a primary factor in the rooting and spread of Islam.

A brief overview of the education factor in the process of Islamisation is necessary. From the outset, there was secret, 'home-based' education: there appear to have been early slaves who were learned in the Qur'an and in Islamic law. Some too were 'mystics' and emphasised Sufi teaching and practice, most of it South Asian. Towards the end of the eighteenth century, the Dutch rulers relaxed some of the restrictions on Islam, which had a number of consequences for Islam in South Africa:

1 1793 saw the foundation of the first Islamic school (the Dorp Street School) and in 1797 the first mosque was built by slaves and exiles (the Awwal Masjid). The school was founded by *Qadi* 'Abd al-Salam of Tidore (who died in 1797) who was the first official imam at the Cape and, like Sheikh Yusuf, a follower of the theology of al-Ash'ari. He brought about a revival or reformation of Cape Islam, and many of the early imams of the first mosques were chosen from the descendants of the family and friends of both Sheikh Yusuf and 'Abd al-Salam, perpetuating a particular tradition. The direction of Cape Islam was of a certainty influenced by their teaching and al-Ash'ari leanings, and it was they who trained the first group of South African imams. Furthermore, this first school gave rise to numerous satellite schools, mostly in the homes of the imams.

2 In 1805 the British did away with the Statutes of India and initiated religious freedom. At their request, Sheikh Abu Bakr Effendi arrived from Turkey (introducing yet another cultural strand into Cape Islam) and established a school for girls and the Ottoman Theological School (for higher Islamic learning). In 1863 Effendi instituted a Muslim mission school, open to all, with an Afrikaans/Cape Dutch medium (this was partly a result of church schools being closed to coloured children, and Muslim parents not wanting their children to receive a Christian education).

3 Arabic Islamic literature began to flow into the Cape, once so isolated from the outside Islamic world, from Egypt: this was translated into Afrikaans, the language of the Cape developed from Dutch, but using Arabic letters. Early in the nineteenth century, some young men from the Cape went to Mecca to study *tafsir* and *qira'*. Upon their return, they were to play an influential role in Cape Islam.

4 In 1912 the first *madrasa* (independent from the mosque) was established. By 1959 there were nineteen in the Cape and Natal, following the same curricula as secular schools, but offering Islamic studies. Many of these enjoyed government assistance and had the same status as Christian mission schools.

5 The 1948 imposition of the apartheid laws had a devastating effect: relocation meant the abandonment of hard-won mosques, *madrasa*'s and schools.

6 The 1960s saw the establishment of new *madrasa*'s, different from the earlier ones in that these only supplemented public school education.

7 Finally, the 1970s witnessed the introduction of Arabic and Islamic studies into some of the public, secular schools, and in the 1980s the first exclusively Muslim secondary schools were established.

We will see this theme of education again in dealing with the history of Islam: suffice to say that it played a primary role in the rooting and establishment of

Islam in South Africa, with the early educators influencing the direction Islam would take. Many of their traditions and particular theological and spiritual leanings have been perpetuated in Cape Islam. Also clear is the pivotal role played by Sufi masters and traders in the process of Islamisation, and the ingredient of restriction and hardship, the context into which South African Islam was born and took root and which, together with education, shaped and determined the type of Islam which was to develop in the country.

History prior to 1960

So it was that the first century and a half (1657–1804) of South African Islamic history were years of hardship, oppression and struggle: the earliest Islam was rooted in the banning and punishment of practice and propagation, and in the forbidding of public manifestations and institutions. But Islam grew and developed despite this, kept alive secretly with a powerful impetus from slaves who were learned in the Qur'an and shari'ah, of mystics and of Sufi exiles. This secret growth, with its steady rate of conversions, put a strain on the Dutch slave trade: Muslim slaves came to be regarded as 'unpredictable' and their importation was halted in the Batavian empire. In spite of slight relaxations by the Dutch at the end of the eighteenth century, restrictions continued until 1805, as did the many forms of private Islamic manifestation. The Sufi masters at the Cape continued to strengthen the deep-rooted devotion to God (*tasawwuf*) among the adherents there, and Sufi practices dominated Cape Islam.

One cannot overestimate the role played by the mosque and the imam in South African Islamic history, for the latter is firmly rooted in these two 'institutions'. After the long struggle to establish one, the mosque took a central role as a place of learning, worship and protection: it was partly the protection of their hard-won mosques that brought the Islamic community into open conflict with the apartheid regime from 1948 onwards. A complex mosque organisation, quite obviously influenced by the structures of the Christian church, developed at the Cape, with the imam (chief priest), *Moota* (the deputy imam), *Khatib* (preacher), *Bilal* (deacon) and *Mabut* (imam and sexton). At the centre of the mosque activities, worship and learning was the person of the imam, who played an important pastoral role (not unlike that of the Christian clergy), and especially in the days when the Muslim community came into painful conflict with the government and policies of apartheid. If, 'the first mosque in Islam . . . was the place from where the Prophet controlled the political and religious community of Islam'[9] then the same can certainly be said for the South African mosques and their imams.

In 1805, in response to Napoleon's manoeuvres, British forces invaded the Cape and repelled the Dutch, replacing them as colonial masters. They put an end to the Statutes of India and introduced some longed-for liberties. But these contained wariness in the English Protestant mind of 'unchristian' teachings regarded as harmful, so that in the move towards religious liberty and tolerance, there is a strong sense of 'better the devil you know!' Despite their doubly disadvantageous position (colour and social status), the Muslims took full advantage of the religious liberty and tolerance held out to them by their British masters.

1862 witnessed a dispute between the Shafi'i and Hanafi groupings at the Cape. A request was directed by a Cape parliamentarian to the British government for a religious guide to be sent to the Cape Muslim community to settle the dispute. Referred to the Turkish embassy in London, the request resulted in the arrival of Abu Bakr Effendi, a Hanafî, to resolve this and later disputes among the predominantly Shafi'i Cape Muslims. Effendi established schools and produced the first Islamic works in Afrikaans, but he upset the Shafi'i Muslims in the Cape who eventually demanded his removal.

Generally speaking, the years prior to 1948 were a time of growth, consolidation and establishment. But the imposition of the 1948 apartheid laws, with their consequent forced removals (people, depending on their racial classification, were forced to move to designated areas) was devastating, disrupting the Muslim community, splitting close-knit families, dividing the *umma*, and resulting in the loss of homes, properties, mosques and *madrasa's*. People were uprooted and forced to begin all over again – as if the first history of South African Islam was being re-enacted. The close-knit Muslim communities were now dispersed into various parts of the different provinces, a diaspora which mixed Muslims with Christians – again, the early mixture of Muslim and Christian slaves, also the result of injustices, being echoed in this new hour of Islamic history. As at the beginning, new boundaries for the *umma* had to be drawn up. Until the 1960s, there was little resistance, although the spirit of resistance, present from the beginning, was evident. But the devastation wreaked by the laws of apartheid had numbed the Muslim community: their unity and strength had been disrupted and would take years to restore and revive. Further disruption of unity resulted from the variance of political stances within the Muslim community. Hard-won mosques and *madrasa's* had been lost. The diaspora together with Christians led to an opening-up to non-Muslims as the realisation dawned that apartheid did not only affect Muslims, and had to be fought.

Yet a catalyst was needed: something that would revive the spirit of resistance and unite the Muslim community. It would take thirty-five years of pain, hardship and loss before this catalyst would catapult the South African Muslims into the heart of confrontation and struggle with the forces of injustice. But from 1948 until 1960, the Muslim community was disrupted, disunited and disabled, firmly under the heel of the apartheid government, police and army.

The spirit of resistance: 1960 onwards

1960 and the years that followed were years of Muslim politics and movements, and of a spirit of resistance which would later receive impetus from the worldwide Muslim resurgence after the Iranian Revolution. In discussing the post-1960 history of South Africa, we need to bear in mind what has already been said about education, mosque and imam: all three were to play a pivotal role in the development of the Islamic political conscience (and contiguous action). The post-1960s saw the rise of the spirit of resistance and the politics of defiance (not only among Muslims) and especially in the Cape. Farid Esack writes:

> While there were numerous Muslim individuals from the other provinces who made common cause with the people of South Africa in the struggle against

apartheid, the contribution of Cape Muslims was different in two respects: a) as a community they became a part of the struggle while the pro-apartheid elements were marginalised individuals, and b) Islam played a prominent role in inspiring their involvement and/or in its legitimation.[10]

There is no doubt about the role played by South Africa's minority Muslim population in the country's history and especially in the struggle for liberation: Muslim theologians like Esack[11] have formulated a 'Muslim liberation theology' based on the Exodus archetype in the Qur'an. The role of Muslims after the 1960s is seen primarily in the formation of a number of Islamic movements and organisations, all of which had a twofold justification:

1 They were an attempt to represent all Muslims in the light of a divided 'ulama.
2 They were an attempt to fill the gap created by the silence of the 'ulama bodies in issues of politics and justice.

The following can be regarded as the most influential and prominent of these movements:

1 The Islamic Council of South Africa (est. 1975). The Council lost much support over the years due to its unclear stance on the Iranian Revolution and because of some ill-considered political strategies. As such, it is no longer regarded as a 'progressive' movement, and played a diminished role within the spirit of resistance and the struggle for liberation.
2 The Muslim Youth Movement (est. 1970). This movement has, since its foundation, given birth to at least ten other Islamic movements, and is certainly the oldest, largest and strongest of the progressive bodies. It has always considered itself as part of the international Islamic movement, and has been strongly influenced by the Pakistani *Jamaat-e-Islami* and the Egyptian brotherhoods. Its famous 1984 document entitled *The Muslim Response: Our Vision for South Africa* was issued at the height of the politics of defiance, and attempted to express an Islamic understanding of the Muslim role in the resistance to apartheid. But while the movement believed in political involvement, it remained more committed to establishing 'the order of Allah' in South Africa, and consequently remained politically indecisive for a long time.
3 The Call of Islam (est. 1961). This 'first' Call of Islam (for a 'second' one would later follow it) was a short-lived movement in opposition to the devastating Group Areas Act, which split the Muslim *umma* with its practice of relocation. The later-martyred Imam Abdullah Haron led the movement.[12] Despite being short-lived, this movement was the first real attempt to rally the Muslim community into action against apartheid. It aimed at fighting oppression and intolerance, in a battle based on Islamic principles of social justice. Its foundation met with surprise in the white parliament, because it was the initiative of what one parliamentarian (A. Z. Berman) called 'the most law-abiding, the most loyal, the most peaceful section of our non-European [i.e. non-white] population'.[13] This statement is understandable in light of the long and peculiar history of South African Muslim loyalty to local government, clearly

expressed (for example) in the 31 July 1964 Muslim Judicial Council declaration in the *Muslim News* which spoke to Muslims of 'our' government and urged them to realise that they were well-off, had religious freedom and should be content. This collaborationist stance, worse when seen in the light of the devastation which the apartheid laws had wreaked among Muslims, was part of the Muslim Judicial Council's fluctuating political involvement. In fact much of the increased organisational activity from the 1960s onwards was a reaction by young Muslims, disenchanted with the older, conservative Muslim generation in the context of a developing self-awareness, something which the Muslim Judicial Council would call 'youthful impetuosity' in its unfavourable reaction to the 1961 foundation of the Call of Islam.

4 The Call of Islam (est. 1983). The first one being short-lived, this second Call of Islam sprang up in the desire to establish a politically and socially relevant Islam against the apartheid system. It was an offshoot of the Muslim Youth Movement, led by former Muslim Youth Movement leaders who were unwilling to sever their ties with the United Democratic Front (one of the political groupings, now defunct, that was heavily involved in the liberation struggle). This second Call of Islam was therefore smaller and younger than the Muslim Youth Movement, and was deeply involved in the fight against apartheid, with strong links to the United Democratic Front. The importance of this second Call of Islam was its insistence that non-Muslims had experienced the same hardships as Muslims under the apartheid system, and that whilst the search for Islamic solutions may be a sacred duty, the search for solutions without reference to 'at-oneness' with others in untenable.[14] This cooperation between Muslims and non-Muslims during the years of struggle is one of the profound elements of South African Islam, springing perhaps from the early mix between Muslim and non-Muslim slaves. It was expressed in a redefinition of Qur'anic hermeneutics and in the declaration that South Africa's problems were 'human', not 'religious'. The 1983 Call of Islam became vociferous and organised, with senior members of the 'ulama in its ranks and links to the Muslim Judicial Council. Their activities included mass rallies, public meetings, funerals of the victims of police brutality and the publication of pamphlets: they had, wrote Farid Esack, 'chartered for themselves a specific and well-defined understanding of Islam which enables them to respond in a fairly predictable manner to different issues'.[15] Nevertheless, their willingness to work alongside non-Christians in the liberation struggle has made their role crucial.

5 Qibla (est. 1980). This movement was based on the premise that only devotion to Islamic principles of social justice would bring about liberation: it was intended to be a great movement of 'super-conscious' Muslims with the aim of Islamic revolution in South Africa after the example of Iran. It was hoped that the shortcomings of the liberation movements would disillusion people, so that Islam could be offered as a viable alternative. Qibla started therefore as a socio-religious group, small, but deeply involved in the liberation struggle (producing a host of pamphlets and publications). As an alternative to the United Democratic Front, Qibla aligned itself to the Black Consciousness and Pan African movements, and in the mid-1980s emerged as a militant, revolutionary Islamic force. However, it remained active from the outskirts of the

liberation struggle which, unlike the Call of Islam, it saw as tainted by un-Islamic elements. Qibla was based at the famous al-Jami'ai mosque in Cape Town, where the martyred Abdullah Haron had once been imam, and which became a centre of anti-apartheid activity. Qibla faded out in 1987, only to re-emerge in the mid-1990s with the PAGAD issue.

6 The Muslim Judicial Council (est. 1945). The Muslim Judicial Council was established for the purpose of jurisdiction over Muslim affairs, and was a representative body, with all Cape Muslim leaders invited to be in its ranks: this resulted in a body in which there was a great variance of theological training and political awareness. Its primary task was to safeguard the shari'ah: it was one of four South African bodies (the *Jamiatul 'Ulama* in Gauteng and Natal were both Hanafî, while the *Madjlisul 'Ulama* in the Eastern Cape and the Muslim Judicial Council in the western Cape were both liberal Shafi'i). It was precisely because there was no united 'ulama body that so many organisations sprang up. The Muslim Judicial Council attempted to be politically involved in matters it perceived to be unjust and contrary to human rights. Its primary task obliged the defence and promotion of justice: so, for example, it expressed itself clearly after Sharpeville in 1960 and after Soweto in 1976 – in the latter case, three months after the event.[6] But there was continuous fluctuation and inconsistency in the council's political role: for example, its 1961 'Call of Islam' statement was the first to declare apartheid a heresy, and yet in 1969 the same council failed to give support to Imam Haron in detention, or to register protest at his death in police custody. In fact, between 1961 and 1964, years of brutal repression, the Council issued only five statements condemning acts of apartheid and held only one public meeting. As recently as 1997, Cape Town theologian Farid Esack castigated the Muslim religious leadership before a hearing of the Truth and Reconciliation Commission, accusing them of marginalising and betraying the struggle against apartheid and labelling their contribution as 'one of betrayal'.[7] There had been, claimed Esack, 'a denial of space for all those who opposed apartheid and who were a part of the anti-apartheid struggle'.[8] In the early 1980s the Muslim Judicial Council aligned itself to the United Democratic Front (later withdrawing from this alignment) and made a concerted effort to be 'politically relevant'. But it retained a low profile, with little activity to match its rhetoric. It was hampered by the great variance of theological training and political awareness in its ranks, by a feeling of inadequacy in political matters and by the fear of crossing the political boundaries which Cape Muslims had drawn up for themselves.

In synopsis, the post-1960 period, and especially the 1970s and 1980s saw the foundation of numerous Muslim organisations, for the most part in opposition to the apartheid regime. The 1980s saw (especially) the Western Cape Muslim community identifying with those seeking liberation from apartheid. It was equally a time when the worldwide Islamic movements made great impact on South African Islam, and of new trends in theology and in the self-awareness and understanding of South African Muslims (so, for example, the question of interfaith cooperation, detailed later in this chapter, came to the fore at this time).

1983 was really the crucial year, and the necessary catalyst of which we spoke earlier. It was the year of the 'new deal' and the fateful tricameral system. Already by 1983 the apartheid government was more than aware of the growing storm of resistance. In a conciliatory move, the President's Council (a group nominated by the state president and seen as collaborators by the resistance movements) proposed a new constitution: there would be two new parliaments, one for coloureds and one for Asians, to be added to the existing whites only parliament. These two new bodies would govern their own affairs, while the white parliament would look after black affairs. This indignity was the final provocation, causing Cape Muslims to erupt into the heart of the struggle with such force and vigour that the BBC described the Western Cape in terms of 'shades of Beirut'. 1983 onwards saw a protracted, violent struggle against apartheid, characterised by mass rallies and protests, banning and exile, mass detention, torture and death in police cells, the police and army on standby in the townships,[19] enormous loss of life and the proclamation, at various times, of a state of emergency. For ten years this struggle and violence continued all over South Africa: it culminated in the release of Nelson Mandela, the imprisoned leader of the banned African National Congress, the unbanning of the Congress and, in 1994, the fall of the apartheid regime with the first democratic elections.

In these crucial post-1960 years, South African Muslims, disunited and weakened by the imposition of the apartheid laws, grew in self-awareness and understanding, a growth characterised by the impatience of the younger Muslim generation with the older, more cautious generation, known for their peculiar loyalty to local government. The energy of the younger generation was channelled into the foundation of various Islamic organisations in which, for the first time, Muslims gained a voice in the political arena. Concomitant with this was a progressive opening-up to the non-Muslim community, backed by a new breed of Muslim theologians who offered innovative models by which the struggle and interfaith cooperation could be justified and legitimised. When the history of the liberation struggle in South Africa is written, the Muslim community must be recognised as being, despite their minority status, a vociferous and major player in the fall of apartheid and the rise of the South African democracy.

The coloured community

It is impossible to speak of South African Islam without speaking also of the coloured community, the descendants of the first Indonesian Muslim slaves and the community in which Islam continues to find its most popular support. So much so, that it would be almost impossible to understand South African Islam without some understanding of the dynamics of the coloureds.

Within the South African population (42 million), about 8.9% (4 million) are classified coloured; 85% of this grouping live in the western Cape, with roughly 81% professing Christianity and 6.5% professing Islam. The so-called 'Cape Malay' is included in this grouping, although they have, on the whole, maintained their Malay identity and features. The various coloured communities in South Africa have their roots in the Dutch colonial policy and the importation in the seventeenth century of slaves, mostly from Indonesia and Malaysia. A new gene pool was created through the offspring of settlers and soldiers with slaves and indigenous peoples (Khoikhoi, San and Xhosa) and was added to by slaves imported from West Africa: the term coloured eventually came to be applied to all people of 'mixed race'. The form of Dutch spoken at the Cape gradually changed significantly from that spoken in Holland, and this Cape dialect came to be called 'Afrikaans'. While the language of the churches, courts, educational institutions and government circles remained Dutch, Afrikaans became increasingly the language of the common people (today, the coloureds share Afrikaans with white Afrikaners, although separated from them by strong social and class distinctions).

The coloured population thus represents a wide range of genetic and cultural backgrounds. Most speak Afrikaans, but their rich cultural mix has added to the development of Afrikaans as a distinct language (since Afrikaans was also the language of the apartheid government and of the white Afrikaners, the protagonists of apartheid, many coloureds joined black South Africans in consciously fostering English as a form of protest).

When the British replaced the Dutch as colonial masters at the Cape, the white Afrikaans-speaking farmers moved north to escape British rule, leaving the coloured population with more social and political freedom than before. But while the coloureds benefited under the more benevolent British rule, they were still treated as socially inferior, and this isolation grew as British settlers began to establish themselves at the Cape. This isolation was increased when the British banned the use of Afrikaans.

In 1948, the Nationalist (white Afrikaner) government introduced the policy of apartheid in order to maintain white supremacy in South Africa: apartheid was actualised by numerous laws and bannings, and had a devastating affect among the coloured population, which was divided by the variance of its political stances. Compared to the black peoples in South Africa, the coloureds were given an ostensibly privileged position under apartheid rule, although their rights were severely limited. Despite political indecisiveness, the coloureds were vocal and visible in the struggle that led to the fall of the apartheid regime and the first democratic elections in 1994.

In the light of their origins, history and make-up, the coloured people are hard to define. But perhaps we might start by reminding ourselves of two points made earlier:

1 The words of Karen Armstrong, quoted at the very beginning, are of great relevance here: she claims that a 'loss of cultural roots' can produce an 'aggressive, defiant religiosity as a means of asserting the beleaguered self'. If anything, one has to say that the coloured community, with its radically mixed gene pool and multicultural make-up is a community that has 'lost its cultural roots'.
2 One of the distinguishing marks of South African Islam is that, from the beginning, it offered the slaves, who were economically and socially marginalised, a status and identity that was secure and distinct. The coloured community continues today to be a community marginalised in some respects, and it is precisely in this community that Islam has received its warmest, widest acceptance and its greatest numerical growth.

Islam has spread rapidly in the coloured population, with many Christians converting, and continues to attract followers primarily from this community. Concomitant with Islam, many coloureds have embarked on a wholesale adoption of Arabic culture: they are a 'lost' community, apparently devoid of their own culture, neither white nor black, regarded as socially inferior by some blacks and whites, unsure of their place and even of their own history. As a result, they have borrowed liberally from numerous other cultures, so that the coloured community is a melting pot of variation and a bundle of contradictions. It appears highly attracted by fundamentalism, whether it is American Pentecostal or Islamic. Within this male-orientated, patriarchal and fundamentalist-leaning community, Islam is highly attractive, offering a secure status and a distinct identity, a culture and a point of reference. And yet the coloured community contains within itself both this strong pull to Islamic (Arabic) lifestyle as well as to those very things which are diametrically opposed to everything Islam stands for: high incidents of divorce and family break-up, alcoholism, drug addiction and criminality. The coloured community is at once pro-Islam and pro-American (in the sense of west), with the coloured youth especially attempting in many ways to emulate American cultural trends in food, clothing, language and music.

All these things, like the racial classification at the very beginning of South African Muslim history, are regarded as constituting an assault on the Islamic world-view and self-understanding. The coloured community is thus a divided community: in religion, in the sense that the most Islamicised community contains within itself those things most opposed to Islam; in politics: the political instability of the coloured community is seen, for example, in the fact that after forty-six years of oppressing them, the National Party retained power in the strongly coloured Western Cape in the 1994 elections, thanks to a strong coloured majority vote. The coloured community, then, is politically and socially fragmented and unstable: if anything, Islam is the one thing that unites large sections of it (although even within Cape Islam there is a diversity of religious and political opinion). The coloured Muslims are very Islamic (the defiant, aggressive religiosity mentioned earlier) and the coloured Christians and non-Muslims tend strongly towards anti-Muslim bias (the Christians especially, possibly because of the fragmentation of Christian families and communities through conversion to Islam). In fact, the same 'fear' of black domination which caused Cape coloured voters to maintain the National Party status quo is seen in the anti-Muslim bias of many (often fundamentalist Protestant) coloured Christians, dividing the community even further.

Presently, Islam is beginning to take root and grow within the black community of South Africa (whereas Christianity is not): but among the white community, kept in ignorance and suspicion by the South African press, and rooted in Calvinism, Islam has found little welcome or support. The Calvinist Dutch Reformed church still dominates the South African white community. On 23 October 1986, the General Synod of the Dutch Reformed church declared Islam to be a false religion, and proposed that all members of the church should witness in every area of life to the Gospel, as the only possible means of stemming the Islamic onslaught. The aggressive Synod declaration, which included attacks on various Christian churches and groupings that were in opposition to apartheid, was answered on 27 October with a statement from the South African Chapter of the World Conference on Religion and Peace, calling the document a 'stark revelation' to the world of South's Africa's bigotry, intolerance and racism.

Currently, in post-democratic South Africa, Islam is becoming ever more public and prominent. For the first time, and rooted in its experience in the post-1960s era, Muslims are finding a voice and a self-identity. This is seen, for example, in the presence of Muslims in government and parliament, in the Muslim radio stations and publications, and in the fact that two Islamic parties stood in the first democratic elections. The diversity in theological and political opinion continues: this, in turn, has results in the levels and intensity of inter-faith cooperation and dialogue.

To complete this historical survey, we need finally to turn our attention to a wave of Islamic resurgence and defiance that erupted in the 1990s from a now stronger and more self-confident South African Islam.

PAGAD:[20] Islamic resurgence and defiance in the new South Africa

As a context and background for the PAGAD phenomenon, we need to draw together some elements already mentioned:

1 The 'aggressive, defiant religiosity as a means of asserting the beleaguered self' which, as we have seen, aptly describes a strong trend in South African Islam and in its reception in the coloured community.
2 The high incidence of alcohol and drug abuse, with the concomitant formation and activity of gangs (as a means of controlling the traffic and trade in drugs) and crime within the coloured community.
3 The dissatisfaction with negligible government efforts to deal with the problems of crime, gangsterism and the drug trade, exacerbated by the fact that many Muslims see the government as secular and thus unable to answer Islamic needs.
4 The continuing influence of worldwide Islamic resurgence.
5 The growing self-awareness and self-confidence of South African Muslims, together with the ever-present spirit of resistance.
6 And finally, with the fall of apartheid, the strange vacuum left in a community which since its first beginnings had been engaged in a struggle against all that it perceived to be a threat to or assault upon the integrity of Islamic life.

PAGAD provides an example of Islamic resurgence and resistance in the post-democratic South Africa, and one can trace in its rise the elements of aggressive religiosity, political dissatisfaction and the ever-present spirit of resistance, all of which may help to make PAGAD's appearance a little more understandable.

It has already been noted that the coloured community of the Western Cape is ravaged by a number of destructive elements. One of these is the growing traffic in and usage of drugs, and the other is the violence and activity of drug lords and gangs, who have been formed to control the drug trade. It was primarily these two factors which were the catalyst for the emergence of PAGAD (and, within PAGAD, elements of Qibla which had faded from the political scene in the late 1980s). The growing dissatisfaction with increased crime and violence, and the new government's apparent inability to remedy the situation, brought large Muslim crowds onto the streets for demonstrations early in 1995. Unlike the political demonstrations of the 1980s, these protests were characterised by a number of factors. For one thing, the protestors were almost entirely Muslim; for another, the slogans and chanting were not political but religious – in other words, from the very outset PAGAD was conceived as a religious rather than a political phenomenon.

In a series of follow-up meetings, PAGAD came to be born, and the government was given a thirty-day ultimatum to begin dealing with the crime situation. When neither the ultimatum, nor a meeting between the PAGAD executive and the Minister of Justice appeared to have the desired results, large groups of PAGAD supporters began to march at night to the homes of known gang leaders and drug lords, demanding an end to their illegal activities. In these early days, PAGAD received widespread support, not only from the Muslim community, who saw it as a Muslim religious phenomenon, justified and legitimised by the Qur'an, but even by the non-Muslim press and community, who hoped it would bring about a radical change in the drug and crime situation.

Late in 1996, during one of these night marches, the crowd publicly executed a well-known drug dealer and gang leader. This was a turning-point for PAGAD: it lost much public support, and was more and more driven into violent confrontation both with gang leaders and with the police. This confrontation continues today, although on a very small scale, as the remnants of PAGAD attempt to continue the battle against gangs and drugs, ever trying to win back the popular support which it has lost.

From the beginning, PAGAD was perceived as an Islamic, religious organisation: its meetings were held in mosques, its slogans were Islamic, its justification Qur'anic. Despite this, the PAGAD leadership urged and invited Christians to be part of the initiative, an invitation that received little positive response. Many Muslims were, in turn, disturbed by certain elements and ill-judged strategies within PAGAD, so that once again the Muslim community found itself divided. At the same time, PAGAD was a vehicle for Muslim resurgence, making Islam more prominent in South Africa than ever before. The war against drugs is seen as a 'holy' one, based on Qur'anic principles and for the good of the whole community.

As recently as December 1997, in the wake of violent gang reprisals against the Muslim community, Muslims clerics and representatives of the western Province Council of Churches appealed to Christian and Jewish communities to support the Cape Muslims. Calling for a 'dramatic and prophetic shift', the spokespeople invoked memories of the liberation struggle, when Christians and Muslims had worked in harmony, and invited a new solidarity against the violence of gang and drug related crime.[21]

Conclusion

The aim of this chapter was not to offer an in-depth analysis of Islamic history in South Africa, but to show how South African Islam has, from its very beginnings, been shaped and directed by a number of characteristics that were present from the start.

Its severely disadvantaged begins, under the shadow of slavery, political exile and religious restriction, comprising as it did an assault upon the integrity of Islamic principles, the presence of Sufi strands and its rapid reception among the coloured population, led to a distinctive and distinct South African Islam. Its further disruption with the 1948 imposition of apartheid led to a weakened, disunited *umma*: but the spirit of resistance, present from the start, catapulted the Muslim community into the forefront of the struggle for liberation and justice.

The scarcity of literature about South African Islam further suggests that it is only now that Muslims in that country are finding an identity and a voice, a factor no doubt influenced by the necessity of its political involvement in the 1970s and 1980s. This identity and voice are seen in the role Muslims play in the social, economic and political framework of contemporary South African society, as well as in the Islamic resurgence seen so recently in the country.

Its continued reception among the marginalised and politically unstable coloured community hearkens back to its very first reception among the slaves at the Cape, where it offered them a longed-for identity and security. Furthermore, the coloured community's loss of cultural roots and identity has led to an often severe religiosity, despite the presence of so many factors in that community which militate against the Islamic way of life.

In spite of its minority status, the South African Islamic community has, in recent years, asserted itself and has proven that both now, and in the future, it will remain a force to be reckoned with.

Notes

1 Apartheid is a word, unique to the South African situation, meaning 'separateness', and refers to the official policy of racial classification practiced there from 1948 until the 1994 democratic elections.
2 Armstrong, K., *Muhammad* (Victor Gollancz Ltd, London 1992), p. 23.
3 Lubbe, G., 'The Soweto Fatwa: a Muslim response to a watershed event in South Africa', *Journal of Muslim Minority Affairs*, 17: 2 (1997), 336.
4 In mid-December 1997, during a state visit to South Africa, Indonesian President Muhammad Suharto officially elevated Sheikh Yusuf to the status of National Hero of Indonesia at a special ceremony held at his kramat in Faure, Western Cape. The President saluted Yusuf as 'the father of Islam in South Africa'.
5 This information was gleaned from reflections in the *Cape Press* (December 1997) by Achmat Davids, Cape historian and researcher.
6 Sonn, T., 'Middle East and Islamic studies in South Africa', *Mesa Bulletin*, 28 (1994), 14.
7 Hiskett, M., 'Islam in South Africa' in *The Course of Islam in Africa* (Edinburgh, Edinburgh University Press, 1994), p. 174.
8 See Lubbe, G., 'Muslims and Christians in South Africa', *Islamochristiana*, 13 (1987), 123.
9 See Lubbe, 'The Soweto Fatwa', 336.

10 Esack, F., 'The Exodus paradigm in the Qur'an in the light of re-interpretative Islamic thought in South Africa', *Islamochristiana*, 17 (1991), 85.

11 Ibid.

12 Found dead in police detention on 27 September 1969. His story is recounted in Desai, B. and Marney, C., *The Killing of the Imam* (London, Melbourne and New York, Quartet Books, 1978).

13 Naude, J., 'South Africa: the role of a Muslim minority in a situation of change', *Journal of Muslim Minority Affairs*, 13: 1 (1992), 18.

14 Ibid. 19.

15 Lubbe, 'Muslims and Christians in South Africa', 119.

16 Sharpeville in 1960 and Soweto in 1976 were both occasions when police massacred large numbers of innocent victims: as such, they were both catalysts in the struggle for liberation.

17 *Cape Argus* (18 November 1997).

18 Ibid.

19 The name commonly given to 'non-white' areas.

20 'People Against Gangsterism and Drugs'.

21 *Cape Argus* (15 December 1997).

14

Christians and Muslims in West Africa

Stanisław Grodź

Media reports have recently predisposed us to see Muslims as dangerous, fanatical and violent people. In this way the old bad western-Christian stereotype of Islam and Muslims re-emerges in a modern disguise. The western perspective, antagonistic towards Islam, ignores non-western points of view and experiences, and tends to impose its own reading of Christian–Muslim relations worldwide, as David Kerr has pointed out.[1] It is not surprising that in such an atmosphere many people perceive Christian–Muslim relations as mainly (even only) confrontational and often violent regardless of the actual region where they take place. From this perspective West Africa has its own local Christian–Muslim conflict, with the situation in Nigeria as the most obvious example. To readers who know more about the Nigerian situation beyond the media reports it is obvious that it is far more complex and that the Muslim–Christian encounters, especially in West Africa, are not confrontational by definition. Moreover, the fact that Christian–Muslim relations in West Africa take place within a specific context (or one should even say contexts) is of primary importance.

West Africa is a vast and diverse region. For that reason this short overview should not in any way be treated as exhaustive. Its principal aim is to trace strands of Muslim–Christian contacts in West Africa and concentrate on some of the main issues. Attention will be given to the way Islam and Christianity have spread in the region and to the consequences of specific conversion processes. The problem of Muslims' and Christians' attitudes towards the African cultural milieu, as inherently related to the spread of Islam and Christianity, will be examined closer. Politics, i.e. the access to power and the way related economic and social problems are handled, could be compared to a rotating platform on which conflict or examples of cooperation between Muslims and Christians can equally be staged. Encounters where 'religious' concerns feature in a prominent way do not always provide realistic hopes for peaceful coexistence and cooperation, thus fuelling the accusations of those who see the root of violence in religion. In spite of all this, we shall not be too pessimistic as rays of hope are visible in the rather too darkened horizon of Christian–Muslim relations in West Africa.

The present state of research

The literature on Islam in West Africa is vast. Research began during the colonial era when the European administrators needed information concerning the local population and how they could secure European domination.[2] Then came the time of independence of African states and the period for 'rediscovery' of African history. Researchers focused on recovering old Islamic manuscripts from private collections bringing to light the rich history of the Islamic presence in West Africa. Even if the research was not as objective as its authors claimed, giving a somehow glorious picture of the Muslim presence and achievements in the African milieu, still it produced important material on the many phases of co-existence.[3]

The advance and presence of Christianity has also been described in many of its aspects and dimensions, ranging from missionaries' reports and information provided by colonial administrators to scholarly publications treating topics meticulously researched and analysed by a diverse group of historians, social scientists and theologians. The literature is vast, too.

In contrast to the above-mentioned literary abundance, the problem of Muslim–Christian relations in West Africa still awaits to be described and analysed in its variety of dimensions in the whole region. Articles with a continental perspective contribute to a better understanding of the situation, yet out of necessity, their horizon is often too wide.[4] The situation in Nigeria has been extensively treated by various researchers but this country stands out on many levels in the region.[5] Apart from that there are only a few publications focusing on the general situation in certain countries (e.g. Chad, Senegal). Others take up specific local issues, e.g. rivalry between missionaries and 'ulama in Burkina Faso, women's status in Cameroon, converts' actions in Ghana, or focus on prominent West African personalities, e.g. Amadou Hampâté Bâ.[6] The vacuum in the description and analyses of Muslim–Christian relations in West Africa in an overall regional perspective, pointed out in the late 1990s by Josef Stamer, was partly filled by Henry Coudray a few years later, yet still exists.[7]

Difficulties in forming a regional perspective

This absence of a regional perspective is probably due to the fact that although the area can easily be distinguished in geographical, linguistic, ethnic or political terms, it lacks the homogeneity required for conducting comparisons or drawing conclusions. Diversification of the whole region was further strengthened by the colonial division of West Africa, setting an additional language barrier (French/English) that separated not only the local populations but various representatives of the metropolises as well, including scholars.

The region is comprised of highly Islamised areas like Senegal, Guinea, Mali, Chad, Niger, northern parts of Nigeria and Ivory Coast, together with places where Islamic influence, though visible, has never been unquestionably dominant, like in the chiefdoms of the present day northern Ghana, and areas where the local ethnic groups were resistant to Islamic influences, like the Bambara, Mossi and Ashanti kingdoms. The presence of Muslims and the extent of Islamisation of different areas and ethnic groups varies depending on very local circumstances. Similar things – *mutati mutandis* – can be said about Christianity. There are highly Christianised areas like the costal regions, parts of the interior where Christians have a strong though minority presence, e.g. Burkina Faso or Mali, and places where it was not preached or it was strongly resisted. Emissaries of both universalistic religions came generally from opposing directions (from inland and from the sea)[8] and although their respectively most distant northern and southern points of presence can be identified, there is hardly any clear distinguishable border line across West Africa between Christian and Muslim zones. Even in areas where violent clashes occur, like in Nigeria, the territorial border line is blurred. Muslims and Christians together with adherents of different African religions live not only as neighbours but often even as members of the same extended families.[9] The British and French colonial authorities initially prevented Christian missionaries from entering the so-called Muslim northern territories but at the same time allocated some of the regions inhabited by adherents of indigenous religions to the jurisdiction of the northern Muslim emirs.[10] In southern coastal regions, e.g. in present day Ghana and Nigeria but also Ivory Coast, Togo and Benin, the Muslim presence dates only from the colonial period when the Europeans imposed a new order and removed obstacles that kept Muslim traders at bay, far away from the coast.[11] Recent statistics show that the population of southern coastal cities like Accra is about one third Muslim and the numbers have been constantly growing.

Internal diversity and divisions within Islam and Christianity have become another factor inhibiting the presentation of an overall comparative regional picture of Muslim–Christian relations. Every country has its own specific atmosphere in which contacts between believers from different religious traditions have been taking place. The overwhelming majority of Muslims in West Africa are Sunnis belonging to the Maliki law school and the way Islam spread in the region contributed to the appearance and development of the Muslim religion in a rather ethnic garb (saturated by local customs). The role of Sufi brotherhoods (*turuq*) in West Africa cannot be overlooked. The brotherhood members contributed significantly to the Islamisation of the local people, but at least two of the *turuq* – the Qaddiriyya and the Tijaniyya – became engaged in a bitter struggle for domination in the region from the mid-nineteenth century. Al-Hajj Umar Tal and his legacy cast a long shadow on this aspect of intra-Muslim affairs from Senegal to Nigeria. Contemporary trends brought in still further diversification of the West African Muslim scene. Reformist groups of Arab provenance appeared with the aim of 'cleansing' Islam from unlawful innovations and challenging the Sufi brotherhoods. This goal features high on their agenda.[12]

Christianity is not in any better position. It did not appear on the West African coast as a monolithic entity. Anglicans, Presbyterians and Methodists were later joined by Roman Catholics and various Protestant groups not belonging to the so-called mainline churches. Diversification of Christianity was further extended by the rise and proliferation of the so-called African Independent (Instituted) Churches. They came into being as splinter groups from the existing churches, or were formed anew as parallel structures, or even appeared as a sort of 'side-effects' of the prophetic/catechetical activity of indigenous prophets like William

Wadé Harris.[13] Reinvigoration of Christianity in recent decades comes from the Pentecostal movements and contributes significantly to the 'Pentecostalisation' of the mainline churches. While the latter have recently been more prone to enter into a dialogical relationship with adherents of other religions, the former harbour some die-hard evangelists who favour a very radical and antagonistic approach towards non-Christians.

The appeal of universalistic religions (conversion)

The appearance of heralds of universalistic religion in a milieu characterised by ethnic religions often causes turmoil. New questions, broader perspectives for answering the old ones, access to new knowledge, contacts and associations with a wider structure that can boost feelings of self-assurance with the new identity can be named as some important factors of an incoming change. Apart from political, social (and often economic) gains offered by the new contacts, genuine religious needs also play their own role. It cannot be overlooked that there are people who adopt the new perspective out of their own inner deep convictions. Yet, such an acceptance is hardly ever followed by a total rejection of the former (ethnic, local) worldview. The influence of the latter may be significantly reduced but cannot be completely superseded. Its strength in persistence will often be shown at times of affliction.[14]

Islam, spreading in West Africa from the ninth and tenth centuries, made provisions for a long transitory period of conversion. Muslims appeared on the southbound trade routes and gradually settled along them. Their skills and goods made them attractive at least to some strata of local societies and that led to their incorporation into the local social systems. Islamisation of African societies was a slow, gradual but also reversible process with different dynamics among various ethnic groups. Most of the merchants, and even the 'ulama, were not driven by a missionary zeal and the long transitory conversion period for the local converts was simply a part of everyday life.[15] Muslims who temporarily or permanently settled in a place often married local women. Their presence influenced the local population and also attracted other Muslims to come and stay. Local merchants accepted Islam also as a new significant feature of their profession if they wanted to become engaged in the long distance trade. In some centralised political entities, like the Songhay empire, Islam reached a prominent position in society but the rulers still held those of their subjects who adhered to traditional local religions in high esteem and often rulers themselves refrained from being Muslims, at least overtly. In other political units, like the Ashanti empire, Muslims were incorporated into the social system with hardly any prospects of social promotion.[16]

Christianity was a late comer in the region, becoming a more significant element in the local context only from the mid-nineteenth century. It came from the coast and from the later part of that century its advances were often associated with the European colonial conquest and presence. The actual relationship between Christian missionaries and the colonial administration was not always amicable. Both the French and the British obstructed missionary activity, at times. On the other hand, the missionaries were not always eager to be associated with the colonial administration either and sometimes criticised it openly. When they cooperated it was usually, though not always, 'a marriage of convenience'. Whatever we say about their relationship, Christianity spread rather rapidly in parts of the region. Different reasons could be given for this fact. Knowing the openness (not to say eclectic character) of African religions towards new elements or even new trends that brought about an aura of power and success, acceptance of Christianity could also be attributed to the appeal that the achievements of European civilisation had for Africans. However, the same openness could have contributed to the reception of the Christian message on the spiritual level. Given the variety of positive responses on the part of Africans, in spite of heavy organisational demands made by the churches, one could say that the Gospel has resonated deeply with Africans.

Attitudes towards the African cultural milieu

Local Muslims kept in touch with the wider Islamic world through trade, travels for acquisition of knowledge, and pilgrimages to Mecca. These activities gained recognition from the Middle Eastern and North African Muslims for some centres, people and families.[7] Though there were instances of radical powerful extra-regional ideological interference in the West African Muslim thinking before the late eighteenth century (e.g. Al-Maghili)[8] the general attitude towards the African traditional milieu was rather tolerant. The jihad movement that swept across West Africa from the late eighteenth century proved to be a very destructive force concerning Islamic co-existence with the adherents of African religions. That eruption of politically motivated religious zeal strived to eradicate forms branded as syncretistic, i.e. mixed with local customs. However, it should be remembered that the West African Islamic revival of the eighteenth and nineteenth centuries was led by members of Sufi brotherhoods (mainly Qaddiriyya and Tijaniyya) who were themselves West Africans. There was hardly any expatriate participation. The strong and unquestionable position the brotherhoods enjoyed in West Africa has been challenged only recently by new Islamic movements of Arab provenance accusing the *turuq* of being too African and deviating from 'true' Islam.

The practice of peaceful penetration of Islam into the African cultural milieu led to the development of 'ethnically coloured' brands of Islam. They were not generally perceived as sects, though. One could say that there were different circles of participation in the Islamic milieu, a situation described by J. Spencer Trimingham in his theory of three stages of assimilation of Islamic culture by African societies: a preparatory stage ('the infiltration of elements of Islamic culture into animist life'), conversion ('the break with the old order [rather] then the adoption of the new') and 'the gradual process by which Islam changes the life of the community'.[19] The accuracy of his theory, as too simplistic and unidirectional, was later questioned by other scholars researching the spread of Islam in West Africa, yet Trimingham rightly stressed the long transitory period of conversion.[20] There are reports, for example from northern Ghana, that some local chiefs, though not Muslims officially, were described as 'praying' and thus associated with the Muslim milieu. Formally, though, they belonged to a different social stratum (chiefs and warriors, Muslims, peasants) and did things not associated with Muslims, i.e. drank alcohol and shed blood.[21]

The radical negative attitudes of European Christian missionaries towards the African cultures has been widely described. Trying to gain a balanced view of the issue one should remember that this attitude has not been constant throughout the period of contact. Especially early nineteenth-century missionaries seemed to have been more open towards the local culture, though for them it was only a vehicle for transmitting the Christian message. The hardening of the negative view on indigenous cultures in European missionary circles coincided with the colonial period. African cultures were perceived as useless at best and as 'devilish' at worst. Converts to Christianity were expected to cut all their ties with their cultural context and were often treated as a *carte blanche* which could be written completely anew with the Christian message and morality in its European understanding. Even singular elements of African cultures were seen as unfit for being used in the Christian liturgy and theology.

Compared to what was happening when an African was being drawn into a Muslim milieu, the rupture between the Christian world and the African indigenous one seemed to be abrupt, setting the two of them radically apart. The insistence of Christian missionaries on that sudden change contributed (among other things) to the proliferation of the above mentioned African Instituted Churches.

Though one is prone to think that there were no Afro-Islamic groups at all, Harold W. Turner writes about orthodox and Africanised types of new religious movements springing from the Muslim milieu in Africa. In the latter, Turner included the Lâye Fraternity of Seydina Limamu, the Mourides of Senegal (though he underscored that the personal religion of the founder was rather an orthodox form of Islam) with their sub-group of the Bay Fall, and the Hamalliyya together with the Sylla branch. He also pointed out some small nineteenth-century Islamic-Christian synthetist movements, like a group founded by T. B. Freeman in the Gold Coast, the Isawas (the Jesus people) in Nigeria, and the Ijebu Islamic Reformation Society in mid-twentieth-century Nigeria.[22]

The striking contrast between hundreds of Afro-Christian groups or churches and a tiny number of Afro-Islamic ones was explained by Turner with five basic reasons. The close link between religion and politics in Islam meant a tighter control of religious developments, while the separation of these two realms in Christianity created a space for setting up new groups outside the official control. Islam provided more opportunities for local people with leadership charisma (it was easier for them to reach an important status), while in Christianity the local charismatic leaders, being constrained by the ecclesiastical structures, often found an outlet for their energy in setting up an independent group. The gradual process of becoming a Muslim and the acceptance of various local cultural elements was inclusive, while Christianity, not being able to 'find bridges into African cultures', '[presented] conversion in more demanding terms'. Easier contact of Islam with African religions lacked depth and masked 'a deeper indifference or profound disdain towards' them, while the interest of Christian missionaries in African languages and cultures, despite the rigidity of the official ecclesiastical structures, opened ways for creating Africanised forms of Christianity. The access to the Qu'ran was much more difficult for the Africans because of the principle of non-translatability, while translations of the Bible or its parts into vernaculars gave an easy access to the source and opened the gates to indigenous interpretations.[23]

The great imbalance in the number of Afro-Islamic and Afro-Christian groups, has been sometimes interpreted and explained in favour of Islam as a religion much closer to the 'African spirit or mentality' than Christianity. Others pointed to the difference in methods of propagation, indicating that Muslims opted for conversion from ethnic religions to Islam in stages and accepted a long transitory period, while Christian missionaries, especially in the second half of the nineteenth and the first half of the twentieth centuries often demanded a sudden and complete rupture with the traditional past. However, in the long run both conversion processes bear similar traits. The long transitory period of conversion to Islam could be seen as paralleled to what was happening within the African Instituted Churches, with the significant difference being the formal allegiance of converts or potential converts. In the Islamic milieu they were being gradually drawn towards the centre, i.e. full acceptance of the Muslim faith, while in Christianity baptism incorporated them into the centre (the new faith community), but because of heavy demands (rupture with their cultural milieu) put on them by the missionaries, an outward movement was taking effect, i.e. creating independent structures that would have provided space for a transitory period in the long process of conversion. This is an example of opposition or 'reversibility' between Christianity and Islam in the West African context, i.e. approaching the same issue from different (often opposing) directions or being in another phase of dealing with the same or a similar problem. This sort of disharmony can be seen in another instance.

The 1960s witnessed the beginning of a new paradigm shift. The mainline Christian churches started modifying their perspective on the African cultural milieu and began seeing it in a more nuanced way. For a growing group of thinkers the liturgical and theological experiments of the African Instituted Churches ceased to be condemnable effects of religious syncretism but became 'signposts' or creative challenges to the way the Gospel should be implemented in African societies. Elements of African cultures have been drawn into the liturgy and theology of the mainline churches.

Meanwhile, an opposing trend, as far as the attitude towards the African cultural milieu was concerned, had been developing among some Muslim groups. Arab Wahhabi influences contributed to the growth of anti-Sufi moods and at the same time were hostile towards everything that had a mark of local customs. Reformist influences have been growing in the West African Muslim circles since the late colonial period (1945–1960), and were strengthened by later Libyan and Iranian stimuli. With the recent reports of the increasing activities of various reformist groups we can observe another attempt at reformulating Muslim identity. This shows that the issue of primary identity for the adherents of a universalistic religion in Africa (are they Muslims in Africa or African Muslims?)[24] is still at stake. Yet, a more nuanced approach to the struggle between the *turuq* and new reformers can help to sustain a hypothesis that access to power has been the main issue in the conflict. Local forms of

Muslim practice and belief serve generally as an excuse for challenging the brotherhoods.

The paradigm shifts are yet another example of an unfortunate disharmony between Muslim and Christian circles. Both do similar things but hardly ever at the same moment in history. One could say that it concerns the rivalry between Muslims and Christians. Though the rivalry can take on a form of noble competition in goodness, it can also degenerate into heated debates and fierce struggles for power and domination.

Opinions about the apparent closeness of Islam to the African mentality and the incompatibility of Christianity were pronounced in certain circles and localities with force and conviction during the colonial period and after independence, when it turned out that most of the governments opted for a secular state model.[25] These opinions, if repeated without awareness of their original political context, distort the picture of religious dynamics in West Africa. Statistics show that the number of Christians in Africa grows more than twice as fast as the number of Muslims.[26] Repetition of these opinions also requires a conscious limitation of the historical horizon of reflection to very recent abuses committed by European colonisers, while turning a blind eye on the Muslim excesses against the African traditional religions.[27]

Politics – rotating platform of conflict and cooperation

In the popular perception in the western world one can expect troubles wherever the political and the religious meet and overlap. This is so because contemporary westerners are used to drawing a border line between the two, though it does not mean that they have always been consistent in doing so, or that they would have always drawn this border along the same lines. African governments have partly adopted this perspective but in general they operate in a context still retaining the traditional outlook that knows no separation between the sacred and the profane.[28] Islam has been quite at ease with such a situation. In the early North African conquests political submission equalled conversion to Islam.[29] Similar attitude seemed to have been adopted during the nineteenth-century jihads. Yet, during the long periods of the peaceful spread of Islam in West Africa conversion was the work of the men of religion. Some of them were politically neutral, others were very much involved in politics, yet both groups were very apt at converting their charisma or spiritual capital into economic power that eventually had political implications.[30] From a contemporary western perspective such practices would be called 'instrumentalisation of religion'. It would be mistaken, however, to attribute them solely to the traditional African and Muslim milieus. Christian missionaries did not refrain from using their influence in the political establishment whenever they could strengthen their position in the area, or play on the administration's fears of Muslim activism. One could even detect tendencies to re-create Christendom with traces of a medieval blending of religion and politics. Reasons for this were diverse and the goal (creating Christendom) not always consciously adopted. Christian missionaries were also occasionally used by the colonial administration as a source of information on the local issues or as agents who could convince the locals to adopt certain colonial policies. In contacts between a political authority and a religious body it is not always easy to establish who is using whom. Opinions have been expressed, for example in the present situation in Nigeria, that it is the religious groups that manipulate the politicians and not vice versa.[31]

People who have time only for a quick glance at the political situation in West Africa, as far as Christian–Muslim relations are concerned, often focus on the situation in Nigeria. The struggle for dominance on the federal level between the 'Muslim north' and 'the Christian and traditional African south' with its various stages (joining the Organisation of Islamic Countries (OIC), the shari'ah debate, proselytic activism) could lead to the conclusion that Christians and Muslims have been engaged in a bitter struggle in West Africa. However, 'Nigerian lenses' are not suitable for reading the situation in the whole region.

In a way the struggle in Nigeria has been the follow up of the jihad era and the British colonial legacy of dividing the area first and then making it one independent country. The situation in the Ivory Coast, bearing some resemblance to the Nigerian case in the division between the north-east Muslim Mande-speaking region and the traditional and Christian south, was kept under control by the crafty Ivorian President Felix Houphuët-Boigny. Apparently, he was constantly aware of the political imbalance in the country between different sectors of Ivorian society, deepened by economic migration, and feared a danger of 'Muslim dissatisfaction'. Yet, he managed to secure stability also by maintaining close contacts with some prominent Muslim figures. The economic crisis of the late 1980s and his loosening grip on power resulted in the escalation of problems. Houphuët's death created a vacuum that his successor Henri Konan Bédié, a southern Christian, could not fill. Afraid of the political challenge posed to him by Alhassane Ouattara, a Muslim northerner belonging to Houphuët's political establishment, Bédié undertook legal actions in order to exclude Ouattara and his companions from competing for the presidential office. In spite of the support given to him by the official Islamic establishment Bédié managed to pass a bill that made the condition of being a 'pure Ivorian' (i.e. belonging to an ethnic group that lives only within the borders of the country) an obligatory requirement for presidential candidates. Taking care of his political career Bédié antagonised the Muslim Juula who understood the bill as a move to reduce them to second-class citizens. The bill was also criticised by some Christians. In that way the politics instead of continuing to be a scene of cooperation of different ethnic and religious groups became a battleground. Presidential actions resulted not only in splitting the official Muslim leadership (a parallel national Muslim organisation to the existing pro-government one was created) but also in reinvigorating Islam as a powerful vehicle of political opposition.[32]

The territory of the present day Senegal has been inhabited by an overwhelming Muslim majority. Yet, because of the French changeable attitude towards the Muslims, resulting from the actual level of suspicion or fear of their alleged subversive activities, and the fact that Dakar was made the capital of the colony, the tiny Christian presence in the coastal region rose to prominence. Leopold Sénghor, the first elected president of the independent Senegal, though a Roman Catholic, won the election with a strong backing from the leaders of Muslim brotherhoods. His government managed to create an atmosphere of cooperation with various Muslim groups operating in the country giving them access to the public media, responding to Muslim expectations concerning education and fostering good relationships with Christian communities.[33] The leadership of Christian and Muslim groups is considered as not interested in open confrontation, though apparently the relations between both faith communities 'are more often characterized by mutual suspicion and competition'. The change of guard in the brotherhood's ageing leadership and the problems arising from progressive urbanisation will influence the situation in the near future.[34]

Religious encounter

The struggle for political and social dominance is linked with religious affiliation. Religion has often been used as a mobilising factor in all sorts of conflicts or disputes. The way social and economic conflicts have been presented in regions distant from Africa, for example in Poland, often exposes the religious affiliations of their participants. Thus, the media reported a conflict as a Christian–Muslim clash, which on closer investigation turned out to be a dispute over access to grazing grounds and arable lands in the Nigerian Middle Belt.[35] Regardless of whether this distorted perspective comes from ignorance due to the lack of contact with the Nigerians, or from an intentional projection of Muslim–Christian relations as based only on conflicts, it is sad and frightening that the antagonistic reading of contacts between Christians and Muslims comes to many people as the most obvious perspective.

Unfortunately, negative stereotypical perception of the current situation has been detected not only among people who do not know the African reality. Henry Coudray reported the existence of an 'advance of Islam in Africa' syndrome among Christians or at least in certain Christian circles. The syndrome is based on a conviction – again, proved false at closer investigation – that Islam is rapidly spreading in Africa and Christianity is losing grounds. Coudray pointed out that the alleged advance of Islam on the one hand concerns the areas and peoples already Islamised and is a form of re-Islamisation of Muslim societies; on the other it is mistakenly equated with the migrations of the Islamised groups into new regions, which does not make the local population Muslim.[36] Even the visible activity of various Muslim organisations of local or foreign origin subsidised by Muslim countries (like Saudi Arabia, Libya or Kuwait) that results, for example, in the construction of mosques, cultural and health centres, does not support the hypothesis of the rapid Islamisation of Africa, even if a certain aggressiveness on the part of some Muslim organisations is taken into account. According to the data presented by Coudray, the number of Muslims in Chad and Nigeria has stayed more or less on the same level for the last fifteen years, while the number of Christians increased significantly.[37]

The reinvigoration of Islam pointed out by Coudray is attested to by Lansiné Kaba in his account of changes among the Mandinka. He argues that radicalism acquired for them a meaning of a struggle to improve adherence to the fundamentals of the faith transmitted either by a Sufi sheikh or a Wahhabi teacher. Each individual should strive for this first in his own life, and then in the life of his particular Muslim community. This goal, common for all Muslims, contributes to mutual respect and unity. Prohibition of religiously motivated violence, giving more visibility to Islam in media broadcasts, and the overt association of local politicians with Islam contributed to the reinvigoration of Islam. Kaba pointed out that a newer type of Muslim leadership had been emerging, active in giving an example with their own way of life and engaged in missionary and conversion activities (though not on a big scale).[38]

Hope for the future

It should be noted that this change of a mutual attitude among the Muslim groups took on an interesting shape drawn from the indigenous African culture – a joking relationship well known (not only) to the Mandinka. It offers another way of defusing and venting tensions, while respecting differences.[39] Could the indigenous African cultural milieu perhaps offer more means for building family ties or friendly relationship not only within one religious tradition but also among adherents of various religions?

Coudray refers to the feeling of deterioration of the general atmosphere of Christian–Muslim relations in Africa in recent years and sees several groups of reasons for this state of affairs. Though at first glance quite a lot of these reasons seem to come mainly from the Muslim side, a more careful reading of his text shows that Christians also contribute to the present pessimistic atmosphere, e.g. by printing and distributing anti-Muslim pamphlets, or calling the organised rallies 'crusades' and preaching against Islam.[40]

Initiatives taken up and promoted by the PROCMURA (the Project for Christian–Muslim Relations in Africa) deserve special appreciation. The organisation coordinates various projects that strive to promote peaceful coexistence and work at the grassroots level. At the same time the need for giving a genuine Christian witness is underlined. In his concluding remarks at the 2004 Birmingham Conference on Christian–Muslim Relations in Africa Johnston Mbillah, the general advisor of PROCMURA, underlined that Africans should be more concerned with working out their own models of coexistence rather than adopting problems imported from other parts of the world.[41]

Coudray sees hope in the recent events in Chad where – according to him – one could observe a growing interest in Christian–Muslim relations not only among lay Christians but also among the candidates to the priesthood. Even the Roman Catholic bishops were able to speak with one voice on these issues. Certain educational projects started together by Muslims and Christians were also reported. They contributed towards mutual appreciation and better understanding.[42]

On a social level one could point out that everyday contacts between adherents of different religions become the most obvious platform of cooperation. In many places extended families have been composed of people belonging to various religious groups and usually this does not pose a big problem. The African eclectic or open mentality provides a basic framework for such a coexistence. Even in a struggle-torn Nigeria the Yoruba, one of the three dominant ethnic groups composed of significant numbers of adherents of traditional religions, Muslims and Christians, are reputed to minimise conflicts and promote

217

coexistence. The religious studies department of the University of Ibadan publishes a journal *Orita* devoted to interactions between adherents of universalistic and African traditional religions.

Development projects could also provide a platform for cooperation, although in this sphere there is a greater possibility of entering into competition using religious affiliation as a distinctive element. Muslim organisations have entered the scene occupied for a long time mainly by groups of western and Christian provenance. One should note, however, that competition does not necessarily need to be hostile rivalry.

Certain tendencies present in both Muslim and Christian thinking still seem to treat Africa as a new battleground for the old struggle, either turning a blind eye to the cultural context in which it takes place, or treating it as a corruptive factor that needs to be removed. Both Christians and Muslims have displayed ambivalent attitudes towards African culture throughout the centuries, though Muslims (given their long presence in the region) have a more positive record in this respect. With the old and new experiences has the time not come when both Christians and Muslims should begin to look at the African cultural milieu with greater appreciation and use it as a platform for building their peaceful coexistence?

Notes

1 Kerr, D., 'Christian–Muslim relations: lessons from history', in Ipgrave, M. (ed.), *The Road Ahead. A Christian–Muslim Dialogue* (London, Church House Publishing, 2002), pp. 27–8.

2 For example: Marty, P., *Études sur l'Islam au Sénégal* (Paris, Editions Ernest Leroux, 1917); *Études sur l'Islam et les tribus du Soudan* (Paris, Editions Ernest Leroux, 1920); *L'Islam en Guinée* (Paris, Editions Ernest Leroux, 1921).

3 See J. A. Azumah's remarks on a privileged treatment given to African Islam by some European scholars in his *The Legacy of Arab-Islam in Africa. A Quest for Inter-religious Dialogue* (Oxford, Oneworld, 2001), pp. 7–18.

4 Hock, K., 'Christian–Muslim relations in the African context', *International Journal for the Study of the Christian Church*, 3 (2003), 36–57.

5 For a brief overview of the situation see e.g.: Miles, F. S., 'Religious pluralism in Northern Nigeria', in Levtzion, N. and Pouwels, R. L. (eds), *The History of Islam in Africa* (Athens OH, Ohio University Press, 2000), pp. 209–24.

6 Coudray, H., 'Chrétiens et musulmans au Tchad', *Islamochristiana*, 18 (1996), 175–234; Kouanda, A., 'Marabouts et missionnaires catholiques au Burkina à l'époque coloniale (1900-1947)', in Robinson, D. and Triaud, J.-L. (eds), *Le Temps des marabouts. Itinéraires et stratégies islamiques en Afrique occidentale française v. 1880–1960* (Paris, Karthala, 1997), pp. 33–52; Dovolo, E. and Asante, A. O., 'Reinterpreting the straight path. Ghanaian Muslim converts in mission to Muslims', *Exchange*, 32: 3 (2003), 215–38; de Benoist, J.-R., 'Amadou Hampâté Bâ: homme de dialogue religieux', *Islamochristiana*, 19 (1993), 1–16; Grodź, S., 'Towards universal reconciliation: the early development of Amadou Hampâté Bâ's ecumenical ideas', *Islam and Christian–Muslim Relations*, 13: 3 (2002), 281–302.

7 Stamer, J., 'Littérature sur l'Islam et les relations islamo-chrétiennes en Afrique de l'Ouest', *Jahrbuch für kontextuelle Theologien* (1998), 208. Coudray, H., 'L'Avenir

des relations islamo-chrétiennes en Afrique noire', *Islamochristiana*, 27 (2001), 157–73.

8 This is very general and schematic because Christian missionaries in the French West Africa came to some parts of the region (e.g. Mali, Burkina Faso) via communication routes along the Senegal and middle Niger river valleys.

9 The Yorubas of south-western Nigeria provide one of the most obvious examples in this respect.

10 For the French see e.g. Triaud, J.-L., 'Islam in Africa under French colonial rule', in Levtzion and Pouwels (eds), *The History of Islam in Africa*, p. 179; for the British see Hiskett, M., *The Course of Islam in Africa* (Edinburgh, Edinburgh University Press, 1994), pp. 114–17.

11 The Ashantis controlled the trade and generally kept the Muslim merchants at bay on the northern frontiers of the empire allowing only a small number of them to cross the borders and travel south. The British conquest of the Ashanti empire and introduction of the so-called *pax Britannica* not only allowed the Muslim traders free movement in the areas formerly closed to them but also allowed them to settle in the southern towns. Wilks, I., 'Asante policy towards the Hausa trade in the 19th century', in Meillassoux, C. (ed.), *The Development of Indigenous Trade and Markets in West Africa* (London, Oxford University Press, 1971), p. 136; Levtzion, N., *Muslims and Chiefs in West Africa* (Oxford, Clarendon Press, 1968), p. 32.

12 These groups were created by the young generation of Muslims educated in Egypt, Sudan and Saudi Arabia. The challenge they posed to the *turuq* differed in scope in various countries, showing that 'religious' zeal was only one aspect of their activity. Political goals seemed sometimes more important. Kaba, L., *The Wahhabiyya: Islamic Reform and Politics in French-speaking Africa* (Evanston, Norhtwestern University Press, 1974).

13 Harris did not found any churches. Calling for repentance he directed his listeners to the already existing churches. However, in places where the mission churches had not been established yet, Harris' converts formed new churches, though without involvement from Harris himself. Haliburton, G. M., *The Prophet Harris* (Longman, 1971).

14 For an example illustrating a particular case see: Kirby, J. P., *God, Shrines, and Problem-solving Among the Anufo of Northern Ghana* (Berlin, Dietrich Reimer Verlag, 1986).

15 Many sources confirm that the Manding-speaking traders exposed local African populations to Islam and external influences, and made Islam a means of trust building among merchants, but they themselves did not take an active part in the propagation of Islam. See e.g. 'Introduction', in Levtzion and Pouwels (eds), *The History of Islam in Africa*, p. 3; Kaba, L., 'Islam in West Africa: radicalism and the new ethic of disagreement, 1960–1990', in Levtzion and Pouwels (eds), *The History of Islam in Africa*, p. 191: 'Until the era of the jihad in the nineteenth century [...], conversion was achieved mostly through trade and other peaceful means'.

16 Bakary, the son of Biton Kulibali and ruler of the early eighteenth-century Bambara state, was deposed and killed when he became a Muslim because he contravened a delicate balance between Islam and local indigenous tradition. Levtzion, N., 'Islam in the Bilad al-Sudan to 1800', in Levtzion and Pouwels (eds), *The History of Islam in Africa*, p. 75. Osei Kwame, the king of the Ashanti

(*Asantehene*) who became a Muslim at the end of the eighteenth century, was deposed on similar grounds. Wilks, I., 'The position of Muslims in Metropolitan Ashanti in the early nineteenth century', in Lewis, I. M. (ed.), *Islam in Tropical Africa* (London, Oxford University Press, 1969), p. 334.

17 Centres of learning like Timbuktu; families like the Kounta or some of the Juula clerical families, e.g. Al-Hajj Salim Suwaré and the Jakhanke.

18 On Al-Maghili see e.g. Hunwick, J., *Sharia in Songhay: The Replies of al-Maghili to the Questions of Askia al-Hajj Muhammad* (London, The British Academy, 1985). The eleventh and twelfth century movements of Almoravids and Almohads, though radical and destructive for the early African states, like Ghana, developed into a more Arab and Imazighen society of the Maghreb, and eventually diverted their attention to Muslim Andalusia.

19 Trimingham, J. S., *Islam in West Africa* (Oxford, Clarendon Press, 1959), p. 34.

20 See e.g. comments by I. M. Lewis in the introduction to his *Islam in Africa* (Oxford, Oxford University Press, 1966).

21 'Introduction', in Levtzion and Pouwels (eds), *The History of Islam in Africa*, p. 4.

22 Turner, H. W., 'New religious movements in Islamic West Africa', *Islam and Christian–Muslim Relations*, 4: 1 (1993), 7–24.

23 Ibid., 24–6.

24 Christians face a similar identity problem – are they first Christians in Africa or African Christians? For the Muslim milieu the issue was extensively treated in Westerlund, D. and Rosander, E. E. (eds), *African Islam and Islam in Africa. Encounters Between Sufis and Islamists* (London, Hurst & Co., 1997).

25 Blyden, E. W., *Christianity, Islam and the Negro Race*, 2nd edn (Edinburgh, Edinburgh University Press, 1967); Kaba, 'Islam in West Africa', pp. 194, 196; Triaud ('Islam in Africa under French colonial rule', p. 181) pointed out that the Muslim religious elites 'were ousted lastingly from their politically determined positions by elites who had a French education'.

26 Coudray, 'Les relations islamo-chrétienne', 164, note 15.

27 See the argument presented by Azumah, *The Legacy of Arab-Islam in Africa*, pp. 1–6.

28 See e.g. the discussion in Sanneh, L., *The Crown and the Turban. Muslims and West African Pluralism* (Boulder CO, Westview Press, 1997), pp. 179–231.

29 'Introduction', in Levtzion and Pouwels (eds), *The History of Islam in Africa*, p. 2.

30 Ibid., p. 4.

31 Such an opinion was expressed e.g. by Matthews Ojo at the International Conference on Christian–Muslim Relations in Africa, Centre for the Study of Islam and Christian–Muslim Relations, Birmingham, April 2004.

32 Kaba, 'Islam in West Africa', pp. 198–201.

33 Ibid., p. 198.

34 See Quinn, A. and Quinn, F., *Pride, Faith, and Fear. Islam in Sub-Saharan Africa* (Oxford, Oxford University Press, 2003), p. 100.

35 *Wiadomosci KAI* (23 May 2004), 27.

36 For example the number of Muslims in the Ivory Coast increased in the last fifteen years because of the influx of immigrants from the neighbouring countries. In Chad Muslim groups settled in the south fleeing the war-stricken north. Coudray, 'Les relations islamo-chrétienne', p. 163.

37 The number of Christians in Chad increased by 10% in the last fifteen years. Coudray, 'Les relations islamo-chrétienne', pp. 163–4. It should, perhaps, be noted that similar fears *à l'envers*, i.e. about a 'Christianizing attack on Africa', have been expressed by the Muslim side. See: Johnston, P., 'An Islamic perspective on dialogue. Articles from Islamic journals', *Islamochristiana*, 13 (1987), 160–3.

38 Kaba, 'Islam in West Africa', pp. 202–4. If the picture drawn by a Malinke novelist Ahmadou Kourouma in his *Les Soleils des indépendances* (Montreal, Les Presses de l'Université de Montréal, 1968, p. 72) is accurate, they have a lot of work to do first within their own faith community: 'Are they fetish-worshipers or Muslims? A Muslim heeds the Koran, a fetish-worshiper follows the Koma; but in Togobala, everyone publicly proclaims himself a devout Muslim, but everyone privately fears the fetish'. Quoted in Harrow, K. W., 'Islamic literature in Africa', in Levtzion and Pouwels (eds), *The History of Islam in Africa*, p. 538.

39 Joking relationship 'assumes equality among partners and recognizes each one's identity in his defined group and role. By lowering the tensions in the community, it has encouraged a free expression of ideas and promoted a general sense of brotherhood – regarded as a cardinal value'. Kaba, 'Islam in West Africa', p. 203.

40 Coudray ('Les relations islamo-chrétienne', pp. 158–64) writes about: 1) planned actions (in the West African case: adoption of the shari'ah by the six states in northern Nigeria; spreading anti-western = anti-Christian ideology by the new Islamic NGOs and Islamising the public space by making Islam visible; preaching crusades, often anti-Islamic, organized by various Protestant groups); 2) spontaneous movements that turn violent in reaction to certain events (disturbances in Nigeria and Ghana); 3) exerting social or economic pressure on people in order to convert them; 4) instrumentalisation of religion (especially of Islam but also of Christianity); 5) fears of 'advancing Islam'.

41 www.procmura.org.

42 Coudray, 'Les relations islamo-chrétienne', p. 166.

15

Christian–Muslim relations in the Sudan[1]

John Flannery

The forgotten history of Christianity in Sudan

The notion that Christianity is a recent import to Africa is a misconception more widespread in the continent (and further afield) than might be expected, and the subtle impact of such an assumption within African Christianity must not be under-estimated. As Paul Bowers points out, 'it is vital to African Christian self-understanding to recognise that the Christian presence in Africa is almost as old as Christianity itself.'[2] Such self-understanding has a vital part to play in the Sudan, where successive Islamist governments have continued to portray Christianity as a foreign religion imported alongside European colonialism in the nineteenth century.

It is widely known that Christianity flourished in North Africa before being wiped out by Arab Islamic invasions beginning in the seventh century, and that Christianity in Ethiopia is both an ancient and a surviving tradition. The survival of Christianity in Egypt in the Coptic church may be less well known, but the fact that there was also a powerful Nubian strand of Christianity, a Christianity which lasted for over a thousand years in what is now Northern Sudan, is something familiar only to a few. Curiously, it was the construction of the great Aswan Dam in Egypt which gave a new impetus to scholarly research into Nubian Christianity. An international appeal by Unesco in 1959–60 resulted in a remarkable collaborative effort to rescue as many archaeological remains and to examine as many previously unexplored sites as possible before they were submerged beneath the waters of the Nile. This exercise produced a vast amount of fresh information on Nubian Christianity, since fully half of the sites investigated were from that particular period of Nubian history.

Ancient Nubia (approximately from Aswan south to modern Khartoum) is frequently mentioned in the Old Testament as 'Cush' or 'Ethiopia', and the 'Ethiopian eunuch' of Acts was not from the land which now bears that name but from Nubia (since the title 'Candace' given to the queen in Acts 5:27 was peculiar to the Nubian kingdom of Meroe). The three Nubian kingdoms officially became Christian around 540CE, and remarkably the Arab conquerors of the following century failed to extend their power south from Egypt into Nubia. The kings of Nubia continued to hold out against the Islamic rulers of Egypt, and at times came to the diplomatic and even military assistance of beleaguered

Egyptian Christians. The Nubian church appears to have been largely monophysite in Christology, following the theology of the Egyptian Copts, but there is also strong evidence of Byzantine Christianity. It would seem, from recent research, that Christianity was still officially functioning in Nubia in the late fifteenth century,[3] and it is suggested that tiny Christian communities may have survived until the middle of the eighteenth century. Catholic missionaries passing up the Nile in the nineteenth century still encountered traces of a folk-memory of a Christian past. The question of Christian influence spreading southwards and westwards from the Nubian kingdoms still needs further enquiry, but some scraps of data support the possibility. Ottoman Egypt had conquered the Sudan in 1821, giving new impetus to the process of Islamisation. The Egyptians failed, however, to penetrate to the south, principally due to problems of transportation, and to the presence of the tsetse fly. Christian missionaries succeeded in reaching the south by other routes and worked to evangelise the region. Later in the nineteenth century, the Catholic church sought to establish a presence in the Sudan, sending missionaries from a number of Orders and from the Propaganda Fide, but it would be the Italian Daniel Comboni (1831–81), first bishop of Central Africa and founder of the family of Comboni Missionaries, who truly deserves the title of 'father' of the Catholic church in Sudan.

The limited success of the missionaries among the non-Muslim peoples of the south was interrupted when the Egyptian rulers of Sudan were defeated by the followers of the *Mahdi* ('the divinely governed one') in 1885.[4] The *Mahdi* died shortly afterwards from ill-health, but his movement held power until it was defeated in 1898 by a joint Anglo-Egyptian force. The country was governed as an Anglo-Egyptian Condominium until 1956, and it is in this period that the contemporary Christian presence developed. The Comboni missionaries returned, and in 1903 the government assigned separate territories to the three denominations (American Presbyterians, Catholics and Episcopalians) which had applied for permission to evangelise.[5]

British policy in the Sudan was effectively to divide the country into two, with separate administrations in the north and south. In 1946, however, under pressure from Egypt, they decided, without consulting the people of the south, to establish a single state. Administration was unified and a Legislative Assembly established in Khartoum in 1948, giving the north considerable control over the south.

Despite Egypt's claims, and attempts to annex its former colony, the Sudan achieved independence on 1 January 1956. As was so often the case in Africa, the Sudan, the largest country on the continent and a creation of colonial imperialism, contained different and disparate elements which would almost inevitably lead to conflict after independence. The balance of power was largely concentrated in the more developed north, predominantly Arabic in language and culture and Islamic in religion, in contrast to the south, largely African and following traditional African religions, with small Christian and Muslim communities.

Even before the coming of independence, the south was aware that it was likely to be subordinated to the north,[6] and was demanding a degree of autonomy through a 'federal solution'. With the progressive withdrawal of the British in 1955, all the administrative and military posts passed directly to northerners, causing a mutiny in the south (at Torit, 18 August 1955), the creation of the Anya-Nya guerrillas, and the beginning of the first civil war, which would last for seventeen years. Southern members of the government, fearing that the north might attempt to dominate and exploit the south, as had been the case in the nineteenth century, demanded constitutional guarantees that their region would keep its African identity, without fear of being absorbed into the Arab world. Their fears would prove well founded, as the north decided to speed up the process of Arabisation and Islamisation of the south in order to ensure the loyalty of its inhabitants. The slogan 'One language (Arabic), One religion (Islam), One country' accurately encapsulated government policy. To many in the north, the English language and Christian religion present in the south were seen as obstacles to national unity. This programme was often forcibly applied, and no educated southerner could fail to perceive the at least implicit violation of fundamental human rights. When, for example, the southern MP Ezboni Mondiri requested that the English language and Christian religion be recognised as legitimate, he was sentenced to seven years imprisonment for 'incitement to disaffection', on the basis that his views were seen as an affront to northern views and a seditious attempt to divide the country.

During the 1958 election campaign, Sheikh Abdel Ali Rahman, a leader of the Khatmiya Islamic sect and a cabinet minister, reportedly claimed that the Sudan was an integral part of the Arab world, and that anyone dissenting from this view should leave the country. Another minister, in a speech at Juba on 25 May 1962, reasserted that national unity implied the universal adoption of Arabic as the national language and Islam as the national religion.

The main steps by which the Arabisation and Islamisation of the south were to be effected included: the seizure of all mission schools in 1957, the change of the weekly holiday from Sunday to Friday, the Missionary Societies Act of 1962, the expulsion of foreign missionaries from the south in 1964, and the destruction of major centres of church influence.

Seizure of mission schools

Christian missionaries had long feared that Arabic might be the Trojan horse by which Islam would try to make inroads into the south. In 1922 the Sudan government, nominally Anglo-Egyptian, but effectively a British colonial administration, had ordered that English should replace Arabic as the language of administration in the south. In 1950, as British policy responded to the wishes of Sudanese nationalists, the Minister of Education ordered that Arabic should be introduced to all intermediate and secondary schools in the south within two years.

Catholic missionaries obeyed this order, while fearing its consequences, even sending some of their personnel to the Lebanon to learn Arabic. A further step on the planned process of Islamisation took place on 13 February 1957, when the Minister of Education summoned to Khartoum all church leaders with missions in the south, and announced his ministry's intention to take over all mission schools in the Southern Sudan, with effect from April of the same year. The result was that 350 schools (300 Catholic and 50 Protestant) with some 30,000 pupils came under the direct control of the ministry of education. The minister gave 'national interests' and the 'national goal' as reasons for the takeover. At the Khartoum meeting he absolved the mission system from being under suspicion by the government for being disruptive of 'our national harmony', and promised that the religious instruction of Christian pupils could continue in the nationalised schools. None of the promises he gave to remove the concerns of the missionaries were kept, however, and the true purpose of the takeover soon became clear. In the Upper Nile Province, the schools were rapidly made to conform to the model of the *khalwa* (Qur'anic school), with Islam taught as the main subject and no provision for Christian pupils. In the provinces of Bahr el-Ghazal and Equatoria, missionaries were permitted, even as late as 1961, to give Christian instruction in schools. Increasingly, however, the missionaries were denied access to the schools, and their influence was eliminated in an outright attempt to transform the schools into positive instruments for Islamisation. In the Kapoeta district of East Equatoria a process of intensive, accelerated Islamisation was attempted. Village chiefs were pressured by government officials to declare themselves Muslims, and having done so were required in turn to put pressure on parents to register their children in the schools as Muslims, or, at least, as non-Christians. In this way schools became Muslim schools, and missionaries were strictly forbidden entry. Only the religion of Islam could be taught, and was made a compulsory subject.

The loss of the schools was a serious blow to the church, and only the escalation of guerrilla warfare in the region and the subsequent collapse of the whole system of education in the south prevented the spread of Islam through these former mission schools.

A Muslim Friday instead of a Christian Sunday

In February 1960, the military dictatorship of General Abbud, which had seized power in the Sudan from the elected government in 1958, decreed that, in the south, Friday rather than the hitherto customary Sunday should be observed as the weekly holiday. Both Christians and the followers of traditional African religions resented this imposition, an unmistakable sign that the government intended to impose Islam in the south. Faced with protests by students and villagers, the government resorted to force to impose its decision. The students of the Rumbek secondary schools, who had signed a written protest against the change, were tried and sentenced to terms of imprisonment of ten to twelve years (later reduced to three to four years). Only with the fall of the military dictatorship did the government admit its mistake and restored Sunday as the day of rest in the south.

The Missionary Societies Act

In May 1962, the military government promulgated the Missionary Societies Act, forbidding all missionary societies in the Sudan to exercise any missionary activity, except in accordance with the terms of a licence granted by the Council of Ministers (art. 3). Special provisions prevented the propagation of Christianity among followers of traditional African religions, since the law declared all missionary work illegal 'in regions or places other than those specified in its licence, or towards any person professing any religion or sect or belief thereof, other than that specified in its licence' (art. 7). Missionaries were also forbidden to adopt abandoned children (art. 8), and even such activities as the formation of social clubs, appeals for and collection of monetary assistance, famine and food relief, and the distribution of audio-visual media were all to be regulated by the Minister of the Interior.

The act was clearly intended to cripple the church in the south, as demonstrated by the fact that it was only in the south that it was implemented, and not in the north, where such flagrant violation of human liberties would have been too apparent to foreign eyes. None of the applications made by the missionary societies was ever granted, yet the act had an unpredicted consequence, with more southerners than ever joining the church. In 1962 alone, some 100,000 inhabitants of Equatoria requested baptism.

Expulsion of the missionaries

At the time of independence, some 460 missionaries were serving in Southern Sudan (360 of them Catholic). With the conviction on the part of some government officials that Islam would be unable to make adequate progress in the south as long as Christian missionaries remained, a policy for their expulsion was gradually introduced. First to go were those missionaries employed full time in the schools, with the government arguing that since schools had now been nationalised, their presence was no longer justified. During 1958, thirty missionaries, half of them Catholic, were asked to leave the country, while others engaged in pastoral activity were allowed to remain.

Between 1958 and 1961, other missionaries were expelled, often on the basis of fabricated charges brought against them, while between October 1962 and May 1963 (i.e. after the Missionary Societies Act) a total of 143 missionaries were ordered to leave, on the sole basis that they were 'redundant'. In 1963, the Minister of the Interior is reported to have stated that, 'They [the missionaries] had entered the Sudan as teachers . . . there is no reason for them to stay after their jobs have been Sudanised'.[7] Commenting on the minister's statement, the editor of the *Sudan Daily* provided an insight into government thinking. 'Much harm', he said, 'has been done in the past by foreign-based elements promoting hatred and disharmony among the people of this land. If, under the cloak of religious zeal, activities likely to produce divisive tendencies are pursued, the Government of the Sudan will not shrink from its responsibilities of protecting the unity and security of the State, even if it is forced to resort to expulsion'.[8] Sayed Ali Baldo, governor of Equatoria Province was even more forthright, declaring, 'It [is] as clear as the sun that the Catholic priests are the source of all the government's troubles in the South . . . [because of their spreading Christianity in a territory the government wanted to gain for Islam] . . . Therefore, it was necessary to throw out all the *Italian* [sic] missionaries'.[9] On 27 February 1964, the minister of the interior announced the decision of the Council of Ministers to expel 'all foreign missionaries from the southern provinces', attempting to justify this action by charging the missionaries with conniving with the 'rebels', a suggestion largely rejected by world opinion, although instances of humanitarian support for the guerrillas could certainly be cited. Some believed that the true reason for the expulsion of the missionaries was to prevent foreign witnesses to what was planned for the region, nothing less than a desperate attempt to put a stop to guerrilla activity in the south by fire and sword. Commenting later on the fall of the military dictatorship (in October 1964), the Sudanese prime minister attributed it to 'God's punishment for all the cruelties the military junta perpetrated in the South'.[10]

The departure of the foreign missionaries revealed the extent to which they had been responsible for the pastoral care of Catholics in the Sudan, and the lamentable lack of indigenous Catholic clergy. (The fact that both the Anglican and Presbyterian churches were much better placed to take over administration must raise questions about relations between the Catholic missionaries and the people they served, and about the model of mission under which they operated.[11] It must be said, however, that an apparent reluctance to develop an indigenous clergy was by no means peculiar to the Sudan.) One bishop and twenty-eight priests were left with the task of ministering to some half a million Catholics. On the positive side, however, there were ninety-four students in the major seminary of Tore in 1964. Under normal circumstances a reasonable proportion of these students would have swelled the ranks of the Sudanese clergy: it would, however, be years before the south experienced anything approaching normality, and then only as a temporary respite before the resumption of civil war.

Destruction of church property

From May 1965 onwards, following the creation of a coalition government under Muhammad Ahmad Mahjûb, a policy of military repression in the south led to mission buildings becoming targets of both sides in the continuing war between guerrillas and government. The major seminary and the two junior seminaries at Okaru and Porkele were attacked by the army and set ablaze. Priests and seminarians fled under bullet-fire, and walked through the forest until they reached Uganda or Zaire. In September of the same year, the Sisters of Our Lady of Victories at Mupoi had a narrow escape when their convent was attacked during Mass. They sought safety in flight and spent the day in hiding, while the soldiers searched the mission buildings, and their convent burned to the ground. On the following day, the nuns began a fifteen-day march through the forest until they reached the Central African Republic. A total of sixteen mission stations were destroyed, seventeen badly damaged and pillaged, and five suffered minor damage. One bishop, two apostolic administrators and some twenty priests remained in the south, while all the others fled to safety abroad.

It was in the face of such difficulties that the Christian churches in the Sudan came together in 1965 to form the Sudan Council of Churches, in order to coordinate their activities and to give witness to their solidarity and brotherhood.

Military conflict escalated between 1966 and 1969, with no prospect of decisive success on either side. On 25 May 1969, Colonel Gaafar Mohamed Nimeiri seized power in Khartoum by a bloodless military coup. He had previously served in the south, and describing his experience there, he spoke of seeing 'churches without prayers, schools without pupils, fields without farmers, empty houses without a fireplace, orphans without a father . . . attackers and defenders, killers and victims, all children of the same country . . . the northern troops stationed in the swamps of the South to kill their brothers and save the pride of politicians who sat in comfortable chairs in Khartoum'.[12]

Two weeks after the coup, he announced a revolutionary new policy for the solution of the 'southern problem'. The south was to have self-government. His plan was thwarted, however, by Communist elements within his government, who wanted to ensure that their party had a strong position in the south before the elections for self-government took place. In July 1971, the Communists fell out with Nimeiri and themselves staged an abortive coup, leaving him free to implement his plan for the south. Christian organisations collaborated with the government by persuading guerrilla leaders abroad to cooperate with Khartoum, and eventually an agreement was thrashed out at Addis Ababa on 27 February 1972. Henceforth, all local affairs in the south were to be managed by the southerners themselves: never before had the people of the south enjoyed such freedom nor looked forward to such a bright future.

1972 and beyond: an opportunity for the church

The Addis Ababa Agreement dealt mainly with political and administrative matters related to the southern provinces. To dispel any fear of forced Arabisation, article 6 of the agreement stipulated that Arabic was the official language of the Sudan and that English was the principal language for the southern region, without prejudice to the use of either language. Moreover, freedom of religion was guaranteed in Appendix A, n.4 (1): 'Every person should enjoy freedom of religion, opinion, conscience, and the right to profess them publicly and privately . . . and to establish religious institutions, subject to reasonable limitations in favour of morality, health, and public order, as prescribed by law. Parents and guardians should be guaranteed the right to educate their children in accordance with the religion of their choice'. This agreement was incorporated in the 1973 Constitution of the Sudan Republic, which also guaranteed religious freedom to all citizens, Muslim, Christian or 'pagan'. More important than the legal guarantees enshrined in the constitution, was the fact that implementation of this policy in the south was entrusted to southern administrators, almost all Christian and formerly educated in the mission schools. There were no longer difficulties in opening church-related schools, hospitals and dispensaries, repairing buildings, organising religious associations, visits by priests to outlying villages, or the evangelisation of 'virgin areas', for which consent had previously been needed and routinely refused. The regional government welcomed church initiatives which brought material and moral development to the area.

Only three months after the Addis Ababa Agreement, the government took the surprising step of establishing diplomatic relations with the Vatican at ambassadorial level, and the Pro-Nunciature of Khartoum was established.

In view of this new situation, and in response to a request from the Sudanese clergy, the Holy See established a local hierarchy for the Sudan. The *ius commisionis* of the missionary societies was replaced by a national church on the model envisaged by the Second Vatican Council, with the local clergy responsible for the *plantatio ecclesiae*. Khartoum became the Metropolitan See for the north, and Jura, with four suffragan dioceses, for the south.

It must be admitted, however, that the fledgling church struggled in the face of the enormous challenges presented to it in the aftermath of years of civil conflict, and the new bishops had little choice but to turn to foreign missionaries for help, with the result that a number of religious institutes again came to play an important role in pastoral work, health care and education in Sudan. The churches, however, continued a process of Sudanisation of the Christian communities and their leaders, in contrast to the approach of the earlier missionary period. In the north, meanwhile, the Catholic church initiated programmes of cooperation with Muslims, fostering everyday dialogue among the ordinary people.

Party divisions resulting from the process of reconciliation led Nimeiri to suppress all opposition, and particularly the Islamist Muslim Brethren. In 1977 he was forced into a 'National Reconciliation', whereby other factions were integrated into the government. From this point, Hasan al-Turabi, leader of the Muslim Brethren, began to exercise influence on the government. He headed the committee for the revision of the Sudanese legal system in accordance with Islamic shari'ah law. Adding to this the implementation of an Islamic banking system, the scene was set for a sort of Islamic revival, which strengthened Islamic fundamentalism in the Sudan, and to which Nimeiri came to ally himself increasingly in the late 1980s.

The 1980s: imposition of shari'ah law and a return to civil war

The proclamation of Islamic law in September 1983 led to deep dissatisfaction among both the Islamic opposition and the Christian communities. Sudanese Muslims and Christians would both suffer under the new legislation. The Catholic Archbishop of Khartoum, Gabriel Zubeir Wako, wrote a pastoral letter condemning the unacceptable implications of shari'ah law, and instructing his faithful on how to react to it. Since this time the Sudanese Council of Churches has spoken out on issues of peace, justice and human rights, and in 1984 the Catholic bishops of Sudan issued their message, 'Lord, Come to Our Aid', on appropriate Christian behaviour in view of the situation in the country.

The imposition of Islamic law was by no means the only reason for civil war to break out again in the Sudan; significant political and economic causes also came into play.[13] The Sudanese People's Liberation Movement under the control of John Garang demanded a federal and secular system for the whole country as the only way to ensure equality for all Sudanese. Numeiri's support dwindled, even in the north, and he was ousted in 1985 by a group of army officers who set up a transitional military council. Shari'ah law was suspended, and free elections held after one year. A coalition was established under Prime Minister Sadiq al-Mahdi (great-grandson of the *Mahdi* who defeated General Gordon at Khartoum). In 1988, the National Islamic Front entered the coalition, with its leader, Hasan al-Turabi, appointed as deputy prime minister and minister of foreign affairs. The inability to end the civil war was a major cause of the *coup d'état* engineered by General Umar al-Bashir in 1989, which resulted in power going to the National Islamic Front under al-Turabi. As the country entered a new decade, the government, now the Revolution of National Salvation, returned to a deliberate policy of forced Arabisation and Islamisation.

The 1990s: Islamic fundamentalism and interreligious dialogue

Through its National Comprehensive Strategy, the Revolution of National Salvation had as its goal the building of a 'new Sudan', an African, Arabic and Muslim Sudan, with the various Muslim groups in the country united under the flag of a pure Islam, based on the principles of Islamic law. While the stated intention of the government may be seen as the establishment of a federal system, an Islam claimed to be federalist and modernist, a popular and participative democracy, in fact, the many attempts to introduce shari'ah law, the declaration of jihad against the rebels in the south in 1992, and the creation of a Popular Defence Army, all contributed to a continued Arabisation and Islamisation of the Sudan, even if its Constitution clearly recognised the multireligious nature of the country. Under the leadership of al-Turabi, the National Islamic Front played an important part in this process, and he more than once stated his wish to convert Sudan into an Islamic state as a model for the rest of Africa. For al-Turabi, 'The Sudan is a country open towards the whole of the African continent and at the same time towards the Arab world. Its ethnic structure constitutes a miniature model of Africa at large. Thus, if Islam and the Arabic language should succeed in spreading out over the whole of Sudan, it would then become very easy to open to them also the East, the Centre, and the West of Africa. And – who knows – the whole African continent'.[14]

Despite this unpromising background, and the widespread abuse of human rights in the Sudan, the 1990s saw a vigorous response from the bishops of the Sudan, and the cautious development of Sudanese–Vatican dialogue. The establishment of Islamic law governing banking and civil cases in the North from the beginning of 1991 appears to have been the impetus for a visit to Khartoum in March 1991 of the pope's envoy, Cardinal Roger Etchegaray. The Pastoral Letters of the Catholic Bishops' Conference of the Sudan, 'The Truth Shall Make You Free' (November 1992), and 'United and Faithful' (December 1992), were highly critical of the government and its treatment of non-Muslims. On 6 October 1991, the Apostolic Pro-Nuncio in Khartoum sent an open letter to the Sudanese government and the Holy See, describing the difficulties being experienced by the Catholic church at the time. The letter is based on reports from the Archbishop of Khartoum and pastoral workers, and refers to specific cases of persecution. The Pro-Nuncio emphasised his deep disappointment that earlier promises by the government of a new political system in which 'all citizens will be equal, without any discrimination by reason of colour, religion or sex' and that 'in future, all religions will be equal and free in their religious activities' had failed to lead to any perceptible change.[15] In November 1991, the Council for International People's Friendship (a Sudanese NGO) organised its first Interreligious Dialogue Conference, attended by religious leaders from around the world.

In September 1992, the papal ambassador to the Sudan met with an official from the Sudanese Foreign Ministry to re-examine issues of peace and religious minorities in the country, while in October of the same year the Vatican criti-cised the violation of human rights of church workers in Sudan. Also in October, the Sudanese bishops gathered in Rome for their *ad limina* visit.[16] In his prelimi-nary address, the Archbishop of Khartoum, Gabriel Zubeir Wako, referred to the absence in Sudan of 'a system that honestly respects human rights, that acknowl-edges and respects the diversity among our people in terms of religion, race, language and culture; that promotes true freedom, particularly the freedom of religion and its practice, the freedom of expression and association'. He described the situation of the Catholic church in Sudan as 'one of the worst moments of her history', but also painted a picture of 'a Church that is growing to maturity through the Cross' in which '[m]ost of our faithful, instead of showing fear and discouragement before what we can rightly call religious persecution, have begun to live and profess their faith more meaningfully and courageously'.[17] In his own address, the pope insisted that, 'Any hindrance of the exercise of reli-gious freedom, in that it calls into question the inviolable transcendence of the religious subject, injures the cause of peace'. He refers to the unacceptable situ-ation of 'discrimination in education, the harassment of priests, religious and catechists, the expulsion of missionaries, the obstruction of the legitimate expression of the faith, the lack of true freedom in conversions', while exhorting the bishops 'to continue to work for peace and reconciliation in the spirit of the Beatitudes'.[18] On 4 December 1992, a strong condemnation of the human rights record of the Sudanese government was issued by a UN committee, followed later the same month by UN Resolution L77. The Resolution had the support of the Vatican, and owed a good deal to the intervention of two Sudanese bishops who had visited the US to meet the UN Secretary General, calling for a UN intervention in the name of humanity. The bishops also visited the US Depart-ment of State to press the case for UN action. Their intervention appears to have been effective, as it would be the US which drafted and introduced Resolution L77 to the UN General Assembly.

During the same month that the Sudanese government was criticised by the UN, the Vatican announced that Pope John Paul II was likely to visit the country in February of 1993. The brief visit, at the end of a papal tour of Africa, took place on 10 February, and the pope met with the Chairman of the Revolutionary Command Council, Lt. General al-Bashir.[19] The significance of the date of the papal visit would not have been lost on Sudanese Catholics, occurring as it did on the feast day of Josephine Bakhita. A black southerner, she was born in the Darfur region in 1869, kidnapped at the age of nine and sold into slavery, later converting to Christianity and spending fifty years as a member of the Institute of Canossian Sisters of Charity. Her beatification had, coincidentally, taken place in 1992 (she would be canonised in 2000).

The Sudanese government clearly hoped to gain the maximum benefit from the pope's visit, and it was preceded by public shows of religious tolerance. An editorial in a Khartoum daily boasted, 'The Pope will see that the Sudan is the land of dialogue between Islam and Christianity',[20] travel restrictions were lifted, and promises were made that the Missionary Societies Act would finally be repealed, and entrance and exit visas granted to missionaries.

Among Sudanese Christians, there was some concern that the pope's visit could be seen as giving support to a regime which had become something of an international pariah (at least one southern bishop spoke out against the visit) and that the government would attempt to make capital from the visit.[21] However, an indication of the pope's intentions was given in a speech to the diplomatic corps in Kampala, Uganda, saying, 'I wish to raise my voice in support of peace and justice for all the Sudanese people, and to comfort my brothers and sisters in the faith, so many of whom are affected by the conflict going on in the South'.[22] The pope did not mince his words: in his official meeting with President al-Bashir, he invoked international human rights charters, stressing the need for a 'constitutional formula' to end the war and for 'a legally guaranteed respect for human rights in a system of equal justice for all'. At the open air Mass attended by tens of thousands of Christians and Muslims, he declared that 'only the perversion of religious sentiment leads to discrimination and conflict'.[23] Faced with such stern criticism, al-Bashir responded by saying, 'Respecting human rights is not a political choice, it is a religious obligation',[24] a statement which could not but ring hollow in view of the government's record on this issue.

During his visit the pope also met and addressed the leaders of other religions in the Sudan, emphasising the need for citizens to accept one another 'with all their differences of language, customs, culture and belief'. He stressed the high regard of the Catholic church for the followers of Islam, hoping that 'this meeting will contribute to a new era of constructive dialogue and goodwill', ending by saying that 'the Catholic church is irrevocably committed to ecumenical and interreligious dialogue'. In his more irenic leaving discourse to government leaders, the Catholic bishops, and the diplomatic corps, John Paul II ended by saying 'I depart with the hope that a better relationship between North and South, and between the followers of different religious traditions, will soon be a reality'.[25]

From the Christian perspective the visit was largely seen as a success, leaving Christians in the Sudan with the feeling that they were not alone and forgotten. There was, however, no apparent attempt to differentiate between the rampant Islamism of the government and the attitude of the majority of Sudanese Muslims, in fact, rather the opposite, with the pope continually referring to the 'breakdown' of relations between Muslims and Christians.[26] The opinions expressed in the Saudi paper *Asharq al-Aswat* and in the London-based Arabic daily *Al-Hayat* offer some insight into other views of the papal visit. In the former, the Sudanese columnist, Othman Mirghani, complained that the purpose of John Paul II's visit was not easy to establish, given its timing and brevity. In his opinion, such a short visit made it impractical to discuss relevant issues in any depth. He went on to wonder whether a parallel could be drawn with the pope's visit to Poland, which would prove instrumental in the fall of Communism. From the pope's statements about the conflict in the Sudan springing from the search for a national identity in a country whose north and south have deep ethnic, cultural, linguistic and religious differences, Mirghani drew the conclusion that the hidden agenda of the visit was to show support for southern secession, finding it significant that the Sudan visit coincided with a meeting in Uganda of those southern leaders who favoured secession and opposed the federalist approach of the SPLM leader John Garang. The writer also questioned the fact that the visit focused on talks with the government, to the exclusion of the moderate majority.

Writing in *Al-Hayat*, the editor, Jihad Khazen, agreed with Mirghani that the inspiration for the visit was political, but saw a certain 'exchange of benefits' between the pope and the Khartoum government, with the pope seeking better conditions for Sudanese Christians, and the government desperate for a degree of international credibility.

Claiming that Khartoum would try to milk the visit all it was worth in terms of global propaganda, he referred to the planned meeting of a Sudanese inter-faith committee which it was hoped would turn the spotlight on the government's 'angelic face'. Khazen pointed out, however, that the government may be disappointed, as the days when papal visits made the headlines were long over, particularly in view of John Paul II's fondness for globe-trotting.[27]

The promises made by the government before the visit failed to be honoured, and in a pastoral letter the Sudanese bishops declared that following the pope's visit to the country, despite what seemed to be a more serious commitment for dialogue for peace, nevertheless, many citizens were still persecuted 'deprived of their fair share in the political, social and economic life of the country' and of their basic rights.[28]

In a visit to the Vatican on 13 October 1993, Hassan al-Turabi, the influential Islamist leader, met the pope in the Vatican. It would appear that he proposed to the pope that they should set up a common religious front in order to stop the world becoming less religious, less moral and more materialistic.[29] The same theme is apparent in the resolution of the Second Popular Arab and Islamic Conference in December 1993,[30] which speaks of unifying 'the views and efforts of people of faith against secularism', and of the 'high moral values' which religion confers. Interestingly, both the Vatican and Sudan would criticise the proposals on sex and abortion of the UN population conference held in Cairo in 1994. In October 1994, the Second Interreligious Dialogue Conference was held in Khartoum. The speech there by Cardinal Arinze, head of the Pontifical Council for Interreligious Dialogue, drew considerable attention. He told his hosts frankly, and in forceful language that left no room for misunderstanding, that 'the success and durability of your Muslim–Christian Association will depend much on your willingness to put the emphasis on facts, rather than beautiful statements'.[31] The conference decided to establish an NGO, the Inter-religious Dialogue Association, as a permanent and independent body. It is clear that the cardinal had been a driving force behind the establishment of this specifically Sudanese body for Muslim–Christian dialogue, having strenuously rejected the attempts of the government to 'internationalise' the dialogue[32] for reasons of political propaganda. If the cardinal had been outspoken at the conference, no less so was the Archbishop of Khartoum who insisted on the need to recognise that Christians were victims of government discrimination.

Immediately before the beginning of the conference attended by Cardinal Arinze, the government passed a decree cancelling the Missionary Societies Act of 1962. However, when the text was provided to the churches some weeks after the cardinal's departure, it became clear that it went hand-in-hand with a new

decree which changed their status to that of 'associations' or NGOs. The Sudanese Episcopal Conference drew attention to the 'danger residing in the power
of oversight given to the Minister to amend the constitutions and statutes relating to the aims of each society'.[33]

While the 1990s saw a number of initiatives in the field of interreligious dialogue at government level, it must be questioned how genuine was the commitment to dialogue, particularly when President al-Bashir had openly declared to
the delegates after the official closure of the 1994 conference that 'the government in Khartoum was following a long term plan to convert Sudan into an
Islamic state, by every possible means'.[34]

Despite the rhetoric directed at an international audience, the situation of
the Christian churches in Sudan remained dire, with Christians falsely accused
of involvement in anti-government terrorism, the abduction, imprisonment and
torture of clerics, catechists and lay Christians, and the demolition of Christian
schools and centres. In 1997, the Sudanese Council of Churches was still demanding that government ministers should act in accordance with their earlier promises since despite the repeal of the Missionary Societies Act, the churches had
noticed no effective improvement as regards religious freedom.

The Sudanese churches nevertheless continued to call for peace and for the
establishment of a genuine dialogue among equal partners. Their wish for a
cessation of hostilities was realised when, after several years of stop-start negotiations, pressure from Europe and particularly the US finally brought about a
somewhat fragile peace agreement between the Sudanese People's Liberation
Movement led by John Garang, and the Khartoum government.

The Comprehensive Peace Agreement finally signed on 9 January 2005 provides for a federal system, with a two-chamber central government and a regional
government for southern Sudan which will have substantial powers.[35] This structure will remain in place for six years, after which southern Sudan may chose to
become independent through a referendum vote. During this interim period, a
government of national unity will administer the country on a national basis.
The agreement addresses many contentious issues, including the question of
power-sharing in government, administration of the contested regions, and
wealth-sharing, particularly in respect to oil revenues. Importantly, the agreement provides that shari'ah law will not apply in the south or in the capital,
Khartoum. This issue had been a major sticking point in the peace negotiations
and a stumbling-block for official Muslim–Christian dialogue. Significantly,
both parties to the agreement reiterated their determination to continue resolv-
ing the root causes of the conflict and violence in Sudan which inflict hardship
and suffering on the people of Sudan and seriously hamper the prospects for
economic development and the attainment of social justice in Sudan. The Draft
Constitution for the national government dated 16 March 2005 promises that
the government will respect the religious right to 'worship or assemble in connection with a religion or belief and to establish and maintain places for these
purposes', freedom to 'communicate with individuals and communities in
matters of religion and belief at national and international level', and 'to teach
religion or belief in places suitable for these purposes' (Ch. 1, §6 (a) (e), and (i)).
The Draft Interim Constitution of Southern Sudan (September 2005) declares

the south to be 'a multi-ethnic, multi-cultural, multi-lingual, multi-religious and multi-racial entity' (Ch. 1, §1 (1), where 'all religions shall be treated equally' (Ch.1, §8 (2)).[36]

As signs of peace grew stronger, the Catholic bishops of Sudan issued a pastoral letter, 'I Will Make Everything New' (Apoc. 21:5), addressed to all people of goodwill, and setting out steps which would be needed for a just and lasting peace. In their 'Statement Regarding the Signing of the Comprehensive Peace Agreement', they reiterated the same themes, stressing the need for forgiveness (requiring both justice and a change of heart on the part of all parties involved) and reconciliation (based on the model of the South African Truth and Reconciliation Commission).

The end of the devastating civil war, which cost the lives of some two million people and resulted in the displacement of up to four million, will bring enormous challenges to the Sudan, not least that of achieving lasting peace in the Darfur region. The Christian churches will also face new challenges. No longer the focus of opposition, they will need to build a positive new role in a rapidly changing society,[37] lest they run the risk of marginalisation. New structures will also need to be created to facilitate a genuine Muslim–Christian dialogue, but perhaps the greatest hope for such dialogue comes from the people themselves. As the Archbishop of Khartoum pointed out, in Sudan, 'Muslims work and live side by side with Christians. It can be said with some truth that tolerance and mutual respect is part and parcel of the Sudanese culture as a whole'.[38] With the end of conflict they will be able increasingly to express what Guixot refers to as those 'rarely known realities'[39] of Sudanese life which give evidence to the vitality of that 'dialogue of life' between Muslims and Christians so deeply rooted in the majority of the population.

Notes

1 This chapter will concentrate on the Sudanese Catholic church, the largest Christian community.
2 Bowers, Paul, 'Nubian Christianity: the neglected heritage', *Africa Journal of Evangelical Theology*, 4: 1 (1985), 3–23 serves as an excellent brief introduction to the topic, and includes numerous bibliographical references.
3 The decline and extinction of Nubian Christianity is now understood to have been the result of a complex of disparate economic, political, geographic and religious factors, rather than simply caused by the spread of Islam. Bowers discusses the issue in the article referred to above.
4 The treatment of the Christian minority in this period is considered in Camillo Ballin 'The Dimmis in the Sudanese Mahdiyyah (1881–1898)', *Islamochristiana*, 27 (2001), 101–29.
5 Some British administrators feared that missionary activity would cause local security problems and such separation was thought desirable. On the lessons to be learned from the early missionary period, see Voll, John O., 'Imperialism, nationalism and missionaries: lessons from Sudan for the twenty-first century', *Islam and Christian–Muslim Relations*, 8: 1 (1997), 39–52.
6 Representing more than a quarter of the population, the south had only thirteen deputies out of a total of ninety-five. In the commission charged with establishing

the Constitution, only a single southern delegate was present to argue for federalism.

7 'The Catholic church in Sudan: a golden opportunity lost', *Pro Mundi Vita Dossiers*, 1 (1984), *African Dossier*, 28, p. 9.

8 Ibid.

9 Ibid.

10 Ibid., p. 10.

11 On criticism of foreign missionaries by Sudanese clergy, see the article by Roland Marchal, 'Remarques sur le développement de l'Eglise catholique et la 'vernacu-laristion' du christianisme au Soudan', in Bleuchot, Hervee, Delmet, Christian and Hopwood, Derek (eds), *Sudan: History, Identity, Ideology*, IREMAM and The Middle East Centre, St Anthony's College Oxford (Reading, Ithaca Press, 1991), pp. 181–96, esp. pp. 187–8. On the specific problems of missionary education during the period of the Condominium, see the article by Lilian Passmore Sand-erson 'Education in the southern Sudan: the impact of government–mission-ary–southern Sudanese relationships upon the development of education during the Condominium period, 1898–1956', *African Affairs*, 179: 315 (1980), 157–69.

12 'The Catholic church in Sudan', p. 10.

13 See the article by Heraclides, A., *The Journal of Modern African Studies*, 25: 2 (June 1987), 227–8.

14 *Al-Ahram Hebdo* (28 February–6 March 2001), 13. Quoted in Guixot, Miguel Angel Ayuso, 'Christian–Muslim relations in the Sudan: a survey through Sudanese politics', *Islamochristiana*, 30 (2004), 131–51, see p. 144.

15 The English text as published by the General Secretariat of the Sudan Catholic Bishops' Conference is reproduced in *Catholic International*, 3: 1 (1–14 January 1992), 5–8.

16 Two of the bishops from the south had been unable to travel to Rome, remaining behind in the besieged southern capital of Juba. For the background to the affair see the news item, 'Missionaries ordered out of Juba', *The Tablet* (5 September 1992), p. 1112.

17 The archbishop may well have had in mind the case of the church at Damazin in the Blue Nile province. After the expulsion of the parish priest, Fr Debertolis, two remaining Sudanese priests were told to stop preaching and ordered to hand over the keys of the parish premises in order that they could become a police station. The faithful reacted by occupying the premises for several days to prevent the takeover, and the local authorities backed down. The archbishop congratu-lated the people in a pastoral letter of 28 November 1991, in which he praised them for opening a new page in the history of being church in the archdiocese, giving an example of 'a Church that is gradually acquiring its identity and internal strength'. This and other incidents are described in the article by Michael Campbell-Johnston, 'Cross and crescent in Sudan', *The Tablet* (1 February 1992), 133–4.

18 *Osservatore Romano*, 40 (7 October 1992), 3 and 5.

19 It is curious that on this occasion the pope did not meet with the most powerful and influential Islamist leader, and *éminence grise* of the Sudanese government, Dr Hassan al-Turabi. A possible reason was Vatican support for the recent critical UN resolution. Dr al-Turabi did, however, meet with the Ghanaian Cardinal Francis Arinze, head of the Vatican department responsible for interreligious dialogue.

20 *The Tablet* (20 February 1993), 252.
21 This fear would in all probability be responsible for the change of plan by the Archbishop of Canterbury on his visit to Sudan in December 1993. He had initially intended to visit Khartoum, but in fact went only to the rebel-held south. His actions resulted in something of a diplomatic incident, with the mutual expulsion of ambassadors to Britain and Sudan.
22 See the news article in *The Tablet* (20 February 1993), 252.
23 Quoted in the article by Gill Lusk, 'Tough words from the pope', *Middle East Journal* (19 February 1993), 13.
24 *Middle East International* (19 February 1993), 13.
25 *Osservatore Romano* (11 February 1993), 25–28, XXV–XXVIII, carried the texts of the pope's address to the president, his address to religious leaders, the homily of the Mass in honour of Blessed Bakhita, and his leaving address.
26 In reality the papal visit had given moderate Muslims the hope of a future in which their rights also would be respected.
27 These opinions are summarised in *Mid East Mirror* (11 February 1993), 17–18, in the article 'The pope and the Sudan'.
28 See the news item, 'Bishops plead as civil war goes on', *The Tablet* (12 June 1993), 763.
29 This information results from a private interview with al-Turabi conducted by Masaki Kobayashi and reported in his article 'Inter-religious dialogue between the Vatican and Sudan', *Islam and Muslim-Christian Relations*, 7: 3 (1996), 285–95.
30 With al-Turabi as secretary general.
31 Faruqi, M. H., 'Bhamdoun to Khartoum: from ceremony to serious agenda', *Impact International* (December 1994), 16–17, cited in Kobayashi, Masaki, 'Inter-religious dialogue between the Vatican and Sudan', *Islamochristiana*, 7: 3 (1996).
32 The cardinal's views are forthrightly expressed in his interview with Kobayashi, 'Inter-religious dialogue between the Vatican and Sudan', 289–92.
33 Quoted in the article by Hubert Barbier MAfr., 'Un cri d'alarme des Eglises chrétiennes', *Les Cahiers de l'Orient*, 48 (1997), 19–30.
34 Ibid., 26.
35 A signed copy of the 260-page agreement can be found at the website of the United Nations Mission in Sudan, www.unmis.org/English/cpa.htm.
36 These and other important texts are available in the 'Documents' section of the *Sudan Tribune* website: www.sudantribune.com.
37 As, it can be argued, has been the case of the Catholic church in Poland after the fall of Communism.
38 Address given by Archbishop Gabriel Zubeir Wako to the French bishops at Lourdes (7 November 1999), *Islamochristiana*, 26 (2000), 238–41, see p. 240.
39 Guixot, 'Christian–Muslim relations in the Sudan', 150.

16

Christianity and Islam: the way forward?

Emma Loosley

Throughout this book the various contributors have returned time and again to the fact that the world changed irrevocably on 9/11. It is a cliché, but nevertheless true for that, that since 2001 the world has lost its innocence. In the aftermath of the destruction of the Twin Towers many people were quick to adopt Samuel Huntingdon's predictions of 'a clash of civilisations'. Since then further atrocities have been perpetrated in Bali, Madrid and other places around the world but perhaps the most significant attack for many of the contributors to this book were the 7/7 attacks in London in 2005. For the first time the act was committed by 'people like us', British-born and educated young men, who happened also to be Muslim. This proved a turning point for many, as it was finally realised that disaffected Muslims are part of all societies today and we cannot dismiss the actions of Osama Bin Laden and Al-Qaeda as those of a few isolated extremists in the Afghan mountains anymore. Until the misunderstandings and social isolation of some young Muslims in western society are addressed these problems will continue to escalate.

While there has been a growth in sensationalist, provocative literature claiming to penetrate the mysteries of 'the Real Osama Bin Laden', 'what Jihad really means for the West', 'my Time in the Mujahedin', and so on, very little serious scholarship has looked at the cause of this problem. This book has been intended as a two-pronged approach to examine some of the issues facing the Christian community, or more accurately communities, across the globe as they all face the task of seeking to live in peaceful co-existence with Muslim neighbours. At the beginning of this volume Michael Ipgrave sought to set a framework for ecumenical Christians in Britain to utilise in their dealings with British Muslims and Barbara Mitchell concentrated on the steps taken by the Anglican church to bring Christian and Muslim congregations closer together. After beginning with a discussion of Britain, a society that is nominally Christian, but also widely acknowledged as a relatively successful example of multiculturalism, the remainder of the book set out to examine Christian–Muslim relations in the rest of the world.

Andrew Unsworth's chapter further introduced the theological framework underlying the Christian–Islamic dialogue process by chronicling the history of the Vatican's approaches to Islam since Vatican II (1962–65). Surprisingly this is a subject that has not been widely studied in its own right before and Unsworth's future publications on this subject, based on his PhD thesis, will be eagerly awaited. The situation of western Europe as a whole was considered by Philip Lewis, who sketches a history of European attitudes to Islam since the fall of Granada in 1492. He explored where Muslim immigrants to Europe have come from and how their attitudes have changed as they have become more entrenched in European society, before finally discussing what different churches have done to foster a spirit of openness and welcome for Europe's growing Muslim population.

While aiming for inclusivity, the constraints of time and space meant that some areas of the world had to be neglected in this volume and, despite aiming to sketch a global picture, the American continent was not included. On the other hand, some chapters have addressed Christian–Muslim relationships in countries about which remarkably little is known. Basil Cousins's chapter concentrating on Tatarstan in the former Soviet Union, and which is still part of contemporary Russia, gave a very different impression of Russian policy. We are all aware of the ongoing struggles for Chechnya and, having watched in horror atrocities such as the Moscow Theatre siege and the attack on a school in Beslan, the rest of the world could be forgiven for assuming that there is no part of Russia where Muslims and Christians co-habit in a relatively peaceful manner. Cousins's chapter demonstrates the inaccuracy of this assumption and sheds light on a relatively little-known society.

The same can be said for my own chapter on Syria. As a country dubbed part of 'the axis of evil' by George W. Bush, most people view Syria through the prism of the Arab-Israeli conflict and it is often forgotten that Israel has been occupying the Syrian Golan Heights since 1973. Yet despite Syria's restrictive political regime, in fact largely because of this regime, Syria remains perhaps the most religiously tolerant society in the Middle East. No serious research has yet been conducted on how the Al-Assad led Ba'ath Party has upheld stability among a bewildering array of religious minorities in a predominantly Sunni Muslim society, but as my chapter points out, it is a system that works and the biggest challenges facing contemporary Syrian Christians are economic rather than religious. The relaxed view of the Syrians towards their compatriots of different religions can be contrasted with the tensions that bubble under the surface of Egyptian society. Fiona McCallum's chapter chronicles the highs and lows of the Coptic church's relations with the Egyptian authorities during the twentieth and into the twenty-first centuries. Her chapter proves particularly apposite at a time when these problems seem to be occurring with more frequency, a fact brought to world attention with the murder of Christians attending Good Friday services in Alexandria at Easter 2006 and the growing tensions in the country caused by an influx of Christian refugees from Sudan.

The problems of Sudan were addressed by John Flannery, who sketched a complex history that goes back far farther than the nineteenth century, the point at which most people assume Christianity entered Sudan. At the time of writing there seems no possibility of a solution to religious strife in Sudan at present, but Flannery's chapter does enable us to understand the reasons for the ongoing violence in the country. In contrast to the problems of Sudan, Stanisław Grodź argues that, with the exception of Nigeria, Christian–Muslim relations in West Africa have largely been non-confrontational. His consideration of how both religions have been adapted to better fit the African cultural milieu perhaps answers the question of how West Africa has managed to better avoid the Christian–Muslim conflicts that have been so disastrous in other parts of the continent.

Another African perspective is offered in Christopher Clohessy's chapter on South Africa where Islam had a valuable role to play in the struggle against apartheid. Here Islam has not so much offered a challenge to Christianity as been an important part of the identity of a persecuted and marginalised people; a role it continues to play in today's still disadvantaged coloured community. The state of Islam in South Africa is also another area that has not been seriously studied before and Clohessy's chapter is a serious attempt to stimulate study and debate of this subject.

While anyone interested in Islam will be aware that Indonesia is the state with the largest Muslim population in the world, media concentration on Indonesia means that Islam in other countries in the Far East is often neglected. Peter Riddell's chapter on Malaysia discusses how a Muslim majority has been struggling with the tendency towards fundamentalist rule and how this has impacted not only on Christians and other religious minorities, but also affected the lives of moderate Muslims. A key theme that emerged in his chapter was the disunity of the Christian response to Islamic persecution. This is a subject that has surfaced time and again throughout the book and one that will be discussed later in this chapter.

The situation is slightly different in the Philippines where, as Rocco Viviano indicates even in the title of his chapter, the Christian population of the country is so overwhelmingly Catholic that it is very much a Catholic-Muslim issue. Viviano also highlights an issue that is increasingly overlooked or deliberately avoided in the name of political correctness: the issue of proselytism and conversion. He clearly points out that it is only when, in his words, the Catholic church works 'with' Muslims rather than 'for' them that progress is made in dialogue.

Staying with the southern hemisphere Anthony Johns' chapter considered the Muslim population of a continent perceived to be entirely without Muslims: Australasia. While many of us have traditionally believed Australia to be inhabited by Aborigines and people descended from European settlers, Johns points out that Muslim immigrants have made Islam the second largest religion in Australia after Christianity. However, their relatively recent presence in the country has led to alienation and friction and he argues persuasively that tensions between Muslim youths and other groups will continue unless a coherent government response to integrate and protect Australian Muslims is formulated.

Finally the Middle East was largely omitted due to the fact that so much has already been published on interfaith issues in that region and the intention was to concentrate on less well-known examples. Despite this Anthony O'Mahony's chapter on Iran demonstrates that Iran is far from being a monolithic single-religion state, as most outsiders assume. He explains that contrary to public perception, some elements in Iranian society are eager to establish relations with other religions and this openness has even spread to parts of the Iranian establishment.

Where do we go now?

As the above summary demonstrates, there is a multiplicity of what we should perhaps call 'Islams' rather than Islam singular. On the other hand the same can be said for Christianity. It is wrong to assume that both religions are single monolithic entities, when both are religions that embrace a wide spectrum of beliefs and practices under the umbrella of faith. If we acknowledge this simple, but often overlooked, fact, then it becomes clear that we must examine a series of responses rather than assume one approach will be equally efficacious in all cases.

The chapters dealt with a variety of societies ranging from those that are predominantly Christian or perhaps more accurately post-Christian (Britain, western Europe, Australasia) to those that have an overwhelmingly Muslim majority (Egypt, Iran, Malaysia and Syria to name but a few). In between are more mixed societies where the balance of faiths is more precariously maintained. What is automatically clear is that strategies should be tailored to fit each individual circumstance. We read how Muslim minorities feel threatened in some western societies and indeed, Johns attributes this feeling of persecution as the main cause of violent behaviour among Muslim youths in Australia. On the other hand similar emotions among Copts are one factor that have inflamed passions in Egypt and led to disproportionate outbreaks of violence in response to provocation by Muslims. Therefore the clear conclusion to be drawn in this instance is that religious minorities must not only be protected by the state, but they must also be treated in a manner that respects their dignity. If a minority feels degraded as well as threatened, the propensity for violence is increased; this is a message that is increasingly repeated by young British Muslims and one that we should move quickly to accept and seek to remedy.

In a more evenly balanced society, cultural norms can provide the key to religious tolerance. Grodź's chapter on West Africa underlines the point that, in societies with a relatively recent conversion story (in this case the nineteenth and twentieth centuries), religious tensions can be avoided if the religion is absorbed into an existing cultural system. In fact cultural assimilation seems to be the key to smooth relations in a number of other, extremely diverse, societies. South African Muslims were leading players in the battle against apartheid and this common cause acted as an aid to integration. In Syria Christians voluntarily observe Islamic dietary laws on what is *halal* (permitted) and abstain from keeping or eating pigs. They also adhere to local dress codes so that it is extremely difficult to tell Muslim and Christian apart. This kind of cultural sensitivity causes a diminution of tension in society and removes many petty causes of conflict.

One problem on both sides of the religious divide, which relates to all the societies discussed in this book, is the lack of unity among co-religionists when discussing how to initiate a relationship with the 'other side'. While there are the obvious difficulties of getting Sunni to collaborate with Shia, or Catholic to work with Anglican, the problems are far deeper than this and the multiplicity of groups working on dialogue sometimes threatens to overwhelm the process itself. For example, taking a personal standpoint, in the past year I have been involved in: the Community of al-Khalil in Syria, the Ampleforth-Qom Catholic-Shia discussion group, the Anglican-Shia consultation group. I have also been invited to a conference hosted by a group that uses meditation to bring religions closer together, and been asked to get involved in a women's interfaith forum. With all these groups rapidly mushrooming it is obvious that many, if not all, are simply going backwards and forwards over the same ground. It is also the case that many of the same people are present in a significant number of groups, adding to this duplication.

Both sides must address the pressing issue of ecumenism. Until Christians and Muslims can put aside mutual antagonism towards their co-religionists, it will be difficult to create movements that can significantly contribute to the Christian–Islamic dialogue process. Good intentions are not enough and personal prejudices must be kept under control so that fewer, larger groups come into being; until this is realised we risk squandering the admirable impulse and valuable time offered worldwide by serious Christians and Muslims wishing to engage in a meaningful relationship.

One big step forward in the dialogue process is the increasing growth of Christian–Islamic dialogue as a serious subject for academic study. Andrew Unsworth's chapter on Vatican policy on dialogue since Vatican II is the result of his doctoral research and the increase in topics like this means that we are generating a significant body of work allowing us to examine which approaches have been fruitful and which have failed over the last forty years. Armed with this knowledge we should, if prepared to collaborate, be able to build on the trial-and-error method to see which projects and conferences have proved most successful in the past and should therefore be used as the basis of future strategies.

If any further evidence of the importance of such research was needed it has been provided by current events. At the time of writing Lebanon is being decimated by Israeli forces and there are no signs of a ceasefire because, from the very beginning of hostilities, dialogue has played no part in the events unfolding before us.

This book has demonstrated that there are many ways of approaching Christian–Islamic dialogue, some more successful than others, but this is an issue that will become one of the most important political factors of the twenty-first century and it is perhaps not overestimating the case to say that the lives of millions of people may depend on the formulation of a dialogue process to bring Christians and Muslims closer together. The book has been intended as an introduction to this issue for a wider audience than the few academics and clerics who are normally involved in the process. It is hoped that by more open and frank discussion of the dialogue process we may be able to arrest the trend of using violence rather than discussion as the first response to friction.

Index

CPSIA information can be obtained at www.ICGtesting.com
Printed in the USA
BVOW010920270312

286155BV00002B/42/P

9 780719 086687